Female
GANGS
IN
America

Female
GANGS
IN
America

Essays on girls, gangs and gender

*Edited by Meda Chesney-Lind
and John M. Hagedorn*

LAKE VIEW PRESS · CHICAGO

Lake View Press, P.O. Box 578279, Chicago 60657

Copyright 1999 by Meda Chesney-Lind and John M. Hagedorn.
All rights reserved. Published 1999

Printed in the United States of America

Library of Congress Cataloging-in-Publication Data

Female gangs in America:
    essays on girls, gangs, and gender / edited by Meda Chesney-Lind and
    John M. Hagedorn.
    p. cm.
Includes bibliographical references and index.
ISBN 0-941702-48-0 (alk. paper).
ISBN 0-941702-47-2 (pbk.: alk. paper)

    1. Gangs —United States.
    2. Female juvenile delinquents—United States.
    3. Female offenders—United States.
    I. Chesney-Lind, Meda.
    II. Hagedorn, John M. 1947- .

    HV6439.U5F46 1999

    364.1'06'60820973—dc21   98-53160
                                                                 CIP

7/00

Contents

Tables and Charts

Acknowledgments

A book like this is a genuine collaboration, and as a result we have many folks to thank. First, the editors want to express the pleasure that they have had filling what both of us regard as a huge need to get good work on girls and gangs together in one place. We also regard this as a "work in progress," since we deeply appreciate the work that has come before, and we welcome good work that we hope will appear in the future. For this reason, we want to first thank all the authors that have contributed to this volume or allowed their work to be reprinted here, and we also want to thank the publishing houses who allowed us to reprint their fine work.

We also both want to thank our tireless and very supportive editor, Paul Elitzik, for the willingness to go the extra mile on this project. As one small measure of our appreciation to him, we've promised to stop arguing about what to put on the cover. That was easy, because of the fine cover designed by Michael Miner. We also greatly appreciate the design work of Ann Eidson and Merle Welkomer and the meticulous copy editing of Eileen Favorite.

No work of this sort happens without the labor of others, often women, whose contributions are largely invisible but also invaluable. Meda particularly wants to thank Joell Hokulani Yuen and Konia Freitas for the hours of work scanning, retyping and proofreading articles. Her colleagues, both in the Women's Studies Program, the Youth Gang Project, and in the College of Social Science have also provided her with intellectual and emotional support, particularly Karen Joe, David Johnson, Dave Mayeda, Nestor Batalon, Howard Reyes, Anna Rockhilll, and Vickie Paramore. John particularly wants to thank Paula Evans and Jenjee Sengkhammee for their long hours scanning, editing, and fixing the manuscripts. Veronica Ejma lent her organizational support to this effort as did Beki Cook in getting staff of the University of Wisconsin-Milwaukee Center for Urban Initiatives and Research to provide support. Irina Sharer, Felicia White, Jennifer Bannach, and Rod Scheib also lent a hand. John also wants to acknowledge his intellectual debt to Joan Moore and thank her for her support over the years.

A broader network of support within the American Society of Criminology also deserves mention. The meetings serve as a vital and important venue for the sharing of ideas as well providing as the generative soil in which projects like this one take seed and eventually grow. We want to express particular appreciation for the "gang" panels that have been convened over the years at these meetings. We've met many of the authors published or reprinted here first at these meetings, and we hope that our students and theirs will extend the work we have begun.

Finally, and most importantly, we want to thank the young people who have been involved in gangs for taking time to talk with both of the authors. Most of these youth—female and male—are of necessity nameless, but we owe them a tremendous debt of gratitude for sharing their lives, their insights, and their troubles with us so generously. It is our deepest hope that because they have told their stories so powerfully, we can as a nation move past the mean spirited and clearly racist policies regarding gangs in America.

Female
GANGS
IN
America

Introduction:
Why This Book?

We began talking about putting this book together because we both recognized the existence of decades of rich, scattered, and sometimes fugitive research efforts on the subject of girls and gangs. We were also aware of exciting new work that is building on the best traditions of past research. Some of this new scholarship is applying new perspectives in feminist and other theories to the no longer invisible female gang (for a complete review, see Moore and Hagedorn, in press).

We have also tried, in four articles introducing each section, to lodge the pieces included in this book within a much larger literature on gangs. As you will see examining the chapter headings, these include discussion of the history of female gangs, the impact of economic restructuring, the special way in which gender works in gangs, and female violence and victimization.

Knowing that girls in gangs have long been "present but invisible," the book fully explores how our understanding of gangs might be enriched if we listened to the girls themselves. As a result, the majority of articles in this volume are field research, ethnography, or other kinds of articles that let female gang members speak for themselves. Understanding the need for geographic, methodological, and ethnic diversity, we built this volume with an eye toward the richest collection of readings possible. The selections included here reveal that girls of different ethnicities experience gang life differently, that gangs vary by geography, age, and other variables. The volume also shows that girls in gangs must be understood on their own terms, and that difference, as well as similarity, characterizes girls' participation in gangs. Finally, many of these articles imply that it is vital that we stop constructing images of girls' participation in gangs that endlessly compare them to boys and their gangs, or worse, get caught up in notions that girls, and their groups, are simply appendages or mirror images of boy's gangs.

How do we respond to girls' involvements in gangs? Several selections argue that the media fascination for the hyper-violent girl of color distracts from the necessary and long overdue focus on the needs of all youth in gangs, girls as well as boys. A careful reading of these articles reveals critical and unique themes in girls participation in gangs. Clearly, most gang girls grow up in economically marginalized neighborhoods. But economic marginalization means something different for girls is also clear—poverty, violence, and victimization take on special meanings in girls' lives, and many of these themes emerge in girls' choices to join gangs. Moreover, girls who join gangs pay a price for being born a girl of color in a society that short-circuits the choices of these girls in particular. In this complicated social and economic terrain, gangs clearly play a complicated role in girls' lives, both protecting them from some victimization, while putting young girls at greater risk in other ways.

This volume should be understood as a start on a long overdue research agenda. We are keenly aware of the many questions that the articles in this volume, old and new, leave unresolved. For example, there are no articles in this volume on female gangs in prison, while there is a rich literature on male prison gangs. Despite our best efforts, we were not only unable to locate any articles on female prison gangs, but we were not able to gather any reliable reports that there is any significant number of female gangs in prison. Owen (1998), in her ethnography of women in what is likely the world's largest women's prison (Central California Women's Facility), notes that "gangbanging" is seen as "childishness" by the older women prisoners and this attitude seems to pervade the institution. It is also possible that the family structures in adult women's prisons may interfere with gang affiliation. Still, this phenomenon needs exploration and explanation; it is rich in implications for the different roles of gangs for males and females. With the war on drugs increasingly catching more women into its steel net, however, could this situation too be changing? We need to investigate the matter and construct theory.

There is also little literature on programs for female gang members, for much the same reasons as the lack of studies of female prison gangs. David Curry reports on a few such programs in his article for this volume, but the main fact is that girls typically get left out when communities face the issue of gangs. Given what we know about the way the male gang problem has been approached, maybe that's not such a bad thing. Still, we hope this volume raises the visibility of female gangs and serves as a call for gender-specific programs that meet the needs of these girls and their communities.

This volume devotes considerable attention to gang girls' violence, not simply their victimization. The various chapters explore female fighting and violence as one way gang girls "do gender," but none of the more recent authors sees female violence as simply girls "acting male." In general, many of the selections included in this volume explore how racism and patriarchal privilege shape (or distort) girls' lives and their choices. They disaggregate the gang experience, showing how girls and boys live both together and apart in marginalized communities. There is evidence from several studies that, on the whole, girls come from more troubled families than boys. The female gang acts as a kind of refuge for many girls, while for most boys the male gang is an extension of a mainstream, aggressive, male role.

Solutions to the gang problem in the United States, we believe, are inextricably tied up with larger questions about how economic restructuring has impacted segments of our communities. The problem of female gangs is also linked to profound questions of gender equality. As we've noted, there are few programs developed specifically for women, and stereotyping and overreaction are more common than solutions based on good research.

If girls have an opportunity to attend good schools; if we can build on the cultural strengths present in their neighborhoods; if we can protect children from sexual and physical violence; if we can provide youth who cannot stay at home with safe places to live; if we can help resource-strapped families nurture their children; if we can offer economic security for all parents and hope for the future for their children—only then will our nation's gang problem shrink to more manageable proportions.

If, on the other hand, we ignore violence against children; if we ignore the gendered experiences of boys and girls growing up in hostile environments; if, in the name of "welfare reform," we force poor girls and boys onto the streets either in reaction to stress or as a desperate attempt to aid their families; if we offer young adults few profitable avenues in the formal economy; if we offer poor children a bleak, rather than a bright future—we should not be surprised if our gang problems not only will not go away, but take on even more troubling and violent forms.

We may be naive, but we believe that the starting point in tackling this task is to assemble what we know about female gangs. We have tried to present as much of it as possible in this single, usable, volume as our contribution to improving girls' lives.

1 Historical Perspectives

Introduction:
Present but Invisible

What would the world of gangs look like if it was viewed through the eyes of a girl or young woman in the 1920s, 1960s, or 1970s? Given how indisputably "macho" gang life was (and is), such a question is almost unthinkable. Yet as the pieces you are about to read ably demonstrate, girls have long been "present but invisible" in American gang life (McRobbie and Garber 1975). The pieces also ably document what Campbell (1990) has called the "gendered habits of researchers," since all the pieces but one are written by men. Particularly the earliest pieces in this collection reflect the privileged male gaze on the behavior of young women very different from themselves. The one exception to this generalization is Laura Fishman's piece, and in her work she worries about the fact that she was the only African American woman among her entire group of researchers and workers documenting gang life in Chicago.

The pieces included in this section cover gang life from 1927 to 1977 in different parts of the country and examine gangs of different ethnicities. One could argue that some (particularly the earliest accounts) are atheoretical, racist, or sexist, since they represent beginning attempts by white male social scientists, social workers, and journalists to describe a phenomenon in which they had little interest. In this regard, please note that we have not edited these pieces to delete dated language or perspectives, believing that these constructions, although inaccurate by today's standards, are worth reading as they were originally written. Bernard's sensationalist account of female gangs should be of particular interest in this respect. Despite their age, these selections nonetheless establish some extremely important themes.

First, these papers document that girls have long been a part of the gang scene, and that their behavior has always been more complex and diverse than the incessant focus on girls' sexuality in the literature would permit. The fact of female gangs emerges even though many male researchers ignored or dismissed them and gang intervention programs discouraged work with them (see Hanson 1964, 43). Willam Bernard, for example, in his 1949 book *Jailbait,* states (without documentation) that for every 1 female gang there are 300 male gangs. Perhaps Bernard's uncited source was Thrasher (1927), who could find only 5 or 6 female gangs among 1,313 in Chicago's gangland.

Were there really so few female gangs, or did sexist researchers just not see them? We can't know for sure. Thrasher, in the piece reprinted here), offers the first sociological explanation for why girls don't have what he calls the "ganging instinct" of boys. The "great weight of tradition" keeps girls in line, and besides, the father of gang research argues, girls are more closely supervised than boys. Thrasher goes on to state that while girls may form "sets" or "cliques," they do not form "gangs" because they don't fight as much as boys. Since for Thrasher conflict was the glue that held the gang together, and since he believed conflict was missing for the girl clique, therefore, by definition, girls could not form gangs.

The real issue of interest for early gang researchers is captured by the title of Thrasher's chapter—"Sex in the Gang." Female delinquency, for most social scientists of that era, was really about sex, not violence. Bernard's (1949) aptly titled *Jailbait,* in a section reprinted here, goes luridly on and on about the sexual promiscuity of delinquent girls. He is particularly horrified by lesbian gangs (he calls them "Florabels" in a different part of the book) who force themselves on innocent girls. Bernard spends much of this titillating book describing various sexual acts, including shocked descriptions of "honeying up"—lesbian relationships between white and Black girls. Kitty Hanson (1964, 143), describing New York gangs of the 1960s, insists that the main difference between male and female gangs is the female gangs' focus on "sexing." Therefore, for both Rice, in this volume, and Hanson, the way to handle female gang members was to set up "charm schools." "If they learn to be girls," Hanson advises, and we suspect most of the early writers would agree, "then they won't imitate the boys."

The studies reprinted here, however, cast some doubt on the proposition that pre-1980s female gangs were only about sex, and were not violent. As an example, Thrasher (1927, 225) observes gang girls "have some ability in the line of physical prowess." Indeed, one young woman he profiled was involved in seventy-five robberies. Rice's profile of an African American girl gang in New York also documents the role of fighting in girl gang behavior, and he even describes one girl "fighting gang." Miller (1975), in his oft-cited article on the Molls, also discovered a fighting female gang, the "Queens." Carla and her "Dagger Debs" in Hanson's (1964) account were tough street fighters. In this volume Brown reports a fighting female gang, the "Holly Hos," who "greatly resembled the warring Amazonian women referred to in ancient mythology." For both Quicker and Fishman, violence was a central part of both male and female gang life.

These pieces, then, establish that girls' violence has long existed, even though the official preoccupation with their sexuality ("promiscuity") eclipsed concern for this behavior. The focus on girls' sexuality, however, did not extend to protecting girls from the sexual and physical violence of boys in their neighborhoods. Most of the early ethnographies talk rather matter-of-factly about "gang shag" or gang rape of girls (e.g., Thrasher, p. 20 this volume), but it is the *girls'* sexuality (or pregnancy) that is condemned.

The lack of studies makes it difficult to generalize about female gangs of the past. The collection of articles in this section, however, strongly suggests that female gangs, like male gangs, appear to vary widely. In fact, to shamelessly paraphrase Thrasher, we might declare that "no two female gangs are alike." Echoing the weaknesses of the male gang literature, however, we also find little appreciation of variation within gangs. Anyone who reads the descriptions of each of the "Dagger Debs" in Hanson's *Rebels in the Streets* will realize that female gangs, like their male counterparts, are made up of different kinds of kids, not just the abused child or the poor student.

For all of the writers in this section, you'll note, female gangs are male auxiliaries, and thus in a way can be seen as "pale imitations" of the male genuine article. Brown addresses this issue squarely, pointing out that both boys and girls in Philadelphia's poor African American ghetto face the same conditions, but girls are socialized differently. Male gangs, Brown seems to say, with Thrasher and Miller, are more of an extension of the riskier, more aggressive male role. But if girls are less pressured to join the street life and are more home-centered, why do they join gangs? "Excitement," Brown exclaims, but he doesn't follow up and more closely examine the functions of the gang for girls.

That task is left to John Quicker, in a previously unpublished piece made available for the first time in this volume. He explains that the Chicana gang was a male auxiliary, but had considerable independence. In fact, the female gang existed as an alternative institution for the girls, sort of a substitute family. In Quicker's work we get a clearer picture of the female gang as filling needs for girls, rather than just being used by the boys. In looking at the female gang as its own entity, Quicker represents a qualitative leap from earlier male-centered views like Bernard's, who wrote: "Principally, however, the young ladies act as camp followers, supplying the lads with such sex as they required." While early female gangs may have been horribly dominated by males, they also are likely to have played important roles in poor girls' socialization, as Quicker found.

Laura Fishman, in an article rewritten for this volume, ties many of the themes of prior research on female gangs together and adds one new one. For Fishman, the Vice Queens were a solution to problems of gender, race, and class for young African American girls. Fishman's perspective of the Vice Queens' behavior as a response to the needs of poor, young African American females sharpens the focus of the picture taken for us by Quicker.

Fishman not only discusses lower class conditions, but also gendered oppression, giving uncomfortable descriptions of how the boys felt free to assault the girls. She examines ethnicity by looking at how African American women both had more free-dom but also had less protection than women of other ethnic groups. The Vice Queens, in Fishman's account, represented a subservient notion of femininity and were thoroughly dominated by the Vice Kings. One wonders about variation within that gang, or whether other female gangs of that time were as traditional in their alle-giance to men. We simply don't have research of Fishman's quality on other gangs to answer those questions.

One new theme Fishman strikes is the issue of "survival"—the integration of eco-nomics with gang life. None of the other accounts make this a central concern for girls, but the Vice Queens were focused on making money, and in this, provide a link to gangs today which are forming under conditions of economic restructuring. We still have very few studies of the economic functions of female gangs.

To conclude, these pieces demonstrate that gangs are shaped by class, age, gender, and ethnicity. Gangs, girls' gangs included, are chiefly about economic and political mar-ginality. These papers suggest that gangs are also a violent by-product of neighborhoods that are, themselves, the products of that lethal mix of poverty, neglect, and racism that has long haunted America. And this "other America" has haunted our country even during its best times.

The rest of this book will deal with the manner in which gender works in these kinds of neighborhoods. We will consider how factors such as early motherhood, domestic violence, gang rape, and boredom shape the unique world that girls inhabit in these communities, and how the choice of gang membership is a way that girls who find themselves in this world survive.

Sex in the Gang

Frederic M. Thrasher*

The influence of sex upon life in the gang varies with the age and biological development of its members. In some of the younger gangs a girl may play the same role as a boy. Among the gangs of younger adolescents, there is a definite indifference or hostility to girls as such, although sex interests may be evident in various types of auto-erotic activity. The members of the older adolescent or young adult gang usually have a definite though half-concealed interest in girls. Dates and dancing become important, girls' groups may enter into alliance with the gang, and certain girls may be taken under its protection or in other cases may actually become members of the gang in their sexual capacity.

On the whole, however, it is safe to say that sex represents a decidedly secondary activity in the gang. In the adolescent group in particular, it is subordinated to the primary interest of conflict and adventure to which it is extraneous. As the gang grows older, however, sex gets more attention, in most cases ultimately supplanting the gang entirely to the extent that its members marry and enter into family relationships.

Sex in the Younger Adolescent Gang

In the gang of younger adolescent boys, the usual attitude is one of indifference, scorn, or open hostility to girls and their characteristics which are classified as "sissy."

"A Hard-Boiled Egg"

129. The leader of our gang was what is usually termed a "hard rock." He was the leader because he was the "hardest" and because he had a strip clipped off through the hair on his head so that he might show the girls how little he cared for what they thought of his looks.[1]

Most adolescent gang boys are emphatic in denying that they go with girls: they "don't like no girls." When asked why, they give a variety of reasons: They are too young; the girls do not like them; there are no girls around; they get nothing out of it and all girls do is spend money and get them into trouble. In many cases there is evidence of sex hostility: the girls stick their tongues out and "tattle."

"I Kill the Girls"

130. "Do you like the little girls, Tony?" I asked a boy of fifteen.

"Naw! I never love no girls. I don't want to monkey around wit' girls. Dey give me troubles. I kill de girls."

*Reprinted from the unabridged edition of Frederic M. Thrasher, The Gang (Chicago: University of Chicago Press, 1927/1936), pp. 221–47. Copyright 1927, 1936 by the University of Chicago. All rights reserved. Reprinted by permission of the publisher.

He has several sisters, so I asked him if he hates them too.

"What, should I hate my sisters? Dey don't give me no troubles. Dey're my sisters."

This attitude toward his sisters is significant of the strong family bonds of Tony's group (the Italians).

"Oder girls report me to teacher for t'rowing t'ings—snowballs. One said I jumped on her . . . I just push her—like dat. All de oders jump on her; she don't report dem; only me. . . . Why don't dey go straight home?" He asked complainingly; then, to demonstrate what great trouble-makers girls are, he added, "Dey have to wait for somebody."[2]

The reasons for this group attitude against women seem to be in the main that they have interfered with the enterprises of the group, have weakened the loyalties of its members, or in demanding time and attention have impaired the gang as an effective conflict group. Thus gang tradition discourages any but the most casual contacts, and if a boy's clandestine interest in girls becomes manifest or overt, he is usually subjected to most unpleasant ridicule, upbraided for his lack of loyalty, or more definitely disciplined by the gang.

Punishment for Interest in Girls

131. As soon as a member of our gang of high-school Freshmen showed any desire to walk home from school with girls or attend one of their parties, he was automatically dropped. If he fell from grace but once, he could sometimes be reinstated by taking a "billy wedging."[3]

Although the gang at this age affects to despise girls, it sometimes has its own code of chivalry with reference to them.

The Code of Chivalry

132. The boy who attempted to fight with a girl was punished by the other boys. A girl might slap a boy in the face and all he could honorably do was to dodge the second blow, or, if he was very religious, as was seldom the case, he might turn his head around and ask to have the inequality rectified by a similar blow on the other side.[4]

In one case, considerable alarm was caused among women workers in a social settlement by the fact that gang boys followed them at night. The fear was alleviated, however, when it was found that the interest of these boys was in protecting the women in accordance with the Irish idea of chivalry.

In spite of the general lack of attention to girls and women, much informal "sex education" takes place in the adolescent gang.

Sex Education

133. The gang developed in the boy a distinct point of view, so that he considered it somewhat of a disgrace to play with girls. At this stage he would be the subject of

derision if caught playing, or even conversing familiarly, with any girl except his sister. The older boys, however, became instructors of the younger boys of the gang in sex matters, and in many of them a premature interest and curiosity was inculcated. There was a large amount of obscene literature and art, which was circulated very freely among the boys, copied many times over and handed down to the next "generation" as a social legacy.[5]

In one case the chief interest of the group was in learning about sex matters. These boys were finally brought into court because of a sort of polyandry carried on with a girl in their hang-out. The dominance of this interest in the adolescent gang, however, is very rare.

The Gang Which Includes Both Sexes

How may we understand then the instances of juvenile gangs which have a girl as a member? The real explanation is that the girl takes the role of a boy and is accepted on equal terms with the others. Such a girl is probably a tomboy in the neighborhood. She dares to follow anywhere and she is ill at ease with those of her own sex who have become characteristically feminine. Sooner or later, however, sex differentiation arises: the whole situation is changed and the girl can no longer assume her role in the gang.

A Girl's Role in the Alley Gang

134. My entrance into the alley gang occurred soon after my family moved to a small town of five thousand population. I was eight years of age at the time, a small but strong and agile girl quite capable of taking care of myself and of my younger brothers and sister. The first few days I watched the boys playing in the alley beside the church where my father was to act as a pastor. One morning I found one of the boys surrounded by a delighted group of onlookers, torturing a frog. I could not countenance such cruelty, and I squirmed my way into the group.

"Stop that!" I commanded.

The boy looked up in astonishment, grinned, and continued his activity. I sailed into him and soon sat astride his stomach, directing vicious jabs at his head.

"Say enough!" I demanded. He wiggled uncomfortably and looked sheepishly at the interested circle of boys.

"Nuff!" he said, and I left him go. The next day I was invited to take part in a game of Piggy; I had made my debut into the gang as an equal.

Nearly all the boys in the neighborhood of the church belonged to the gang, the number varying from fifteen to twenty. For a short time I was the only girl, but after I had become "friends" with Marion, who lived around the corner from my home, I saw to it that she also became a member, although she was never accepted on a status of absolute equality. "Cliff," the oldest of the boys, was the recognized leader, and the gang followed him unquestioningly.

The requirements for joining the gang varied and, although never expressed, were definitely understood to include some ability in the line of physical prowess. Some contribution to the gang's welfare was sometimes sufficient for temporary membership. Forest, whom we knew as rather a sissy, was admitted for a time because of his new football. Marion, too, enjoyed membership for a considerable period, partly because I insisted on it and was able to back up my arguments, partly because her mother was generous with oatmeal cookies, and also because she came in handy as a captive maiden when we were conducting Indian wars. She drew away from the gang gradually when I realized that she did not belong, and withdrew my claims.

The only other gang with which we came in contact was the Sunnyside gang, a group of older boys, more commonly known as "toughs," from the South Side of town.

It was in an effort to hold his own against an arrogant Sunnyside that Cliff first swore. We were rather startled, and I, being encumbered with much religious training, waited for him to be struck dead. He wasn't. He repeated the fearful words mouthing them as though he enjoyed the taste. Art tried it, and then Glenn; and then, the gang meaning more to me than salvation, I followed suit. After that, we swore occasionally and nonchalantly but always in the privacy of our pals.

The Sunnyside gang had a meeting place, a haunted house, and from them we got the idea of establishing headquarters. Hitherto we had not felt the need, but a meeting place now became a necessity. We chose the haymow of a barn and used it for a base.

The lack of sex difference in the gang was significant. I was always accepted on terms of absolute equality. In the instance of playing Indian, as mentioned before, I was as bloodthirsty and terrible a warrior or as stalwart and brave a pilgrim defender as any of the boys. I should have been insulted to have been relegated to the role of captive maiden, and I doubt if the boys thought of such a thing. Marion's submission to the part is perhaps one reason why she never really belonged. I could shinny up the walnut tree in less time than any of the boys; I took my turn at bat, and played tackle or end in our hodgepodge football struggles. Girls, except Marion, were to me silly and nonessential; and I took delight in shouting derisively with the gang, "George's got a gurrl! George's got a gurrl!" when George carried Mabel's books home from school.

My personality outside the group was very different. The most uncomfortable afternoon of life was spent at the birthday party of one of the girls in my Sunday-school class. I was distinctly out of place among the pink and blue frills. It was evident that my attitude toward the boys was quite different from that of the other girls, and that in a party atmosphere the boys regarded me in a different light from what they did in the alley. I suffered the agonies of the damned on these occasions. I sat by myself on the stair steps—and I spilled my lemonade.

My exit from the gang occurred the spring when I was eleven years old. I fell in love. It is significant that I did not "fall" for another member of the gang but for a boy who had just moved into the neighborhood. The experience changed everything for me. Boys became boys, not fellows, and I became self-conscious. I didn't understand the process or the result, but I realized that things were different. I remember that a heavy rain had left a large puddle—almost a pond—of water in the alley. When I came home from school some of the boys were already wading.

"Come on over!" they called. A week before that time I should have dropped my books on the steps, jerked off my slippers and stockings, tucked my skirt into my bloomers, and waded in. This time I blushed furiously, flung at them a confused excuse about my helping my mother, and hurried into the house. The object of my affections stood watching the gang.[6]

Another interesting case is that of a gang composed largely of girls who had transferred their interests from sewing to playing in a large sand hill with a protruding plank. Forced to defend their play place against other gangs, they waged wars in which combat took the form of rock battles. They took the roles of boys until they began to wear their hair up and put on long skirts.

It is interesting to note in this connection that the Girl Scouts organization is developing a new type of literature for girls. It is said that little girls want the same thrill in their reading that is so persistently sought among adolescent gang boys— "tales of blood and thunder, detective stories, and mystery yarns." This seems to show that boys and girls are much more alike than the differences which are developed by traditional social patterns would indicate.

Do Girls Form Gangs?

This is a question very frequently asked, but one not difficult to answer. Gangs composed entirely of girls are exceedingly rare. Not more than five or six have been discovered in the present investigation. One of these was a group of colored girls in Chicago having baseball as their chief interest; another was organized for stealing; and the others were marginal cases, probably more really clubs than gangs.

It might seem quite plausible to say, therefore, that the reason girls do not form gangs is that they lack the gang instinct, while boys have it. This explanation lacks analysis of the problem. There are two factors: first, the social patterns for the behavior of girls, powerfully backed by the great weight of tradition and custom, are contrary to the gang and its activities; and secondly, girls, even in urban disorganized areas, are much more closely supervised and guarded than boys and are usually well incorporated into the family group or some other social structure.

The analogue to the boys' gang among girls is probably the clique or the set, but this must be regarded as an entirely different type of collective behavior. In certain groups where girls are allowed a greater degree of freedom as they grow older, there is a trend toward a type of club which corresponds to the athletic club among the boys and is sometimes affiliated with it. This, however, is not a conflict group and it does not exist in most immigrant communities on account of the close supervision to which the girls are subject.

The Immoral Gang

What have commonly been reported as "immoral gangs," composed of both sexes, are probably of the orgiastic type, such as the Fusileers,[7] rather than true conflict groups. Their chief activities seem to be what are commonly called in college circles "petting, necking, and mugging," and often include illicit sex relations. Cases of this sort are not rare.

The Tulips

135. This was a mixed group of boys and girls of the unorganized type, whose gang name suggests its activities. Its members were drawn from the elite of the juvenile delinquents of two of Chicago's smaller satellite towns and had their meeting place at the post-office.[8]

The Lone Star Club

136. This was a mixed gang whose interests were immoral. The group was well organized and carried on its activities systematically. Its members met in the open fields under the stars. One of the girls was ultimately sent to the Juvenile Psychopathic Institute for examination.[9]

An "Under the L" Gang

137. The Juvenile Protective Association has received a report of a mixed gang of boys and girls meeting nightly under the elevated tracks at and streets. There is some reason to believe that bad practices are engaged in here.

Special conditions may tend to develop this type of gang. A group called the "Night Riders," of which a complete account was obtained from the members themselves, was the product of a rooming-house environment. The boys and girls, living with parents or relatives in cramped quarters, were anemic and not of the type to form a rugged conflict group like those often found in the slums. The impression from such a study was somewhat similar to that obtained from seeing pale insects crawling about in the bleached grass upon turning over a board that has lain for a long time on the ground in some damp unwholesome place.

Many cases of the "petting clique" or so-called "immoral gang" have been reported in grade and high schools and sometimes in colleges. When cases of this sort get into the newspapers, as they sometimes do, they are widely heralded as "vice rings" and their sensational aspects are played up to the nth degree.

A Mixed Gang

138. The main purpose of this gang was sexual, and the indications are that not only normal but many unnatural and degenerate methods of sex gratification were in vogue. The boys of the group were as a whole stronger or tougher than the other boys in the school, and they succeeded pretty well in dominating the rest of us and playing the part of bullies.

In seasonable weather the scene of the gang's activity was a vacant lot on the South Side, or else a half-block of meadow land east of the I.C. tracks. The lot was at one time raided by the police and a number of the group were taken, but no punishment followed so far as I am able to discover. In rainy or chilly weather the gang assembled in some deserted barn. Members of the group also managed to get together on other occasions such as a picnic to Ravinia given by members of the eighth-grade class, when five or six disappeared and did not return until time to leave for home.

Of the fifteen or more members of the gang, some seemed to be quite normal mentally and physically while others were subnormal or worn out by excesses. There was not much conscious organization in the group, but the biggest boy was the apparent leader. The ages of the members were from thirteen to sixteen.

Most of the members of this group had bad records: some had been in the reform school; most of them had been suspended from school at least once; and others were eventually expelled. One boy was brought before the principal for flourishing a revolver on the playground. Scholastically they were below the average, but they dominated physically and in athletics, partly due to their greater size.

The only rule which the gang had, to my knowledge, was that no member should indulge in relations with outsiders. On the whole, they made no effort to conceal the nature of their activities and seemed to take pride in flaunting them before the rest of us. They possessed certain signals by which one of the boys could "ask" one of the girls while in class. These signals soon became known to the rest of us, and it is probable that even the teacher was not entirely unaware of what was going on.

The attitude of the rest of the class toward the group was largely one of disgust mingled with hatred. This was especially true of the boys, although there was a small group on the border line that looked upon the gang with admiration.[10]

Groups of this type are probably far more common than is ordinarily supposed. The facts suggest that these boys and girls suffer from a lack of wholesome work and recreation. There is every indication that ease of obtaining parental permission for the free and unchaperoned use of the family automobile, or ready access to the cars of friends, is one of the most important elements in the situation.

Conventional Sex Life in the Older Gangs

The conventional sex relations of members of the older gangs, especially of the conventionalized type such as the athletic club, usually take the form of picnics or hilarious truck parties to the forest preserves and dances.

Dances are exceedingly popular and a source of considerable income. The club dance is held in the club's own rooms or in a rented hall and is often patronized by other clubs. The dance programs are elaborate and contain a great deal of advertising by local business men and also by politicians who in addition often act as patrons, make speeches, or lead the grand march.

Gangs virtually control certain of the public dance halls of the city.[11] The conventionalized gang may take the name of its favorite dance hall and organize an athletic team bearing the same name. The clubs often have special "pull" with the management of these halls, which may depend largely upon such patronage for their receipts. Special nights at the dance halls are set aside for particular gangs or clubs; special concessions and privileges are granted with reference to exclusiveness and the use of liquors. In return the gang protects the management from the ordinary bum or loafer and is liberal with its patronage. Clashes between gangs in or about the dance halls are not uncommon occurrences.

Special Bar Permits

In the days before prohibition it was customary for these groups to obtain special bar permits, and sell intoxicants at their dances, which, on such occasions, tended to be unspeakably bad. The liquor produced complete relaxation of all restraint and the wildest debauchery often followed the dance with no attempt at control by the police, who themselves had often imbibed freely at the improvised bars. Some dances of this type, promoted by the larger clubs, were mammoth affairs and were held even in the Coliseum (one of Chicago's largest auditoriums).

Before Prohibition

139. . . . .While many of the club dances are well conducted, the majority are openly dangerous, and they are nearly all marked by extreme disorder and open indecency.

Our city ordinances require that no organization or individual shall be granted a special bar permit more than six times during the year, and yet the Juvenile Protective Association has evidence showing that organizations frequently secure three or four times this number in one year. In 1914, 5,601 special bar permits were secured; in 1915, 3,650, and from May 1916, to February 1917, 2,673 were secured. Over one hundred permits are issued each week in Chicago during the winter.

In the latter part of 1914 an attempt was made to pass an ordinance in the City Council which prohibited the sale of liquor in any dance hall. There was so much objection to this ordinance on the part of aldermen representing foreign-born constituencies that a compromise ordinance was introduced and passed April, 1915. . . . So carelessly, however, have permits been issued that in one case the man in whose name the permit was granted had been dead for several weeks. The result of this great laxness is that many bar permits are granted without investigation to "fly-by-night" clubs who have no financial or moral standing, sometimes to organizations without even an address. . . .

It sometimes happens that after investigation, the police refuse to grant a special bar permit. For instance, in one case they refused a permit to a certain club because at one of their previous dances two young girls had been outraged. The officers of the club then secured the services of the aldermen of their ward who interceded for them with the chief of police, and a permit was granted by him over the heads of the police committee which made the investigation. . . .

All the investigations report that up to about 11:00 p.m., generally speaking, the dances are well conducted; the crowd then begins to show the effect of too much liquor. . . . One investigator said in speaking of a dance, "These young people did not appear vicious but rather like children who, with blood aroused by liquor, their animal spirits fanned to the winds in a manner they would never do elsewhere. Rigorous supervision and no liquor would have made this dance almost an innocent party."[12]

The Stag Party

A favorite form of entertainment with certain so-called athletic clubs and gangs of similar type is the stag party. The nature of these affairs which are exceedingly demoralizing is described in a report of the Juvenile Protective Association.

Stag Parties

140. . . . While some stag parties are legitimate and unobjectionable affairs, others are characterized by conduct too obscene to permit description. . . .

It is impossible to describe in this bulletin the immoral practices permitted at some of these parties which rival the extreme depravities formerly prevailing in the commercialized vice district. Only hints of certain scenes actually observed by Protective Officers can be given. Stories of the most obscene character are related by a woman to a crowd of men and boys. Indescribably filthy jokes are perpetrated by a ventriloquist with the aid of a puppet. Degrading dancing—vile beyond description—is indulged in by girls some of whom are apparently scarcely out of their teens, while a woman gives nude an unbelievably debasing dance. After these demoralizing exhibitions girls circulate through the audience taking up a collection and assuring the patrons that, "the more you put in the more the girls will take off." Then follows the climax of the evening. Women dancers appear, first singly and later in groups entirely nude and proceed to participate in a licentious debauchery in which the men near by join. The scene finally culminates in a raffle of one of the girl performers, the man holding the winning ticket being awarded the girl for the balance of the night.

The Juvenile Protective Association has concerned itself with these unspeakable exhibitions because of their corrupt effect on young boys and girls. An investigation of a dozen so-called entertainments has invariably revealed the presence of minors. At one affair held in the Loop the names and addresses of twenty-two boys from fifteen years of age and up were secured. At another "smoker" given on the West Side attended by many minors a girl of ten years and a nine-year-old boy were exhibited in a pugilistic contest refereed by the children's father. Immediately following the bout a nude woman danced. Women entertainers whose performances were most obnoxious have acknowledged in open court that they had children of their own.[13]

The frequency of this type of entertainment, which is not confined to the gangs, is not generally known since great precautions are taken to maintain secrecy and only occasionally are such parties raided.

Suppression of the Stag Party

141. Storytelling palled on the guests at the ninety-second anniversary celebration of the Eagle Oriental club.... They wanted the big attraction of the evening. It came. Eight young women began to dance while, little by little, they disrobed in time to the music, until they had nothing on but their shoes.

Police, having seen all there was to see, decided it was time to act. They admitted other policemen from outside and in a few moments the 8 women and 197 men were arrested. Yesterday the men were all fined $1.00 and costs each. The case of the women was continued for a jury trial, together with that of the announcer, the pianist, and the doorkeeper.[14]

Certain politicians, perceiving the popularity of the stag party, have not hesitated to capitalize the sex appeal and employ this sort of entertainment for political rallies attended by hundreds of men and boys.

Sex Delinquencies Among the Older Gangs

Among the members of the older gangs there is evidence of looseness and promiscuity often involving the obliging sweetheart or the clandestine prostitute, as well as inmates of disorderly houses. Some of the clubs have been accused of harboring women in their rooms, but ordinarily this practice is avoided as being too dangerous.

A peculiar form of sex delinquency in a particular gang area may be in the tradition of the groups of that community. This is illustrated in the so-called "gang shag" which is in vogue among the older adolescent gangs in a certain disorganized immigrant community in Chicago.

The Gang Shag

143. The gang shag is an institution peculiar to the gangs and clubs of this neighborhood. There are few sex perverts among the boys, but there is a great deal of immorality. This does not begin, as a rule, before the age of sixteen or seventeen.

The gang shag includes boys from sixteen to twenty-two years of age. It is a party carried on with one woman by from fifteen to thirty boys from one gang or club. A mattress in the alley usually suffices for this purpose. This number of boys have relations with the woman in the course of a few hours.

As a result of this institution and other irregular practices of a like nature, venereal disease is very high among the boys. One physician in the district has had as high as twenty boys from a single club of forty members under treatment at one time.[16]

The semi-criminal gangs and clubs of older adolescents and young men are sometimes guilty of attacks on women. The victim may be attacked incidentally in the process of a holdup or may be enticed to the hang-out of the gang.

The Bear Claws

144. The Bear Claws, composed of about fifty members ranging in age from seventeen up, had a clubroom in an old barn in the South Side badlands. Some of its members were roughnecks and sluggers and its hang-out was also frequented by pickpockets and other criminals, who lowered the moral tone of the club.

One night the man who was renting the barn to this group heard a woman screaming, "Murder, murder, they're killing me!" When he ran to the barn, he saw the members of the club running out. In the loft he found an elderly colored woman wired to the floor with her hands behind her head. Her body was covered with blood and scratches. She had been attacked by the whole group.[17]

There is a common practice among young men in Chicago, and this is by no means confined to boys of the gangs or the underprivileged classes, of picking up girls, utter strangers, on the street and taking them for a ride in an automobile. During the course of this ride it is customary to indulge in passionate petting, and often the affair culminates in the sex act. If the girl refuses, it is commonly supposed that she is put out of the car some place in the country and asked to walk back. So widespread is this practice that allusions to it have become a common joke on the vaudeville stage. Many a girl voluntarily or involuntarily begins a delinquent career in just this manner; in some cases she is made the victim of a brutal attack after accepting such an invitation.

A Pool Room Gang

145. A Jewish girl eighteen years of age on her way home from work flirted with two young men and finally accepted a ride. Instead of driving her home, they stopped in front of a poolroom where soft drinks were served and coaxed her to come inside.

This was the hang-out of a gang of about seventeen Italian boys ranging in age from seventeen to twenty-one. The door was locked and the girl was attacked by six or seven of the group. The proprietor of the poolroom in the meantime called up the remainder of the gang, seventeen in all, and the girl was attacked by this number within an hour. The girl was three months in a hospital before she recovered. The men were sent to the Joliet penitentiary.

This is the type of poolroom gang that loafs consistently and whose members are always on the lookout for a way to make some easy change. They gamble and are out for any excitement.[18]

"Cherchez La Femme"

Women have come to play an increasingly important part in the criminal gang. While wives of successful gangsters are well protected, sweethearts and paramours often take part in criminal enterprises, sometimes acting as lures, sometimes actually holding a gun and participating as any other gangster in a holdup. Robbery is no longer taboo for women, that is, women who live in an underworld atmosphere. Since the occupations of men, formerly closed to women, have been opened to them, what is inconsistent about their entering the time-honored profession of the highwayman? They may do it for thrills; they may do it because hard pressed to make a living;

they may do it simply as a matter of course; but at least it is more wholesome than becoming a prostitute.

Yet this sort of activity for women who live on an urban frontier should not occasion surprise. The frontier of the pioneer often created conditions favorable to the entrance of women in criminal gangs. Women were usually attached to the bandit gangs that created such terror in the early days of Illinois. Then there was Kitty Kelly, as hard boiled as any member of the notorious gang of Australian bushrangers; and Texas had its Belle Star, who has been compared and contrasted with the modern Brooklyn gun-girl.[19]

Cases of this type indicate how a woman, abandoning what are conventionally regarded as feminine traits, may play the role of a man in a gang and be accepted on terms of equality with the other members. It is quite possible in some of these cases that she may play the dual role of gangster and sweetheart, but ordinarily one part or the other seems to dominate. So well, indeed, does a girl sometimes play the gangster role that she may qualify for a share in the leadership of such a group.

"Honey's" Gang

146. A diminutive, bobbed-haired girl of twenty-one, who thrilled with pride on being told she resembled Clara Phillips, the hammer-slayer, but wept with shame at the thought of bringing sadness to her mother, last night confessed to the Evanston police that she was the brains and sometimes the brawn of a bandit crew responsible for seventy-five North Shore robberies and hold ups.

———— ———— is her name, but she particularly requested that it be given as "Honey," explaining that that was what "the fellows" called her. In jail with her is ———— ————, while Tom ———— is out on $2,000 bonds, being named by Honey as her crime lieutenants. Glen ————, whom she coyly terms her sheik; Connie ———— and Roy ———— are sought.

Honey mingled her story with many a "My Gawd!" and "That's the hell of it!" and resentfully explained that her arrest came when a "bunch of those damn police overheard me telling about one of the jobs I pulled."

"My gang didn't have the nerve, that was the trouble. My sheik, Glen, was O.K., but I had to steer him. But that ———— ———— was yellow. One night we were waiting to pull a stick up at Ridge and Dempster and he got cold feet. I stuck my gun to his head and said:

"'I'll blow your brains out if you try to quit now.'

"That brought him across all right.

"Glen started me on this stuff, I guess. I worked in my mother's confectionery store. I'd go out with him and sit in the car while he pulled stickups, but he didn't know how to work them, so I took charge. Then we annexed the rest of the gang and put over some swell jobs."[20]

Marriage and the Gang

Ultimately the biological function of sex serves, perhaps, as the chief disintegrating force in the gang. Marriage is the most powerful and dominant social pattern for mature sex relations even in the disorganized region of gangland. Consequently it represents the ultimate undoing of most gangs with the exception, perhaps, of the distinctly criminal groups of the professional type which specialize in rum-running, banditry, and similar activities. For the gang boy, marriage usually means reincorporation into family groups and other social structures of work, play, and religion which family life as a rule brings with it. The gang which once supplanted the home, now succumbs to it; for the interstitial gap in the social framework has been filled. Conventionalization of the gang indicates that this process of disintegration is not far distant. When members begin marrying there is a loss of interest and the club's charter and equipment are eventually sold or passed on to a younger group destined to repeat the same cycle.

The Gang and the Moral Frontier

The different types of sex life in the gang, which it appears vary all the way from ordinary conventional contacts to the utmost depravity and perversion, depend, in the first place, upon the age of the group. The indifference or hostility to girls found among younger adolescents, where the sexual appetite is immature, is later strengthened by gang discipline. The most rigorous discipline, however, is not long able to suppress the sex responses which are the result of developing biological mechanisms and functions. The form the sex behavior takes depends pretty largely upon the attractiveness and general character of their other activities, the nature of their leadership, the degree of their conventionalization, the nature and prestige of the social patterns to which they have access, and the general conditions of social control in their environment.

Space forbids the elaboration of all these points. It is important, however, to indicate the great significance of the situation complex in this connection. The gang boy lives in a disorganized social world where loose sex life is a matter of common observation. Sometimes he sees it in his own home where brothers, sisters, and lodgers are all crowded into the same sleeping quarters.

Overcrowding and Immorality

147. A good deal of the immorality of the ――― district, located in the South Side badlands, is explained by the terrible housing conditions. There are many vacant lots

and open spaces between the structures, but the congestion within the house is almost unbelievable. This is due to the attempt to reduce rents by subdividing apartments and by taking roomers and boarders.

This crowding results often in forcing the children of a household to live and sleep with adults and roomers in intimate relations that are very demoralizing in their effects. The children also see their parents and other adults disrobe. They often observe their parents in the sex relation. One woman made the significant remark that she did not mind this in the parlor in the presence of the children, but it was too much when company was present. Children living under such conditions early become inured to these things and fail to develop standards of decency and shame.[21]

Gang boys come into ready contact with the social patterns presented by vice, for gangland is largely coextensive with these areas.[22]

The Moral Frontier

The area of deterioration about the business center of the city has always provided the natural habitat for the brothels. The slum, just because it is the "scrap heap" of the community, furnishes a region—perhaps the only region within the city proper—in which this ancient and flagrant type of vice resort can flourish. The brothel, on account of its underworld business organization and its open appeal to a large public patronage, has always been the most obnoxious form of commercialized vice. It not only finds cover in this area of deterioration but also is in close proximity to the demand. Although the brothel in modern times has noticeably declined, giving place to a freer type of prostitution, and although the policy of public repression has accelerated this decline, yet the slum still harbors the vestiges of this institution. The most open and public type of vice resort within the city at the present is found there. The so-called "protected" and "syndicate" houses of prostitution in Chicago, which are remnants of a brothel prostitution, are in this area of deterioration.[23]

It becomes readily apparent, then, that these conditions of congestion and intimate contact with vice, coupled with widespread promiscuity which seems more or less traditional among the young men of these areas, present patterns of life to the gang and its members that easily promote sexual irregularities.

A Theory to Explain Life in the Gang

A certain type of explanation for the activities of the gang that has enjoyed a considerable vogue in the past has been based upon the so-called psychological recapitulation theory popularized by G. Stanley Hall. Puffer in his study of gangs has taken over this theory with all its instinct implications.

The Recapitulation Theory of Boyhood Activities

Obviously the instinctive activities of the boys' gang are the necessary duties of the savage man. The civilized boy hunts, fishes, fights, builds huts in the woods, stands loyally by his fellows and treats all outsiders with suspicion or cruelty, and in general lives the life and thinks the thought of the savage man. He is, for the moment, a savage; and he instinctively "plays Indians" as the real savage lives them.

General opinion has it that the boy instinctively plays Indians and follows the so-called tribal occupations as the direct result of his inheritance from some thousands of generations of savage ancestors who, willy-nilly, have been doing these things all their lives. We commonly believe that the normal boy is possessed to throw stones at every moving object because his forebears got their livings or preserved their lives by throwing all sorts of missiles at prey and enemies, so that the fascination of sticks and clubs is but the reverberation of the not so very far-off days when sticks and clubs were man's only weapons.[24]

Puffer continues to apply this theory in the explanation of the various activities that make life in the gang. Baseball is supposed, for example, to embody an epitome of man's prehistoric activities, such as throwing accurately, running swiftly, and hitting a rapidly moving object with a club. Between the ages of ten and sixteen it is assumed that the interests, the body, and even the soul of the normal boy recapitulate the stages passed through by our savage and barbarian ancestors in northern Europe from the glacial period to the early Middle Ages.

Many objections to this theory are advanced in biology, psychology, and sociology; it is not acceptable in the light of modern knowledge. So far as the innate predispositions of the modern boy are concerned, they are probably little different from those of the savage boy; but the make-up of the modern boy is not similar to that of the adult savage, whom he is supposed to resemble.

The energies and impulses of boys are much the same the world over; they are simply functions of the organism in the period of growth. They are certainly not instincts; for they are far more inchoate than such predetermined and definite patterns of behavior. The organism of the normal boy demands activity and change; puberty brings sexual promptings; rest, food, and bodily protection are among the needs of the boy. Such innate predispositions as these are generalized and flexible. They do not become specific until they are developed in particular directions by all the stimulating forces in the boy's environment.

But the boy is not to be regarded as a passive structure, receiving the stamp of his environment like a lump of wax. If he is healthy, his energies are keenly active and his wishes are often imperative; they must get some sort of expression. Yet the direction they take depends upon the environment. The boy is plastic; his energies and impulses may be directed in a multitude of different ways. Just as the natural resources of a region or a country determine in a general way the occupations of its inhabitants, so the habitat of the gang shapes the interests of its members. The group, responding to its human environment, develops along definite lines. Its activities in general tend to follow the patterns which have prestige in its social milieu and which at the same time appeal to its love for adventure or to other wishes of its members.

Thus, life in the gang is a product of interaction between the fundamental nature of the group and its members on the one hand and the environment on the other. Neither factor may be neglected in explaining it.

A Reporter At Large: The Persian Queens

*Robert Rice**

Out in the Brownsville section of east Brooklyn, three-quarters of an hour from Times Square on the subway, there are seven gang girls, from fourteen to nineteen years old, whom I got to know something about earlier this year when I spent three or four evenings a week for quite some time observing the professional activities of a woman worker for the New York City Youth Board, the municipal agency responsible for coping with juvenile delinquency. The girls are the members of a club I shall call the Persian Queens. It is a club that professes to be "social," in the specific local sense that makes "social" the antonym of "fighting," and, indeed, none of the members, as far as I know, has a police record or is conspicuously delinquent in any way except sexually; among them the Persian Queens have produced four babies, and another is on the way. The reason I call them gang girls is that a gang girl, as the Youth Board uses the term, is a girl who has chosen to identify with—in other words, bask in the glory of—a gang of fighting boys, and only a few months before I met them the Persian Queens had not been Persian Queens at all but Mohawk Debs; that is, members of the ladies' auxiliary of a particularly active fighting gang called the Mohawks. This auxiliary was a big group, perhaps thirty strong; like most "deb" groups in New York, it was loosely organized, if it could be said to have been organized at all, and it was composed of girls who, in their relationships with each other, were enemies just as often as they were friends. The only qualification for membership in the Mohawk Debs was that a girl be attached to a Mohawk and proud of it.

In personality and in character, the Persian Queens are as different from one another as any seven people with similar backgrounds and living in similar circumstances would normally be. Perhaps the two crucial respects in which they are alike are that they were all born Negroes and were all born poor. Of course, many more poor Negro girls than not conduct themselves with what both policemen and schoolteachers concede to be propriety, so it is hard to be sure how much their empty pockets and dark skins had to do with impelling these particular girls to join street-gang society. As far as I can tell, no Persian Queen is more than vaguely aware that being either poor or Negro is an unlucky, or even a special, circumstance, and Youth Board people with whom I discussed the matter have the same impression. "These kids are so far down and so far out that they're doing well to get from today to tomorrow in one piece," a Youth Board worker told me. "Freedom? Man, if you lived the way they do, what would that word mean to you?"

One thing the Persian Queens do know, though, is that once they had joined street-gang society they had a third congenital disadvantage: they were born female. For street-gang society is a society organized by males, operated by males, and devoted to traditionally male pursuits—chiefly fighting and carousing—and the special problem facing gang girls is that there is simply no way for a girl to gain a significant amount of power or prestige in a gang. If a girl fights as well as a boy—and Youth Board workers know girls who do—boys don't like her, and in no walk of life is a girl whom boys don't like an object of admiration or envy to other girls. By the same token, the one kind of status that carousing can confer is manly status, and to the extent that gang girls carouse they merely lessen the possibility that they will achieve the womanly status of being considered desirable mates. In short, because gang girls aren't boys, they are, in their own view, barely people, and this low self-esteem is naturally reflected in their personalities. I dwell on this fact because it is the one that most concerns the Youth Board. It is also the one that most surprised me during my evenings in Brownsville. As I started commuting on the New Lots Avenue line, I did not suspect that girls who drank and fought and shoplifted, who declined to go either to school or to work, who were as likely as not to have caught a venereal disease or have had a baby, or both would be dim. The Persian Queens are very dim, and one way of describing what I saw the Youth Board worker do in Brownsville is to say that she was conducting an experiment in social work whose object was to learn whether the techniques Youth Board men had developed to keep gang boys from fighting could be effectively applied by a woman to the less showy but possibly more complicated task of helping gang girls to brighten up.

The name of the Youth Board woman I saw in action is Mrs. Virginia Noville, and she is anything but dim. A handsome, handsomely got up young Negro woman, she majored in sociology at Central State College, in Wilberforce, Ohio; put in some time with the Welfare Department in Dayton, Ohio; came to Brownsville to work in a community center that is part of one of the housing projects there; and then, feeling strongly that the girls who went to community centers were in much less need of her services than the girls who strayed—or were kept—outside, moved to the Youth Board, which specializes in doing social work on the streets. It is fair to describe Mrs. Noville as a militant feminist, who is appalled when she sees other members of her sex being treated as, or thinking of themselves as, second-class. It is also fair to say that no group of girls in Brownsville are more certain that they are second class—and therefore in greater need of her kind of help—than the Persian Queens. At this point, I must make it clear that the one condition Mrs. Noville imposed when she consented to allow me to do her footsteps in Brownsville was that I would do my best not to describe the girls I became acquainted with in such a way that they could be identified. In this report, therefore, the names of all girls and groups are invented ones, and a good many other identifying details have been falsified. I will add that the name I have invented for the club is not a wholly improbable one, for the reason that the real names of the New York street gangs are so various, and often so fanciful, that inventing a wholly improbable one is wholly impossible. Some real gang names are factual (the Forsyth Street Boys), some are romantic (the Dragons, the Apaches, the Vikings), some are candid (the Sinners, the Stompers), some are boastful (the Mau Maus, the Untouchables, the Hellburners), and some are mendacious (the Jolly Midgets). The church is represented by the Bishops and the Chaplains, the state by the Viceroys, the arts by the Jazzmen, and the paraphernalia of power by the Swords, the Sceptres, and the Crowns. The gamut of the nobility is run, from Knights, through Lords and Counts and Dukes and Princes, to Kings. Geography is extensively drawn on by Frenchmen, Scotchmen, Romans, Egyptians, and even Bohemians and Canadians. And so, somewhere in the city, there may well be Persians, though I don't happen to have heard of them. At any rate, the non-Persian Persians in Brownsville are also, as I have said, extraordinarily unqueenly Queens. To begin bluntly, their appearance is exceptionally unattractive, not because their faces or figures are in any way odd but because every one of them habitually sits in a slouch and walks with a swagger, looks at and plays with their middle sweater button and mumbles when she talks, dresses in skirts that create the impression that her anatomy consists principally of knees and hips, and apparently does her hair with her left hand while looking away from the mirror. I know it is rude to disparage the way a girl looks and walks and dresses and grooms herself, but it is impossible to report what I saw of Mrs. Noville's work without discussing the appearance of her girls. One of her convictions is that a girl's looks and a girl's self-esteem are inextricably intertwined. On the theory that if she could teach girls to look like ladies there was a chance that they would start to act like ladies and think of themselves as ladies, she devised an extensive program of advice to the beauty-lorn. A few months before I came along, she had presided over a Charm Clinic, at which, one evening a week for four weeks, about fifty girls crowded into the local Youth Board office, which consists of a central room (during the day, it houses six street-club workers, two secretaries, a water cooler, and a switchboard) with a conference room on one side of it and a supervisor's office on the other. During the clinic's two-hour sessions, the girls heard, saw, and apparently enjoyed experts giving advice and demonstrations on such matters as Complexion Care, Basic Makeup for Every Girl, Simple Clothing, Selection of Accessories, and—to end with the most elementary—Personal Hygiene. The members of the Persian Queens were among the pupils at the clinic, which is how Mrs. Noville first made their acquaintance. Later on, while I was in Brownsville, Mrs. Noville staged quite an elegant fashion show in a local dance hall, in which more than thirty of her girls, including the Persian Queens, participated in one way or another; twenty or so served as models, and she had drilled them so well that during the show only one was chewing gum. Like any technique of character-building, turning gang girls into ladies takes time, and not one of the Persian Queens had sufficient self-confidence to model in the fashion show; they elected, as a group, to form the backbone of the refreshment committee, and spent the evening behind a counter dispensing soft drinks and slices of cake they had baked—and not baked very well. But Mrs. Noville is not the proprietress of a cooks' and bakers' school, and she was delighted with the Persian Queens that night. Never before, as far as she knew, had they so much as attempted any concerted project. What's more, the occasion had inspired them to preen themselves almost beyond recognition. By the time they got together for their next club meeting, five days later, their strenuous chic was gone, but they had made a first appearance as gracious hostesses, and Mrs. Noville had seen to it that they were photographed behind their counter, so that the transformation, however fleeting, would be a matter of record.

The Persian Queens' organizer and moving spirit—indeed, the only spirit in the club that seems capable of much motion—is Ethel, a burly, dark-skinned seventeen-year-old, with big hands and feet and powerful shoulders. Though she looks as if she could lick any kid on the block, there is no evidence that she has bothered to try; she apparently has a pacific nature. The expression that was most often on Ethel's face when I saw her was the smug one that little girls assume after they have said, "I know a secret." And Ethel unquestionably does know many secrets that you and I don't know, and, more to the point, that the Youth Board doesn't know, for she is an almost totally mysterious character, in a way that, I learned, most of such girls are most of the time. There is a lot more than simple peasant suspiciousness in the determination with which they try to conceal the circumstances of their lives. To a degree that a middle-class person can barely comprehend, they and their families are the subjects of dossiers on whose contents their very existence depends. Even assuming that they do nothing that might find its way into a police blotter—and this is quite an assumption to make about people who have plausible reasons for feeling that the purpose of the criminal code is to threaten rather than to protect them—they are likely to be under eternal scrutiny. If they are receiving financial assistance from the Welfare Department, as the households of all Persian Queens are, every dollar or pair of shoes or bottle of whiskey in their lives is a matter about which the City of New York is entitled to be inquisitive. If they live in a housing project, as three of the Persian Queens do, the Housing Authority has a statutory right to keep their morals under surveillance. Some aspect of the domestic problems of many of them is recorded in the files of the Family Court. School guidance counselors keep track of them, and so do the admitting officers of the clinics in the city hospitals, and so do the directors of the neighborhood community centers, and so, for that matter, do Youth Board street-club workers. And unfavorable entry in any dossier can have consequences that range from the merely annoying, like being refused admission to a community center, to the catastrophic, like being excised from the relief rolls. The environment is not one that stimulates candor. In fact, it is safe to say that much of the material in the dossiers, since it has necessarily been supplied by the subjects, is fabricated and therefore of little use to someone interested in acquiring accurate information about any given case. Presumably, as Ethel gets to feel that Youth Board workers are trustworthy and sympathetic friends, she will reveal some of the facts of her life, but at the moment there is almost no fact about Ethel that can be stated with assurance—except that Ethel is running the club. Even Ethel's first name is a matter of doubt, since her friends call her by at least two other names as the fancy strikes them, or maybe strikes her. Mrs. Noville has occasionally visited Ethel at a housing project apartment, and this is probably where Ethel lives, but it may not be, since mail that has been sent to her there has been returned by the post office stamped "NOT AT THIS ADDRESS." Whether she has a family, and, if so, who its members are, poses a similar enigma. There are two other apparent inhabitants of the apartment in which Ethel apparently lives. One is a toothless little old lady, a Welfare client, who, one tends to assume, is Ethel's mother or grandmother or aunty, but who may be no relation at all, since Ethel introduced her to Mrs. Noville and me, when we called the apartment one afternoon, as "Mrs. Betty." The other is a three-year-old boy named Andrew, who dances the Twist charmingly, and who, on the basis of the one reference Ethel made to him in my hearing—to wit, "Yes, Andrew stays with us"—could be her brother or her nephew or her son, or none of these. There is no telling how Ethel spends her days. From time to time, Mrs. Noville questioned her about this, but the answers that came forth were transparent fictions. It is almost certain that she doesn't go to school, for she once told Mrs. Noville she didn't, and Mrs. Noville can't imagine her lying about that. She also said she didn't work, which is probably true but could be a lie if Mrs. Betty is receiving money from the Welfare Department for Ethel's maintenance. In any case, Ethel always seems to have five or ten dollars, which she carries in a pink plastic wallet, and she says she has a prosperous brother who visits her almost every weekend and in the course of each visit gives her a ten-dollar bill. The whole subject of where an adolescent's money comes from is one that Youth Board workers find it prudent not to speculate about—or not until they have acquired enough influence to follow up any speculation they verify with remedial action.

Mrs. Noville told me about the ambiguities of Ethel's biography on the night of my first visit to Brownsville, and they did not appear to vex her; she found them normal and not especially important. However, Ethel did furnish one puzzle whose solution then seemed to Mrs. Noville to be of consequence: Why had she organized the Persian Queens, and why did she insist on maintaining the organization? It was a club whose only visible reason for existence was that Ethel willed it to exist. There was not evidence, to begin with, that its members were a group of old friends. Ethel, it appeared, was fond of one of the other girls, and had been for years. This girl is Lucretia, an inarticulate, delicately built fifteen-year-old, who favors turtleneck sweaters in which she can bury her chin, who is still going to school, and who lives in the same project, one flight up from

Mrs. Betty. (Or whose mother, at least, lives there. On not one of a dozen or more occasions when Mrs. Noville had knocked at the apartment door had Lucretia been inside.) On the other hand, two of the Persian Queens seem to be only casual acquaintances of the rest. These are the Robinson sisters—a lethargic seventeen-year-old named Elizabeth, who bleaches her hair an amazing shade of orange, and who dropped out of school in the middle of the seventh grade to go to work and then found that no employment agency would recommend her for a job, because she couldn't multiply past the three-times table, and a garrulous fourteen-year old named Jacqueline, whose shoulders are usually hunched up to her ears, and whose style of dancing to slow music would be considered extreme by an Eighth Avenue belly dancer. Grace, the next girl on the club's roster (nobody knows how old she is), never showed up while I was around, and was barely known to Mrs. Noville, who suspected that the most that Grace was willing to do as a Persian Queen was to allow her name to be on the roster, and then only if Ethel paid her dues, of a dollar a week. (There is some reason to believe that Ethel pays, or helps to pay, everybody's dues. After a meeting at which Lucretia had rather ostentatiously produced a dollar bill from her wallet and deposited it in the treasury, she quietly borrowed twenty-five cents from Mrs. Noville.) The sixth member of the club, a fourteen-year-old named Kelly, also did not show up at any meeting I attended, since she had delivered herself, only a few weeks before, of an eight-and-a-half-pound boy. I did meet her one afternoon, though, when I accompanied Mrs. Noville on a visit to the project apartment that Kelly shares with her mother and the baby. Kelly is a jolly character, who seems to find premature motherhood considerably more of a laughing matter than, say, Mrs. Noville does, though I'm not sure that her good humor is going to be of much solace to her son. She was holding the baby on her lap while she talked with Mrs. Noville and me that afternoon and at one point he began crying. Mrs. Noville suggested that he was thirsty. Kelly allowed that he probably was, but added that if she gave him something to drink he would wet his diaper and she just didn't feel like changing his diaper right then. Kelly is a well-known and popular girl throughout the neighborhood, but apparently her two or three best friends are members of a girls' club that is a sort of rival to the Persian Queens, so her presence on the roster is as mysterious as anyone else's. The seventh, and oldest, Persian Queen is Frances, a sullen and slipshod nineteen-year-old, who is the mother of three children by three different fathers, who seldom rises before noon, and who spends much of the rest of her day and of her public assistance money at a local bar of extremely bad repute, leaving the children, the youngest of whom is eight months old, in the care of a local eleven-year-old boy, who is also of extremely bad repute. Between Frances and Lucretia there is a dislike so intense that it prevents even conversation. One night, on the way home from a club meeting, the two girls had a fight on the sidewalk while Ethel watched with interest, declining to intervene, because, she said later, the girl in the middle always gets hurt, especially if either combatant is armed.

(In this case, Frances was armed with her fingernails, and Lucretia with a tote bag.) A few days before the fight, Lucretia, with many giggles and much squirming and casting of her eyes to heaven, had confided to Mrs. Noville in my hearing the cause of the bad blood between her and Frances. At a party several weeks earlier, Lucretia had sat herself in the lap of the boy who was the father of Frances's third child. He had responded by kissing Lucretia roundly. This had so enraged Frances that she had taken off a ring he had given her and hurled it at him. He had caught it and handed it to Lucretia. Later, out on the street, Frances had met Lucretia and demanded the ring back. Lucretia, though she had no particular interest in the boy—and, in fact, felt sentimental about another boy— had refused to give it to her, on the ground of etiquette. It was the boy's ring, she had pointed out loftily, and he was entitled to dispose of it as he chose; if *he* asked her to return it to *him,* she certainly would, and meanwhile Frances could just go to hell. As I listened to this tale, it struck me that the incident, probably barring the existence of the baby, could just as well have arisen at an adolescents' party in the playroom of a twelve-room Colonial mansion in Greenwich, Connecticut, as at one in the kitchen of a three-room cold-water flat in Brownsville. Even the fact that the two girls ultimately came to blows was not one that seemed to me demonstrably characteristic of street-gang society and no other. However, I did not expect that the club would be disrupted by so savage an antagonism between two of its members, and I was astounded to find that both Frances and Lucretia showed up phlegmatically at the very next meeting, Lucretia with the marks left by Frances's fingernails still visible on one cheek and Frances with the lip and eye still puffy from the wallops of Lucretia's bag. Mrs. Noville was not at all astounded. Though she was in the dark about why Ethel was determined to have a club and how she influenced the other girls to cooperate with her, Mrs. Noville was sure that the determination was fierce and the influence was powerful, and that it would take more than an outbreak of intramural philandering, and the contusions and abrasions that resulted, to smash the Persian Queens.

If the personalities of the members and their relationships with one another do nothing to explain the existence of the Persian Queens, neither do the club's aims. Gang children may have a number of reasons for "going social." A chief one in almost every case, I would guess, is to persuade a more or less gullible public, including themselves, that they are "good," not "bad." After that, the two most common reasons for the existence of a social club are the declared purpose of building a large enough treasury to buy each member a sweater with the club name emblazoned on its back, and the undeclared purpose of milking as dry as possible the Youth Board's, or some other social agency's, supply of free movie tickets, dance bands and dance halls, buses and station wagons for excursions to parks and beaches, and other forms of free entertainment. The Persian Queens have shown no interest in either sweaters or excursions. As I have said, the club exacts dues of a dollar a week—a figure that Mrs. Noville thinks is scandalous for girls on relief—and Ethel, whether or not she is merely keeping track of her own money, records dues collections rigorously. Yet during half a dozen meetings that I sat in on, no member advanced a proposal for doing anything with the money, or even inquired why it was being accumulated; one of the odd things about the club was that the question of sweaters never came up. The girls seem to believe that a club member is a dues-paying animal and let it go at that. Certainly Ethel has no nefarious plans for the funds, since she cheerfully allows Mrs. Noville to have custody of them, perhaps because she once was in a club that entrusted its treasury to one of the members and one day that member's mother, being short of food and rent money, appropriated the entire hoard, which amounted to forty-five dollars. But Ethel doesn't seem to have any non-nefarious plans, either. The Persian Queens have no more visible interest in being entertained than they have in their money. At one meeting, Mrs. Noville cajoled them (all except Lucretia, who was willing to sit at a club meeting with Frances but not to go on a junket with her) into agreeing to go as a group, the following Sunday afternoon, to the Radio City Music Hall—a project whose expenses were to be shared by the club and the Youth Board, and whose adventurous nature I can make clearer by adding that although most of the girls were vaguely aware that there was such an establishment, none of them had any notion of what or where it was. Once they had consented to carry out this drastic plan, Mrs. Noville asked them to meet her at two-thirty sharp on Sunday at the entrance to a subway station close to all their homes. At three-fifteen, Ethel showed up, alone, and said that she had scoured the neighborhood and hadn't found another Persian Queen anywhere. The project was called off.

Scouring the neighborhood for her members—usually with more success than on that Sunday—occupies a fair amount of Ethel's time. She generally manages to round up a quorum and to convoy it to the Youth Board headquarters no more than an hour after the weekly club meeting is scheduled to start. On one meeting night, though, she didn't have her usual luck. She appeared at the headquarters at seven-fifty—fifty minutes late—with only Lucretia in tow. And Lucretia wasn't happy. She was hungry, she said, and, as the result of certain amount of interrogation by Mrs. Noville, it emerged that she hasn't had any breakfast, because eating breakfast always made her sick, and hadn't had any lunch, because the menu at the school cafeteria that day had displeased her, and hadn't had any supper, because she hadn't gone home after school. She had been about to go home, she said, squinting at Ethel in what was the slowest thing to a display of insubordination I ever saw her make, when Ethel had located her and insisted that she come to the meeting. Mrs. Noville offered to take her across the street for a hot dog or a slice of pizza, but she declined, and appeased herself by drinking at least eight cups of water from the cooler. Ethel had seen Frances earlier in the day and had learned that she wasn't planning to attend the meeting that night. Neither (naturally) were Grace or Kelly, but the Robinson girls were expected any minute. For an hour or more, we waited and chatted (it was that night that Lucretia, taking her mind off her hunger pangs for a few minutes, described her difficulty with Frances), but the Robinson girls didn't show up. Ethel and Mrs. Noville, to Lucretia's evident but silent disgust, weren't discouraged. They thought that the Robinson girls might be dancing or playing cards in the housing-project community center across the street from the tenement they lived in, and that we should look for them there. So, in a cold drizzle, we walked seven or eight blocks to the community center, with Lucretia still adamantly refusing to take any nourishment.

The first two blocks were on Brownsville's main shopping street, Pitkin Avenue, one of the few remaining streets in New York where if you hear a foreign language spoken it is as likely to be Yiddish as Spanish. For Brownsville was until fifteen years or so ago an almost totally Jewish neighborhood, and, according to the 1960 census, it is still one of the New York neighborhoods with the highest percentage of foreign-born residents. Pitkin Avenue must look much as it did thirty years ago. There are certainly no new buildings on it, and the stores can't have changed much, either: a proliferation of cheap shoe and clothing stores, the inevitable Woolworth's, a Loew's theater, a few branch banks, a scattering of hot-dog stands and clothing stores and Chinese restaurants, and a single bar. There are practically no elevators in Brownsville, except in the housing-project skyscrapers. A typical Pitkin Avenue building is a four-story structure, with a store at the bottom, the offices of a lawyer or a doctor or a chiropodist one flight up, and apartments on the two top floors. Some of the residential streets are linked with one and two-family houses, often frame ones, and even contain a few trees and an occasional patch of grass, and others are given over to the kind of brick tenements that were designed when they were built, fifty years ago, to be as squalid as possible; there are still plenty of cold-water flats on streets like those. There are a lot of synagogues in Brownsville, some of them functioning, some of them abandoned, some of them converted into Pentecostal churches. Almost every thing in Brownsville is dilapidated—the one-family houses, the two-family houses, the tenement houses, the synagogues, even the trees and the grass. At night, the neighborhood is quite spooky. The blocks are long, the sidewalks are narrow, the street lights are dim. On most Brownsville streets at night, every approaching pedestrian looks like a cut-throat until he gets close enough to turn out to be, say, a venerable Jew with a long beard, or a stylishly dressed Negro girl whose expression indicates that she has been as apprehensive about you as you have been about her. It is a neighborhood that I found myself getting used to but am sure I could never learn to love. As we approached the community center that night, I found myself observing with surprise that for the first time in my life I was looking at a housing project and finding it good.

We entered the community center, which is in the lee of a thirteen-story apartment house, and inquired for the Robinson girls, but they weren't there, so Ethel volunteered to go over to their apartment and try to arrange for the meeting to convene there. She'd be right back, she said. Half an hour later, Mrs. Noville and Lucretia set off to look for her. With the possible exception of bars in Spanish-speaking neighborhoods, housing-project community centers are the most deafening places in New York. In this one that night, a phonograph was rocking and rolling at top volume, ping-pong balls were being slammed out of time with the music, and the recreators, just to make themselves heard, had their volume turned up, too. Preferring the cold drizzle as an environment in which to kill time, I walked out onto the sidewalk to await word on whether I would be welcome at the meeting at the Robinsons', if there was going to be a meeting at the Robinsons'. In perhaps ten minutes, Mrs. Noville reappeared and said that the meeting was about to start; the fourteen-year-old Robinson, Jacqueline, was at home, though in bed with the grippe, and the seventeen-year-old, Elizabeth, had just stepped around the corner for some groceries. It was almost ten by then. The Robinsons live in three rooms on the top floor of a lopsided four-story building that is an almost total disgrace. No doubt the landlord wasn't responsible for the powerful smell of molasses that filled the halls that night, but there isn't much else that can be deducted from his account. The walls are cracked, chipped, gouged, grease-stained, and scribbled on. The banister wobbles alarmingly if one is injudicious enough to grasp it. On the first and third flights of wooden stairs—I can't vouch for the second flight, because it was in darkness—I saw a comprehensive collection of splinters, dust balls, cigarette butts, chewing-gum and candy wrappers, paper sacks, and wine bottles, along with a pint bottle whose label declared that it had once contained a good grade of bonded bourbon. The Robinsons' apartment is tidier than the halls, but it is in no better repair. Except in the corners, the linoleum that covers all the floors is worn through to its tarry backing. Several windowpanes are cracked. If a painter has worked in the apartment during the past ten years, he must have used invisible paint. I had heard previously that the Robinsons—or, rather, the Welfare Department of the City of New York, through the Robinsons—paid someone seventy dollars a month for the three rooms. When I saw the rooms, I thought, not for the first time, of the eccentricity of a system under which slum landlords are provided for out of the public treasury.

The Robinsons' front door opens into the kitchen—a room that, like many Brownsville kitchens, contains a bathtub that is equipped with a wooden lid so that it can serve as counter space when it isn't being bathed in. Mrs. Noville and I were admitted by Mrs. Robinson, a small woman with a flustered expression, who was holding a mop in her hand. Mrs. Robinson smiled vaguely and said the girls were waiting for us in her room and would we please excuse her, because she had to get on with her cleaning. If the way the apartment is furnished and fitted out means anything, the Robinsons are poor beyond imagining. A table and three plastic-covered chairs, two of them with rips in their seats, are all the furniture in the kitchen. Mrs. Robinson's room, where the girls were, contains a ram-shackle double bed, a bureau from which one leg and most of the drawer knobs and paint have disappeared, and a straight chair with a piece of board laid across a hole in the seat. From what I saw of the third room, it also had a decrepit bed and a decrepit bureau, plus a small radio, a tarnished wall mirror, and an overstuffed chair whose springs rested on the floor and whose stuffing was emerging from a number of holes in the arms and the back. Nowhere did I see a picture, an ornament, a rug, a lamp, or, for that matter, an ashtray. I do not mean to suggest that this is the way people—even people on relief—ordinarily live in Brownsville. Quite the contrary. I have been inside a dozen apartments there, most of them occupied by Welfare families. Almost all of these flats are reasonably comfortable, and none looks anything like the Robinsons'—none except Frances's, that is, and I am certain that in the case of Frances squalor is an expression of personality as much as of economic status. The Robinsons do not seem to be temperamentally squalid, for the girls are always neatly turned out and the apartment is clean. They seem to be suffering from some extraordinary shortage of funds. The only clue to the nature of the shortage, if there is a shortage, is something that Elizabeth told Mrs. Noville a few weeks later. One evening during the previous summer, which the girls were spending at their father's apartment, in another part of Brooklyn, their father had got into an alcoholic dispute over a woman with a man next door and stabbed him to death as the girls watched. The father is now in jail, awaiting trial. Mrs. Noville thinks it possible that before his arrest he was helping to support his daughters. Fathers who have left their children sometimes do, whether by order of a court or on their own. Certainly the fathers of many Brownsville children have left their families. No Persian Queen lives in a household of which a man—any man—is a permanent part, at least officially, though I did come across several hints that the official situation in this respect does not always jibe with the unofficial one. For example, on the Saturday afternoon Mrs. Noville and I paid our unannounced call on Kelly, Kelly's mother and a man to whom we never were introduced were sitting at the kitchen table when we arrived. Both of them had their elbows on the table and their chins in their hands. Both were freshly groomed and freshly dressed, Kelly's mother in a crisply ironed house dress and the man in a spotless white shirt, dark-blue trousers with sharp creases, and gleaming black shoes. There was a brown paper bag on the table between them. It was quite evident that there was a bottle in the bag. (A good deal of the drinking that is done in housing-project society is done without ever removing the bottle from the bag, perhaps because so much of it is done on sidewalks or on park benches.) In any case, both Kelly's mother and the man were drunk, the man to an extent that had put his steering mechanism quite out of commission. Kelly's mother was wobbly, but when she saw that her daughter had visitors she was able to escort her companion to the back of the apartment, where they remained during our stay. It is not unreasonable to suppose that one reason that Kelly's apartment is comfortably furnished and pleasantly decorated is that a man who can afford good clothes and whiskey is a fixture there.

If I have so far avoided describing what usually happens at a meeting of the Persian Queens, it is because remarkably little happens. At one meeting, as I have indicated, most of the time was spent in earnest discussion of a trip that one intended to make. Another was taken up chiefly by an attempt to compose a three-sentence letter of thanks to a beauty parlor that had given free hair-cuts to Ethel, Lucretia, and the Robinson girls the day before the fashion show. The letter was never composed. To begin with, the girls simply couldn't cope with vocabulary and syntax, and Mrs. Noville, as a matter of principle, gave them as little help as she could. For another thing, the attention span of an average Persian Queen appears to be about forty-five seconds, and so every attempt at serious composition rapidly deteriorated into a series of jokes, gossiping remarks, and giggles. No sooner had Jacqueline, who is the club secretary, laboriously written "Dear Madam" at the top of a sheet of ruled paper than all the other girls began hooting derisively. "Well, it sure isn't 'Dear Sir,'" Jacqueline said defensively. That provoked more laughter, and several facetious suggestions about the proper salutation. Finally, Mrs. Noville got the girls' minds back on their work, and they agreed that the polite thing would be to salute the beauty operator by name. It turned out, however, that none of the girls could remember her name. The discovery provoked three or four minutes of silent thought. At last, ten minutes later, they agreed on "Dear Madam." Even so, they might have got the letter written if another special difficulty, which proved utterly inseparable, hadn't arisen: the letter absolutely had to be circumlocutory, because all the girls were slaves to a superstition that neither Mrs. Noville nor I had ever encountered before; namely, that offering direct and specific thanks to a person who has done your hair will make your hair fall out. The meeting at the Robinsons' was necessarily short, because it was late and Jacqueline was ailing; besides, there was no place for most of us to sit, so everyone stood up. Consequently, it accomplished even less than usual. Ethel, as she always did, bookkept at some length. Mrs. Noville suggested that since warm weather was approaching and the girls might need money for some new clothes, the club dues be cut in half. That was too much of a startler for the girls. They postponed action on it and adjourned. Elizabeth never had shown up with her groceries. Jacqueline, who looked peaked, and who hadn't said a word all evening, though she was ordinarily the most conversational of the Persian Queens, went back to bed in the other room. Ethel, Lucretia, Mrs. Noville, and I said good night to Mrs. Robinson, who was still busily mopping, and picked our way down to the street. After we had walked two blocks in the direction of the Youth Board headquarters, Ethel announced that she was going to take Lucretia to a Chinese restaurant for something to eat, and the two of them sloped off in the direction of East New York, which was neither the direction in which any one of the three nearest Chinese restaurants was situated nor the direction in which the girls lived. Three blocks farther on, Mrs. Noville and I ran into Elizabeth. She didn't have a bag of groceries, which wasn't surprising, since the store she had supposedly gone to was one block away from her home, not five. Elizabeth's orange hair was as tidily arranged as I had ever seen it, and she was wearing quite a stylish fitted coat, yellow gloves, and what looked like a new pair of shoes. Mrs. Noville asked her why she hadn't been at the meeting, and she answered that she had "had to help a friend move some dishes"—a provocative explanation, if ever I heard one. Mrs. Noville, however, did not allow herself to be provoked. She did not ask Elizabeth where the dishes had been or where they were now or who their owner was. "Well, good night, Elizabeth," was what Mrs. Noville did say, and Elizabeth started on her way again.

There is one postscript to that evening. A week or so later, Jacqueline sought out Mrs. Noville to tell her that she hadn't had the grippe at all but evening sickness. She was two months pregnant.

After a while, the fog began to fade away a little from the principal Persian Queen mystery—why the girls had formed the club in the first place. In this instance, as in many others, things were just about the opposite of what they seemed. Apparently, the Persian Queens did not think of themselves as Persian Queens, or as being social; what they believed they really still were, and took pleasure and pride in being, was true-blue Mohawk Debs. Their line of reasoning may become faintly intelligible if it is related to a smattering of the recent gang history of Brownsville as it is known to Mrs. Noville and those of her male colleagues who are serving with the local boys' gang. At the time the Youth Board established a separate Brownsville street-club unit, in July of 1960, it had in its files the names of twenty-four local groups of adolescents that could conceivably be called gangs. Of these, about half were quiescent and needed no more attention than an occasional visit from a Youth Board man to make sure that they were staying that way. Five or six others were largely defensive in character; they were prepared to resist invasion of their territory but were disinclined to sally into anybody else's. Four or five quite aggressive gangs occupied the borders of the neighborhood and brushed frequently with similar groups from the surrounding areas of Bedford-Stuyvesant (to the north), East New York (to the east), and Canarsie (to the south). Inside Brownsville, the principal conflict was—and in somewhat different form still is—between two bellicose gangs, the Mohawks and the Famous Dukes. They were strategically placed in what might be called the center of Brownsville's natural gang territory—the largest housing project (actually three separately administered but contiguous projects, in which almost four thousand families, nearly all of them Negro, live) and the surrounding slum streets, which are a reminder of what the neighborhood was like before the projects were built. The dividing line between the two groups was definite. It was a wide street—which, for the sake of concealing the identities of the gangs, I shall misname Montgomery Street— that runs north and south through the area. Montgomery Street itself, if it wasn't exactly neutral ground, was at best no man's land, but everything for several blocks east of it was under firm Mohawk control and everything for several blocks west of it was in the hands of the Famous Dukes. Travelling between the east and west ends of Brownsville by any other route than Pitkin Avenue—which, since it contains the business establishments of the neighborhood's most prosperous citizens, is well policed—could be a perilous undertaking for a young person, male or female, whose motives weren't transparently nonpartisan. The conflict between the Mohawks and the Famous Dukes was entirely territorial. As far as the Youth Board people could see, the only obvious difference between a typical Mohawk and a typical Famous Dukes was that one lived on one side of Montgomery Street and the other on the other side. All the Famous Dukes and all the Mohawks were Negroes. Just about all were from families with Southern backgrounds. (And if the ones I saw were representative specimens, all were enormous, which may be some sort of evidence that a home-relief diet is not deficient in vitamins.) However, there was a slight but perceptible difference in the character of the two gangs: the Mohawks appeared to be better entrenched and more self-assured, the Famous Dukes to be more pushing and savage. This may have been because the Famous Duke territory had been inhabited by Negroes only since 1948, when the first project opened, whereas the Mohawk territory, or a part of it, had been a small Negro enclave as long ago as the twenties, when Brownsville was otherwise Jewish. It must be added that Brownsville was not Elysium when it was all Jewish. Even ten miles away on the west side of Manhattan, when I was growing up there thirty years ago, Pitkin Avenue, which must have been less well policed then, had the reputation of being one of the roughest streets in New York. And the accuracy of that reputation was confirmed a few years later, when the existence of Murder, Inc., whose headquarters were in Brownsville and most of whose operatives were Brownsville Jews, became known.

Naturally, there were girls associated with both the Mohawks and the Famous Dukes; there were Famous Duchesses as well as Mohawk Debs. The Famous Duchesses were an atypical and outrageous band. They were a bona-fide fighting gang—one of the few girl fighting gangs the Youth Board has ever come across—and their depredations in the neighborhood were the original reasons for the addition of a female street club worker to the Brownsville staff. (The reason the street-club project was all male until a couple of years ago was not that the Youth Board was unaware of the numerous problems gang girls have and present but that the Youth Board's limited resources of time and personnel had to be allocated to work with boys because boys do so much more physical injury than girls to property and to other people. Even now, only nine of the hundred and fifty-odd street-club workers in New York are women, which is why I have called Mrs. Noville's work an experiment.) By the time I got to Brownsville, though, the Famous Duchesses had misbehaved themselves virtually out of existence. A couple of them had become pregnant, a couple of others had been evicted, on the ground of general unseemliness, from the housing project they lived in and had left the neighbor-hood, and the two most ferocious had been nabbed by the police as they were conduct-ing a purse snatching operation, and were at the State Training School for Girls, in Hudson, New York. One of these was a girl named Ruby, who, Mrs. Noville told me, with what I can only describe as professional enthusiasm, was the most extraordinary person (though she may have meant case) she had ever met. Ruby, who was just twelve years old when she was arrested, and was not big for her age, was apparently the fighting heart of the Famous Duchesses. She was fearless and fierce. She would fight regardless of the size or the number of her opponents, and when she fought she fought to win, with any weapon that lay to hand, though her favorites were a length of two-by-four and her fingernails, which she kept long and sharp. Ruby almost always wore pants rather than a skirt, and she habitually kept her head tightly bound in a black bandanna. It is question-able whether Ruby could have been reformed by street-club work alone, rather than by some more heroic treatment, but in any case Mrs. Noville did not have enough time with her to make much progress. The Charm Clinic had some effect on her, however. Before she disappeared upstate, she had been sufficiently influenced by Mrs. Noville's femininity campaign to snatch the bandanna off whenever she came into Mrs. Noville's presence. I once asked Mrs. Noville if Ruby had ever been pregnant. "Why should Ruby be any different from everybody else?" she answered, and went on to say that Ruby was pregnant when she was arrested. Then, at Youth House for Girls while she was awaiting transfer to Hudson, she helped organize, and participated actively in, a riot. At the height of it, she lost her baby.

Unlike the Famous Duchesses, the Mohawk Debs were a conventional group—an informal association of girls who, in their eagerness for the glory they thought the Mohawk name would reflect on them, were delighted to drink with the Mohawks, sleep with the Mohawks, and, if the occasion demanded, carry weapons and furnish ali-bis for the Mohawks. At about the time the Famous Duchesses were chewing them-selves to pieces, the Mohawk Debs began to disintegrate in an unobtrusive way. Probably the principal cause of the disintegration was that the Mohawks themselves were losing some of their fighting spirit. The gang's leaders had reached nineteen or twenty and had out-grown mass sidewalk belligerence, and intensive street-club work had frustrated the formation of a leadership cadre of younger boys. More important, the changes in gang organizations that were taking place all over the city were taking place in Brownsville, too. Today, indeed, the era of the big gang and the full-fledged "bop," when battles involving forty or fifty boys on a side were fought in the streets, seems to be over. Now the characteristic juvenile group is the clique (the members' own word for it), numbering five or six, and the characteristic juvenile outrage is the ambush, in which the members of a clique waylay a putative enemy and deal with him without any immediate risk to themselves—just the ultimate risk of retaliation. Cliques don't give themselves names; their membership and their alliances with other cliques shift bewilderingly; and, of course, they make street club work—and police work—a good deal harder than gangs did, which may be why they are replacing gangs. In any event, one of the side effects of the changeover has been to leave the ladies' auxiliaries of the big gangs without sustenance, since being an auxiliary of a nameless, secret group is no way to acquire glory. That, fundamentally, was what happened to the Mohawk Debs. Another thing that happened to them was that the group's three most influential members all got pregnant at the same time. I suppose I seem to be harping on the subject of pregnancy. If I am, it is because every authority I have discussed the matter with agrees that sexual promiscuity is practically a built-in trait of girls who associate with gang boys, or who are themselves delinquent in other ways. Among the girls Mrs. Noville has worked with, virginity is nonexistent. Anyway, it was not extraordinary that three Mohawk Debs should become pregnant at the same time, though the fact that the three happened to be the group's top leadership was a disruptive coincidence.

The heiresses-apparent to the girls who went out of action were Ethel and a certain Hazel. Because they were mortal enemies, they couldn't work together, and neither was powerful enough to run the Mohawk Debs on her own. And so, during the late spring and summer of 1962, while the Mohawks, prodded by their street-club worker, were making an elaborate show of rearranging themselves into social clubs with comprehensive bylaws and sweet-sounding names, the Mohawk Debs evaporated. In the fall, Hazel and eight or ten of her adherents formed a social club of their own, which they said (and apparently they meant it), represented the breaking of whatever connection they had with Mohawks or Mohawk Debs. One day, after I had been going to Brownsville for quite a few weeks, Ethel described these girls to Mrs. Noville as "traitors," and not long after that Mrs. Noville became convinced that the act of treason was what had goaded Ethel, in a forlorn attempt to administer restoratives to the Mohawk Debs, to rally her adherents into the Persian Queens. (It is possible that the reason the Persian Queens are so oddly indifferent to the notion of acquiring sweaters is that the only name that it would give them any satisfaction to see on sweaters is Mohawk Debs, and that is out of the question.)

While I was in Brownsville, I saw something of Hazel and her group, too. Considering that the members of both clubs started out in life as Mohawk Debs, the contrast between the two is startling. Hazel's club calls itself the Athenian Ladies, acting on a suggestion from the boy friend of one of the members—a young man who is a profound enough scholar to have earned the local epithet of "heavy." I once asked a few of the girls what the name "Athenian ladies" meant to them, and discovered that they had a quite adequate idea of the implications of the word "Athenian" (I'm substituting names again, of course, but the real one had scholarly implications, too), even though a couple of them weren't very clear as to the exact location of name of the city involved. The

Athenian Ladies want sweaters, like to go on trips, and don't let Mrs. Noville hold their money. Most of them are still in school, at least half of them are from families not on relief, and three of them live in households that include fathers. One of the things about them that struck me particularly, now that I had seen a lot of Brownsville girls, was that most of the time most of them wore neat pleated skirts, which indicated that they were the objects of a certain amount of maternal solicitude. The Persians, to a girl, wear short, tight skirts.

It is quite understandable that Hazel and Ethel don't get along. In almost every respect except economic status—Hazel's home is in an abominable building, next door to and identical with the building where the Robinsions live—the two girls are totally unalike. Ethel is placid and Hazel is jumpy. Ethel is good-natured and Hazel is irascible. Ethel is unaffected and Hazel is self-conscious. Ethel is brawny and Hazel is frail. Ethel is frumpy and Hazel is chic. Ethel is dull and Hazel is bright. Ethel runs her club by being president and issuing orders, and Hazel runs hers by declining office and making sugges-tions. But probably the most significant difference between them is that Ethel looks like a person who will be a member of housing-project society all her life, while Hazel is clearly—to borrow a phrase that social workers seem to enjoy using—"upward mobile." The phrase doesn't mean that Hazel is well-behaved. She certainly isn't that. She is, or at least, was a committed gang girl, and, indeed, it is likely that because of her unstable tem-per, not to mention the visible rudiments of a persecution complex, she has been in more scrapes than Ethel ever has. Hazel's attitude toward Mrs. Noville has been demanding to the point of being infantile. For example, a few days before the fashion show she became furious with Mrs. Noville because she felt that Mrs. Noville hadn't given her her rightful share of tickets. Hazel's story was that she had been in the crowd of girls around Mrs. Noville, when the tickets were being distributed, and that every time Mrs. Noville saw her she had quickly looked away and given tickets to someone else. I had been in the room at the time and had seen what happened; Hazel had been lurking in a far corner, almost out of sight, waiting for Mrs. Noville to notice her and make a show of calling her forward for her tickets, and Mrs. Noville never had noticed her. Mrs. Noville made a point of calling Hazel's house as soon as she could and giving her the tickets. Hazel accepted them, of course, but not without stating explicitly that she wasn't particularly impressed by the fact that Mrs. Noville had gone so far out of her way, since that was no more than Mrs. Noville's duty as a social worker. It was a perceptive remark, and came close enough to the truth to leave Mrs. Noville with little to do in response but smile and say, "You're welcome, Hazel." As I have said, Hazel is bright. She is taking a commercial course in high school, and doing well at it. I watched her at the typewriter one evening at the Youth Board office, and it seemed to me that she was already qualified for a job. The reason it is important for the Youth Board to work with her, and work fast, is that Hazel's upward mobility, once she is out of school, may well take some such form as working her way up through the ranks to the position of booking agent for a string of party girls. For Hazel is determined to say goodbye, one way or another, to Welfare checks and tenements and wine parties and three-dollar shoes and community-center dances—in fact, to Brownsville and all that it represents. Whatever she does she will leave the Persian Queens far behind.

And this brings me to what is essentially, the antagonist against which Mrs. Noville and her colleagues have been struggling. It is Brownsville itself, one of the lost neighborhoods—the many lost neighborhoods—in New York. In the course of moving around the city over the years, I have devised a number of lost-neighborhood tests, which may not be definitive, but which I find give me an idea of the way a neighborhood is regarded by the authorities and by its inhabitants, too. Brownsville passes them all. There is the garbage-pail test: On almost any Brownsville street—except Pitkin Avenue—at almost any time of almost any day, there are dozens of full, if not overflowing, garbage pails. There is the sidewalk test: Most Brownsville sidewalks—except on Pitkin Avenue—are cracked and pitted. There is the coin-machine test: Not one chewing gum, peanut, or candy machine that I put money into in any Brownsville subway station was working. Most importantly, there is the passerby test: Almost everybody I saw on Brownsville streets—including Pitkin Avenue—looked as if he belonged in Brownsville and nowhere else. It is this last phenomenon that makes Brownsville, though it looks like New York, seem to me not like some other place but like no place at all. I suppose geography has a good deal to do with it. Though Brownsville is in the heart of the city, it is a backwater. It is a neighborhood quite without museums or monuments, office building or halls of justice, docks or railroad stations, bridges or tunnels, roller coasters or cabarets, or anything else that might attract someone who doesn't live or work there. It isn't even on the way to or from anywhere, except Canarsie. And so Brownsville is not only a neglected neighborhood and a poor neighborhood but a dull neighborhood as well, and the dullness all too often amounts to positive lethargy—or more accurately, to hopelessness—as in the instance of the Persian Queens: Frances, sitting in a saloon while her three babies do whatever it is they do in their squalid room; the Robinson girls, without furniture, without a father, without prospects; Lucretia, who in another environment might be an ordinary girl but is too ordinary to deal with the environment in which she finds herself; Kelly humming a merry tune to herself while her baby cries for his bottle; Ethel, who more than likely has been a working prostitute for years. There, dully waiting for Brownsville to be retrieved from outer space, I must leave the Persian Queens.

Jailbait: The Story of Juvenile Delinquency

William Bernard *

One alarming aspect of the situation is the growth of the girl gang. These first became prominent during the war, when they invaded the bright-light areas, lured soldiers and sailors into side streets where boy accomplices too young to be drafted would "roll" the uniformed men for their wallets. One court report tells of a Bronx gang which assigned girl members to waylay the leader of a rival Manhattan gang, lead him to a loft and seduce him. While the program was under way, the Bronx boys called the police, had the Manhattanite hailed for rape.

According to Bradford Chambers, a delinquency expert who made a survey of girl gangs at the time, they showed a low incidence of venereal disease and illegitimate births.

This still holds true. But in every other respect the situation has become worse since the end of the war. More girls are engaged in gangsterism; and they are committing crimes more severe. Gang offenses among girls between the ages of 14 and 17, in 1948 and the first six months of 1949, ran almost ten percent higher than during the peak-delinquency war year of 1943; but what police complain of most is that the girls are even more difficult to handle than the boys! Bronx magistrates call girl offenders more violent than ever before. Manhattan police state, "these junior gun-molls are tougher than the guys!" In Brooklyn, an emergency meeting in 1949, attended by magistrates, representatives of the district attorney, police officials and senior probation officers, emphasized that the adolescent girl gangster, in that borough, too, excelled her boy colleague in sheer viciousness.

Only rarely does the girl gang function without affiliation. In the great majority of cases it exists as the auxiliary of some boy gang, to which it gives fierce loyalty. One important duty, as described at the 1949 conference of Brooklyn law enforcement officers, is to act as weapons carriers to the boys, who thus escape seizure and charges. The girls also supply alibis, claiming that suspect boy was with them at a "session" or in bed at the time of a crime's commission. Principally, however, the young ladies act as camp followers, supplying the lads with such sex as they require—and fulfilling duties as lures and spies.

These bands of girls go under such names as "Robinettes," "Chandeliers"— after a peculiar hair-do—and "Shangri-la Debs." They comfort themselves viciously in

*From William Bernard, Jailbait: The Story of Juvenile Delinquency *(New York: Greenberg Publisher, 1949).* Copyright 1949 by Greenberg, Publisher.

street-fighting, although rarely using guns. A favorite weapon is the lye can and bottle of pop. When the girl slept with a boy member of an opposing gang, girls of her own group set out to punish her with the lye-and-soda mixture—detectives, fortunately, interfering before damage could be done. On another occasion, during a battle involving boy gangs and their respective auxiliaries, one tender lass hurled the mixture at a boy enemy. It missed him, struck a wall, bounced back, and horribly burned the girl's face, neck and shoulders. Another girl, a 15 year-old described in the press as "a pretty little miss, apparently sweet as the breath of heather," was in the habit of attacking with broken beer bottles. A week after being paroled for mashing up an 18-year-old girl with such a weapon, she was arrested with three child companions for beating a second girl, 16, with fists, kicking her in the stomach, burning her with cigarette butts.

The sex practices of these gangsterettes are particularly revolting. Homosexualism seems to be unknown, but any member over 12 is expected to give her favors to the boy gangsters. Older girls, to curry favor or by command, have been known to procure younger ones for the pleasure of their male gang leaders. One recorded case concerns a Manhattan girl, a Negress, caught by white girls in an East Bronx bailiwick. The girls dragged her to their cellar clubroom, where she was forced to submit to fourteen young mobsters.

Probation reports describe the initiation ceremony of the Shangri-la girls as requiring each neophyte to have intercourse with one of the boys of the Tiny Tim gang. Often girls thus initiated are no older than 12. It is said that the honor of performing the rite usually goes to a specific member of the Tiny-Tims—known to his fellows as "Willie the lover."

Judge John F.X. Masterson of Adolescent Court, attempting to awaken the public to action, recently released this story to the press:

> A prospect was enthusiastic about joining a certain girl gang—until the induction ceremony was explained to her. Then she rebelled.
>
> The recruiting agent and her friends promptly beat the girl, tied her up and proceeded to brand her chest with lighted cigarettes. They got as far as "Bi—" in their nasty little word game when the girl's screams scared her torturers off.

The sordid life of these degenerate girls stands well revealed in an incident which took place in the Bronx—at about the time the enforcement officers were holding their meetings in Brooklyn:

> Warfare broke out between the "Comets" and "Happy Gents" at Claremont Community Center, P.S. 55, with the stabbing in the abdomen of Carl, a 16-year-old Happy Gent. From what police could learn, the trouble between the two gangs

started when the Comets took some girl friends away from the Happy Gents.

The Comet leader, a 17-year-old, was held in $15,000 bail. He had a zip gun in his possession.

Others held included Leroy, arrested with a sawed-off carbine hidden in his trousers leg. He lived with one of the girls in the gang clubrooms. Another girl is expecting a baby fathered by one of the gang.

The magistrate observed that gangster movies and comics were to some extent responsible for youthful gangs. He added about the arrested boys: "They come from sub-standard homes… possibly from the lowest run of the economic ladder. Ultimately, I suppose, they will be sent to jail. That will be punitive action. What is being done about corrective action?"

One form of "corrective action" is the establishment of recreational and social facilities, based on a threefold idea. First, such facilities keep kids off the streets, where they get into trouble. Second, athletic and social events, such as dances, furnish thrills and excitement substituting for those otherwise sought in delinquent behavior. Third, a supervised environment is provided to make up, in part, for the lack of home life in slum areas.

The Chicana Gang: A Preliminary Description

*John C. Quicker**

The relative dearth of literature pertaining to female gangs is not altogether surprising, given the less frequent and less violent activities of the girls when compared to the boys. This apparent differential influenced Tuck in 1946 to make an even more interesting analysis when she stated "practically no Mexican American girl is ever arrested by the police." (1946, 219) Well, "the times, they are a changing," to quote an old Dylan song, or more accurately here, the times have changed. Girls are appearing not only more frequently on police blotters, but also in the probation departments, the courts, and the mass media.[1] Nevertheless, attempts at any systematic study of girls' groups, particularly Chicanas, are still notably absent from the literature, indicating a type of research lag period.

This paper is an attempt to begin filling that void. It is an exploratory venture whose concern is with the Chicana gangs of the East Los Angeles area, which in the past several years has been the battleground for some of the bloodiest gang warfare in Southern California. The data comes from an ongoing study of working with groups in this area over the past year. During this period, I have talked with various school personnel, teachers, probation officers, youth workers, police types, administrators, and youths themselves. Individual, focused interviews, ranging from one to two hours, conducted with thirteen gang girls, which were taped and transcribed, provide a significant portion of the data base for this paper. Due to the time limitations on presentation, I have limited the paper to a brief discussion of four areas which I felt could most succinctly portray the major characteristics of the gang. In particular, I will be concerned with the nature of the relationship of the girls to the boys' gangs, how one becomes a member, the process of decision making, and gang loyalty.

The Relationship of the Girls to the Boys' Gangs

Studies as far back as Thrasher's (1927) work have indicated that girls have always had some kind of an association with boys' gangs as a unit. These early Chicago years had the girls as members with almost no distinction as to sex. That is, if the girls could demonstrate physically that they were at least as powerful or skillful as the boys within the boys' own activities, they were given equal membership in the gang. These girls were warmly referred to as "Tom Boys," or "just one of the boys." More recently, studies have indicated that girls will sometimes act as assistants for the boys,

*Published here for the first time, this essay was originally presented at the annual meetings of the Pacific Sociological Association, San Jose, California, 1974. Special credit is acknowledged to the Los Angeles Human Relations Bureau and Ms. Alice Williams for providing technical assistance in the preparation of this study.

carrying their weapons in case they are stopped by the police and hiding them when they are searched. Other studies (Dawley 1973, Keiser 1969, Miller 1973) have shown that the girls actually form their own groups that act as auxiliaries to the boys' gang. In certain of these latter instances the girls may also have a sexual function, an apparently exploitive relationship with the boys.

The Chicana groups of East Los Angeles demonstrate some similarities to the auxiliary type of a relationship, though they are not actually auxiliary units. They appear to never achieve independence from the boys, although their relative autonomy does vary from group to group. In this sense, each girls' gang is an affiliate of a boys' gang, this latter having been formed first with a subsequent influential role in the determination of the existence and form the female affiliate was to take. I have not encountered any instance of a girls' gang existing independently of a boys' gang, though there are some boys' gangs that do not have associated girls' gangs. In general, however, the overwhelming majority of gangs seems to be mixed, with the trend being toward increasing female membership both within existing groups and for newly forming groups.

As an indication of this association, it is of interest to note that the girls' group always derives its name from the boys' name. For example, the Marianna Maravilla gang's female affiliate is termed "Marianna Maravilla Mona," the suffix being the female noun "monkey." For Loyo Maravilla, the female group was called Loyo Maravilla Gansas, which means "goose." There were also age-differentiated cliques within the groups that shared names such as the "chicos" for the older boys, and "chicas" for the older girls, or "locos" for the younger boys and "locas" for the younger girls. In some cases the girls' clique would have a name that was not just the female noun for the boys' clique. For instance, there are the boys' cliques "Pee Wee Cherries" and "Little Cherries," with the equivalent girls' cliques of "Santas" and "Ciclonas."

Often the girls will assist the boys with their activities, accompanying them on fights, to fight the girls of the other boys' gang that might be there, and occasionally carrying a few easily concealable weapons. However, as with the boys, they also have their own activities where only girls can attend. For instance, almost all internal disagreements or external conflicts are settled primarily by the girls themselves, except in instances where the decision directly affects the boys.

There appears to be considerable ambivalence on the part of both sexes concerning the acceptability of the girls affiliates. In effect, the boys are not certain that it is in anyone's best interest that girls should belong to a gang, although they seem to enjoy the presence and assistance the girls give. The girls for their part do not seem to know what the boys, in fact, want, a situation that is not at all uncommon in our society. As one of my respondents put it, when I asked her how the boys felt about the girls being in the gang:

I don't know, I've asked my boyfriend and they all come up with the same answer: I don't think a girl should be in. It's all right for a guy, but she shouldn't be in the fights. That's what they all say, yet they are happy to have their own girls. They're proud. They say our girls do this, our girls are bad. They say it's right for a guy, but it's not right for the girls, it doesn't look right. But I don't know what they're talking about cause they get happy. If it wasn't for them we wouldn't be around cause the guys first started M——. The girls never start the gang the guys did. And the girls that liked them or back them up started it with their permission.

Confounding these ambivalences are the boyfriend-girlfriend relationships. The boys almost categorically do not want their girlfriends to join the gang, while making exceptions for other girls. On the other hand, if the girlfriend joins, the boy makes little effort to convince her to leave.

There appear to be no clear-cut rules regarding dating patterns among gang members. Gang girls usually date boys who are in their gang, although they can also date boys in other gangs and boys not in any gang at all, without any negative sanctions, providing that the gangs are not doing battle with one another. This, however, seems to be somewhat related to the cohesiveness of the gang. That is, the closer the gang, the more likely are exogamous dating patterns to be proscribed. In a certain sense, to date or want to date someone outside the gang is an affront to one's "homeboys," who theoretically are more dear than any other boys. Where girls are in the periphery of the gang structure or in a weakly organized gang, exogamous dating patterns are not as traumatic. When asked if boys go out with girls not in the gang, the following response was given:

Yeah, but we get mad. The homegirls get mad. Like when we go out with the guys to drink from C——, the guys use to get mad. They use to tell us, get out of M—— if you want to be with the guys from C——. Go get in C——, and they get hurt. They get real mad. Cause, you know, once you're their home girl, they feel close to you, they feel as if you belong to them, not in no other way. They have respect for you. That's the way it is in our barrio. (S (1) p. 6)

Initiation: Getting into and out of the Gang

As a general rule, no one is coerced into joining a gang. That is, girls are not threatened or even cajoled into becoming a member if they are opposed to it. When they join it is because they want to. Prospective members are on occasion courted by the gang, but the usual procedure is for the girl herself to request membership, either personally or through friends already in the gang.

No one has to, it's willingly. Sometimes they don't even ask you, you go to them and ask them because a lot of times if a girl who hangs around with me a lot and I tell her how come you don't get into my neighborhood, you know. But there is also a lot of time you don't even know nobody and you still go to that person and say, "Why don't you get me in," and all that. But a lot of people, I've heard it from a lot of grown-ups who'll say, "Why he had to get in," and, "No, they made him get into a gang, and he didn't want to," but that's not so, because nobody gets into something they don't want to, you know.

Membership is not open to all who desire to join. There seem to be at least three basic criteria for qualification. The first is that the girl must not be interested in joining for protection only, or to have the gang fight her battles for her. Second, there must be some indication that the girl will not fold under pressure but will support the banner of the gang under adverse conditions. She must not "rank out," or give any signs that she might when she gets "hit up." This concept seems to be similar to Cloward and Ohlin's (1960, 24) idea of "heart" for a gang boy in the conflict subculture. Third, she must be able to "throw," or fight. Girls who are physically weak or unable to defend themselves are not an asset to the gang and often will not be allowed to join. If these criteria are met, the girl will then be ready for the final step, a ritual granting her full status as a gang member.

This ritual is termed, being "jumped in." The following dialogue I had with a gang girl gives a vivid account of the procedure:

Q: What happens when you get jumped in? What do they do?

R: When you get jumped in, what they do is they get around you, and then there'll be a girl counting, and it depends what gang you're getting into and how well you know the girls really, on how far they count and how slow they count.

Q: What do you mean count?

R: They count till 10 and they start jumping you and they'll start counting 1 then when they finish at 10, that's all, they jump you.

Q: What do you mean they count and they start jumping you?

R: Aja. Well, like they'll be a girl out there and she'll go okay, and then they'll start jumping you. She'll count to 10 and when she finishes counting, they'll stop.

Q: Do you mean they'll jump you one at a time, or a whole bunch of them?

R: No, a whole bunch.

Q: And what? They'll all jump on you and a girl counts to…

R: 10, and when she finishes counting, they're up.

Q: What do they do when they jump you?

R: They hit you all over.

Q: They do! Can you hit back?

R: Aja. If you want to hit back. Sometimes you… well, it depends on the girls that are jumping you, because some girls will get scared when you're swinging back, cause you're swinging anywhere, just to get them off you. Other girls won't be scared. Those who are scared will kind of back away.

Q: Do you get it worse if you swing back?

R: No, I don't think so.

There are two other ways of joining, though these are much less frequently used. The first is what is called a "fair fight." Here the novitiate "throws" with one of the gang members until her skill has been amply demonstrated to the rest of the gang. The second procedure, termed being "walked in," involves no fisticuffs at all, but rather occurs by agreement. This latter is not only quite rare, but in some gangs is absent altogether. Whatever way the girl enters, her final acceptance is signified by having all the girls present embrace her warmly and welcome her as a new member.

Leaving the gang is a much more complicated procedure than entry. It can be characterized by two types of departure, active and passive. In the former instance, either the girl or the gang initiates procedures that will unequivocally remove her from the gang. The latter instance occurs when the girl gradually stops hanging around with the gang, or the gang itself begins to slowly disintegrate.

Active departures are the most violent kind, where the ordeal is at least as difficult as the initiation, and in some cases more difficult. If the girl decides to leave, she will—at the least—have to throw with a number of girls in which she can expect to lose.[2] Usually it's not a simple loss where the girl cries "uncle" and the others stop, but rather she will be thoroughly beaten, often suffering some kind of injury.[3] When the gang wants the girl out, the violence appears to be at about the same level, although the instance of girls being removed in this fashion is quite rare.

The violence component of an active departure can be attributed in part to the fact that the remaining girls view such an act as a betrayal. To want to leave the gang bears similarities to wanting to leave the marines; the upstart is violating the trust of a group who has been like her family. For the gang to want a girl to leave, she must have violated—probably repeatedly—a deeply held taboo. Cases of "ranking" (to be considered in another section) or repeated sex with somebody else's boyfriend are usually severe enough to warrant disbarment.

Passive departures, probably the most frequent type, are relatively easy. In some instances girls never do leave the gang, even though they may not have actively participated with them for years.[4] Generally, as the girl gets older her activity with the gang becomes less frequent; certain status changes for the girl, such as marriage, a baby, graduation from high school, or getting a job bring about a more sudden reduction of gang activity, but are not interpreted by the gang as an active departure. Passive departures seem to have no ceremony at all involved with them. They are seen as natural developments not requiring any kind of retribution. The girl also receives an emeritus status, is given an honorific title—*veterana*—and is sought after for advice and council.

In the case where the gang itself is dissolving, leaving is accepted as a natural consequence. Besides, if the group that leaves at any one time is sufficiently large, it will rival the power and interest of those remaining to do anything about it. As the cohesiveness of the group decreases, anomie tends to characterize their relationships.

Decision Making

The female gangs tend for the most part to be democratically functioning units. Decisions that concern the group are rarely autocratic, but usually accomplished via the vote. An interview with one of the girls disclosing the gang's policy on removing undesirables is indicative of the concept of fairness most gangs utilize.

> . . . when we want to get someone out of M——, we have a meeting, you know. We take a vote. We see the reason we want to get them out. Most of the time we give them a chance, you know, and we talk it over and we talk in front of the person that's there, you know, and we tell her, "Hey man, there's a meeting and whoever doesn't come is going to get out," and that makes them all go to the meeting. We say, "So and so said you should be out of the barrio," and we tell them in front of everybody, everything is out in the open, why we want to get them out and everything like that.

The element of secrecy, so characteristic of many of our institutions, seems to be absent within the gangs. They are, as it were, "up front" about business pertaining to the gang or any one of its members.

Leadership within the group is diffuse. While some will deny that there are any leaders at all, by stressing the idea "we are all equal," others acknowledge the recognition of certain girls as leaders. One girl said that within the W——— gang some of the older girls are considered leaders; "They have been there longer and know girls from other gangs." (R (l) p. 10). In many cases the veteranas are looked up to as leaders, though as I mentioned, this is not an active role. What seems to occur is that they act more as advisors than leaders, whose opinion is sought because of the high esteem they have in the gang.

Two of the firmest denials I received regarding the existence of leaders came from girls who in my estimation were clearly leaders themselves. In this sense, they initiated activity, called most of the meetings, had key voices on decisions regarding who was to be allowed into the gang or removed, and by far carried on some of the most audacious of all activities. My feeling is that they were not denying the existence of the important roles that they were playing, but were rather not interpreting these roles as ones of leadership. To insist on equality, however, is contradictory to the admission that some are more equal than others.

Loyalty

Perhaps the most impressive quality of these groups is the overwhelming emphasis on group loyalty. Its closest analogue on this dimension is the family. In fact, the similarities of the gang to the family were drawn by most of the girls interviewed, as evidenced by the following:

> ... but to us, we're like one big family, if they do wrong to my home girl or home boy, it's like they're doing wrong to me and it hurts me.

At another point, she was explaining her feelings toward a group who had hurt some of her gang members, attempting to indicate to me how easy it is to retaliate in these situations:

> ... they are like our sisters you know, and how would you feel about them if they come home and told you somebody did this and this to you or one of your relatives, someone you're really close to. You'd get mad...

In a certain respect, then, the gang appears to take on the same kind of affect that one's family has. No sacrifice is too great; if you are a homeboy or homegirl, you are part of the *familia*, you are always right when challenged by an outside group.[5] Even the references to the male and the female members—homeboy and homegirl—take on an affective quality that is found in the family.

Other writers (Thrasher 1927, Cohen 1955, Cloward and Ohlin 1960) have indicated the intense loyalty of gangs to one another. For the Chicanas, coming from a tradition of extended family relationships, where there is considerable loyalty, the concept seems easy to grasp. Blood ties run deep. When these ties are transferred to another group having the same type of meaning that the family had, the loyalty goes along too. If we can accept the analogous functions of these groups, then it becomes clear why there exists this shift of emotions. In effect, the gang taking on the functions of the family receives the affect ordinarily exclusively reserved for it, sort of an in-group type transference.

A question I was particularly concerned with here was the source of one's friends. That is, how many of the girl's friendships were with gang members and how many were not, and what was the quality of those relationships? In general, it seems that the closer one is to the gang, the more likely are one's close friendships to come from the gang. The following is illustrative of how inclusive gang relationships can be:

... all the girls that go down to my house are from M———. All the guys that I know that I am close to are from M———.

Don't you have any friends that aren't from M———?

... Ya, from school you know there are always people who aren't from the gang. But they are the ones that are my friends, my real friends, the ones I consider my friends, they are all from M———.

A second illustration indicates in part why these relationships are so inclusive. As one girl said to me when I asked her why all of her friends were in the gang:

I don't trust anybody else, that's why. They're the only ones I can depend on, cause I know if I get into hassles they'll help me, and the other girls. Like one time we went to B———, we use to go to hang around there, and some girls there were going to jump me, and all the girls I was with took off and they left me there alone. I was in W——— too, but it was not the girls from W———. That's when I said I was only going to hang around with my homegirls.

In effect, then, for many of these girls a major portion of their support comes directly from other girls in the gang. For these girls any meaningful relationships outside the gang are rare. Further questioning concerning the depth of these relationships indicated that when these girls have a serious problem, they are more likely to seek a gang peer to talk it over with than anyone else. The gang here is not only a primary group, but perhaps the most important primary group in the girl's life.

At times the norms of the gang come into conflict with the norms of one's family. In a number of instances, I encountered girls whose parents did not know they belonged to a gang. They did not want to tell them because they knew they would disapprove. In other instances a girl would lie to her parents by telling them that the gang forced them to join. They could not quit because it would go badly for them when they met anyone from the gang again.

Resolutions to these conflicts were not always easy. One girl told me of a time when her father threatened her in front of some of her homeboys. She called on them for protection, which they gave, and in the ensuing tussle, the father hit one of the boys. The boy did not return the punch because he "had respect for" him, but the father never forgave the girl for forcing such a difficult situation. She was glad that the battle ended when it did, as she felt she would have been unable to choose between the gang or her father had she been forced to make a decision at that point.

For the most part, the gang serves some extremely valuable functions for the girls and is not something they take lightly. To want to join badly enough to be willing to be roughed up at an initiation or to be beaten up defending it, or to allow it to separate them from their families, and sometimes to die for it, is indicative of the exalted position in which it is held. This could suggest that the gang may be a substitute institution for things that the girls are missing from their lives. In a hostile world where the family is breaking down and conventional institutions such as school and work are becoming increasingly meaningless, the gang provides meaning and identity for these girls. (See especially Penalosa 1967; Rubel 1966, and Ramirez 1970.) As Cohen (1955) argues, it is a place where their status is unambiguous, but it is much more. It is a substitute for all those other things that they do not have, a place where they can receive warmth, friendship, understanding, education, and protection. Were the gang unable to provide these things, it would not be so acceptable an alternative, but rather it is precisely these functions which lend it its vitality. When girls coming from a traditional environment such as this are able to cast off those traditions sufficiently to become involved in activity previously allowable only for men, there are some very powerful dynamics occurring. We cannot divorce these dynamics from the social upheavals that are occurring. Unable to cope in a world that does not want them or cannot give them what they need, where being poor and non-white limits their opportunities, the gang appears as an attractive alternative. The gangs are structures that have existed for long periods of time, appearing to grow in recent years as their value for members increases. They are a solution, an enigmatic solution perhaps, but one nevertheless that is superior to the other institutional alternatives. To the extent, then, that they continue to bring satisfaction to the expanding group of anomic Chicanas, their growth will continue in the upward spiral we are witnessing.

Black Female Gangs in Philadelphia

*by Waln K. Brown**

Subcultural delinquency among females has suffered from a paucity of reportage when compared to the plethora of extant accounts concerned with male delinquency. As one source has been quick to point out (Cowie, Cowie and Slater 1968, 44), subcultural delinquency seems not to have been explored at all in relation to females. The truth of this statement has been partially dispelled in the last few years due to the recent women's movement for the equality of the sexes. The women's movement has helped to spawn some studies on female criminality, such as the insightful works of Freda Adler (1971; 1975b), but for the most part there is still a lack of information relative to the study of female delinquency in general and female gang involvement in specific.

Over 20 years ago Otto Pollak (1950) argued that female crime is more likely than male crime to go undetected and unreported, and he also raised the possibility that women may very well be as involved in crime as men. Despite Pollak's thesis many of the studies that post-date his work continued to claim that the delinquencies of females differ from those of males. The pronouncements of these researchers were most often based on the findings that they could acquire from official statistics such as police and court records. These researchers (e.g., Gibbons and Griswold 1957; Morris 1964; Vedder and Somerville 1970) found an inordinate concentration of sexual offenses, running away, and incorrigibility among female as compared to male offenders. Their studies are indicative of the rather narrow approach taken to the study of female delinquency which tended to concentrate on specific, officially reported areas of female delinquency while relegating other aspects of female delinquency to a modicum of discussion with little accompanying analysis.

More recently Hindelang (1971) has concluded that the pattern of female delinquency parallels does not differ from that of males. Hindelang's thesis has been most extensively verified by Adler (1975) who contends that crime among American women is increasing, more violent, and more varied than ever before. There have been recent accounts of violent female gang involvement in such major cities as New York *(The New York Times,* May 9, 1972), Philadelphia *(The Philadelphia Inquirer,* February 4, 1973), and London *(Time,* October 16,1972).

Philadelphia has long been recognized as a hot-bed of black gang violence. An article presented in *The Philadelphia Inquirer* (February 23, 1975) points out that the gang related deaths in Philadelphia during the ten-year span from 1964 to 1974 officially stands at 305, with an unofficial statistic speculated at about 500. Yet, analytical and statistical

*International Journal of Offender Therapy and Comparative Criminology 21 (1977), pp. 221-28, copyright ©1977 by Sage Publications, Inc. Reprinted by permission of Sage Publications.

sources dealing with Philadelphia's gang problem, be they newspaper or magazine articles, journal articles, or books on the subject, almost invariably neglect to mention the role of females in the gangs, or even that females are involved in the gang subculture.

This absence of research on female involvement in the black gang subculture of Philadelphia seems even more peculiar when we consider that black females undergo the same basic sociological phenomena as do black males from Philadelphia's lower class, inner city neighborhoods. The females live in the same high concentration, low income ghetto neighborhoods as do the males. They are exposed to same ghetto-specific lifestyle (Hannerz 1969) as the males. They encounter the same unstable, unclear nuclear family unit as do their black male counterparts. They are in constant contact with the same expressive culture system (Brown 1974; 1976) as the males. They realize their limited access to the opportunity structure of the larger society (Cloward and Ohlin 1960) at much the same rate as the males. Like the males, the females are even aware of the "turf boundaries" (Davis 1962) that they must traverse as they move to and from school and shopping trips. In short, females encounter the same problems and function in the same milieu that leads males to delinquent acts and gang participation.

Conversely, there are three major differences that distinguish female exposure from male exposure to the gang subculture. First, it is common practice in the lower-class black family to assign the females the task of supervising younger siblings, tending to the sibling's needs, and practicing such domestic chores as house-cleaning, meal preparation, and other household duties. This is particularly true in the single-parented household or in the household where both parents work. This practice limits the amount of exposure the female will have to street life and gang interaction. Second, lower class black females have more exposure to mainstream ideals than do lower class black males due to maternal and other female influences. Black women move more freely between the ghetto-specific and mainstream lifestyle than do black men. This is due to the fact that women can readily find jobs as domestics, waitresses or the like, coupled with the fact that the black women are, generally speaking, better educated than the males (Moynihan 1965). Thus, mothers and other influential females tend to denigrate gang involvement as "low life" that a female should not become involved with if she desires to foster higher ideals. Black males, on the other hand, often receive positive reinforcement from older males such as father, uncle, or brother who have been or are heavily involved in street life or gang activities. The third, and most important, difference is the fact that females are not pressured into joining gangs. They are permitted the luxury of choosing whether or not they desire to participate in gang-related activities. While males undergo pressure to join or be "drafted" by a neighborhood gang to aid in territorial defense, the females are allowed, not forced, to join. This single factor accounts for the major reason why the number of females involved in gang activities is limited. If the males were allowed this same alternative and not pressured to join gang activities, there would be many less black youths involved in Philadelphia's gang subculture.

Why, therefore, do females join the gangs? If they are not pressured by gang members to fill the ranks, and if, in fact, the females undergo certain experiences designed to retard their potential for gang participation, why would they desire involvement in such a violent subculture? The answer to this question is most succinctly presented by two young female informants who are Philadelphia gang members. Peaches, a rather outspoken girl of 15, answered this question with the statement, "The gang's where it's happening; it's where the action is." While Cheese, a large-boned and rather soft-spoken girl of 16 added, "Lots of girls join the gangs to be popular; you're part of a big family then, and you have lots of friends." Although there are a number of other reasons for a female to join a gang, popularity and the lure of excitement were readily agreed upon by my informants as being the primary reasons for a female's involvement in the gang subculture.

The sense of belonging fostered by gang membership fulfills some very basic psychological needs for the female gang members in much the same fashion as for the male gang members. The desire to be popular, to be accepted by other members of one's peer grouping, is not always satisfied in a normative fashion. Because some females are less attractive than others, less sociable than others, less proficient at school work, or new to the neighborhood or school district, an alternative route may be used to satisfy needs for popularity. Furthermore, when the primary family unit fails to supply the needed psychological reinforcement that engenders positive ego formation, or fails to provide an atmosphere of stability, the female may look elsewhere to satisfy her psychological needs. By belonging to the gang, the girl establishes her identity and increases her popularity. She is part of a group that has a corporate identity and which provides for her individual identity within the group according to her specific abilities and specific roles. As Cheese stated, "You're part of a big family then, and you have lots of friends." As a gang member, the female has established her identity as one of the group, thus providing her with a high potential for popularity, while allowing her access to an atmosphere of excitement.

Excitement is a by-word for gang activities. Almost invariably there is something "happening" amongst the gang members. There is the "turf" which must be defended against encroachment by other gangs. There is the potential "war" with a neighboring gang to discuss and for which to prepare. The upcoming party at another gang member's "crib" (home). A casual get together held over wine and "herb" (marijuana). The initiation of a new "young boy" into the gang structure may be held. A "box" (first fight) between two gang members searching for new status within the gang may be taking place. Or, it just may be one of those days to loaf on the "corner" (the gang's meeting spot) and "rap" (talk) with other gang members. If the female is not a member of the gang, some or all of these activities would be denied her.

In most cases joining the gang is easy for a female; she only needs to express an interest in being a gang member and, if she is acceptable to the members, she automatically becomes a part of the gang. Males who wish to join the gang, on the other hand, must be tested. They must give out "fair ones" (fist fights) to specified gang members, and if they prove to have "heart"(courage), and that they can handle themselves in a fight, they will be accepted into the gang. Those males who are forced or "drafted" into the gang, to add to the gang's numbers, and do not exhibit qualities of "heart" or fighting ability will not receive rank in the gang and will be looked down upon by other gang members.

The new female gang member is labeled a "young girl" until she learns the intricacies of the gang and has become "street wise" through gang-related experiences. Once she fulfills this criterion the gang female becomes an "old head," a term used to denote her street and gang experience, not her chronological age. A gang female can be an "old head" at 14 or a "young girl" at 17, depending upon her gang experience, so that just because a female appears young does not mean that she is naive to gang activities. Unlike male gang members who have several classifications (Brown 1974) female gang members are classified only under these two criteria.

The "young girl" takes on a new identity upon her integration into the gang subculture. She learns new roles designed to benefit the gang and new values are internalized that reflect the gang's philosophy. The overriding interest of the "young girl" is the gang and its related activities. She is constantly being educated through her street experiences and gang interactions so that as time progresses and her street savvy increases she will become an "old head." To be an "old head" in the gang is to gain great respect from other gang members, to be part of the gang's elite, and thus to gain popularity within the gang.

To gain this popularity through "old head" status, the "young girl" must become proficient at gang activities. She must establish a "rep" (reputation) that exhibits her special qualities and abilities as a gang member. She must show that her role within the gang is an intrinsic part of the gang's "rep." By establishing this correlation, the "young girl" establishes her identity within the gang while enhancing the potency of the gang's "rep."

The avenues available to the "young girl" for the establishment of a "rep" are quite similar to those avenues available to a "young boy" with only several exceptions. Females are involved with fighting and therefore gain notoriety for their proficiency at combat. In the case of gang wars they will often enter the ranks of combatants. The females will most often fight other female members of the opposing gang in a gang war, but it is not uncommon for the females to fight males of the opposing gang. These females can be just as deadly as their male counterparts in such combats, wielding guns and brandishing knives with great dexterity, or, in many cases, the females will carry weapons for the male gang members to the gang wars so that the males will not be picked up for possession of illegal weapons. Gang members are quite aware of the fact that females are less subject to the scrutiny of police and other authority figures than are the males, so that their role as weapons carriers is of great aid to the male gang members.

Gang wars are not the only form of physical violence a female gang member encounters. Individual and small group combats often occur between one or more female gang members at school or on the streets when one female "sounds" (insults) another female's gang. Inter-gang fights can occur between two females of the same gang who are vying for the attentions of the same male, or in the case of a female who seeks to elevate her status within the gang through "copping" (taking) the "rep" of another female by beating her in a fight. Gang or non-gang females who make the mistake of trespassing on gang "turf" may also be subject to the displeasure of gang females. Some gang females may even have the "gump" (courage) to fight with male gang members who have incurred their wrath, in some cases beating them and many times leaving the males with reminders of their encounter. As can be readily seen, female gang members can be just as violent and just as deadly as the males in their identity search within the gang subculture.

Females also perform some gang related functions that are of great value to the gang but are less available to the male gang members. Females often act as spies who gain information about activities being planned by other gangs. Most often they will establish a relationship with a male member of an opposing gang and extract as much information as possible from him, reporting this information back to the gang's "runner" (leader) or "warlord" so that appropriate adjustments can be made if an impending conflict is foreseen. Females will also establish relationships with male members from another gang so that they can lure the unsuspecting male to a predesignated spot where other gang members can safely assault him without fear of immediate detection. By offering sexual opportunities the female gang members can often bait a male member of an opposing gang, towards whom the female's gang has a specific grievance, into a compromising position that may prove to his demise.

Sex, such as the sexual luring role presented above, is one function of the female gang member. Female gang members do very often provide male gang members with sexual opportunities. However, this is not their only or always their most important role within the gang. Other analysts such as Bernard (1949) have pointed to the importance of the sexual role of the gang females they have studied, and perhaps they have been correct in their assumptions as regards the particular gangs they have analyzed, but in the Philadelphia black gang subcultures sex is only one aspect of the female gang member's role, and quite often this role does not apply. Though some female gang members do succumb to the sexual desires of the male gang members there are also those females who unite only with boyfriends, while others totally abstain. To be a female gang member in Philadelphia's black gang subculture does not have the automatic connotation of being a sexual object subject to the whims of the male gang members. Rather, it means that the female is an intrinsic part of that gang's group identity who participates in gang activities and is involved in various gang functions, rather than just ancillary activities such as sexual fulfillment.

Female gang participation is not always limited to the sexually integrated gang thus far presented. There do exist those gangs totally populated by males and who do not admit females into the gang organization. In such cases female involvement with the gang is only peripheral, limiting itself to social affairs. While, on the other hand, there exists at least one black Philadelphia gang totally organized and populated by females.

The "Holly Whores" (pronounced Holly Ho's) is an all-black female gang. Comprised of females ranging in age from the early teens to early twenties, with a population fluctuating between 20 and 30, these females have organized a gang that functions surprisingly similarly to that of the male-dominated groups. Their activities are primarily centered around aggressive and violent actions. Unlike the sexually integrated gangs previously mentioned, the gang's members are not inducted into the gang's ranks merely by expressing a desire for membership. Rather, aspiring initiates must prove their worth to the gang by undergoing trials designed to select the females who can best exemplify the gang's philosophy and enhance the gang's "rep."

The "Holly Ho's" are a female gang heavily involved in the subculture of violence, with physical combat and aggressive behavior being intrinsic parts of the gang's philosophy. To join the gang the initiate must fight the gang's "runner," either beating her or giving a representative showing of her pugilistic prowess. If the initiate proves her physical combat skills and shows that she has "heart," then she will be admitted to the ranks of the "Holly Ho's." This trial may seem easy enough, but as one informant reported, combating the "runner" of the "Holly Ho's" is quite a bit more frightening than would be assumed.

> "I wanted to join this gang. My girlfriend was a Ho' and she told me if I wanted to join I had to beat the 'runner.' I said I'd fight her. After all, a girl can't be but so big. They set up a date and I went to see that girl. When I saw her, I said never mind! I'm not fighting that girl. She was big and ugly looking with scars all over her face. All the other girls were laughing at me, but I left. I wanted to live."

The "Holly Ho's" are indeed an awesome, fear-inspiring group of females. Described as football players with big shoulders and fight scarred faces, they greatly resemble the warring Amazonian women referred to in ancient mythology. Like the Amazons, the "Holly Ho's" appear to be fearless, aggressive women who will fight men or women alike. Comprised of females from a variety of different neighborhoods, they cluster at 46th and Lancaster, calling this their "turf." Their raison d'être is predicated upon violence. Reputed to enjoy fighting, they have been accused of knifing and kicking pregnant females and especially enjoying badly scarring and mutilating "cute" girls. Their arsenal is said to contain knives, hand guns, rifles, and sawed-off shotguns. "Getting a body" (killing) is also said to be an important part of their "rep." Like the black male gangs of

Philadelphia, the "Holly Ho's" are a violent gang that function in a milieu where aggression has become a symbolic means for establishing an identity.

Females are definitely part of Philadelphia's black youth gang subculture. They are not always confined to peripheral gang activities such as social and sexual affairs, but rather the females often have roles intrinsic to the maintenance of the gang. In the sexually integrated gangs, the females are involved in a multitude of gang-related affairs, and when it comes to inter-gang conflicts, the females will join the ranks of the combatants. The all-female gang, exemplified by the "Holly Ho's," is just as violent and just as aggressive as the all-male gangs, with a "rep" just as potent as that of many male gangs.

Because females are exposed to essentially the same milieu as that of the males in Philadelphia's low income neighborhoods, and because these females also are in search of their identity within a subculture where opportunities are limited to the ghetto-specific lifestyle, violence and aggressive behavior become a viable means for establishing that identity. To become popular and be involved in the excitement of gang activities, females will join and function in Philadelphia's black gang subculture, so that when we speak about the black youth gangs of Philadelphia the female gang member must be included before a representative statement can be made.

Black Female Gang Behavior
An Historical and Ethnographic Perspective

Laura T. Fishman[*]

Background

While male youth gangs have been a popular subject for the media and the focus of social investigations in various academic disciplines, comparatively little attention has been paid to the role of females within the gang subculture. This article presents a systematic description of the multi-dimensional world of the Vice Queens, a black female auxiliary gang to a boys' conflict gang that existed in Chicago during the early sixties.

As an historical account, this article provides some important insights into the attitudes and behavior patterns of poor, black females who choose to join gangs. Such documentation is needed since little has been written about gang girls during the sixties. More has been written about them recently. These contemporary works on female gangs primarily have made Hispanic girls the principle subjects: i.e., focusing on Chicanas in Los Angeles (Harris 1988; Quicker 1983), Chicanos in Chicago (Horowitz 1983), and Puerto Ricans in New York City (Campbell 1984). Fewer studies have focused on black, Asian, or white girls (but see Brown 1977; Campbell 1984; Miller 1973).

According to more recent reports, gangs, since the sixties, continue to inhabit the rotting cores of ghettoes in every major city. These areas have been characterized by the economic decline of urban blacks due to black unemployment and economic restructuring (Glasgow 1980; Hagedorn 1988; Short 1990; Taylor 1990; Wilson 1987). Gang research since the sixties has continued to do some investigation of gang activity in these areas. Within this context, then, researchers have made black males the focus of their investigation. A consistent finding is that much has changed in response to worsening economic conditions. As noted by Short, some gangs have become more sophisticated in crime than their counterparts twenty or more years ago. More lethal guns are available. Drug abuse and drug distribution have become more widespread. Taylor's (1990) study of Detroit black gangs confirms some findings of Hagedorn (1988) and Sanchez-Jankowski (1991) that urban gangs are using drugs as a vehicle for social mobility. He elaborates upon this finding by giving some attention to how the economic decline of urban blacks impacts on black females. He notes that black females are either (1) members of male drug-oriented gangs or (2) members of all-female drug distribution gangs. In contrast, the article presented here provides an historical treatment of how

[*]*This essay is published here for the first time. An earlier version, "The Vice Queens," was published in M. W. Klein, C. L. Maxson and J. Miller,* The Modern Gang Reader *(Los Angeles: Roxbury Publishing Co., 1995) pp. 83-92.*

the conflict-oriented subcultures that surrounded the new black underclass young people (Wilson 1987) during the sixties had shaped some black girls' ways of thinking and doing.

According to some reports (e.g., Adler 1975b), over the past thirty years there have evolved some important differences in girl gang organization and behavior. For instance, girl gangs appear to have evolved from a predominantly auxiliary status—that is, functioning primarily to support male gang groups—to a position characterized by greater autonomy and independent activity. Other recent works (Campbell 1984/1991; Harris 1988) do not support this observation. Instead these works contend that urban youth gang activity has traditionally been depicted as a predominantly male enterprise to which female gangs are auxiliaries and of only marginal importance. Campbell's survey of gang literature indicates that females most frequently continue to be members of auxiliaries to male gangs, occasionally to be members of mixed-sex gangs, and least frequently to be members of independent or unaffiliated female gangs. Harris's survey of Latino gangs in California echoes this theme. Whenever a male Latino gang is active, there almost always appears to be a female auxiliary. Only Brown's (1977) study of gang life in Philadelphia and Hagedorn's (1988) study of gang founders in Milwaukee documented the existence of one wholly autonomous gang of black girls in the respective cities.

Given this, then, earlier studies also report that girl gangs, as traditionally oriented, were completely controlled by males and were almost completely focused upon male activities. For instance, girl gang members were perceived as maintaining traditional female roles, typically by participating in socio-sexual activities with the boys. Thrasher (1927), in his classical study of male gang members in Chicago, discusses two female gangs in which members, in general, conformed to the traditional female role. Short and Strodtbeck (1965)[1] echo this finding in their study of Chicago gangs during the 1960s, describing girl gang members as mainly sexual objects, used by the boys for sexual purposes.

More recently, the literature concludes that not very much has changed. Campbell (1990) and Harris (1988) point out that the role of sex objects still encompasses being a girl-friend to a male member, providing sexual services to gang boys, and so forth. Sanchez-Jankowski (1991) supports this finding in his study of some 37 male gangs over more than a decade (1978-1989) in four cities. He reports that in every gang included in the study population, girls were considered a form of property. Any sexual advances made to a member's woman was viewed by the member as either an attempt to steal his property or as an insult to his ability to protect his property.

Older studies indicated that on the streets the status of girls had traditionally been dependent on that of their corresponding male gangs. In 1963, Rice concluded that the Persian Queens, a female gang in New York City, were doomed to lower status in the street gang society, which is completely controlled by males and oriented towards male activities. There was very little the Persian Queens could do to achieve power or prestige in the gang world.

By the mid-seventies, descriptions of girl gang roles and activities were less likely to be restricted to the traditionally female role. Quicker (1983), for example, reported that, while female gangs were still dependent upon male gangs for their existence, they had begun to function more autonomously and to take initiative in defining the content of their gangs. In his study of female Chicano gang members in Los Angeles, Quicker noted that girl members made their own decisions on internal matters, usually through a democratic process. However, several years later, Brown (1977) observed that, while girls still placed a high value on male approval, relationships with other female gang members were more important in gaining memberships and status.

Campbell's (1984/1991) findings elaborate upon Brown's (1977) observations. She observes that new methods of gaining status appear to have emerged since the sixties, in that, more recently, status is believed to be conferred on the basis of a girl's ability to fight. Campbell reported that girls most frequently listed maintaining personal integrity, safeguarding their tough reputations among their peer group, and impressing other girls with their courage as their primary reasons for fighting. She concludes that female gang members still function as "partial and pale facsimiles" of male gang structures, processes, and behavior. And they still mainly define achievement and status largely in male terms.

Finally, some observers (e.g., Adler 1975; Chesney-Lind 1993; Taylor 1990) have pointed out that as girl gangs have moved away from their traditional female role, they have moved closer to becoming increasingly violence-oriented. In contrast, Mann (1984) points out that prior to the mid-seventies, even in terms of conflict-oriented activities, girls continued to play out such stereotypical roles as weapon carriers for the boys, instigators of male conflict, and as fighters against girls who were connected with enemy boys' gangs.

Hanson (1964), in turn, reported that the Dagger Debs, a female gang in the Puerto Rican area of New York City, were instigators of the boys' fights with enemy male gangs. They spread false rumors and goaded the boys by threatening their masculinity in order to provoke intergang warfare. Miller (1973) observed that the Molls, a female gang in the Boston area, not only manipulated boys in gang fights but encouraged boys to steal cars and take them for joy rides.

Despite their role as instigators, gang girls have reportedly been excluded from the planning or carrying out of male gang activities, especially conflict situations. For example, Rice (1963) observed that a New York City female gang was seldom involved in gang boys' conflict situations. Rather, gang fights were at the behest of the male gang members who allowed the girls to accompany them to intergang "rumbles." On these occasions, they were likely to maintain their traditional roles as females and were relegated to fighting the enemy's girl gang members.

Bowker and Klein (1983) reanalyzed data on black female participation in male gang activity in Los Angeles County during the sixties and found girls still enmeshed in traditional female roles (i.e., girls were not the "cause" but the "cure" for male delinquent behavior). They reported that girls appeared to have a preventive effect on male delinquent activity in that, whenever they were present at the sites of boys' delinquent activities, the boys were likely to terminate such activities. By the mid-seventies, descriptions of girl gang roles and activities were less likely to be restricted to the traditionally female role. Gang girls were more often depicted as being actively involved in conflict situations which, in the past, were believed to be male-dominated, e.g., gang feuds, individual and gang fights. Brown (1977), for instance, also observed that female gang members in Philadelphia's black gang subculture were actively involved, along with the boys, in conflict situations. He concludes that "the female is an intrinsic part of the gang's group identity who participates in gang activities and is involved in various gang functions, rather than just ancillary activities such as sexual fulfillment" (p. 226). Campbell's (1984) observations of three New York City girl gangs support this position. She found girl gangs to be involved in serious personal and property crimes. Furthermore, these girls appeared to take a forceful role in male gang conflict situations and to use "male" weapons such as guns and knives. They fought over boys, but they also fought in other arenas—e.g., in gang feuds, against personal insults, and against the police.

Despite an apparent trend for gang girls to have moved away from traditional female roles since the early 1960s, not all reports are in agreement. For example, Miller (1975) found no evidence that female criminal behavior, in connection with gang activity, is more prevalent or violent than in the past. Rather, he reported in the mid-seventies that female participation was still traditional in content, with girl gangs still functioning as auxiliaries to male gangs, and serving as weapon carriers and as decoys. The status of girl gangs, he maintained, is directly dependent on that of male gangs.

More recent works on gang behavior do concur that the gang "rumbles" of earlier years have today assumed a more lethal form of gang conflict (see, for instance, Hagedorn 1988; Sanchez-Jankowski 1991; Short 1990; Taylor 1990). Campbell (1984/1991) elaborates upon these observations. Her work makes it clear that female involvement in conflict has increased since they, as the boys, live in a highly turbulent and violent world. Harris (1988) notes, in her study of the Cholas, a Californian Latino gang, that Latina girls now carry weapons but none used guns even when the boys did. These same girls shared a commitment to the use of physical aggression as a major mode of personal interaction and a device for solving problems. Accordingly, Harris (1988, 174) reports that "The girls described here will fight instead of flee, assault instead of articulate, and kill rather than control their aggression. 'Being bad,' 'being crazy,' and 'acting wild' earns respect and status."

These findings related here are not surprising given the recent discussion about the underclass employment of survival strategies. The literature suggests that within such communities, black and Latina women and girls develop survival strategies to deal with the multiple oppressions they encounter. Within this context, then, King's (1988,1990) highly relevant comments should be noted here. Accordingly, female gang members, mentions Campbell (1990), are handicapped by class, race, and gender. She contends that black women encounter multiple jeopardy, which refers to the simultaneous oppressions of race, gender, and class. The present article elaborates upon this observation. It documents how gang girls respond simultaneously to being poor, black, and female, and the kinds of survival skills they engage in are shown as both similar yet different from the black male's struggles.

Several authors who have studied the black lower class community (Brooks 1980; Fields and Walters 1985; Glasgow 1980, 1981; Valentine 1978) have noted that most males and females, being offered little from the community in the way of resources or controls, must develop some knowledge of hustling and fighting in order to survive. Low income blacks need to combine income from intermittent employment, welfare and hustling[2] to maintain even a low standard of living. However, less attention has been given to how the survival skills utilized by black gang girls and boys are both similar yet different. The recent literature on gang girls only mentioned that girl gang members must hustle to survive. More recently, several investigators (Bowker et al. 1980; Hagedorn 1988; Harris 1988; Quicker 1983) have observed that available hustling techniques are learned and shared as a way for gang girls to put a few dollars in their pockets. The need to hustle is accepted as legitimate, as necessary to survive.

And within these communities, Campbell (this volume, pp. 248-55) points out that the female auxiliary gang offers lower class girls some protection and relief from fighting alone. It must be noted here that whether or not they are on the streets or in their homes, black women and girls generally are not safe. To survive, they must be constantly alert to male assaultive behavior in such forms as rape, battering, physical assault, and robbery. In response to the unsafe environment, Brooks (1980) observes that the black woman must be socialized to defend herself, her family, and her hard-earned property against aggression because she is not likely to receive protection from anyone, including the police. And Brown (1977, 1978) leads us to conclude that the black female gang serves as a principal agent of socialization for poor black adolescent females, offering girls the opportunity to learn important survival strategies as well as the subtleties of lower class black lifestyle, in order to function effectively within the black community. As girls go about learning the rudiments of these strategies, they also learn the rules by which to compete successfully and gain status. Other investigators also point out that black adolescent girls who learn to handle premarital sexual experiences in a sophisticated manner and/or who give birth are conferred the highly valued status of adult women (see, for instance, Bell 1971; Ladner 1972; McCray 1980; Staples 1973.)

It remains difficult to draw conclusions about possible changes in girl gangs' structures, culture, process, or their activities. The paucity of the existent literature on female auxiliary gangs simply does not permit generalization in the absence of extensive and careful ethnographic study. It is therefore difficult to generalize to "all gangs" or "female gangs" or "blacks" or "Latinas" or any other types of gangs. However, the discussion presented here about the Vice Queens sets the stage for filling in some important gaps in our knowledge. By documenting what the Vice Queens were like in the early 1960s, we can provide an important missing piece as to how black girls actively respond to a social environment which exposes them to multiple systems of oppression and how they are not just passive victims of the system at an economic and social level. This material, then, can be considered as a forerunner to these more recent ethnographic studies which observed female gang behavior as behavior in its own right—or as a subject to be taken seriously. On this basis, we can further conclude that the research reported here and these more recent studies share a tradition of providing rich and detailed descriptions of the structure and culture of female delinquent gangs. However, it would be difficult to speculate whether researchers' perceptions or perspectives of gang girls have changed.

Methods

Data was collected as part of a larger study of male delinquent gangs in Chicago during 1960 and 1963. Sixteen delinquent gangs were assigned detached workers by the Program for Detached Workers of the YMCA on the basis of their generally "troublesome" character to the community, as judged by police complaints, reports of welfare agencies, and by field investigators of the detached worker staff. Later, in collaboration with the University of Chicago program, gangs were selected to fulfill research design requirements in a study of gangs representing major delinquent subcultures.[3] The Vice Kings, a notorious boys' conflict-oriented gang, was selected to be included in the study population. In turn, the Vice Queens, as the boys' female auxiliary gang, also was included to be studied with some depth.

Information gathered from field observations and interviews has been combined to provide an in-depth portrait of the Vice Queens' way of life and the structure and function of this particular girl gang in order to augment the existing literature on the female gang subculture of the early 1960s.

The present paper is based on reanalysis of detached workers' interviews and field observer reports. The availability of detached workers as intimate observers of girl gang members provided an opportunity to gain more complete insights into the behavior of these girls than could be provided by any other methods. Weekly interviews with the workers assigned to the Vice Kings suggested that they not only shared intimately in the ongoing life of the boys' gang but also of the girls' auxiliary gang. These weekly interviews with detached workers began early in the project and continued until August 1962.

Campbell (1990) provides some insights into some biases of this form of data collection which are relevant here. She contends that early research on female gangs was conducted from an all-male perspective; the gang members' roles were described by male street corner workers to male researchers and then interpreted by male academicians. This all-male perspective led to some biased writings in which girls were described only in terms of their interpersonal and structural relations to male gang members.

To some extent, the research project described here suffers from a similar bias. The bulk of information concerning the Vice Queens tended to reflect a male interest.[4] Except for the author, the detached workers and the research staff consisted of males. Not surprisingly, the Vice Queens were accorded secondary status and, when focused upon, the tendency was to give more attention to the girls' roles as what Campbell (1990) refers to as cheerleaders and followers.

To counteract this bias, field observations by the research team were included to broaden the ongoing documentation of the girls' street corner behavior. This direct contact with the girls themselves, rather than once removed, allowed the girls to speak for themselves. Observational data collection was integral to the project.

The author, a black woman, served as a field observer of the Vice Queens during 1960 and 1963, observing the group in its setting and frequently participating in the gang's main activities. While participating in the ongoing activities, her role also consisted of systematically noting the behavior of all participants. The two other black, male field observers were in the field to primarily observe the activities of the boys. At times, they included in their observer reports descriptions of interactional patterns between the boys and girls and among the girls themselves.

All the observers were introduced to the boys and girls by the detached workers assigned to the gang. These workers actively sponsored the field observers. The author's status as a poor, young, black, female graduate student did not seem to engender either persistent hesitation or hostility. Once the girls overcame their initial suspicion, the author was, for the most part, accepted as a peer in whose presence it is assumed the Vice Queens acted normally and unselfconsciously. Rapport seemed good and the author had every reason to believe that both the girls and boys viewed her as a legitimate type whose feet, nonetheless, remained in a world with which they were familiar. The girls were immediately informed that most of the author's growing years were spent in Harlem, New York—a community in which she had lived on the fringe of various kinds of norm-violating behavior such as the numbers racket, juvenile delinquent behavior, prostitution, and so forth. This background facilitated the task of establishing rapport with the girls.

Information from the field observer reports were compared with the detached workers' reports and with information on file at the YMCA. The data were cross-checked and re-examined in the interests of improving their reliability and validity. Not only have field observer reports and the information on file generally corroborated information provided by the detached workers, but they have added depth to the insights gained from the detached workers. The combined reports provide a detailed portrait of a black female gang during the early sixties.

The Vice Queens, An Auxiliary Gang

The Vice Queens lived in a predominantly black, lower income community character-ized by high physical deterioration, poverty, unemployment, illegitimacy, juvenile and adult crime. The girls shared with their male counterparts exposure to deteriorating insti-tutions which were increasingly incapable of delivering decent housing, medical services, education, and accessibility to the job market. The emergence of a new black underclass (see Wilson 1987) and the presence of extensive criminal enterprises and unpredictable death and violence is directed at both girls and boys, cutting across gender differences.

Within this harsh milieu, the Vice Queens, as a female auxiliary gang, represented for its members a collective solution to survival issues. Not only did the gang provide friendship, easy access to boys, and a means of achieving status, it provided girls with pro-tection against undesirable men in the neighborhood. Further, the Vice Queens were not bent on the establishment of "new rules" counter to middle class values, but rather pursued positive status goals within a black lower class cultural system. The Vice Queens thus provided an important milieu in which girls not only learned new roles designed to benefit the gang, but also learned the intricacies of street life.

As a female auxiliary gang, the Vice Queens came into existence after the Vice Kings had been established and took a feminized version of the Vice Kings' name. They were a loosely knit, though seldom harmonious, family for its more than thirty mem-bers, about nineteen of whom formed the "hard core" membership. Comprising girls ranging in age from thirteen to nineteen, the Vice Queens had their own leaders, meet-ings, and activities.

Unlike the Vice Kings, the Vice Queens had no rigid hierarchical or clearly defined leadership structure. Instead, leaders tended to be self-appointed, with girls assuming the role of leader in situations where they could gain or maintain status. Other girls seldom threatened these leadership positions.

The Vice Queens were not a highly cohesive group. Competition among them for the gang boys' attention often led to physical violence and sharp verbal acrimony that sometimes pervaded the entire group. Paradoxically, such competitiveness lent a measure of cohesiveness in that the girls maintained the Vice Kings' interest in them as an auxiliary group as well as individuals. The existence of a female auxiliary was a source of prestige among the Vice Kings.

The major reason for the existence of the Vice Queens was to maximize accessibility to the boys. Given this, the main interests of the Vice Queens were the Vice Kings' achievements in athletics, fighting, and other activities that form the basis of male prestige. Consequently, the Vice Queens had little meaning to the boys outside of the mating-dating complex, since the conflict gang was largely a male world and the girls more often remained on the fringe of it.

However, the Vice Queens also participated in their own activities, which contributed towards maintaining the group. Independent of the Vice Kings, noted field observers, the girls also participated in aggressive and violent actions, some norm-violating activities as well as their own athletic and social activities. Participation fluctuated with their activities. For example, more girls participated in activities that were attractive to the boys, e.g., dance and athletic events, than in conflict situations and other norm-violating activities. In general, however, fluctuations in participation took place in the fringe group rather than the core.

Occupational and Educational Activities

Most of the Vice Queens did not pursue educational or occupational activities. And seldom did any of the girls express interest in achieving academically and/or establishing careers for themselves.

It is not surprising that most of the girls were school drop-outs. The field observer's reports revealed that of nineteen Vice Queens, thirteen had withdrawn from school and the truancy rate of the others was so high that, for all practical purposes, they were students in name only.

The resultant lack of rapport and the social distance between girls and school personnel, combined with the girls' resistance to internalizing middle class educational objectives, effectively removed them from the formal objectives and programs of the school. School, from their accounts, was not a place where they prepared for future occupations or gained knowledge. It was rather another site for gang activities—a place to learn of pending conflicts, to exchange information about the activities of other gangs, and a battleground for physical and verbal fights.

Quitting school did not appear to heighten the girls' motivations to obtain jobs, nor were jobs used as a reason for leaving school. Both school and work interfered with the more enjoyable pleasures derived from participation with their peers in street activities. Again, the field observer noted that only two of the nineteen Vice Queens had jobs at the conclusion of the field research. Of the other girls who had jobs before or during the three-year project, all had either quit or were laid off.

Most of the girls at one time or another, but never persistently, had shown an interest in working but seldom obtained jobs. As one detached worker put it, when explaining the girls' lack of interest in work:

> Some of the girls have stated that their old man will take care of them. The girls didn't want to work nor go to school and further their education. They felt, education or not, they would be able to make it. They felt that they have what it takes: they were talking about sex and they figured that they can get a steady boyfriend who will give them five or maybe ten dollars a week and that would be enough to take care of them. In turn, they might live with him, and this is good enough.[5]

Disassociation from the time-consuming occupational and educational institutions permitted the girls more than ample leisure time to engage in gang activities.

Norm-Violating Activities

A significant amount of the Vice Queens' time was spent with the Vice Kings, "hanging out" on the streets, in vacant lots and at school yards, visiting one another, and attending athletic and social events. Although most of this time was spent in nondelinquent activities, norm-violating activities were also of considerable importance.

Female delinquency often is thought to be extremely specialized and virtually synonymous with sexual delinquency. The Vice Queens, however, were quite diversified in delinquent activities. The group was usually the setting for norm-violating activities and, except for sexual delinquency, the solitary delinquent girl was rare. Workers' interviews indicated that unlike conflict and drinking behavior, these norm-violating activities were most often conducted by very small groups of two or three girls.

Almost all the girls were involved in such delinquent activities as running away from home, truancy, and occasional shoplifting. And most girls committed such misdemeanors as driving without a license, disturbing the peace, and loitering. Additionally, however, some of the girls committed "male" crimes such as auto theft, purse snatching and grand larcenies which involved little planning or skills. As a rule, however, the girls' participation in these latter activities was sporadic, impulsive, and experimental. A detached worker reported that an even less frequent criminal pattern among adolescent girls, but one which was not rare among the Vice Queens, was strong-arming:

> They strong-arm like the boys and would strong-arm anyone who would come around, man or woman. They pick on anyone that would come along, usually three or four girls together. Certain of the girls would not participate. But they don't strong-arm too much.[6]

However, the most important group activities, with their own set of rules, were conflict and drinking. According to both the workers and the observers, with respect to conflict, the Vice Queens acted primarily as agitators and instigators in inter- and intra-gang fights among boys. They frequently manipulated the boys into fighting over real or alleged insults or "passes" from male members of enemy gangs. Fighting over girls was common between the Vice Kings and other conflict-oriented gangs. A detached worker described this pattern vividly:

> In front of all the big fights that the Vice Kings have had, the girls have been involved. They have either started them or signified and lied so as to encourage the boys to go and fight. They have been lookouts and have seen Cobras and Comanches come in the area. They have had a lot to do with everything that had happened in respect to the big fights.[7]

Having brought about the fights in the first place, the girls then served as weapon carriers and "lookouts" for the boys. It was clear from the workers' accounts that as weapon carriers the girls provided an essential service, and the Vice Kings were fully aware that the girls were less likely to be searched by the police than were the boys. Knives, guns, black jacks, and other weapons were frequently hidden in a girl's clothing. For instance, a detached worker described a fight which took place between the Vice Kings and two other gangs when the workers took some Vice Kings and Vice Queens to the amphitheater to see a basketball game:

> As we were going in, we met Sam's group, the Southside Cobras. My boys recognized these boys and so right there in the place they had a fight. It didn't get as bad as some fights I have seen but it was on its way. Blows were passed. Just about the time we had the thing quieted down, then Charlie Brown and his group came in and the thing flared up all over again. When the ruckus started, I heard one of the boys in my group tell a girl, "Let me have the stuff!" Well, this one girl produced a knife, a butcher knife, and I don't know what the other girl had, but she never did get it out. Apparently it got caught in the lining of her coat or something, cause when we got back in the car, I heard him ask her, "Why didn't you give it to me?" and she said, "I couldn't get it out." But the implication is that they insisted these girls go along because they are the ones that carry the weapons for them.[8]

Girls would accompany boys to intergang fights and occasionally they would fight the enemy gang's female auxiliary members. More frequently, however, recalled workers, they participated independently of the boys in their own conflicts with members of other female auxiliary gangs. The Vice Queens' fights with other female auxiliary gangs usually erupted as a result of a quarrel between individual members. Many girls informed the observer that arguments generally involved the passing of threatening notes until one gang, sufficiently insulted and angered, demanded that a time and place be set for a fight. Locations for fights were usually secluded streets, movie theaters, or school yards, and seldom did more than ten or eleven members from each gang participate. Seldom did the girls use any weapons. They usually fought with their fists and much like boys. A detached worker commented:

> They try to specialize in one punch knock-outs. They get their balance just like a
> man would get his and they have nice left jabs. They can almost throw them better
> than the boys throw their left jabs. The boys have a tendency to hook their jabs,
> which is very ineffective, while the girls throw their jabs right from the shoulder.[9]

Fighting other female auxiliary gangs appears closely linked with maintaining loyalty in the group and a sense of solidarity between members. Seldom did girls fight over personal grievances, but rather to preserve the Vice Queens' reputation for toughness.

Both workers' and observers' reports mentioned how the Vice Queens fought with both males and females—in short, with anyone who disturbed them on the street, at parties, or at the movies. Some girls fought with male members as well as males from other gangs, adult males from the community, and even policemen. For instance, one detached worker related:

> The Vice Queens have been known to jump on policemen, they have been known
> to go to K town to fight, whether to fight boys or girls, and they were known to
> handle themselves, they weren't scared of nobody. They would jump on sober
> adults, they were that strong.[10]

Fights generally arose over issues of integrity or loyalty.[11] Integrity issues usually center on girls' perceptions of some threat to or an attack on their public reputation. Issues generally emerged whenever other girl gang members join in on the fight, if present, on behalf of girls whose reputations had been attacked. Many girls were not at all reluctant to fight male opponents over personal grievances, as well as in response to the males initiating a violent confrontation.

The evidence presented here also supports Campbell's (this volume, p. 248-55) most recent observation that among the girl gang members in her study population, instrumental aggression was the norm rather than the exception. The girls' intent, when utilizing this form of aggression was similar to the boys' intent—to cause the other person to back down and withdraw.

There is little doubt that fighting a male, and especially winning, carried a particular status among the girls. Within the black lower class culture, failure to respond in this manner constituted deviance from an implicit norm, e.g., "no one says that and gets away with it!"

The gang thus provided girls with opportunities to learn such traditional male skills as fighting skills and taking care of themselves on the streets. Within their community, there was relatively greater freedom, but also less protection, for girls. It was thus expected that girls would learn to defend themselves against "abusive men," attacks on their integrity, and police who were perceived as thugs, animals, and "head whippers."

Both workers and observers concurred that a considerable number of the girls consumed both alcohol and, to a lesser extent, marijuana. While both were integral to leisure time activities of the community, marijuana was not as regularly available, nor as inexpensive as alcohol. The girls sometimes pooled their money to buy liquor, which was brought either by the Vice Queens who were legally of age or by neighborhood men and women.

Drinking was a recurrent group recreational pattern for the Vice Queens, who occasionally drank gin, but more often inexpensive beverages such as wine. Some of the Vice Queens drank a little every day, usually in the evenings. Usually they drank in small groups, on the streets, in alleyways, but seldom in their homes, and they did not willingly share their limited liquor with the boys.

The functional character of drinking is suggested by the fact that girls often have only half a glass of wine, but they will act drunk for the duration of the evening. The girls are boisterous, they often participate in sexual activities with the boys, and verbal and physical fights are common.

Sexual Delinquency

An important dimension of the girls' participation in antisocial activities is prostitution. The evidence noted that not all of the girls participated in the antisocial activities mentioned earlier, but, according to the workers' accounts, all had prostituted themselves at one time or another, some more often than others. Prostitution, at no more than two or three dollars a customer, was a chief source of income for the girls, although they got money from other illegal activities and, occasionally, from parents. Customers were procured in taverns and on the street or at other locations not connected with organized houses of prostitution. The girls led the workers to believe that they were aware of the prostituting activities of their peers, and prostitution was accepted as standard behavior for the group. However, they seldom discussed with each other the details of their adventures in prostitution. In turn, workers informed the author that those Vice Kings who were cognizant of the prostitution, even though the girls will not prostitute themselves when the boys were present, took no action to discourage the girls from earning money in this manner.

Their prostitution is the strongest indication of the Vice Queens' acceptance of female-oriented, illegitimate hustles. This should not be a surprising pattern, given that the Vice Queens lived in a community where hustling was a requisite for survival. However, hustling appeared to be conditioned by gender, since the Vice Queens' major and most remunerative form of hustling seemed to be prostitution, a traditionally "female" crime. The findings strongly suggest that the Vice Queens, as poor black girls, have begun to establish for themselves a diverse package of illicit activities to produce economic gain. There are too many risks associated with hustling to restrict activities to one method. So rather than specialization in one hustle, they are generalists—building a flexible package of various hustling activities. Thus girls cannot look to focus on only "female" crimes, as they are limited in scope, and consequently must also look to "masculine" crimes in order to broaden their package.

Vice Queen-Vice King Relationships

According to Cohen (1955), female social status often derived from relationships with the opposite sex, e.g., the types of men they dated and married, their role as sex objects, and their ability to manipulate through sexual attractiveness.

The findings presented here elaborate upon Cohen's observations. The detached workers interviewed report the primacy of sexuality in the Vice Queen's relationship to the Vice Kings. Vice Queens had sexual relations with members of the gang in the process of "going with" the boys and they bore the boys' illegitimate children. In general, the Vice Queens' interactional pattern with the boys lacked subtle discretion. That is, rather than engaging in subtle or flirtatious behavior, the Vice Queens unabashedly placed themselves at the boys' disposal and openly encouraged them to fondle and have sexual relations with them. A detached worker observed:

> The girls do not maintain the boys' interest all day, just at night. These boys all want to get a piece of ass when they want to go home at night and the girls are always accessible to them if they like the boys. I can't see certain boys getting a girl like Dorothy or Kay Bear. Some boys could rap all night long and these girls wouldn't drop their pants. But some boys, whom they like, could rap to them and they might hold out a little bit but they would come through with the goods. The girls would drop their pants just like that for a certain boy.[12]

Within this context, then, a field observer commented:

> The Vice Queens tend to accept the boys' fondling them constantly, pulling on them and beating them up. In fact, one boy entered the worker's car, dragged one of the girls out, and proceeded to beat her up. This girl was not going with the boy at the time and had never expressed any interest in the boy. After this incident, as she was rubbing her puffed up lips, she stated that he "sure was cute." A day later she was going with him. This frequently happens. The boy beats a girl up and then she becomes interested in him and so they are going with each other.[13]

A consistent finding emerged from these accounts. According to the workers, the amount of actual dating was limited. The boys, on the whole, only paid attention to the Vice Queens when they wanted to have sexual relations. The girls, knowing this, had "steadies of the moment" with whom they had relations. It was considered usual practice that their "steadies of the moment" handle them, curse them, and beat them, and little more is expected of the boys. Couples seldom shared activities and seldom did the boys treat the girls to other favors (e.g., hamburgers, Cokes, or flowers).

Although some couples did "go steady" in the conventional sense, neither the Vice Kings nor Vice Queens perceived each other as future marriage partners. The Vice Kings perceived the Vice Queens as useful for premarital sexual relations, but for a steady girlfriend, they preferred, noted a detached worker,

> ...a girl that's unusual, who does not hang with the Vice Queens. Usually the girl they
> talk about is a girl who doesn't come out on the streets very often. The Vice Kings can
> go to her house anytime of the day and she will be there. They like this quiet life that
> the girl plays, instead of the girl who runs on the streets, drinks, and will swing on them
> at any time.[14]

On the other hand, the Vice Queens felt that they could get a steady boyfriend, not necessarily a Vice King, who would take care of them monetarily but not necessarily marry them. Consequently, the relationships between the Vice Kings and the Vice Queens were neither future nor marriage oriented.

The Vice Queens' interaction with the Vice Kings occurs within a relatively free courtship system—free in that it exists within the context of a community which is culturally permissive of such behavior. The girls' associations with the Vice Kings do not take place under parental or other adult supervision. For instance, a central meeting place of the Vice Kings and Vice Queens was an apartment where one of the girls lived. The girl's parents were rarely home, and the apartment consequently became a place to participate in such norm-violating activities as gambling, fighting, and sexual promiscuity. The observer, who visited this apartment, provided the following report:

> We arrived at this particular apartment house. The building was quite run down.
> The windows in the door were broken, the mail boxes were open, and the foyer was
> quite shabby. As we walked up the bleak stairs, I noticed the many obscenities writ-
> ten on the wall, as well as the names of the Vice Kings....We entered the apartment.
> The dining room, crowded with kids, was the only room lit by candles. The rest of
> the apartment was completely dark.... The shades were torn but neatly covered the
> windows so that no one could see into the apartment. Sensuous giggles and mur-
> murs came, intermittently, from the darkened bedrooms....The apartment afforded
> the opportunity for everything and anything to happen.[15]

And finally, within this relatively free courtship system, many of the girls, at the end of the field research phase, turned to homosexual behavior as a source of satisfaction. Several of the girls who engaged frequently in prostitution later became involved in homosexual activities. An observer reports:

It seems that the homosexual activities are continuing among the older girls and beginning to spread to the younger girls. Amy, an older girl whom I do not know, was seen riding Judy, a younger Vice Queen, on her bicycle down the street. Amy was seen kissing and petting Judy who seemed to be enjoying it. Also, the older Vice Queens were importing white lesbian girls into the area in order to increase their circle. This would be the first time the girls have participated in any activity with white girls.... The same girls who are involved in homosexual activities are still prostituting and still having sexual relations with the boys.[16]

From informal conversations with the girls, the field observer learned that the girls sometimes continued homosexual patterns encouraged by matrons at correctional institutions where they had been confined. The reasons given by the Vice Queens for continued homosexual activity embraced a certain logic. First, they could be assured of not breaking their probation on grounds of pregnancy. Second, the girls were tired of treatment received from both Vice Kings and other neighborhood men, e.g., assaults, taking their money, and simply using them as sexual objects. Third, when they did become pregnant (eleven of nineteen girls interviewed had been pregnant), the Vice Kings claimed as the fathers proved indifferent to the girls' predicament. Thus, the Vice Queens felt that relationships with other females could be more rewarding than their experience with male-female relationships had led them to expect. In fact, an ideal homosexual relationship was based upon values and goals romantically assumed to be characteristic of middle class male-female relationships, i.e., love, trust, tenderness, and kindness. Homosexual relationships allowed relief from the demanding and competitive world of the Vice Kings and other men.

Status Seeking

The Vice Queens' role might be viewed as a traditionally female one, and, to a large extent, status was gained through sexual relationships. Workers' interviews revealed that the granting of sexual favors to the Vice Kings did not necessarily confer status to the girls among their female peers. Rather, maintaining status depended on being able to keep four or five boys "on the string" without any boy's knowing of the others, but at the same time, avoiding sexual relationships with too many boys at one time. Further, going from one sexual involvement to another in rapid succession, public acknowledgement of a lack of emotional involvement with the partner, or restricting sexual relations to only one boy could all result in loss of status. Under such circumstances, recalled a detached worker, the other girls may react in the following manner:

I think this girl rates a bit higher than the rest of the Vice Queens. Although the girls accept her, they still feel some hostility towards her. It became obvious to me that they were intent on having her taken through the mud this night.... The girls were anxious to see her brought to their level, so to speak, and have her share every boy in the group so they would be able to say she had been had…. She was drunk and I knew the other girls would have made it very convenient for as many boys as were available to pull a train on her.[17]

Status was seldom acquired by sexual liaisons with high-status Vice Kings (since these boys had relations with most of the other Vice Queens); however, status could be obtained by having a baby by a high-status Vice King. These fathers-to-be rarely assumed responsibility for their pregnant girlfriends, but were more apt to assume an air of righteous indignation followed by indifference. Eventually, they would usually terminate the relationship. As a field observer recounted:

> Linda then began to tell me that Duke was acting very funny toward her since he learned that she was expecting. She went over to him and informed him that she was pregnant. They then proceeded to argue about her becoming pregnant and about what responsibility he should assume. The argument ended in Duke hitting her. Now Linda is afraid to talk to Duke.[18]

Regardless of the attitude of the expectant father, status was conferred on the pregnant girl by the other Vice Queens and Kings. As one of the girls told the observer:

> Everyone comes up and hugs me, boys and girls. They tell me that they are so happy for me and it is great that I am going to give the group another Vice King or Vice Queen.[19]

The girls' incentives to proudly announce their pregnancies are the gaining of attention from the other gang members, publicly achieving adult status, and hopefully strengthening the bonds between themselves and their boyfriends. All of these incentives are culturally supported by the group. This finding strongly suggests that the girls are responding to a specific black lower class cultural pattern which confers the status of adulthood upon young women who become pregnant. They are no longer considered "little girls" but adults with all the privileges inherent in the adult status.

According to one detached worker, another means by which a Vice Queen could attain status was by being assaulted by a high-status Vice King:

> Pep, the President of the Vice Kings, has a girl. Well, her ego swells like a Peacock because she is Pep's girl. What she most likely doesn't know is that Pep has 8 or 9 girls. She has status, not in the girls' group for going with Pep, because that's nothing. Pep will take a nap with any of them. But when Pep's old lady got her ass beat by Pep, she digs this. "Pep beat my ass, you know"… She'd tell me and the other girls this…. They then recognize that she got her ass beat by her old man… and she gets status.[20]

There is a strong suggestion, stated the worker, that the violent forcing of physical intimacy is perceived as an indication of "true love." Assault by a high-status Vice King alerts the girls as well as other Vice Queens that he really must like her; going with such a man might lead to a "happy ending."

Outside of the mating-dating complex, the girls could derive additional status from their participation in norm-violating activities. For example, status was gained from the girls' abilities in conflict situations, e.g., the perfection of fighting techniques, the number of times the girls willingly fought and with whom they fought. A detached worker summed this up as follows:

> Keep the game up tight in the street, whipping other girls and boys in the street. Girls that keep going into Imperials' territory, keep whipping those guys there, going to K town, keeping their stuff going. The boys will probably get so excited, the girls will have all kinds of status. What it would do is create a chain reaction and then the boys would start feeling their oats and they would go too.[21]

But there was little status derived from excelling at school or in performing well in a job. In general, the girls' status within the group was achieved primarily by sexual activity and by fighting.

Discussion

Although the Vice Queens share some common elements with other urban female gangs prior to the seventies, it is not possible to generalize from this group to the situation of urban female gangs in general. Data on the Vice Queens, however, challenge these earlier ethnographic accounts' narrow focus upon a few gang girl roles: i.e., gang girls were mainly observed as sexual objects, as agent provocateurs, and as "cat fighters." It would be tempting to speculate that this narrow focus reflected the prevailing cultural bias that (1) girls' delinquent behavior is synonymous with sexual delinquency or (2) that the male delinquent subculture serves as the nucleus around which girls orbit.[22] It is not possible to draw such conclusions in this regard. Instead, the account of the Vice Queens leads us to conclude that the material on the Vice Queens provides a more complex and multi-dimensional description of the nature of one female gang, during the early sixties, than previously assumed. The Vice Queens perhaps simply provide a more detailed, more revealing portrait.

The picture of the Vice Queens that emerges suggests that they bear some resemblance to other documented gang girls prior to the mid-seventies, but also that they were more autonomous and more prone to conflict and violence than these girl gangs were generally perceived to be. (See for instance, Bowker et al. 1980; Bowker and Klein 1983; Hanson 1964; Miller 1973; Rice 1963; Quicker 1983.) As with other documented girl gang members, it does appear that the Vice Queens were enmeshed in traditional female roles within a male-dominated delinquent subculture.

Specifically, the Vice Queens' existence was traditional in several ways. As an auxiliary to the Vice Kings, the girl gang members' major activities centered around providing the boys with sexual favors. The Vice Queens also sought out the status conferred through successfully keeping several Vice Kings "on the string." When the Vice Queens participated in boys' conflict situations, they usually acted as instigators and as weapon carriers and occasionally fought against the enemy's female gang members. In this respect, the Vice Queens support Bowker and Klein's (1983) observation that girl gang members could be viewed more as a "cause" than a "cure" for the boys' violent activities.

However, this portrait of the Vice Queens also challenges the stereotypical image of gang girls. The evidence presented here strongly suggests that the Vice Queens can be characterized as more autonomous than mere auxiliaries, but not fully independent of the Vice Kings. Some autonomy is expressed by the girls when they made some of their own decisions on internal matters, participated in their own social and sports activities, as well as participated in conflict situations and other norm-violating activities. The Vice Queens also were actively involved in crimes traditionally viewed as "male" (e.g., strong-arming, car theft, etc.), and they engaged frequently in aggressive and violent behavior. Clearly, these black gang girls fought their own battles and took pride in their ability to look after themselves. They also competed with each other in such status-conferring arenas as conflict situations and the skillful employment of their sex.

Of particular interest here is that membership in the Vice Queens is associated with a high probability of involvement in aggressive and violent behavior as well as in more serious "male" crimes, supposedly a characteristic of black female gangs who came after them (Brown 1977; Campbell 1984/1991; Chesney-Lind 1993; Giordano 1978; Taylor 1990). Some observations offered in the current criminological literature to explain black females' illegal behavior as approximating the masculine crime model are of relevance here.

First, the findings presented here strongly suggest that black lower class girls share the same subordinate position—as members of the new black underclass—as do males of their race and class. Both sexes equally experience the consequences of racism, poverty and structural constraints, share subordinate positions, and have limited access to legitimate opportunity structures. And both sexes share similar characteristics which typify members of the underclass: they are young, badly educated, and intimately connected to crime as perpetrators or as victims (Glasgow 1980; Short 1990; Taylor 1990; Wilson 1987). Brown (1977) elaborates on this position which is as relevant to the situation of the Vice Queens as to black females who joined gangs in Philadelphia during the seventies. He points out that since girls are exposed to essentially the same milieu as boys in low income neighborhoods, and since these girls are in search of their identity within a community where opportunities are limited to the ghetto-specific lifestyle, violence and aggressive behavior becomes a viable means for establishing identity.

Second, unlike the boys, however, the Vice Queens also find themselves handicapped by gender. The evidence presented here clearly indicates that female gang members are victims of at least one form of gender discrimination: e.g., the beatings, gang bangs, early pregnancies, the sexual double standard which render them as unsuitable "traditional" girlfriends. Given this, then, the results further suggest that the female auxiliary gangs serve to both expose Vice Queens to gender discrimination as well as provide some collective solutions to triple jeopardy.

Third, within this context, then, Campbell (1990) contends that the multiple oppression of black girls is a crucial factor in determining black female gang members' participation in hustling and in more serious "male" crimes. It needs to be noted here that in response to being black, female, and lower class, the kinds of hustles and crimes the Vice Queens engaged in were both similar yet different from the males' crimes. They might participate in aggressive crime, grand larceny, and sex crimes, but they tended to bring to these activities their gender identities as girls. It is this identity that created a divergence from the kinds and manner in which the Vice Kings committed crimes.

Fourth, the literature on the black female offers "distinctive socialization" as a crucial characteristic that may be a factor in the criminal and delinquent behavior of black females (Brookes 1980; Datesman et al. 1975; Lewis 1981; Mulvihill et al. 1969). Unlike their white counterparts, lower class black males and females are both socialized to be independent, assertive, and to take risks with the expectations that these are characteristics that they will need to function effectively within the black low income community. Given this, there is no tradition separating large areas of social life of black lower class boys and girls. As a consequence, black girls demonstrate, out of necessity, a greater flexibility in roles. The accounts of the Vice Queens, as well as more recent accounts of black gang girls, lend credence to these observations. The girls in these study populations participate in lower class street life and tend to participate in activities similar to those of gang boys. And thus these gang girls come to be active in "male" crimes because of their social position, a position that appears to permit these girls a great deal of freedom and lack of supervision. Within this context, the findings reported suggest that the Vice Queens utilize the female auxiliary gang as a means to acquire some knowledge of such adaptive strategies as hustling and fighting in order to be prepared to survive as independent adult women within their community.

These factors, however, do not directly address the following issue. Although the Vice Queens participate in conflict situations, current research provides a mixed bag of evidence that, since the seventies, black gang girls' involvement in conflict situations and drug distribution has increased (Adler 1975b; Bowker 1978a; Campbell 1990; Chesney-Lind 1993; Hagedorn 1988; Taylor 1990). Yet Campbell (1990) alerts us that perhaps they have not changed all that much. She points out they are still mainly involved in girl fights and act as accessories to male violence. All that can be concluded here is that our assessment of gang norm-violating behavior among girls suggests that girls today continue to be involved in violent behavior and more recently to be involved in drug trafficking.

Given this, some researchers have suggested that perhaps black gang girls today are responding in a violent and aggressive manner to the economic conditions facing lower income blacks as well as the ambiguity of their future. They concur that there has been little improvement in the economic situation of the black community since 1965. Similar to poor black girls today, as black females growing up, the Vice Queens' situation was bleak. They lived in a black lower income community characterized by high chronic unemployment and intermittent employment as well as high homicide, crime, drug addiction, and alcoholism rates. Current examinations of the black lower income community shows that the problems of twenty years ago remain the problems of today only they are more attenuated (see, for instance, Cross 1984; Glasgow 1980; Hagedorn 1988; Short 1990; Taylor 1990; Wilson 1987). According to recent research on gang behavior, the situation for teenage black girls today is even bleaker than it was for the Vice Queens during the early sixties. The findings suggest that as black girls are increasingly exposed to the worsening conditions within their low income neighborhoods where legitimate opportunities become increasingly restricted and drug use and distribution have become a "normal" way of life, then they will increasingly turn to black female gangs which provide these girls with the opportunity to learn the skills to make adaptations to poverty, violence, drugs, and racism. Thus black girls who join gangs today perhaps are not very different from their sisters, the Vice Queens, but they have gone one step further. In response to the economic crisis within their communities today they have become more entrenched and/or more oriented to "male" crime. All of this is by way of saying that if black girls are engaging in more crime, it is not as much a sign of social equality but due to economic desperation and high levels of violence within poor black communities. Thus as poor black girls, the Vice Queens as well as the black girl gangs today, respond to their forced "emancipation" which stems from the persistent economic crisis within the black community.

2 Emerging Theoretical Perspectives on Gender and Gang Membership

Introduction:
Boys' Theories and Girls' Lives

The articles in this section represent the beginnings of serious theorizing about female gangs. These selections obliquely address three historic problems with the theories: (1) there are not enough studies; (2) there are even fewer good studies; and (3) criminological theory has been developed almost solely from a male perspective.

First, the reader of this volume has undoubtedly already discovered that there just are not very many studies on which to base a theory of female gangs. Without grounding theory in a large number of good case studies or sufficiently large and worthwhile data-sets (see Curry this volume; Hagedorn 1998c), theorizing is bound to be limited. As an example, the fact that this is the first reader on female gangs ever published speaks volumes. Mainstream theories of delinquency and gang membership have rarely addressed the life situations of girls on the economic and political margins, since social scientists have seldom talked to these girls or studied their lives. Encouraging more social scientists to study female gangs is one of the main purposes of this book.

Second, and related to the problem of the dearth of social science studies, is that the research we do have, including some included in this volume, has serious weaknesses. Many are journalistic accounts (e.g., Rice 1963, Hanson 1964) which make for good reading, but one cannot help but wonder about their accuracy and generalizability. What other kinds of female gangs existed in 1960s New York that may have been different from Rice's Persian Queens or Hanson's Dagger Debs? How different would those studies have been if the observer were a social scientist rather than a journalist or social worker? What would have happened if researchers had tried to snowball sample by looking for female gang members "different" from those observed or interviewed (see Biernacki and Waldorf 1981)? Or what different conclusions might we have drawn if more researchers would have used probability samples from gang rosters like Joan

Moore's (1978; 1991)? All we can safely say is that there were likely to have been many more types of female gangs and gang members than the few that were reported.

Too many of the good studies draw conclusions based on a very small number of cases. Anne Campbell's *The Girls in the Gang* (1984/1991), for example, while, in our opinion, the most outstanding single book on female gangs, has as its "data" life histories of three gang members from four different New York female gangs (one gang member, Sun-Africa, was in two different gangs). Other studies report on data from only a few female gang members, often in a single gang, who may not be even representative of their own gang, much less other gangs. The problems of selectivity are unavoidable considering the meager and still unimpressive literature on female gangs. While there are arguably many more good studies of female gangs today, we still have very few studies based on anything but convenience samples.

The third theoretical problem this section critiques is that mainstream discussions of female gangs have been almost always an after-thought, and sometimes not even a footnote to theories of male gangs. David Curry reviews some of this male-centered literature in his piece in this section, and Anne Campbell has long written eloquently and persuasively on the subject. Despite the fact that every year girls account for one out of four arrests of young people in America (Federal Bureau of Investigation 1995, 226) and have long been involved in gang life, female delinquency is still relatively unstudied and all but ignored theoretically. Moore (1991, 137) uses Connell's (1987) term "cognitive purification" to describe the process whereby gangs, in particular, were constructed as "quintessentially male," despite evidence from her research and others that as many as a third of the youth involved in gangs were girls and young women.

A review of the almost totally male gang literature does not lack for examples of "cognitive purification." The earliest academic efforts to explain gang behavior, for example, were no more than single-minded efforts to study male delinquents. For Albert Cohen, female delinquency was no more than "sex delinquency" (1955, 45), while the real delinquent, Cohen claimed, "is a rogue male" (140). Cohen went on to reason that the male's delinquent response, "however it may be condemned by others on moral grounds, has at least one virtue: it incontestably confirms, in the eyes of all concerned, his essential masculinity."

However, we should not disregard Cohen's work. His essentialist arguments were based on a recognition, not made by most, that there were fundamental differences between male and female delinquency. Unfortunately, Cohen was unable to rise above 1950s middle class masculine stereotypes and prejudice. In this he was joined by Walter Miller, who also argued that the gang is essentially masculine. In Miller's paper, "Lower Class Culture as a Generating Milieu of Gang Delinquency" (1958), "focal concerns" of lower class life, e.g., trouble, toughness, and excitement, predispose poor male youth to criminal misconduct. Miller, at least, also studied female gangs, though the "Molls" and other female gangs are treated as somewhat of an oddity in an aggressive male world. Cohen and Miller, however, stand out from most criminologists of the time who ignored girls, female gangs, and female delinquency as if there really were nothing substantial to explain.

For example, Travis Hirschi (1969), in the influential *The Causes of Delinquency,* relegated women to a footnote which suggested, somewhat apologetically, that "in the analysis that follows, the 'non-Negro' becomes 'white,' and the girls disappear" (35-36). And lest one think that ignoring women is a property of mainstream theorists, the reader can look in vain for any mention of women in Taylor, Walton, and Young's highly regarded 1973 radical classic *The New Criminology.* In another radical study, *Adolescent Subcultures* (1985), Herman and Julia Schwendinger, for accuracy's sake, ought to have added "Male" to their title. Despite an incisive portrayal of rape and analysis of masculinity, their study is almost solely about male peer groups.

Most classic criminological theories simply ignored women and did not find the nature of female delinquent peer groups as interesting or worth explaining. Robert Merton's (1938) highly influential anomie theory stressed the need to consider how some social structures exert a definite pressure upon certain persons in the society to engage in nonconformist rather than conformist conduct. His work influenced delinquency research largely through the efforts of Cloward and Ohlin (1960), who looked at variation in access to "legitimate" and "illegitimate" opportunities for male youth. No mention of female delinquency can be found in their *Delinquency and Opportunity,* except the familiar notion that boys "engulfed by a feminine world and uncertain of their own identification...tend to 'protest' against femininity" (49). Ruth Morris (1965) is one of the few criminologists to attempt to apply "anomie" or "strain" theory to women. Anticipating Carol Gilligan (1982), Morris looked at the relative lack of legitimate means for women to attain their more relational goals than for men to attain more instrumental goals. Few researchers have followed up on her efforts to revise a fundamentally male anomie theory.

Peggy Giordano's (1978) important contribution to the criminological literature, reprinted here, establishes the salience of the female peer group for the girls themselves. Her argument is a corrective for the long-held assumption by criminologists that females in gangs exist solely to service male needs. Giordano's concise article sent a message to the criminological world of that time that something was seriously awry with "social science" thinking which ignored females except as sex objects.

Giordano reviews the self-reported delinquency of about one hundred incarcerated girls in the seventies, and she discovers that despite their incarceration for traditionally female offenses, their actual delinquency is surprisingly diverse. About half the girls report membership in gangs. Finally, Giordano notes that African American girls and white girls report different pathways to delinquent behavior, with African American girls reporting greater delinquency when in female groups, while white girls report more delinquency in mixed sex groups. Giordano supports the findings of Quicker, in the first section of this volume, that the female gang plays some important and positive functions for girls.

Bowker and Klein (1983), in one of the few articles on female gangs written prior to the nineties, also noted that these gangs had positive functions for their members. What the studies of Bowker and Klein, Giordano, and Quicker have in common is something rare in gang research: their studies were based on carefully selected samples with enough variation to give confidence in their findings. What is most significant about these studies is that the importance of the female gang or peer group to young females is firmly established. In other words, there may be something about the female gang to study after all! But if the female gang has importance to its members, how does it promote delinquency?

"Differential association," or the idea that criminal behavior was learned in intimate personal groups, has been the principal theoretical explanation for the transmission of male delinquency. Edwin Sutherland (1934), who developed the concept of differential association, which also influenced Cloward and Ohlin's work, claimed that his theory explained all crime, but there is little mention of women in his work. Eileen Leonard (1983, 108) suggests that the lack of contact with delinquent peers and girls' more closely supervised life results in fewer girls getting involved with gangs, which is "the most appropriate example" of the applicability of Sutherland's theory to women.

Anne Campbell's "Self Definition by Rejection," reprinted here, is an early attempt to study how dynamics in female gangs differ from those in male gangs. Unlike male gang members, who arrive at definitions of themselves by using the male peer group to help them construct a male identity, Campbell argues that female gang members arrive at their own self-definition by default as they reject components of the identities they attribute to others. Campbell notes that the gang girls she interviewed consciously reject certain aspects of traditional Hispanic femininity, specifically the notion that women had to martyr themselves and tolerate male abuse. On the other hand, Latina gang members simultaneously embrace other aspects of the feminine role, such as motherhood. The gang girl, Campbell says, "enjoys her femininity but rejects passivity and suffering." This differs from the more clear-cut identification of aggressive masculinity by gang boys.

James Messerschmidt, in the section of his 1997 book *Structured Action Theory* reprinted here, continues Campbell's argument on a more updated theoretical plane. Like Campbell, Messerschmidt pushes further away from the construction of girls in gangs as either "journalistic curiosities or footnotes" (Campbell this volume, p. 100) and begins to explore the ways in which class and race impact on teenage femininities. Messerschmidt, as well as Campbell, explores the meaning of "fighting " in the context of these girls' lives on the street. Messerschmidt focuses on what he calls "bad girl femininity" and rejects essentialist notions that all girls are incapable of violence. Others (White and Kowalski 1994) have built on this notion, suggesting that girls' and women's violence needs to be explicitly studied within its social context of patriarchy, as well as, we would add, racism.

Traditionally, girls' and women's violence has been alternately demonized or denied, usually in service of either patriarchal or racist interests. The starkest example of this has been the repeated attempt to link female crime, and particularly violent crime, to the women's movement. More recently, the media "discovery" of girls' violence, particularly the violence of young minority women, has been deployed to "de-gender" and demonize these young women (see Sikes 1997 for an egregious example). Female violence has been repeatedly viewed out of context, and we shall return to critique this idea in the last section of this book. Finally, as Curry's concluding article of this section notes, the fact that gang membership can, for girls, "be simultaneously rewarding and destructive" is theoretically possible if one adopts a dialectial perspective (see Maher 1997). What is needed most, of course, are more good studies to produce the solid, empirical base from which good theorizing will emerge.

The four articles in this section approach the issue of gender and delinquency differently, and taken together they present a variety of theoretical perspectives on girls in gangs. Notably, they recognize that girls grow up in a different world than boys (Block 1984; Orenstein 1994), and that while both girls and boys have similar problems, girls "have it heaps worse" (Adler 1986). Likewise, these articles begin to document the fact that minority girls grow up and do gender in worlds very different from that of their white counterparts. Since racism and poverty are often fellow-travelers, these girls are forced by their race and their poverty to deal early and often with problems of violence, drugs, and abuse. Their strategies for coping with these problems, often clever, strong, and daring, but also sometimes destructive, tend to place them outside the conventional expectations of middle class white girls (Campbell 1984; Orenstein 1994; Robinson 1990).

Perhaps in a decade or so, a profusion of research on female gangs may create the conditions for publishing an entire volume about theoretical perspectives on female gangs. But that time has not yet come.

Girls, Guys and Gangs:
The Changing Social Context of Female Delinquency

*Peggy Giordano**

The historic and widely held assumption that delinquency was predominantly masculine in gender has had important implications both in the kind of theoretical work which has dominated the delinquency literature as well as in the continued choice of males as preferred subjects of empirical research. Psychological or "personal problems" explanations have generally been marshalled to explain female delinquency. It has also been assumed that sexual offenses, incorrigibility, and "running away" make up the delinquent repertoire of girls, and that their involvement in more serious offenses is quite limited.

Even where sociological variables have been studied they have typically been interpreted within a psychological framework. For example, while it is widely recognized that coming from a broken home is related to a higher incidence of delinquency, this variable is thought to have an even greater impact in the case of girls. Studies show a more profound sense of loneliness and low self-esteem in girls who have a poor home life[1] or even a psychological reaction against the absent or inadequate father.[2]

Other studies may include social variables, but nevertheless perpetuate the conception that female delinquency is primarily an adaptation to personal problems. These studies deal with the theory, which was first suggested by Cohen,[3] that delinquency in females may be associated with a girl's inability to establish a good relationship with the opposite sex. While for males, long range goals center around achieving success and acquiring material possessions, the primary goal for females is thought to be "catching a man." Thus, the classic Mertonian model, if somewhat stripped of its structural components, can then be applied to understanding female delinquency (usually sexual in character) as a form of "innovation."[4]

The bulk of literature, then, has perpetuated the notion that personal maladjustments characterize the female delinquent—she must have a psychological problem, be unable to adequately perform her proper sex role, or suffer from the ill effects of a bad home life. The recent large increases in both the *number* of adjudicated females and the apparent increased *versatility* of their involvement in crimes make it far more difficult to account for all female crime in such purely psychological terms. For example, between 1960 and 1973 the arrest rate of females under eighteen years of age increased 265% for all offenses, 393% for violent crimes, and 334% for property crimes. This contrasts with increases of 124%, 236%, and 82%, respectively, for males in the same age bracket.[5]

*Reprinted from The Journal of Criminal Law and Criminology *69:1 (1978), 126-32*. Copyright 1978 by Peggy Giordano. Reprinted by permission of the author.*

Explaining the Increase: Women's Liberation?

A ready explanation for understanding females' involvement and, in particular, these rapidly rising official delinquency statistics is provided by "women's liberation."

Freda Adler's book, *Sisters in Crime,* is one work which suggests a rather direct link between sex role changes and increased delinquency.[6] While this work is important in suggesting changes at various levels of society which may be having an impact on female behavior, these ideas are obscured somewhat by an overall ideological stance which has been taken in relation to the problem. Adler sees the rising crime rate as part of the price society must pay for greater involvement by females at all levels. Women are demanding a bigger piece of the illegitimate as well as the legitimate action. While she does not go so far as to suggest that these women are aligned with the movement itself, casting her argument from a feminist perspective nevertheless imputes "feminist" or "liberated" motives to the criminals.

> Like her legitimate-based sister, the female criminal knows too much to pretend or return to her former role as a second rate criminal confined to "feminine" crimes such as shoplifting and prostitution. She has had a taste of financial victory. In some cases, she has had a taste of blood. Her appetite, however, appears to be only whetted.[7]

We would argue that, important as these sex role changes are, it is a mistake and an oversimplification to suggest such a direct link between the "liberation" of females and increased involvement in crimes. This implies a degree of politicization and commitment on the part of the criminals to which she simply may not adhere. It appears, from what we know about the impact of social movements on various segments of society, that not only is it erroneous to suggest any kind of overt politicization on the part of most female criminals, but it is also an oversimplification to accord any kind of casual, delinquency-inducing status to most attitudinal changes generally associated with the movement. At the very least, recent empirical work demonstrates the necessity for viewing sex role orientation or "liberation" as multi-dimensional and finds a negligible or even negative association between certain indices of liberation and reported delinquency involvement.[8]

Alternative Explanations: Theories of Male Delinquency

In attempting to understand recent changes in female crime patterns, then, it is perhaps more useful to conceive of these women and girls as *recipients* of the effects of broad-based as well as micro-level societal changes, rather than themselves being responsible for a new era of sex role equality. We should begin to focus on the ways in which broader changes have filtered down to the point where they have affected the everyday social world of adolescent and particularly lower status girls so that delinquency is one normal outcome. A re-examination of traditionally male theories of delinquency locates particular factors which have generally been associated with delinquent activities on the part of males. To the extent that there have been social changes in the lives of females in these same areas, we should be able to understand and predict increases in female delinquent activity as well.

Aside from labeling and conflict theories which might be invoked to explain recent changes in official *response* to female deviance, control theory, opportunity theory, and differential association (or other variations which have emphasized the importance of friendship networks) all implicitly suggest factors which could account for behavioral changes on the part of females. Hirschi's control perspective, which emphasized the notion that delinquency becomes possible when attachment to societal bonds is weakened, has obvious relevance to changing female behavior patterns.[9] Females have traditionally been more protected by and attached to conventional institutions, i.e., school, family, church.[10] A weakening of these bonds to allow a wider range of behavior generally creates new opportunities where deviance is one possibility. Cloward and Ohlin's classic formulation of Delinquency and Opportunity Theory highlights the fact that opportunity in the legitimate as well as the illegitimate arenas is differentially available.[11] A relaxing of curfew and other tight constraints on females creates a whole host of situational contexts in which delinquency may occur (e.g., driving around in a car, going to local hangouts, going to bars "unescorted"). This should have particular relevance in understanding increases in crimes such as drinking, vandalism, or drug use where situational factors assume such a crucial role. Jensen and Eve did examine the impact of control variables on female involvement in delinquency, and while such factors were associated with it, they did not completely account for male-female differences.[12] Unfortunately, their use of a sample obtained in 1964-'65 may limit the ability to generalize their findings to present day patterns.

However, perhaps most crucial to an understanding of female participation in minor as well as more serious crimes is the role of the *peer group* in transmitting definitions favorable to the violation of law. The importance of group influence on male involvement in delinquency has been amply demonstrated in classic research studies.[13] But the peer group continues to be important in more recent studies. For example, Hirschi's own findings, though emphasizing control variables, suggest the importance of peer influences.[14] The assumption has been that these friendship networks are non-existent or at least not as important in the lives of adolescent girls. This may have always been a somewhat inaccurate view of the social world of adolescent girls,[15] but clearly peer associations must assume a central role in any attempt to understand recent changing patterns of delinquency involvement. Increases in casual cross-sex socializing (not on a dating basis) could provide reinforcement for behaviors which are illegal, as well as provide opportunities for learning more specifics about some kinds of delinquency. This initial learning may occur in connection with males, but it is hypothesized that there would also be a slowly developing tradition of delinquency among female peers as well. Thus, important changes may be occurring not only because girls are being increasingly exposed to delinquent behavior by learning about it, but also because of their perception that there would be peer approval for their engaging in unlawful behavior. It is suggested that at the very least the more delinquent, aggressive girls are receiving some kind of reference group support from other females, and possibly from other reference groups as well. This is contrasted with the transitional situation where girls may have curtailed their behavior in part because of concern over what the other girls thought, or because their boyfriends would disapprove.

This article presents the results of a study which examines (in the tradition of countless male-based research efforts) the role of the peer group in understanding the nature of female delinquency. It is hypothesized that it is within the everyday social context of the friendship or gang networks that we can see perhaps the greatest evidence of change, and that these changing peer associations will have a more immediate impact on female crime patterns than that evidenced by any kind of ideological or attitudinal liberation.

STUDY

Methodology

The focus of the present study is largely descriptive. It is concerned with the social context in which females participate in delinquent acts, their perception of the attitudes of others toward their violating the law, and the association, if any, between the perceived acceptability of certain kinds of acts and actual involvement in delinquency. A longitudinal design would have been an ideal way to assess the extent of change in female friendship patterns; however, as discussed previously, the few early studies involving females tended to emphasize psychological variables. It is nevertheless thought to be important to determine, using a present day sample, what type of social network seems to be associated with high levels of delinquency involvement on the part of adolescent females. To accomplish this, questionnaires were administered to the total population at a state institution for juvenile offenders ($N=108$), and to a comparable sample of eighty-three girls randomly selected from an urban high school in a predominantly lower status area. The high school sample was added to provide a wider range of delinquent involvement—primarily to increase the number who are more "law-abiding." The age range for the institutionalized sample was twelve to nineteen, with a mean age of seventeen; the range for the school sample was fourteen to nineteen, with a mean age of 17.3. Non-whites constituted 50.9% of the institutionalized sample. The school sample included 48.2% non-whites. One of the important limitations of the sample is that the girls came from lower socio-economic status backgrounds (as indicated by the occupations they list for their parents/guardians) and hence, the findings to be reported cannot be generalized beyond this lower class sample.

A revised version of the Nye-Short self-admitted delinquency test[16] was used to measure the extent of the girls' involvement in delinquent activity. A split-half test for reliability yielded a coefficient of 0.95 for this scale.

Several items derived from the literature on male friendship networks and gangs were used in this study to measure the extent of peer group involvement. Two items were identical to the friendship questions used by Lehrman[17] (*Question:* "When you are at home, who do you usually go around with?" *Answer:* Myself, one or two others, or a regular group. *Question:* "How much of your leisure time do you spend with friends?" *Answer:* All, most, or some). Several other single item indicators, which were more descriptive, were also included.

To determine whether changing definitions of what is "acceptable" behavior for females may be accounting for some increase in criminal activity, a series of questions was constructed concerning three reference groups that might be important to the girls. The girls were asked to indicate how various reference groups would react if they were to engage in certain kinds of activity. Three reference groups were selected: "Guys I run around with," "My boyfriend" and "Girls I run around with," realizing that there might be other important reference groups, such as parents. Behavioral items were chosen to represent independent kinds of actions, some of which might encourage delinquent activity (e.g., "Staying out all night"), and others which were actually illegal (e.g., "Using grass once in a while"). The items chosen dealt with behavior that was traditionally proscribed for females but that, it is hypothesized, may be considered more acceptable or even "cool" by today's adolescent subculture. The questions were worded so that there would not be universal disapproval; for example, it is possible to envision approval for one of the items, "Beating up somebody nobody likes," as opposed to something like, "Murdering someone in cold blood." The specific items included were:

- Beating up on somebody nobody likes.
- Shoplifting.
- Running away.
- Staying out all night.
- Stealing a car for a joy ride.
- Making an obscene phone call.
- Using a fake I.D. to get in a bar.
- Tearing up school property.
- Driving around with a bunch of kids.
- Using grass once in a while.
- Picking up guys.

Total "approval" scores for each reference group were obtained by summing the responses for all eleven items. The split-half reliability coefficient for these items using, "Guys I hang around with," as the reference group was 0.93, for girlfriends, 0.93, and for boyfriends, 0.94.

Results

It should perhaps first be noted that the sample of 108 incarcerated girls did produce a wide range of delinquent activities. One of the initial reasons for administering the questionnaire was to see if girls were indeed primarily involved with status offenses, incorrigibility, and the like, as depicted in the literature, or whether there were girls who had gotten involved in crimes typically considered "masculine." While most of the girls in the institution had, in fact, committed many of the "traditional" female offenses (84.2% had run away from home one or more times; 65% had had sexual relations with someone they didn't know too well). Table 1 lists the percentage of the sample of 108 girls who had been involved in crimes which had traditionally been considered "masculine" in character, as well as the involvement by girls in the school sample in these crimes.

In addition, 53.7% of the institutionalized group indicated that they had been part of a group of girls that could be called a "gang." Of these, 51.9% indicated that the gang had a name. The names of these gangs (e.g., The Outlaws, the Cobras, Mojos, Loveless, Red Blood, White Knights, East Side Birds, Power) convey neither a particularly "feminine" image, nor suggest a subordinate position to a male gang.

Friendships and Delinquency

The first item which dealt with friendship patterns, "Who do you usually go around with?" had three possible responses—myself, one or two others, or a regular group. An analysis of variance was computed which indicated a statistically significant difference between groups. Those who were part of a regular group were more likely to be delinquent. For the white subsample, $F = 11.65$ $(p < .001)$; for the black subsample, $F = 4.62$ $(p < .01)$. The second item concerned the amount of leisure time spent with the group.

Table 1

Percent of Institutionalized and School Sample Reporting Involvement (One or More Times) in "Serious Delinquent Acts"

	Institutionalized Sample (N = 108)		School Sample (N = 83)	
	n	%	n	%
Stealing items over $50	85	78.3	3	3.6
Taken part in gang fights	60	55.6	15	18.1
Carried a weapon, such as a gun or a knife	86	79.6	22	26.4
Fought someone using a weapon	64	59.6	6	7.2
Breaking and entering	68	63.5	3	3.6
Used pills to get high	95	83.3	27	32.5
Tried heroin	47	43.5	1	1.2

A significant positive correlation was found between this variable and the extent of involvement in delinquency ($r =.43$, $p < .001$ for whites; $r =.22$, $p < .01$ for blacks). That is, the more leisure time spent in the group, the more likely a girl was to be delinquent. Similarly, those who indicated that they had been part of a group of girls that could be called a "gang" were more delinquent than those who said they had not been part of such a group ($t = 5.17, p <.001$ for whites, $t =3.32, p <.001$ for blacks).[18]

The Context in Which Delinquent Acts Occur

In addition to the general association between group involvement and delinquency, which parallels the findings from most male-based research studies, it was important to try to specify more clearly the actual social context in which females are likely to commit delinquent acts. Respondents were asked to indicate whether they were more likely to go out with a group of "guys and girls" or with just girls. For the whites, those who indicated they were more likely to go out in a group of "guys and girls" or with just girls. For the whites, those who indicated they were more likely to go out in a group of guys and girls were significantly more delinquent than thoses who said they went out more often with girls only ($t =2.40, p <.05$). For blacks, however, this question did not appear to differentiate delinquents from non-delinquents.

In addition, subjects were asked, "When you are out in a group, who would be more likely to start the trouble—a guy or a girl?" While, as expected, most indicated that it would be a male (only 17.6% of the white girls thought a girl might start the trouble), 31.6% of the black girls thought it might be a girl who would be the one to start trouble.

Similarly, Table 2 presents the distribution of responses to an item which asked subjects, "Who are you more likely to be with when you get into trouble?" An examination of this table suggests that for whites, "a group of guys" or "guys and girls" provides the

Table 2

The Social Context in Which "Trouble" Is Likely to Occur

	Whites (N = 91)*		Blacks (N = 95)**	
	n	%	n	%
Group of girls	17	18.7	33	34.7
A group of guys and girls	25	27.5	21	22.1
A group of guys	28	30.8	15	15.8
One guy	5	5.5	10	10.5
One girlfriend	5	5.5	—	2.1
By self	8	8.8	—	12.6
	91		95	
	* 3.3% missing data		**2.1% missing data	

social context in which "trouble" will most often occur. While this pattern exists in the black subsample as well, there is a higher percentage of black females that indicated that trouble would be more likely to occur with a group of girls. It should also be noted that analysis of a different sample group showed that in terms of whom girls actually reported being with when committing particular offenses, the modal category was clearly a group of "guys and girls."[19] While this differed somewhat by the nature of the offense (i.e., it was more likely in the case of robbers (52.7%) or vandalism (54.1%) than for minor theft (28.5%), and as shown here, by race, it is evidence that association with males is somehow tied with many females becoming involved in delinquent acts. It is interesting, however, that this does not *appear* to represent a simple case of the girl adopting a passive role in going along with her boyfriend as earlier depictions of the female criminal might lead to us predict.[20] This picture of the girl negatively influenced by the boy with whom she is romantically involved is challenged somewhat by the low percentage of both black and white respondents who felt that trouble would most likely occur with "one guy." Findings regarding the girls' perceptions of how significant others would react if they were involved in various delinquent acts further complicate this image.

Changing Definitions of What is Acceptable Behavior for Adolescent Girls

Table 3 presents the composite approval scores. This score represents the degree of approval or disapproval the girl thought she would receive from various reference groups if she where to engage in certain behavior. A comparison of the mean scores shows that, in both the white and black subsamples, the highest approval for engaging in these illegal activities came from other girlfriends. Looking at the other reference groups, girls making up the white subsample perceived the least amount of approval from their boyfriends. This lends additional evidence that these girls are not simply following the dictates of a lover when committing delinquent acts. The picture is, however, more complicated in the black subsample. The highest approval score again comes from other

Table 3

Reference Group Support for Delinquency and Its Relationship to Actual Self-Reported Involvement (N = 191)

	Mean approval	Association with delinquent activity		Mean approval	Association with delinquent activity	
	Whites	r	p	Blacks	r	p
Girls I hang around with	29.38	.33	.001	27.00	.29	.01
Guys I hang around with	26.97	.01	.42	24.74	.24	.01
Boyfriend	22.74	.02	.43	26.15	.18	.05

girls. However, while the mean approval is lower for the boyfriend (t = .33, α < N. S.), the gap between the reference groups is narrower. A computation of E^2 produced a value of 0.86 for the white subsample, 0.23 for the black subsample.[21] This statistic indicates that a much higher percentage of the variance in scores is accounted for by the degree of approval or disapproval from various reference groups in the white subsample as compared to the black subsample. This suggests, then, that the black girls in this sample did not differentiate as sharply between how male and female friends would view their behavior. Also, the meaning of the relatively higher approval score from the boyfriend should be interpreted with some caution, due to the very high variance in that category among black respondents (s^2 =463.77). This is contrasted with a variance on the girlfriend scales of 174.50, and 201.49 for the male friends scale. Thus, while there may be strong approval by *some* boyfriends, the high variance points to the existence of some girls within this group who perceived much less approval. It is hypothesized that at least some of the girls who thought the boyfriend would be approving may have been thinking of "pimps" when answering those items.

The correlation between the perception of approval from other reference groups and actual delinquency involvement is also presented in Table 3. There are significant correlations, for both black and white subsamples, between extent of approval from *other girlfriends* and actual participation in delinquency. There is also a significant correlation between perception of approval of male friends (r = .24 α < .01) and a weak but significant correlation between a boyfriend's approval and delinquency in the black subsample (r = .18, α < .05).

The findings regarding the relative importance of *female* approval are interesting, particularly when compared with the earlier findings (see Table 2) that females are quite likely to commit offenses within the context of mixed sex groups. At first this appears to be a contradiction; specifically, that where the whites were more likely to be with males, there does not appear in the white sample to be an important association between approval from males and actual participation in delinquent activity.

However, one possible interpretation of these results is that interaction with males, particularly in a non-romantic way, simply affords the most propitious environment in which girls will *learn* about as well as actually engage in delinquent acts. This does not have to mean that boys are coaxing them into this activity, or that approval from them is a necessary prerequisite. Just as the same sex peer group has offered a source of status and approval in the case of male delinquents, it appears that approval from other girlfriends will also accompany a girl's decision to become involved in delinquent activity.

It could be argued that this approval would be an even greater necessity for girls since their behavior is not as much a part of an established tradition. Therefore, the girls who *do* become involved in delinquency would be likely to first feel that girls in general and themselves in particular are capable of committing certain behavior, that others *like them* (girls) also probably engage in it, and that these girls are not likely to regard them with disdain if they were to engage in that behavior themselves.

Summary and Conclusion

The findings from the present research, which point to an important link between friendship patterns and delinquent involvement, cast further doubt on the assumption that female delinquency represents some kind of personal maladaption. Rather, for both the white and black subsamples, there was a significant association between group affiliation and self-reported delinquency. Especially in the case of white females, a closer examination of the actual makeup of such friendship networks suggests that groups which include both males and females were particularly conducive to delinquency. Due to the more established tradition of male participation in illegal acts it is likely that girls would, at least to some extent, be learning delinquent modes of behavior from males. This would be particularly important in instances in which there is some technical knowledge involved in committing the act. More research is needed on the particular ways in which association with males exerts this delinquent influence. The pattern *appears* to be more complex than the notion that the boyfriend simply uses the female in an "accomplice" or other passive role while he commits the crime. One index of this is that "trouble" is likely to occur in *groups* which include both males and females. Also, further research should address the important racial differences suggested by this exploratory study; for example, in the black subsample there was a somewhat greater likelihood that "trouble" could involve a group of girls alone. This could represent a difference in the kinds of constraints which may have traditionally been placed on white as compared to black adolescent females. To the extent that the black female have had a longer tradition of independence and freedom of action than has her white counterpart, the less likely it seems that the black female would need to learn techniques, values and motives from "the guys."

Finally, while there were some differences in the social context of black and white participation in delinquency, it was found that for both subsamples the perception of approval from other girlfriends was significantly correlated with actual delinquency involvement. This suggests what may be a crucial element of change. While it is unlikely that girls are or will become immune to what the boys think of their behavior, it is likely that *other girls* are the most important reference group, or at least the group to which they compare themselves. This would be consistent with male subculture theories which have documented the important status-conferring, delinquency-inducing influence of the same sex peer group. Girls appear to be no different in this respect.

Self-Definition by Rejection:
The Case of Gang Girls

Anne Campbell★

I use material obtained from a two-year participant observational study of girl gang members to examine how their structural position as poor, Puerto Rican, and female affects their self-presentation in social talk. Much of their sense of individuality results from their rejection of aspects of identity associated with that social position. Their self-definition is realized not through the construction of a fully integrated "deviant" personality but through piecemeal rejection of various components of stereotypes about poor, Puerto Rican women. I suggest that closer examination of gossip and "put downs" can illuminate how one's own identity is constructed through the vilification of others' actions and character.

Although there is evidence that young women have participated in urban street gangs since the mid-nineteenth century (Asbury 1927; Salisbury 1958; Thrasher 1927), it is only recently that they have received attention as a topic of study in their own right. Prior to the 1970s, female gangs were usually treated as journalistic curiosities (Hanson 1964; Rice 1963) or as footnotes to the study of male gangs (Cohen 1955; Cohen and Short 1958; Short and Strodtbeck 1965; Thrasher 1927). Two themes are apparent in much of this early work: the psychological problems and inappropriate sex role behavior of female gang members.

Psychological studies portrayed female gang members as immature, anxious, and maladjusted (Thompson and Lozes 1976), as relatively low in intelligence (Rice 1963), and as socially inept and sexually promiscuous (Ackley and Fliegel 1960; Cohen 1955; Welfare Council of New York City 1950). Thus, this early research attributed many of the same characteristics to gang members which were used to describe female delinquents in general (Smart 1976). However, Bowker and Klein (1983) reanalyzed data from the 1960s and found only trivial differences between gang and non-gang girls on a variety of psychological tests.

Early studies by social workers and sociologists tended to decontextualize the behavior of ghetto girls and to compare it unfavorably with middle-class stereotypes of femininity. Social workers placed particular emphasis upon gang girls' slipshod appearance, their preference for pants over skirts, and their poor personal hygiene, posture, and manners (Ackley and Fliegel 1960; Hanson 1964). Girls' failures in these areas were taken as indications of low self-esteem, prompting remedial efforts to turn them into young ladies (Short and Strodtbeck 1965). These departures from appropriate feminine behavior

★Reprinted by permission from *Social Problems* 34:5 (December 1987), pp. 451-66. ©1987 by the Society for the Study of Social Problems, Inc.

were also seen as the surface manifestations of a more profound problem: their promiscuity. Although the evidence for this was drawn from a highly questionable source—reports of male gang members—the promiscuity of gang girls was highlighted in Cohen's (1955) theoretical analysis of working-class delinquency. He argued that because emotional and romantic conquests are the female counterpart of societal achievement among boys, these young women expressed their rejection of the "middle-class measuring rod" by freely dispensing sexual favors. Thus, while boys boast about delinquent acts in order to achieve masculine status within their own oppositional subculture, girls should logically flaunt their promiscuity, as a badge of their oppositional female identity.

Examination of the slim quantity of ethnographic work on delinquent and gang girls in fact suggests that this is not the case. The social talk of delinquent girls generally shows that they not only reject sexual activity outside the context of a steady relationship but even reject friendships with "loose" girls whose reputation might contaminate them by association (Smith 1978; Wilson 1978). Horowitz (1983) reinforces this point in her examination of barrio lifestyles of teenage girls in Chicago. As part of the Chicano culture, they must maintain the appearance of virginity and restraint even though the broader U.S. culture encourages and condones sexual experience. The girls manage this contradiction by ascribing pregnancy to momentary passion in the context of a love relationship (the use of contraception would imply a cold-blooded and more permanent commitment to sexual experience). They can maintain their "virgin" status even after motherhood if their public demeanor continues to emphasize their commitment to motherhood and rejection of casual sexual adventures.

Female members of New York street gangs described in this paper had club rules which explicitly required serial monogamy, and girls who spread their sexual attentions too far were disciplined by the gang's "godmother." The pejorative potency of terms such as "whore" and "slut" is clearly seen in the way these teenage girls used such terms to characterize their enemies and rivals, and epithets such as these are often the triggers which spark female fights (Campbell 1986). It was this observation that gave rise to the present study: The words and typifications we use to characterize our enemies are often an important guide to the ascriptions we most reject in ourselves. By extension, our self concept may evolve from our rejection of such negative personal attributes rather than from the active construction of a social identity.

Using data from Puerto Rican gang members, I show how the girls' sense of self as gang members is derived from their rejection of various aspects of membership of three interlocking societal identities: class, race, and gender. They arrive at a female gang identity by default rather than by affirmation. The fragmented and reactive nature of their self-definition helps to make sense of many of the contradictions which are present in the social talk of the gang girl. By "backing away" from one aspect of an assigned role, she may run the risk of being cast in another unacceptable role from which she must also extricate herself. For example, in rejecting women's passivity toward men, a girl may endorse her support for abortion. However, in doing so, she risks being seen as cheap or as a bad mother. Her support for abortion in one context may be withdrawn in another. To achieve self-presentational consistency, the individual must have formed a coherent schema of her ideal self to which she refers. As long as her self presentation depends upon rejecting an interlocking set of actions or qualities, she is likely to find herself escaping from one rejected identity but risking entry into another. The point is that not all components of a given role are rejected; indeed, it is hard to imagine what the result of such a total rejection would be. The girls accept the desirability of some aspects of femininity, class, or ethnicity but reject others. Essentially they are saying, "I am not *that* kind of woman," which is very different from saying, "I am not a woman."

In focusing upon self-presentation through the words of the social actors themselves, the present study has much in common with the study of accounts (Goffman 1959; Scott and Lyman 1968). Accounts are usually given by actors in anticipation of or in response to listeners' negative evaluation of the actors' behavior. They are the means by which actors excuse or justify instances of untoward behavior. Stokes and Hewitt (1976) go further to argue that accounts serve to reconcile prevailing norms with innovative or deviant behavior and, over time, can alter group norms. In the case of delinquency, Sykes and Matza (1957) describe various "techniques of neutralization" which deny the wrongfulness of crime or justify it with respect to some superordinate value. My analysis of gang girls' accounts differs in three major respects from this tradition. First, I focus on social identities rather than on discrete actions. Girls see actions as characteristic of certain types of person and they vilify these behaviors not for their own sake but because they are the manifestations of a rejected identity. This idea is tacitly embodied in some of Sykes and Matza's (1957) justifications and excuses. For example, an "appeal to higher loyalties" often invokes reference to the overriding importance of group solidarity, which can be seen from the present perspective as colloquially indicating "I am not the kind of person who deserts my buddies." Second, the accounts I describe are not directed only at anti-social behaviors. The qualities which gang girls reject include passivity, submissiveness, and provincialism as well as drug addiction and prostitution. Tension exists not only between deviance and respectability but also between old-fashioned and modern values, between poverty and glamour. Third, while accounts are usually efforts to justify the speaker's own behavior, I focus mainly on disparagement of others' behavior. That is, I am concerned with gossip and "put-downs." As Moore (1978, 52) notes: "Gossip, heavily judgmental, is at the heart of much sociability at the frequent parties. Gossip is fun. It also means that everybody—adult and adolescent—has a 'reputation' that is continuously shifting and renewed."

This putting-down of others is a crucial component of the establishment of a self-image. To accuse neighboring gang members of being "whores" or "glue sniffers" clearly announces that the speaker denies the applicability of such terms to herself. Analysis of the vilification of others is not only a useful methodological tool, but this process of symbolic rejection may be at the heart of how gang girls arrive at their own self-definition. They do not actively work at constructing a coherent female group image but rather arrive at one by default as they reject components of the identities they attribute to others.

Method

Between 1979 and 1981 I attached myself to three New York City female gangs as a participant observer. During the first six month's of research, I made initial contacts with a number of city gangs through site visits to gang outreach programs and introductions arranged by the New York Gang Crimes Unit. At the end of this period, I selected three gangs for in-depth observation and subsequently spent six months with each of them. In each case, I selected one girl as the focus of the research and spent approximately four days-a-week with her in day-to-day activities—during the course of which I came to meet her fellow gang members, family, and neighbors. Whenever possible I tape-recorded dialogues between individual girls and myself, as well as group interactions between the girls and between female and male members. I augment my analysis of these recordings with material from my field notes.

One of the three groups I studied was the Five Percenters, a black Islamic movement organized into gang-like structures in a number of East Coast cities. However, I restrict my focus here to the accounts of Puerto Rican gang members, the majority of whom belonged to the Sex Girls and the Sandman Ladies.[1] As with female gangs described in other major cities (Miller 1975; Quicker 1983), both gangs were affiliated with previously established male gangs and adopted a feminized version of the male gang's name. Female members constituted approximately 10% of gang membership in the city (Collins 1979). The girls had their own leader and made most of their decisions independently of the males, including the acceptance, initiation, and discipline of their members. Gang members ranged in age from 12 to 28.

The Sandman Ladies were located on the west side of Manhattan with headquarters in the apartment of the female and male leaders (a married couple) in a housing project. They referred to themselves as a club or a family rather than as a gang, and identified themselves as "bikers"—although the 20 male and 11 female members possessed only one working motorcycle between them. Their primary source of income was from street sales of marijuana, augmented by burglary and by hiring themselves out to protect cocaine sellers in the mid-town area.

The Sex Girls were located in the East New York section of Brooklyn and most of the members lived within a few blocks of their clubhouse—one of the many abandoned buildings in the neighborhood. Their male counterparts named themselves the Sex Boys in honor of one of the local streets (Essex Street) when they split from the Ghettos

Brothers in 1972. The male and female gangs were in a state of decline by 1979. A number of members were dead or imprisoned, and the formal structure of the gangs was in disarray. Although the Sex Girls allegedly had 50 members in the mid-1970s, their numbers had declined to about 10 by the time of my research. The gangs' main source of revenue was drug dealing. During my field work they were involved in a dispute with an Italian group of dealers over territorial rights to selling, which resulted in the deaths of three of the male members. Their income was augmented by petty criminality such as stripping cars and abandoned buildings.

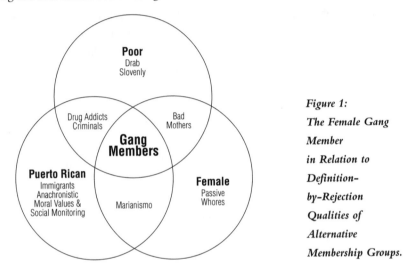

Figure 1:
The Female Gang
Member
in Relation to
Definition-
by-Rejection
Qualities of
Alternative
Membership Groups.

A content analysis of the verbal "put-downs" that appeared in the social talk of gang girls revealed 10 recurrent topics. In each of these, the girls expressed rejection of specific behaviors or qualities and clearly identified themselves as distinct from individuals who could be characterized by them. For ease of presentation, I have conceptualized them as shown in Figure 1 as locations in a matrix of three interlocking structural variables: poverty, ethnicity, and gender. It should be stressed that this conceptualization is mine and did not arise explicity from the girls themselves. Rather these topics of social talk occurred sporadically throughout my fieldwork and the girls themselves did not specifically relate any given "put-down" to these sociological categories. It should also be noted that the diagrammatic representation is not meant to imply that all three components contribute equally to self-definition. For some girls, being female seemed superordinate to being poor or Puerto Rican while for others it was not.[2]

Ethnicity

Anachronistic Values and Social Monitoring

Many gang members were born in Puerto Rico or have visited the island frequently to stay with relatives. As with any immigrant group, their feelings for the homeland tend to be mixed. Often the gang members would talk nostalgically of the sunshine and the fruit growing wild on the trees. Such positive recollections were usually tempered with less pleasant memories of poverty: the lack of indoor plumbing, the perpetual diet of rice and beans, the lack of new clothes or shoes. Aside from the material deprivation they associated with the island, gang members often expressed the views that Puerto Rico continued to adhere to anachronistic moral values and that islanders were old-fashioned in comparison with New Yorkers. For example, many of the gang members who returned to the island for vacations were shocked at the great importance local police attached to marijuana possession. The girls saw tough enforcement and stiff penalties as indicative of the old-fashioned attitude of their homeland. In contrast, they viewed the ready availability of "herb" in corner stores in New York City as an indication of a more progressive and liberal attitude toward marijuana on the mainland. The rigid moral values in Puerto Rico prohibited many of the activities that the girls found most attractive in New York—hanging out in the street, dressing fashionably, flirting, drinking, getting "high," and attending parties. When they stayed with relatives on the island, they were required to come home early and to help with household chores. Some girls said their New York clothing caused consternation among their Puerto Rican kin. The girls' parents seemed to share such views, in that a frequent response to the girls' misbehavior was to send them to stay with relatives on the island. Girls who were associating with undesirable boys, who became pregnant, or who were beyond the control of their parents were often shipped back to Puerto Rico where they would be less tempted by the freedom of the mainland.

The girls also noted that these traditional conceptions of appropriate behavior were enforced by claustrophobic social monitoring which was conspicuously absent in their life in New York. The girls viewed the anonymity and mobility of city life as reflections of the progressive values of the United States. Gang members often complained about the confining tightness of social controls on the island. As one girl put it:

> Puerto Ricans are very simple minded and the atmosphere is very, very close—and that's ideal for whoever likes to be close to people. Not me, I personally, like New York. It's very cold and people think twice about speaking to you. I don't like being watched. Over there, close communities everywhere you go. Everybody knows everything. I can't deal with that. This is the only place where you can come here and be yourself to an extreme but you can still be a faggot—that's an extreme. Or

bitch. Dress that way, and I'm not saying it's going to be accepted by everybody, but you can still survive. Feel your identity—whether it be religion or whatever.

The tension between the sense of belonging associated with these extended networks and discomfort with their tight social monitoring has also been noted by Horowitz (1983) in her ethnographic research on Chicanas.

Immigrants

Gang members more than anything else see themselves as American and identify strongly with the special reputation of New York. They are not "hicks" but street-wise people who cannot be tricked, conned, or fooled. They know all the hustles and are not taken in by them. They strongly reject the old superstitions of the island which they see as evidence of its backward status. For example, many villagers in Puerto Rico continued to believe in *esperititas*—that curses can be placed upon individuals and only be removed through consultation with mediums who locate the source of the curse. The curse can then be lifted by the use of candles and herbs purchased from the local botanica. Although botanicas exist in New York City, they are supported by older Puerto Ricans who are unwilling to openly discount the supernatural. However, gang members saw these beliefs as anachronistic and provincial. In seeking revenge over a rival, they were far more likely to fight it out or "drop a dime" (inform on them) to the police.

In stressing their status as Americans and their superiority over other more recently arrived immigrants, gang members took particular pride in the commonwealth relationship between Puerto Rico and the United States. They viewed the fact that they could come and go from the island without visas as evidence that they were not "immigrants." They saw other newcomers to the city such as Haitians, Dominicans, and Cubans as naive, provincial, and backward in their outlook. As one girl observed:

> America doesn't really want foreigners like me coming in, but right now Puerto Rico isn't foreign. Yeah. Dominican. Cuban. All those kinds of people. They came by boat. They can come on a boat from Santo Domingo or Puerto Rico. A lot of them get caught though, but a lot of them get in. And that's what fucks up the country.... Well, now the Blacks and Puerto Ricans don't have anything to worry about—it's the Cubans now. You know I saw a movie and it said if there were no niggers, we'd have to invent them. Do you know what? The Cubans are taking over the oppressed group now.

A source of particular irritation was the inability of some of these newly arrived groups to speak English. This was particularly striking because many of the gang members themselves spoke "Spanglish," switching from one language to another—sometimes in mid-sentence. Nevertheless, their pride in their children's ability to speak and write standard English was evident, and they were often apologetic about their parents' inability to converse in anything but Spanish. For gang members, assimilation into mainstream American life was demonstrated by fluency in English which at the same time indicated the acquisition of "advanced" material values and skills.

Poverty

Drabness

The majority of gang members came from families that received welfare assistance and lived in communities where this was the norm. The families of many gang members were female-headed, and the mother often represented the only constant parent in the girl's life. Many of the girls themselves had their first child during their teenage years, after which they either lived at home, sharing child-rearing duties with their mother, or moved into a local apartment with the child's father. Gang girls with children were in the more secure position of receiving AFDC checks, but they still relied on their wits (or those of their boyfriends) to provide for any unanticipated expenses. Consequently, males who had successful hustles were a prized commodity, and addicted males were considered a liability since any income they might obtain was spend on heroin. The boys would hustle money on a day-to-day basis by stripping abandoned buildings, selling marijuana, or rolling drunks. Girls did not draw distinctions between legal and illegal income—provided the latter did not invite police attention. The frequent crises of poverty were managed by circles of relatives and neighbors who relied on one another to borrow and lend food or money until the arrival of the next check (Lewis 1965; Sheehan 1976). Life on a shoestring budget meant that there were frequent trips to corner stores to buy items of food, often at inflated prices.

After motherhood, the girls rarely considered taking up employment. They saw their duty as first and foremost to their children, and their role as mothers not only provided a measure of dignity but a legitimate reprieve from the alien world of work. Their low level of literacy and lack of high school diploma meant that they would be eligible only for manual work paying minimum wages. Such jobs would not add sufficiently to the quality of their life to justify leaving their children. Besides, the girls were clearly apprehensive about employment, since most of them had never held a job and doing so would mean leaving their immediate neighborhood. Gang members rarely ventured beyond a few blocks radius from their homes, and the principal source of influence from beyond the neighborhood was television. The girls avidly watched soap operas and game shows during the day. Their favorite shows were filled with images of glamour and conspicuous consumption in which women were either kept in limitless luxury by men or worked in high attractive jobs. It is perhaps not surprising that, when queried about the kind of job they would like, gang members frequently cited dancing, singing, and modeling (see McRobbie 1978). The contrast between these aspirations and their actual job opportunities was striking and typified their rejection of any image of themselves as poor or drab. If work entailed menial labor, they would rather remain at home where their role as mothers engendered a measure of respect.

A good deal of their self-presentation involved an image of devil-may-care casualness about the reckless spending of unanticipated income. They spent unexpected money immediately on drugs or alcohol and on trips to movies and steak houses. Many commentators on ghetto life have taken this as evidence of an inability to plan, save, or defer the gratification of immediate pleasure (see Meissner 1966). When viewed as part of the development of self-image by rejection, the spending of money on glamorous leisure experiences represents the denial, albeit temporary, of the conception of themselves as poor.

Slovenliness.

Gang members also place considerable emphasis upon the purchase of the "right" brand names in jeans, sneakers, alcohol, and stereo equipment. They considered it particularly important that their children dressed well, especially at Easter, and they spent large sums of money on clothes that children would outgrow within a few months. They refused secondhand clothes as indicative of the poverty which they made every effort to deny:

> Your kid might come home and say, "Mom, you got to buy me $30 sneakers, $2.99 sneakers ain't doing it for me. I just can't stand criticism any more. You have to buy me $30 sneakers." What do you do? You go out there and you try to get them for your kids—the best way you can, the best way you know how or something.

Their effort to distance themselves from poverty stereotypes was reflected in great concern about cleanness in appearance. Although they sometimes referred to themselves as "outlaws," they never displayed the disregard for personal hygiene and appearance that has been described among biker groups like the Hells Angels (Thompson 1967). Getting ready to "hang out" often took some time because the girls were so meticulous about their clothing and make-up. Jeans were dry cleaned rather than washed, and boots were oiled and sneakers whitened every day. Some gang girls rejected the wearing of "colors" because they felt it made them look cheap and dirty. They wore the full uniform of boots, jackets, and scarves only when they anticipated a run-in with a neighboring girl gang:

> We used to wear hankies over here, hankies over here. Pockets, on necks, pants, hats, all over. I used to think "Oh that's bad. That's nice." But then I realized, "Look at me. I'm a girl. That doesn't look right." Like, "Look at that little tramp or whore"...You know—my jacket, my jacket, my clothes. I never like to wear them. Only when I'm going to fight or rumble, something like that.

Drug Addicts

The poverty-level Puerto Rican neighborhoods in which these gang members lived had high levels of crime and drug addiction. The fact that the girls belong to highly visible gangs meant that they were viewed by the police and the community as being involved in both of these activities. The girls denied this. When they talked about drug abuse, they drew a clear line between recreational use and addiction. Marijuana was both used and sold by gang members and its place in their life was as uncontroversial as that of alcohol. They occasionally used LSD and amphetamines at parties. However, heroin use was strongly condemned. While some girls had experienced with "skin popping," they viewed intravenous injection of the drug as the index of real dependence. The girls took pains to distance themselves from any such involvement. Heroin users were seen as undependable, capricious, and irresponsible, and they were generally not welcome within the gang. They frequently stole from other members, failed to pay back loans, and were unavailable when needed for defense of the neighborhood. In spite of such vocal condemnation of heroin users, a number of the gang members were enrolled in methadone programs and had relapses into heroin use.

The gang placed firm demands for reform upon such members. As one female leader told an addict who wanted to rejoin the gang after leaving temporarily during a bout of heroin use:

> It's harder coming back the second time. I watch you more. You were fucking up a lot before, you were always nodding. Always told to shut up and you didn't listen. If you blend, you blend. If you don't, you don't. You've been to a different place. So just pretend you never left. Don't be talking about it. I don't want to hear nothing you've got to say.

A few days later, the girl stole three pairs of jeans and disappeared, confirming once again the gang's mistrust of an addict's commitment to anyone but herself. Significantly, a term of disparagement frequently leveled against rival gangs was that they were "dope fiends" or "glue sniffers."

Criminals

The girls did not consider many victimless offenses as criminal in spite of the fact that they might be against the law. These included drug selling, inter-gang warfare, organized crime, prostitution, domestic violence, stripping of abandoned buildings and automobiles, shoplifting, and burglary of businesses. Nevertheless, gang members assumed a condemnatory stance toward people they defined as "criminals." To affirm their own exclusion from this category, they employed a number of self-presentation devices. They symbolically distanced themselves from criminals by reserving the term for "crazy" people—e.g., Charles Manson or David Berkowitz.

Criminals also included rapists and child molesters.[3] Nevertheless, gang members were still left with the problem of accounting for their residential burglaries and robberies which by their own definition were wrong. They achieved this through the use of two favored techniques of neutralization: appeal to necessity and denial of responsibility (see Sykes and Matza 1957). In the first case, they often justified property offenses with reference to a temporary financial crisis which left them no other option. In the second, they argued that they were "crazy" from drugs or alcohol while committing the act. However, neither of these justifications was accepted if the crime was committed on the gang's own turf:

> It was this old lady, she had a bunch of money in her pocket and we was on the corner, you know. We seen the money and I told Little Man, "Come on, Little Man, you want to do it? Let's take the money." So this old lady we know for a long time. She was a little bit crazy. I said, "Come on Little Man, let's do it." Then he walked to the corner and we walked to the corner, right? And then we grab her and took the money but it was on the same block. The cops came and everything but we did it wrong because it was on the same block, so then Danny didn't like it. He started to scream at me, but he wasn't my [the girl gang's] leader, he can't do nothing.

Members accounted for their gang's existence by pointing out the jungle-like quality of city life. Similarly to male members of the Lions in Chicago (Horowitz 1983), they noted the high local crime rate and the need for some form of protection for themselves and their children. Frequently, the presence of rival gangs was given as their raison d'être. They reasoned that since the other gang had "hardware" they had no option but to arm themselves also. As they saw it, they represented a vigilante force on behalf not only of themselves but of friends and neighbors too. In this regard, they felt a sense of cooperative rivalry with the police. The gang too was in the business of maintaining security, and the police frequently came to them to seek information on the perpetrators of neighborhood crime. As one member boasted:

> What the community cannot get to, I can get to. Sometimes the cops come in and nobody will tell them a goddamn thing. Nobody is going to tell nothing—even to save their hide, they won't tell them—but I will come along and they will tell me. They will open up to me because they know, having gone through that shit, everybody opens up willing. They let me know what's up and that way I bring up what happened [to the police].

Because of their cooperation—at least in instances where the crime in question was not committed by them and especially where it was perpetrated by another gang or by competing drug sellers—they saw themselves as under-cover assistants. Accordingly, they were outraged when the police arrested one of them. They felt betrayed and pointed out that the local precinct house would be unable to keep order in the neighborhood without their help.

The Guardian Angels represented a major thorn in their side. The media portrayed the Angels as "good" kids, but the gang members believed that this group received disproportionate credit for its crime control efforts. They often accused the Angels of perpetrating as much crime as they prevented:

> The Guardian Angels got media recognition, they got everything now. They say they're this and they are that, that they're protecting the subway. That's bullshit, man. That's bullshit, right. They've already gotten busted for ripping somebody off on the subway, with their shit on, with their berets and their Magnificent Thirteen T-shirts and all their bullshit.

At the same time, gang members resented their own media image as "bad kids" and believed the press was conspiring to deny them appropriate publicity.

Femininity
Bad Mothers

Much has been written about motherhood as an important rite of passage among disadvantaged teenage girls (Rainwater 1960; Stack 1974; Staples 1971; Sullivan 1985). From an early age gang girls assisted in the raising of their younger siblings, although often with considerable ambivalence, and their own sexual experimentation began early. Many gang girls had their first intercourse at or before puberty and consequently, pregnancy by the age of 15 was not uncommon. In New York City, about half of all teen pregnancies result in the birth of a child.[4] Although the girls' parents may initially react with anger, they usually come to accept the situation and provide practical, if not financial, support. Motherhood means that the girl may now legitimately leave school and receive her own welfare check (although in the case of minors it may be paid through her mother). The young couple may marry but more often they do not; in Puerto Rico there is a long tradition of consensual unions (Fitzpatrick 1971). Although the teenage father takes pride in this public demonstration of his manhood, his commitment to the mother and child is often temporary. Consequently, many teenage mothers face a future on public assistance in which men come and go, offering varying degrees of support or exploitation. As Horowitz (1983) points out, the Hispanic girl is likely to be deeply concerned about her identity as a good mother. To avoid any imputation of irresponsibility as a mother, she must make every effort to demonstrate her dedication to the welfare of her child. A good deal of gossip among gang members centered on girls who failed to take adequate care of their children. Motherhood did not require abandonment of the gang, but it did entail making satisfactory arrangements for the child. Girls who brought their children with them to the corner to hang out were considered irresponsible (also see Horowitz 1983, 128). The appropriate course of action was to leave the child with the grandmother for the night. After an all-night party, the girls would conscientiously return home in the early hours to get their children ready for school. Child care revolved very heavily around physical appearance, and the children's clothes were washed and ironed carefully. Especially with daughters, considerable sums were spent on "cute" dresses and on straightening or perming their hair. Keeping their children in school and off the streets preoccupied the gang members, and much shame was attached to having a child in a "special class." Any failure on the child's part that might be traced back to inadequate motherhood was strongly condemned.

Passivity

Even as they extolled the importance of being a good mother, the girls opposed any view of themselves as being at the mercy of men. They took pride in their autonomy and rejected any suggestion that they could be duped or conned by males, especially in the area of having children. For many of the boys, parenthood symbolized the couple's commitment to one another, and the males would often express their desire to father a child as evidence of their warm regard for the girl. After their first or second child, the girls objected, realizing that ultimately they would be left "holding the baby":

> In Puerto Rico those ladies, boy, they have to suffer a lot. Those men, they play you dirty. All having a bunch of kids. All dirty and shit. And you see a man like that, why you going to keep having kids? For the same fucking man? Having four, six, seven kids like women do in Puerto Rico? I say "Uh-uh, that's not for me." I do me an abortion. And like I tell you, I do four abortions already.

Abortion was a problematic issue for most of the girls. Wholehearted support might be construed as callous disregard for human life and place them in jeopardy of being seen as "bad mothers." On the other hand, too many children could lead to a male-dependent lifestyle and suggest that they were vulnerable to being "conned" by men. Consequently, abortion was accepted as legitimate after the first or second child but was generally condemned in a first pregnancy. Adding fuel to their justification for abortion was the strongly condemnatory stance taken toward it in Puerto Rico; having an abortion was also an acceptance of being a modern American woman.

Whores

Because of the local public perception of the "loose" sexual morality of female gang members, the girls were faced with particular problems of self-presentation in this sphere. The cultural context of Hispanic life places considerable emphasis upon the purity of young women before marriage, although sex in the context of an exclusive love relationship is acceptable (Acosta-Belen and Christenson 1979; Pescatello 1973). In the gang, serial monogamy was the norm and sexual promiscuity was frowned upon. One of the most frequent disparagements of rival gang members was that they were "nothing but a bunch of ho's" (whores).[5] This epithet was one about which the girls were very sensitive:

> People say I'm a whore? They got to prove that. They can't say, "You're a whore" just like that. They got to prove a lot of things. They ain't got no proof, so what's up? Right. So I say I don't live with the people no more. I live by myself. What the people say, I don't care. You know. Let it go.

Although it was in no way a requirement of membership, attachment to the gang often resulted in the girl becoming sexually involved with one of the male members. Once an exclusive romantic relationship had been established, the male would feel free to exert control over her public behavior and demeanor. At parties, for example, girls would sometimes get "high" and flirt mildly with other boys. This behavior usually provoked severe disapproval from their partners. During the summer, the boys would not allow their girlfriends to wear shorts or low cut T-shirts on the street. The girls chafed against these kinds of restrictions since they believed that flirting and fashion did not betoken promiscuity; however, they did accept the general premise that sexually suggestive behavior was inappropriate. Controls which males exerted in their role as boyfriends would certainly have been rejected by the girls had the males tried to impose them as a gang on the female affiliate.

The girls also exerted a good deal of social control over one another's sexual behavior. New girls in the group who, unaware of the prevailing norms, slept around with a variety of men were called to account for their behavior at meetings and instructed that serial monogamy was required. While this was in part motivated by the girls' own self-interest in protecting their exclusive relationship with their boyfriends, members also referred to the danger of losing male respect by this kind of unselective sexuality:

> We think that she's a whore? She's a tramp? We just call her and we tell her, "You got to get down with that one. But don't let everyone go to you. You're going to play with that one? Play with one, but the other ones, they're like friends." They [the boys] used to talk about her. We used to tell her, "Look, they talk about you—this and that. You think you're doing it right, but you doing it wrong. Because they're talking about you like a dog." She cool out in the end.

Marianismo

In their effort to avoid the stigma of cheapness through serial monogamy, the girls ran the risk of becoming overdependent on men. The term *marianismo* describes the qualities of femininity which are reciprocal of those of machismo in men. It refers to the cult of the Virgin Mary. A good woman accepts the dominance of men, values her own compliance and nurturance, and consistently places the needs of her family, especially her husband, above her own (Pescatello 1973). Gang girls, socialized in the United States, strongly rejected this subordinate view of female life. Most girls had seen their mother tolerate, for various periods of time, the blatant abuse and infidelity of their fathers. They frequently expressed disgust that their mothers had remained in the situation:

> Yeah—Puerto Rican women they hurt a lot. Some women they hurt a lot. They suffer a lot because of the man. Or because of their kids. I don't know. Like my mother—I say "Mommy, why don't you leave Poppy?" "Ah, because I love him at the time and I don't want you to have a stepfather." I used to tell her, "Oh man, sometimes you're stupid."

The right of the Puerto Rican male to exercise physical control in his own house has been noted frequently, and the girls' history of physical abuse from their fathers and step-fathers made them unwilling to tolerate similar beatings from their own partners. After violent domestic confrontations, when they saw their boyfriend repeating the same cycle of abuse that their mothers had accepted, they often made exaggerated efforts to assert their own independence:

> I said, "Don't think because I have kids I'm going to put up. I'm not." Like some women will put up, I won't. I'll leave him. I don't have to put up with him. I'll find somebody else that will give me more. I try not to aggravate him so what I do is I worry him a lot. I'll leave him even if it takes killing myself to do it. If I have to escape and that's the only way because he's watching, because he doesn't want me to get away, I'll do it. I'll kill myself.

Infidelity on the part of the male represented an ever present threat to the stability of their social arrangements. Puerto Rican culture emphasizes male autonomy in many spheres including that of extra-marital affairs (Acosta-Belen and Christenson 1979; Pescatello 1973). Although the males' traditional role as breadwinners and the exclusive rights it gave them have eroded, the double standard of sexual morality continues to exist in many New York communities. Puerto Rican women regard men with both fear and condescension as violent, sexual, free, and childish. Men's immaturity and irresponsibility are part of their nature for which they cannot be held fully accountable. Non-gang girls in the neighborhood were often attracted by the boys' outlaw image. The boys felt that to refuse an offer of sex was tantamount to admitting homosexuality and argued that if a girl "put it in his face" they had no choice but to go along. The girls accepted this rogue male image and so had to exert their own control over rival girls. They did this vigorously as if to underline their unwillingness to repeat the *marianismo* of their mother:

> We'll still find out. We'll always find out. They'll swear on their mother, their father, their sister, their brother, "I didn't do it. I didn't do it with that bitch. I wouldn't make good with that bitch." They try to soup. But I already know the deal with them, "Alright, yeah, yeah, yeah." And that's when I go. Then I go up to the girl. And they don't even bother hitting us 'cos they know they're gonna get worse. I would just go up, "Hey, I hear you made it with my old man. This and that. And blat, that's it. The whole thing is over 'cos they don't even raise their hand. They put their head down and they cut out fast.

In this way many romantic disputes involving couples were actually resolved between the young women. The necessity of being attached to a male in order to have sexual relations, combined with a reluctance to challenge the boy directly over his infidelity, had a very divisive effect upon the girls' relationships with one another. As Horowitz (1983) also notes, disputes over men constituted a major source of aggression among the girls.

However, gang girls do take pride in their ability to fight. In rejecting passivity, they stress their aggressiveness and work hard at developing a reputation as a fighter:

> Girls around her, they see a girl that's quiet, they think that she's a little dud. Yeah—let's put it that way. They think they don't know how to fight.... Round here you have to know how to fight. I'm glad I got a reputation. That way nobody will start with me—they *know*, you know. They're going to come out losing. Like all of us, we got a reputation. We're crazy. Nobody wants to fight us for that reason—you know. They say "No, man. That girl might stab me or cut my face or something like that."

Among the Chicana girls studied by Horowitz (1983), aggression was only acceptable when it was directed against other females. Even here, it was seen by the community as an untypical behavior flying in the face of the self-control that was expected of young women. However, Quicker's (1983) description of Chicana gang members in Los Angeles reveals strong similarities with the girls in Puerto Rican gangs. Although aggression was most often directed at females, either "squares" or members of rival gangs, the girls I studied took particular pride in recounting episodes in which they had fought with male gang members from neighboring groups. Hispanic gang boys express considerable ambivalence about the girls' aggression. On one hand they are proud of the girls' "heart," while at the same time they will often intervene in a female fight to prevent injury to the girls (also see Horowitz 1983). Whatever the boys' attitude, the Puerto Rican girls clearly took pride in their willingness to fight and saw it as an indication of their commitment to the gang, to their relationships, and to their self-respect.

More than winning a fight, it was important to be ready to enter one. Before a fight they prepared by tightly securing their hair with oil (so that opponents could not grab it) and donning boots and jeans. Rival gang members were disparaged as hanging out with their men only when times were good and failing to support them during gang wars:

> Tramps. All they think about is screwing. It's true. It's true, shit. They don't fight. They don't go to rumbles with their guys. Nothing. They're punks. They're a bunch of punks. Cuiso, right? The Cheeseburgers are a bunch of punks? They're not tough. They're a bunch of dope fiends.

The importance of not "ranking out" or backing down from a fight was frequently stressed. It was seen as indicative of moral weakness. Fighting was sufficiently highly valued that the initiation of new "prospects" required them to demonstrate their fearlessness in the face of physical attack.

> Well, when we started it was like initiating people—when you take them to the park, like, to see. Like there's some girls that join, like "I get in trouble, I got backup." Now for us this wasn't that. We used to take a new girl to the park. Now that girl had to pick one of our girls, and whoever she wanted, she had to fight that girl to see if she could take the punches. Now if she couldn't, she wouldn't fight. Then we wouldn't take her. Because then we know that someday— you know, somewhere in the streets—she's going to wind up getting hurt. So we knew that she could fight her battles and we used to let her join. She had to fight first. Without crying.

Discussion and Conclusions

Previous work on female gang members has placed considerable emphasis upon their sexuality either as an area for reform through social work, as a symptom of their rejection of middle-class values, or as the single most important impression management problem which they face. While any examination of self-concept clearly must include attention to the management of appropriate male or female identity, I believe it is a disservice to girls in gangs not to recognize other salient features of their self-definition. These young women are stigmatized by ethnicity and poverty as well as gender.

By virtue of their marginal position, both economically and socially, they live their lives within a bounded geographical area where the major sources of influence and support are likely to be families, friends, and neighbors. Without the opportunity to fulfill themselves in mainstream jobs beyond the ghetto, their sense of self must be won from others in the immediate environment. Within this context, gang girls see themselves as different from their peers. Their association with the gang is a public proclamation of their rejection of the lifestyle which the community expects from them. Sociological portraits that deny the girls' sense of differentness from other neighborhood youth deny the validity of the way the girls see themselves.

The sense of differentness experienced by the girls is fragmented and diffuse—as indeed it must be since they do not fully embrace an oppositional deviant identity. They do not buy into a countercultural role that is well-articulated and wholly coherent. Rather they reject bits and pieces of the conventional lifestyle that is expected of them in the local community. Inevitably, the girl finds herself in a contradictory and vulnerable position as she attempts to retain her integrity within her shifting self-definition. She is Puerto Rican but neither provincial nor un-American. She may be poor but her life is neither drab nor criminal. She enjoys her femininity but rejects passivity and suffering.

My evidence suggests that much can be learned from examining how we vilify the traits and actions of others. Much of our social life is spent in talk, and a significant portion of it is concerned not with our own behavior but with that of others. The terms of condemnation in gossip reveal a good deal about our own preoccupations and values. When we criticize others' behavior we assure the listener and ourselves that we are exempt from similar accusations—we set ourselves apart from the object of our decision. Sometimes we level our criticism at figures beyond our acquaintance such as media personalities or politicians; but the most salient reference points for our self-definition are those individuals or groups whose social niche we share. This is particularly true for disadvantaged groups who are caught in a restricted social environment with little hope of mobility.

Important questions remain to be answered about the present approach as about other sociological analyses of accounts. The chronology of gang membership and self-definition by rejection remains uncertain. Do gangs act as clearinghouses for those who have already felt their distance from "straight" lifestyles, or does gang membership encourage and articulate this kind of self-definition? What changes occur in the evaluation of previously rejected qualities when the girl falls from the gang? Answers to these questions will only be found if researchers continue to take disparaging social talk as a legitimate focus of inquiry. Closer examination of the vilification of others may indicate that gossip is a strategic resource for the development of a sense of selfhood.

From Patriarchy to Gender:
Feminist Theory, Criminology, and the Challenge of Diversity

*James Messerschmidt**

In a recent attempt to develop a framework for explaining gendered crime, Darrell Steffensmeier and Emilie Allan (1991, 73) argue that men and women differ significantly in their "moral development," and that "women's moral choices" constrain them from behavior that could be harmful to others. Because women are "bound more intimately into a network of interpersonal ties, their moral decisions are more influenced by empathy and compassion" and this "ethic of care" constructs nonviolence and "suggests that serious predatory crime is outside women's moral boundaries."

Steffensmeier and Allan (1991) ignore the fact that there exists no "scholarship that demonstrates that the greater conformity of women is a function of their special virtues" (Naffine 1987, 133). But beyond this, are females always empathetic and compassionate? In such an analysis, we are hard put to explain the following by a member of the Turban Queens, a "girl" gang in New York City (Campbell 1984/1991, 262):

> But once you're in a fight, you just think—you've got to fuck that girl up before she does it to you. You've got to really blow off on her. You just play it crazy. That's when they get scared of you. It's true—you feel proud when you see a girl you fucked up. Her face is all scratched or she got a black eye, you say, "Damn, I beat the shit out of that girl, you know."

Such violence becomes incomprehensible in an analysis that concentrates exclusively on sex differences. Departures from what is considered "appropriate female crime" are either ignored—indeed, there is a dearth of theorizing about female violence in criminological theory—or are deviantized as inappropriate at best, "masculine" at worst. For example, in the 1970s, Freda Adler (1975b, 15) argued that because of the women's movement, women were becoming more masculine, resulting in an increasing number of women using "weapons and wits to establish themselves as full human beings, as capable of violence and aggression as any man." For Adler (1977, 101), because of "liberation" the "'second sex' had risen" by the mid 1970s and, therefore, women became increasingly aggressive, violent, and masculine. Such a view defines, for example, the member of the Turban Queens quoted here as simply defective and freakish, not authentically female. Moreover, because criminology does not possess the theoretical language capable of representing violence by women, criminologists like Adler simplistically perceive women's violence from the perspective of violent acts by men. As Margaret Shaw (1995, 122) argues, the criminological image of violence by women "is based on that of male violence—macho, tough, aggressive; we have no ways of conceptualizing violence by women except in terms of its 'unnaturalness.'" Thus, criminology lacks theory that does not belittle women and punish them intellectually for stepping beyond the bounds of emphasized femininity; we require theory sensitive to how women/girls as women/girls occasionally commit violence.

A major result then of an exclusive concentration on male-female difference has been to either masculinize women/girls or direct theory away from issues that seriously complicate difference, such as race, age, and female engagement in "male crime." Feminists of color have, of course, berated much of social theory for assuming that all female experiences are similar. Scholars such as bell hooks (1984) have criticized the race bias that occurs when specific experiences of privileged white women are universalized as the experiences of all women. In the same way, criminological theory must not universalize female crime. Although second-wave feminism has disrupted assumptions about men and women and offered new ways to speak of "female crime," when girls and women engage in "male crime" it is as theoretically significant as when they engage in "female crime." Accordingly, such approaches as that suggested by Steffensmeier and Allan obscure a full and complete situational understanding of gender and crime: Where gender differences in crime are the exclusive focus, similarities in crime are often ignored or misrepresented. Abstracting gender from its social context and insensitive to issues of agency, such perspectives mask the possibility that gender patterns of crime may vary situationally, and that occasionally females and males engage in similar types and amounts of crime. As Karlene Faith (1993, 57) recently declared, to concentrate solely on crimes consistent with emphasized femininity "is to deny women's diversity and to promote gender-based objectification and stereotyping."

To comprehend the relation between masculinities and crime we must concurrently grasp when behavior normally thought to be masculine (i.e., interpersonal violence) is *not* a resource for constructing masculinity. As such, through an examination of "girls in the gang," I argue in Chapter 3 (Messerschmidt, 1997) that the gang provides a milieu within which girls can experiment with, and possibly dismantle, the bounds of emphasized femininity. As they do this, however, are gang girls "doing masculinity?" I argue they are not. Partaking in the specific social situation of the gang, girls use the resources available to construct not masculinity but a specific type of femininity and, notwithstanding, challenge notions of gender as merely difference. Conceptualizing gender in terms of social situation and structured action permits a deeper formulation of not only what has been visible but what previously has been hidden or considered atypical "masculine" behavior, such as female violence. It also provides us with a more discerning portrait of masculinities, femininities, and crime.

Girls in the Gang

For both boys and girls, joining a youth gang represents an idealized collective solution to the lived experience of class and race powerlessness. For girls in particular, Karen Joe and Meda Chesney-Lind (1993, 10) point out that

> they exist in an environment that has little to offer young women of color. The possibility of a decent career, outside of "domestic servant," is practically nonexistent. Many come from distressed families held together by their mothers who are subsisting on welfare. Most have dropped out of school and have no marketable skills. Future aspirations are both gendered and unrealistic with the girls often expressing the desire to be rock stars or professional models when they are older.

In addition, alarmingly high rates of physical and sexual abuse have been reported for delinquent girls, ranging from a low of 40% to a high of 73% (Chesney-Lind and Shelden 1992, 90; see also Campbell 1993; Moore 1991). In the social context of a bleak future and the overall violence that surrounds them in the street as well as at home, the youth gang becomes *family* to these girls. One Chicana ex-gang member (Moore 1991, 77) reflects on how, for her, the gang

> was very important. Because that's all I had to look forward to, was my neighborhood, you know. That's all. It was my people—my neighborhood, my homies, my homeboys, my homegirls—that was everything to me. That was everything, you know. It wasn't all about my *familia;* it was all about my homeboys and homegirls.

Similarly, Harris (1988, 101) reported in her study of Latino gang girls that they exhibited a strong need for safety, belongingness, and companionship. One gang girl stated the importance of the gang in the following way: "It was family. We protected each other. We took care of each other. We stole for each other" (119). And in a recent exploration into why girls join gangs in Hawaii, Joe and Chesney-Lind (1993, 20) argue that the gang "offers 'friendship' and a social support system for coping and managing their everyday life problems." One Samoan girl expressed it this way: "We all like sistas, all taking care of each other" (21).

In short, the gang is where many lower working-class girls and boys of color develop strong "family" ties with members of their neighborhood—persons with whom they are not only acquainted but whom they perceive to be "like themselves." In the gang, a collective identity takes shape—they find companionship, safety, and a sense of belongingness (Fishman 1988; Lauderback, Hansen, and Waldorf 1992).

Street Culture and Gender Difference

Nevertheless, coming together on the street, girl-and-boy gang members interact to construct gender-separate groups; this appears to occur regardless of class and race position. Indeed, from the early works of Asbury (1927) and Thrasher (1927), to the more recent research of Quicker (1983), Schwendinger and Schwendinger (1985), Harris (1988), Fishman (1988), Hagedorn (1988), Vigil (1988), and Moore (1991), young females have been found to construct "auxiliary" gangs to the male gangs. Notably, these auxiliary gangs are not simply composed of separate, identifiable groups but, rather, reflect gendered boundaries based on power. For example, Campbell's (1984/1991) important ethnographic study of lower working-class gangs in New York City reported that both females and males assume positions within the group that might be available to them in society at large. As Campbell (266) points out, the "true gang" is composed of young males, and specific female groups "exist as an annex to the male gang, [in which] the range of possibilities open to them is dictated and controlled by the boys." Similarly, Harris (1988, 128) reports that "while the girls purport to be independent of their male counterparts, belief in male superiority and the corresponding deference to male gang members became clear."

Other relevant research reports analogous gendered power relations in youth gangs and the construction of "girl gangs" as secondary to "male gangs" (Fishman 1988; Moore 1991). Thus, although girl gangs have limited autonomy over their own rules and type of organization, they usually are connected yet subordinate to male gangs (Campbell 1993, 132). Youth gangs, then, reflect the gender relations of power in society and the related discourse and practices by which they are reproduced. Consequently, gender difference here is in part related to the social construction of gendered dominance and subordination in gang arrangements.[1]

The realm of sexuality is also an important arena in gang life. Normative heterosexuality is a decisive "measuring rod" for group participation and a means by which gang members construct gendered difference. In the context of the gang, some sexual exploitation seems undeniable. For example, Schwendinger and Schwendinger (1985, 167) found that sexist exploitation of girls is common to both middle- and working-class youth groups. Similarly, a "homeboy" in Moore's (1991, 54) study stated: "I would say 90% was treated like a piece of ass. Usually we just used them as sexual need things, and companions. We needed companions in sex." Another male gang member from the same study echoed this position (55):

Ah, it's just there, you know what I mean. The—you know, when you want a *chapete* (fuck) it was there, you know what I mean. The guys treat them like shit, you know what I mean. And then when they want something you know, get it—wham bam. Sex. Just to have a partner for the time, you know. They were just there, you know, we used to get them in, throw a *linea* (lining up to have sex with a girl), you know what I mean.

Thus relationships of power and sexuality merge within the context of exploitation. Girl gang members are constructed as sexual objects, which concomitantly accentuates difference by emphasizing their "femaleness," and ultimately is an exercise of power over some girls' existence in the gang. Indeed, a female auxiliary gang that is defined primarily through its sexuality becomes a source of prestige and power among males in the gang.

Nevertheless, diversity exists in the way gangs construct heterosexual meanings. For example, Anne Campbell (1990, 179) found in New York girl gangs that "serial monogamy" was the norm and once a girl became involved with a boy she usually remained "faithful" until the relationship ended. These girls, then, construct a femininity that complies with emphasized femininity. Other research, however, indicates that doing difference through sexuality requires neither monogamy nor exploitation and, consequently, girls in gangs construct different types of femininity. For example, many girls effectively avert boys' claim to their bodies and actively negotiate the gang as a site for securing sexual pleasure (Carrington 1993). As one gang girl stated to Joan Moore (1991, 55): "Not *me*, they didn't treat *me* like that. They think we're possessions, but we're not. No way. I pick my own boyfriends. I'll be with anybody I want to be with. You don't tell me who to be with." This girl has constructed an "opposition femininity" through sexuality; she has challenged culturally emphasized patterns. Alternatively, the Vice Queens "unabashedly placed themselves at the boys' disposal and openly encouraged them to fondle and have sexual relations with them" (Fishman 1988, 17). Granting sexual favors to the Vice Kings was a means of gaining status among female peers in the gang, and thus is seen as a reinterpretation of emphasized femininity resulting in the construction of a unique type. Indeed, this type of femininity has its oppositional qualities as well; although the boys thought the girls were simply sexual objects of exploitation, status among the girls partially depended on "being able to keep four or five boys 'on the string' without any boys knowing of the others, but at the same time, avoiding sexual relationships with too many boys at one time" (21).

For both boys and girls, then, the street gang is ideal for "doing gender" in terms of difference. By maintaining and emphasizing the "femaleness" of girl gang members, for example, through specific heterosexual meanings and practices, gender difference is preserved and specific types of masculinities and femininities are both validated and strengthened. Consequently, girl gang members are not simply passive recipients of "patriarchy," but actively participate in the construction of gender relations and they orchestrate the various forms of heterosexuality that result in varieties of femininity. Indeed, these girls do difference differently.

The gang, then, can be a site for sexual restriction and exploitation as well as for sexual exploration and pleasure and, thus, we find variety in terms of accommodation, reinterpretation, and opposition to emphasized femininity. Nevertheless, for the vast majority of girls, their significance in the gang is acquired through affiliation with boys. That is, gang girls accomplish gender in relation to the specific masculinities of the boys. This is so even for girls who develop the type of opposition femininity identified earlier.

Moreover, the street culture provides opposition to what gang girls see as the anachronistic and rigid values of their parents. For example, Campbell (this volume, p. 106) describes Puerto Rican gang girls in New York who reject the "hicks" back on the island (Puerto Rico) and in contrast construct themselves as

> streetwise people who cannot be tricked, conned, or fooled. They know all the hustles and are not taken in by them. They strongly reject the old values and beliefs of the island, which they see as evidence of its backward status.... Gang members saw these beliefs and values as anachronistic and provincial.

Practices such as "coming home early" and "helping out with household chores" are seen as "old-fashioned" in comparison to "hanging out on the street, dressing fashionably, flirting, getting 'high,' and attending parties" (Campbell 1987, 454). Distancing themselves from, and therefore opposing, the provinciality of their race and class, gang girls are practicing a particularized race and class femininity. As agents in a unique historical, social, and situational setting, these girls negotiate a specific gender, race, and class identity and, in so doing, become something distinct from "Other."

Furthermore, members of youth gangs engage in "male" and "female" crimes as a resource for doing gender and satisfying the needs of the "fast life" on the street. For example, elsewhere (Messerschmidt 1993, 108) I describe how, for male gang members, robbery is the most available criminal resource for obtaining money and constructing a specific type of masculinity: "Within the social setting of the street group, robbery is an acceptable practice for accomplishing gender"—and, therefore, doing difference. For girls, however, prostitution seems to be the principal criminal resource for obtaining "fast money" as well as doing difference.[2] A study of youth growing up poor in six different cities across the United States reported that in all of the cities "prostitution is the main occupation for girls" (Williams and Kornblum 1985, 61). Moreover, Fishman (1988, 16) notes that all members of the Vice Queens participated in prostitution as their chief source of income:

> Customers were procured in taverns and on the street or at other locations not connected with organized houses of prostitution. The girls were aware of the prostituting activities of their peers and prostitution was accepted as standard behavior for the group.

Clearly, then, gender is a situated accomplishment in which individuals produce forms of behavior seen by others in the same immediate situation as either masculine or feminine. Within the confines and social settings of the street, economically marginal boys and girls form youth gangs partly to obtain "fast money" for adequate participation in street life. In similar fashion as "Detroit Red" discussed in Chapter 2 [of *Crime as Structured Action*], these youth participate in a street culture where work for "the man" is not the primary signifier of identity; rather, "fast money" is emphasized to pursue "the fast life." As Paul Gilroy (1990, 274) points out, the "hood" becomes the arena for celebrating the body as "an instrument of pleasure rather than an instrument of labor." The street is assertively and provocatively occupied by the pursuit of leisure and pleasure (p. 274). Here gender, race, and class are all salient; girl gang members situationally construct practices that counter their gender, race, and class subordinate position and such social action is the mechanism through which a specific race, class, and feminine identity take on meaning. "Hustling Johns" becomes a means of avoiding wage work and actively participating as a properly raced, classed, and gendered actor of street life. For example, girl gang members spend their "fast money" on food and shelter as well as the appropriate symbols of leisure/pleasure: drugs, alcohol, "trips to movies and steakhouses," and the "right" brand name of clothing and shoes (Campbell this volume, p. 108). Indeed, as Campbell (pp. 457-458) found in her research, girls' efforts to distance themselves from the "drabness" of their structured race and class position were also

> reflected in great concern about cleanliness in appearance. Although they sometimes referred to themselves as "out-laws," they never displayed the disregard for personal hygiene and appearance that has been described among biker groups like the Hells Angels. Getting ready to "hang out" often took some time because the girls were so meticulous about their clothing and make-up. Jeans were dry cleaned rather than washed, and boots were oiled and sneakers whitened every day.

Thus, their criminality incorporated dimensions and meanings of the street culture and, in turn, allowed them to display the appropriate "style" of that oppositional gender, race, and class culture.

Moreover, although the examples of robbery and prostitution show how some members of youth gangs produce "fast money" as well as race and class specific masculinities/femininities, it is through prostitution that these gang girls construct a femininity that both confirms and disaffirms emphasized femininity—yet simultaneously does difference. Prostitution confirms emphasized femininity in the sense that these girls construct themselves as sexually seductive to men and receptive to the sexual "drives" and special "needs" of men. In addition to these conventional aspects of femininity, however, involvement in prostitution also ridicules emphasized femininity by advocating extramarital sex, sex for pleasure, anonymous sex, and sex not limited to reproduction and the domesticated couple. This construction of a specific type of femininity, then, challenges and reinterprets emphasized femininity. The result is a gendered gang in which boys and girls do masculinity and femininity in a distinct race and class way—crime often used as a resource for facilitating the accomplishment of gender, race, and class difference.

Uniting for the "Hood"

In the daily life of the youth gang, girls not only participate in the social construction of difference but also engage in practices common to boys. Although there is a whole variety of common practices, most time is spent in such nondelinquent leisure activities as simply "hanging out" at a favorite spot or attending sporting and social events. In addition, boy and girl gang members partake in such delinquent activities as drinking, taking and selling drugs, committing theft, and fighting (Chesney-Lind and Shelden 1992, 45; Lauderback et al. 1992).

The last activity, fighting, usually considered atypical gendered behavior by females, affords considerable insight into the diversity of gender construction. In fact, one recent feminist text identifies female violence as so rare that it is labeled as an "anomaly" and not in need of much further investigation (Faith 1993, 100). From the point of view of privileged white women, female violence may indeed be infrequent and unusual, but for lower working-class girls of color in the United States, violence is far from an anomaly. Young lower working-class girls of color, in particular, African American girls, commit interpersonal crimes of violence at a much higher rate than do other girls. In a recent review of the literature, Sally Simpson (1991, 117-18) reported that African American girls have higher rates of homicide and aggravated assault than white girls, and that girls of color participate in Uniform Crime Reports violent offenses 5.5 times as often as white girls (see also Sommers and Baskin 1992). Moreover, violent crime rates are highest in lower-working-class communities—urban communities that are disproportionately racial minority in composition (Simpson 1991, 119).

It is well established that the leading cause of death among African American male teenagers is homicide. Less well-known is the fact that homicide is the leading cause of death for African American women between the ages of 15 and 24 (U.S. Department of Health and Human Services 1993, 76-77). In addition, males are not always more likely than females to die by homicide. At every age until the late 40s, an African American female faces a higher risk of death by homicide than a white male (76-77).[3] Although the perpetrators of this homicide are overwhelmingly men,[4] a recent study (Mann 1993, 219) of "sister against sister" homicide in six U.S. cities (with homicide rates equal to or higher than the national rate) found that

> women who kill other women basically resemble the portrait depicted over the past two decades by previous researchers: They are young, black, undereducated, and unemployed. Thus, they reflect the current American portrait of an expanding group of women of color who are marginal to the larger society.

This intragender violence by lower-working-class girls of color generally occurs within the context of the youth gang. Youth gangs confer a dubious prestige on *both* boys and girls with a proven ability to fight—boys and girls to whom street fighting is an essential source of meaning, reputation, and status. The development of this reputation begins during the initiation ceremony, for the gang will not accept just anyone. A female gang member (cited in Campbell 1993, 136) describes one such initiation:

> We used to take a new girl to the park. Now that girl had to pick one of our girls. And whoever she wanted, she had to fight that girl to see that she could take the punches without crying.... Like if I'm walking down the street with you, you have to be able to count that I'm going to throw my life for you. Just like I expect you to do it for me. I have to be able to say, "I'm going to stay here and fight because I know you're going to stay here and fight too."

In East Los Angeles, girls become gang members by being "jumped in." One gang member explained the process to Quicker (1983, 15-16):

> Q: What happens when you get jumped in? What do they do?
>
> R: When you get jumped in, what they do is they get around you and then there'll be a girl counting. Like there will be a girl out there and she'll go okay and then they'll start jumping you. She'll count to 10 and when she finishes counting, they'll stop.

Demonstration of toughness not only gains entrance to the gang but also proclaims oneself a "bad girl." Indeed, in girl gangs "the ability and willingness to fight, facing the enemy, not running from confrontation, to be 'bad,' to be 'crazy,' to be tough... are all prized behaviors" (Harris 1988, 106). "Bad-girl" femininity serves to rank girls in terms of capacity to display physical violence and power; girls who do not "measure up" are ignored and "jumped out" of the gang. Indeed, "bad girls" take pride in their fighting ability and their consequent acquired reputation and status. These girls accomplish gender by specific relational means that violently oppose other girls. Such social practice gains currency in relation to girls who fail to "qualify" and, predictably, constructs power relations among girls, as the following comment (Campbell this volume, p. 115) indicates:

> Girls around here see a girl that's quiet, they think that she's a dud. Yeah—let's put it that way. They think they don't know how to fight.... Round here you have to know how to fight. I'm glad I got a reputation. That way nobody will start with me—they know, you know. They're going to come out losing. Like all of us, we got a reputation. We're crazy. Nobody wants to fight us for that reason—you know. They say "No, man. That girl might stab me or cut my face or something like that."

Differences among girls hinge on how they construct femininity. Thus, "bad-girl" femininity is sustained through its relation to situationally defined "dud" femininity, even within similar race and class categories. Gang girls are distinguished from non-gang girls through different constructions of femininity. Lower-working-class African American girls share the experience of race and class oppression but the notions of "bad girl" and "dud" inflects their commonality with difference. This represents what Friedman (1995, 30) identifies as a partial and situational displacement of the White/Other binary: "The category of Other explodes into its heterogeneous parts while the category of whiteness remains fixed and monolithic." Thus, as agents living out their race and class subordinate position, girls construct power/powerlessness in relation to each other.

Similarly, in gangs that emphasize heterosexual monogamy for girls but not for boys (because it is considered "unnatural" for boys to refuse offers of sex), girl violators are controlled fiercely, as the following example (Campbell 1984/1991, 258) shows:

> "Hey, I hear you made it with my old man." This and that. And blat, and that's it. The whole thing is over 'cus they don't even raise their hands. They put their head down and they cut out fast. 'Cus they know—like if I was hitting a girl and they hit me back and all *these* girls see it, they're all gonna get in, you know? And she's going to get a worse beating. So she takes a slap or two and goes home and cries.

In this situation, not only is a specific type of heterosexuality reproduced, but power relations between girls and femininities are constructed—monogamy is privileged and enhanced through violent attack (and group support for that attack) on situationally constituted promiscuity.

Probably the most positively sanctioned site for displaying one's "badness" is participating in *group* violence. Bonding with peers of common residence, marginalized youths tend to develop a collective race and class loyalty to their neighborhood and to form territorial control over their turf or "hood" (Messerschmidt 1993). The street is inculcated with a powerful sense of locality and a street gang's specific territory, carefully branded and defended at levels of conspicuous absurdity, defines the gang and its perimeters of activity. The focus here is to defend and extend gang space for independence from "the system" and, thus, create a place for self-rule. In fact, turf serves as a boundary between groups and as an arena of status and potential conflict. The "territoriality of identity" becomes simultaneously the "territoriality of control" (Gilroy 1990, 278) and, therefore, street gangs are intolerant of invasions of their space by outsiders. When outsiders do invade their local "hood," this is viewed as inherently offensive. One gang member explains how easily a fight erupts when entering another girl-gang's turf (Harris 1988, 104):

> Like if you go somewhere. Let's suppose we go to San Fernando. And like we don't get along with San Fernando. And like we go to the park and a bunch of girls from

> SanFer are over there, and us Blythe Street Girls. And they're going to give us hard
> looks, and we're going to give them hard looks, and that's where it's going to start.
> And they'll say, "Where are you from?"
>> "Blythe Street. Where are you from?"
>> "Well, fuck you." And then we go. Just for the street. Uno Blythe. Blythe Street's
> number one. That's all it is.

As the quoted scenario indicates, it is not the territory per se that is significant, but the local group's identification with that particular territory. Indeed, support for the group (as representative of the neighborhood) is held in highest esteem and fighting exhibits loyalty to the "hood" and, therefore, to the gang (Fishman 1988, 14). If a gang girl cannot or will not fight, she is summarily rejected. As one gang girl explained to Harris (1988, 109):

> You can belong as long as you can back up your shit and don't rat on your home-
> girls or back away. If you don't back them up and you run, we'll jump that girl out
> because she ain't going to take care of nothing. All she wants is our backup and our
> support but she ain't going to give us none of hers, so what's the use of her being
> around! She has to be able to hold up the hood.

Clearly, one shores up the hood through violence. As Harris (1988, 174) goes on, girls in gangs "will fight instead of flee, assault instead of articulate, and kill rather than control their aggression." Indeed, for "girls in the gang," status is not achieved from excellence in school or at work but, rather, through "the perfection of fighting techniques" and "the number of times the girls willingly fought and with whom they fought" (Fishman 1988, 23). Thus, in relation to middle-class white people, gang girls are lower-working-class girls of color, but in relation to each other they are set apart according to constituency in a particular "hood."

In the world of the street, different gangs are allocated different "hoods" and those who venture out of their socially defined neighborhood are chastised and punished. In this social situation, boys and girls unite on the basis of neighborhood. Because gender is not static but dynamic, in a race and class specific social context where "hood" is elevated to preeminence (that is, neighborhood differences become highly salient) the path for similarity in behavior is much less obstructed. In the context of the street fight, interaction involves at once *caring* (for the "hood" and other gang members) and also *physically* aggressive practices (against another gang) by *both* boys and girls. Moreover, the criteria of femininity are embedded in specific social situations and recurrent practices within them. In the particular context of the youth gang, the criteria of "bad-girl" femininity involve physical strength and power as resources for publicly demonstrating individual proficiency at defending the "hood" by conquering adversary gang girls. Indeed, girls (as representatives of a rival "hood") are the subject of competition in the struggle to secure a situationally specific feminine identity. In other words, what is usually considered atypical feminine behavior outside this situation is, in fact, *normalized* within the social context of interneighborhood conflict; girl-gang violence in this situation is encouraged, permitted, and privileged by *both* boys and girls as appropriate feminine behavior. Thus, "bad-girl" femininity is situationally accomplished and context-bound within the domain of the street.

Girl-gang violence, however, is sometimes subordinated to boy-gang violence. For example, in some gangs girls serve merely as weapon carriers for the boys and, if needed, as "backups" (Chesney-Lind and Shelden 1992, 45-46). As one gang girl expressed to Harris (1988, 127):

> Yah, we back up the homeboys.... And if they were into a fight, somehow it will get to us and we will go and back them up, even though we're girls and we're from the Tiny Locas, we'll still back up our homeboys.

Thus, girl-gang violence in this setting occurs within the context of gender relations of power; these girls are doing femininity in a specific way through their affiliation and, therefore, relation to boys. In other words, they are accommodating to masculine dominance.

Girl-gang violence is not always marginal and secondary, however, to boy-gang violence. For example, with regard to her gang's involvement in violence, one gang girl stated (Harris 1988, 127): "We would do our thing and they would do their thing." In other words, girls are involved routinely in violence without the boys being present. Even when boys are nearby, the boys may actually play a secondary role as "backups" (127-28):

> The guys would back us up sometimes. They'll be there. And they'll watch out like two girls on one or something and they'll get one girl off. Whenever they seen that one of us was getting more hurt. But it usually didn't happen that way. We usually didn't need backup that much.... But they'll be there because sometimes guys came from other gangs and they want to get on the girls too, so like they'll be there in case the other guys came.

For girls in the gang, doing femininity means occasionally, and in appropriate circumstances, doing violence. Because participation in violence varies depending on the setting, girls are, however, assessed and held accountable as "bad-girls" differently. Given that gang girls realize their behavior is accountable to other girls and boys in the gang, they construct their actions in relation to how those actions will be interpreted by others in the same social context. These girls, then, are doing femininity, race, and class in terms of activities appropriate to their sex, race, and class category in specific social situations.

Accordingly, violence by young women in youth gangs should not be interpreted as an attempt to be "male" and "pass" as the other gender. Yet, in the past as well as today some women do pass successfully as men, in part to acquire male privileges.[5] For example, a study of "gender-blending females," young women who pass as men in public settings, found that these women were better treated and were generally afforded more respect in public as "men" than they were in public as women. As Devor (1987, 34) concludes, these women passed as men to obtain greater privileges and freedom of movement while simultaneously avoiding some of "the odious aspects of being female in a society predicated on male dominance."

Arguably, then, girls in youth gangs are not attempting to pass as boys or as "gender-blending females" in the previously mentioned sense. Indeed, these girls value emphasized femininity, for the most part display themselves as feminine in culturally "appropriate" ways, and do not construct an ambiguous gender outside the gang milieu. As Campbell (1993, 133) points out, gang girl concern

> with their appearance, their pride in their ability to attract men, their sense of responsibility as mothers left me in no doubt that they enjoyed being women. They didn't want to be like men and, indeed, would have been outraged at such a suggestion.

Girl-gang violence is but one practice in the overall process of constructing a specific type of femininity, race, and class. Accordingly, femininity is assessed both in terms of willingness to defend the "hood" and on doing difference. Thus, within the gang, girl members do most of, if not all, the cooking and child care, prepare the food and drink for "partying," and are "very fussy" over gender display (clothes, hair, makeup) (Campbell 1984/1991; Vigil 1988, 111-12). By engaging in such practices girl-gang members are not simply preparing, for example, the necessities for adequate "partying"—they also are producing gender difference. As West and Zimmerman (1987, 144) point out, for women to engage in this type of labor and men not to engage in it represents for both an opportunity for doing difference. In addition to carrying out the practices of doing difference identified earlier—separate but connected gendered gangs, specific forms of heterosexuality, and "gender-appropriate" crimes—by engaging in activities identified with emphasized femininity, girl-gang members are assessed successfully as women, even when participating actively in street violence. Accordingly, their "bad-girl" femininity consists of a combination of conventional gender practices (such as cooking and child care) and atypical gender practices (such as violence)—each practice justified by appropriate circumstances. Thus, the case of gang girls exhibits a unique fluidity of gender in which different gender identities are emphasized or avoided depending on the social setting. Indeed, within the social context of the gang, "bad-girls" construct a femininity that secures approval as members of the gang and as women.

This fluctuating femininity bears a striking resemblance to the femininity constructed by women in the U.S. Marines. As the following quote indicates, certain events demand "hard" femininity while others justify emphasized femininity, paralleling the flexibility of gender accomplishment seen among girls in youth gangs (Williams 1989, 76):

> Like when we're marching, the woman part drops out. It's just recruits out marching, slamming our heels down on the deck. When we're not in our cammies or out marching, it's put on your makeup and say yes or no, and don't bend down with your knees apart.

Similarly to "bad-girls," these women are constructing a femininity that wins acceptance as "marines" and as women.

Moreover, Barrie Thorne (1993) recently reported in her important work on gender in elementary schools that when classroom events are organized around an absorbing task, such as a group art project, the cooperation encouraged between boys and girls helps to clear a path toward gender similarity. Likewise, for both boys and girls in the gang, one of the most absorbing tasks is common defense of the "hood." Indeed, the symbolic essence of the gang is triggered and becomes meaningful only through interneighborhood conflict. In this social situation, gang boys and girls unite and work together to protect "their neighborhood" from the threat of adjacent neighborhood gangs. As Campbell (this volume, p. 110) points out, girl-gang members see themselves as part of "a vigilante force on behalf not only of themselves but of friends and neighbors too." Under such conditions *gender* difference becomes secondary to *group* difference and the result is a social site for the construction of "bad-girl" femininity.

Conclusion

Owing to their position in gender, race, and class divisions of labor and power, many young, marginalized girls of color form or join violent street gangs. They adapt to economic and racial powerlessness by competing with rivals of their own gender, race, and class to protect their "hood." For girls in the gang, the struggle with other young women of their class (and usually race) is a means for constructing a specific race and class femininity. As Anne Campbell (1987, 463-64) would put it, these girls are African American, Chicana, or Puerto Rican, but not provincial; they are lower-working-class but not drab; they celebrate emphasized femininity but are not passive. Because girls in the gang collectively experience their everyday world from a specific position in society, they construct femininity in a uniquely race and class appropriate way.

The girls-in-the-gang illustration reveals how social structures are constituted by social action and, in turn, provide resources for doing race, class, and femininity in particularized ways. As resources for doing gender, race, and class, the distinct types of youth crime ultimately are based on these social structures. In this way social structures both constrain and enable social action and, therefore, gender, race, class and youth crime.

Gender patterns of crime are not static, but vary situationally. Outside parental and school surveillance, the gang provides greater space for the negotiation of gender, race, and class. Consequently, females and males engage in "gender-appropriate" crimes yet sometimes commit similar types of crimes. By developing a sense of gender, race, and class as structured action and situational accomplishment, we isolate not only the social actions that sustain but also those that undermine the construction of gender, race, class, and crime as difference.

The gang provides a milieu within which girls can experiment with, and possibly dismantle, the bounds of emphasized femininity. Girl gang members use the race and class resources available to construct gender and, in so doing, challenge notions of gender as merely difference. Thus, rather than conceptualizing gendered crime simplistically in terms of, for example, "males commit violence and females commit theft," we are now able to explore which males and which females commit which crimes, and in which social situations.

Responding to Female Gang Involvement

G. David Curry*

Over the last decade, there has been growing national concern about gang-related crime (Huff 1990, 1996; Spergel 1990; Spergel, Chance, and Curry 1991; Curry, et al. 1994, 1996; National Institute of Justice 1992; Cummings and Monti,1993; Howell 1995, 1997, 1998; Office of Juvenile Justice and Delinquency Prevention 1997; Thornberry 1998). Though gang-related crime has often been viewed as a predominantly male phenomenon, research, program practice, and law enforcement strategies have increasingly focused on the role of females in gangs (Campbell 1984/1991, 1990; Moore 1991; Candamil 1992; Cosmos 1993; Miller 1996; Deschenes et al. 1996; Chesney-Lind 1997; Hagedorn and Devitt this volume; Decker and Curry 1998; Curry 1998). While some senior male researchers have continued to emphasize that female gang involvement is less prevalent and less lethal than that of males (Spergel 1990, 1995; Klein 1995), Joan Moore (1991) has argued that the social costs of female gang involvement and the magnitude of what remains to be learned about the behavior of females in gangs justify continuing to expand research on this phenomenon. Moore has continually insisted that gang involvement by females has more long-term effects on the lives of the female gang members and a more serious impact on the lives of their children (and perhaps consequently for community and society) than gang involvement by males.

In this chapter, I examine responses to female gang involvement from research, social service, and criminal justice sectors in an effort to provide (1) an updated representation of the level and nature of this response, and (2) what can be determined about the changing nature of female gang involvement based on information from these three sectors. Two principles guide this examination: (1) response is an integral part of the development of gang problems at the community and national levels; and (2) the response process has to be perceived as including the development and dissemination of perceived knowledge to and from other sectors of the response process.

Research

Considering research as a "response" to a social problem may seem a novel approach, but I contend that research on a subject increases in conjunction with increased public and policy concern and, perhaps just as important, funding resources. At the same time, research results play a role in conditioning and shaping the level and nature of program and law enforcement responses to a social problem. In the case of research on

*This essay, published here for the first time, was presented at the American Society of Criminology meetings, Boston, in 1995.

female gang involvement, it is possible to suggest a comparatively linear transition from androcentric research drawn from male gang member perspectives on the problem to research that draws on the perspectives of the females involved in gangs themselves.

Androcentric Research: "Male" Gangs and Females

The first systematic studies of gangs in the United States were conducted at a time when women were struggling for far more important rights than the recognition of their perspective in the works of criminologists (Thrasher 1927; Asbury 1927). A majority of contemporary researchers on gangs with little or no reservation pay homage to the contributions of Frederic Thrasher who studied 1,313 Chicago gangs just after the turn of the twentieth century (Hagedorn 1988; Decker and Van Winkle 1996; Curry and Decker 1998). (I must note, though, that there is a dearth of such reverence for Thrasher in the works of women who have conducted research on gangs.) It was Thrasher who laid the foundation for the dismissal or minimization of "woman's place" in the world of gang activity. It is to Thrasher that most of what Campbell (1984) called "myths" and of what Moore (1993) called "stereotypes" must be attributed.

According to Thrasher (161), girls did not form or participate in gangs, because ganging and gang activity were antithetical to the norms and traditions that were defined as "appropriate" behavior for females and because girls were subject to greater parental supervision than boys. The comparatively rare cases in which girls participated in gangs Thrasher identified as involving the comparatively young "tomboy" (151) or the older female who served as an object of sexual gratification for the male members (155). The true role of females in gangs was for Thrasher that of "the chief disintegrating force in the gang" (170). As girlfriends and particularly as wives, females pull males away from commitments to their gangs and into commitments to their emerging responsibilities as husbands, fathers, and breadwinners.

Between Thrasher and the 1970s, research on gang involvement can be placed under one of two categories—ignoring female participation altogether or substantiating Thrasher's conclusions about the role of females in gangs. Among those ignoring female involvement in gang activity are the major theorists in delinquency who modeled their theories on adolescent male gang involvement, such as Cohen (1955), for whom gang members were *Delinquent Boys,* and Cloward and Ohlin (1960), who constructed a theory of gang involvement dependent upon the structure of legitimate and illegitimate opportunities for males.

At least two major studies of gangs supported Thrasher's perspectives on females and gangs. The first was the research of William F. Whyte (1943), who is best known for his classic study of the Norton Street Gang. The Nortons were adult, white, lower-class, male "corner boys" trapped by the Great Depression in a world of prolonged adolescent relationships and behavior. The one view of a comparable group of females offered by Whyte could have been directly taken from Thrasher (155), who suggested that as male gangs become older, "Dates and dancing become important, girls' groups may enter into an alliance with the gang." For a period of time during Whyte's observation, the Nortons entered into such an alliance with the Aphrodite Club. As a result of their association with this female group, relations within the structure of the male group experienced strains and, in some cases, permanent rearrangements.

As a result of methodological decisions on his part, Irving Spergel (1964) in his ethnographic study of male gangs and delinquent groups in three New York City neighborhoods described the females who associated with his gang members from these males' perspectives. Given Spergel's male sources, it was not surprising that images of females failed to challenge any of the images presented by Thrasher. The roles of women in the gang, or more accurately for the gang, were either ones of utility associated with their gender or sexuality or as a threat to the integrity of the gang through marriage. Spergel reported the services rendered to gangs by girls acting as "weapon-bearer" or "spy." He also identified females as instigators and manipulators in the cycles of gang conflict and violence.

> "Particularly the member of the Deb group, or the girls' group affiliated with the gang, played various roles, contributing highly to the maintenance of the gang-fighting system. She was the carrier of tales—the magnifier, the distorter, and fabricator of derogatory remarks which served to instigate conflict among the various clubs." (pp. 88-89)

Again, supporting Thrasher's findings, Spergel emphasized the capacity of females as gang destroyers. As Spergel concluded (148), "Marriage and employment, in particular, compel the patterns of orientation and behavior previously developed during the stage of adolescent delinquency to change."

Academic researchers were not alone in their treatment of female gang involvement. Two journalistic studies of female involvement in gangs were Rice's (1963) *New Yorker* article and Hanson's (1964) *Rebels in the Streets*. According to Campbell (1991, 17), these accounts elaborated on the theme that female gangs and their members were "marginal and parasitic" to the greater social world of male gangs.

Research Discovers the Girls in the Gang

The works of three male researchers have generally been identified as laying the groundwork needed to transcend the male-centered stereotypes introduced by Thrasher. Walter Miller (1973) reported the results of his study of two female gangs, one white, the Molls, and one African-American, the Queens, in the 1950s and 1960s.

Brown (1977) recorded the gang-related activity of African-American females in Philadelphia. And Quicker (1983) studied Chicana involvement in gangs in southern California. The findings of each researcher portrayed females participating in gang activity that was to some degree independent of the male gangs and gang members with whom they associated.

Miller's Molls were eleven white, Catholic, teen-aged girls whose gang-involvement he followed for approximately three years. Though the Molls were affiliated with a male gang, especially in their involvement in criminal activity, they were not completely subservient nor totally dependent on male gang members for their decision-making. In particular, the Molls were not, as a rule, readily sexually available or sexually controlled by male gang members. While leadership among the Molls shifted over time and with changing situations, organization for action usually centered within a subset of female leaders.

The Queens, a female African-American gang, also studied by Miller, differed from the Molls in several respects. The Queens were less cohesive than the Molls and more dependent in terms of relationships on their affiliate male gang the Kings. Seven of the members were sisters of King members, and having a boyfriend who was a King was very common. Though Miller observed that the Queens were less involved in money-making criminal activity than the Molls, he noted that they were more likely to be involved in aggressive behavior, especially assault. Again, easy sexual access to the members of the Queens was not a condition of the gang's affiliation with the Kings. In reviewing Miller's description of their behavior years later, Campbell (1984, 22) characterized Queen members as being socialized to become "good wives."

Brown (1977), himself an ex-gang member, described among the African-American gang females that he studied in Philadelphia, the members of an autonomous female gang the Holly Ho's. From Brown's narrative, the Holly Ho's were what other researchers would have labeled a "fighting gang," with their own level of participation in the community cycle of intergang and intragang violence. Even in mixed-sex gangs, the female gang members observed by Brown attained their own individual status positions within the gang hierarchy based on their own performances in furthering the reputation and integrity of the collective entity. With such avenues of gang participation open to them, it is not surprising that Brown (1977, 226) depicted a gang world where a female member was not "a sexual object subject to the whims of male gang members" and was not strictly limited to participation in "ancillary activities."

In his study of Chicana female gang involvement in East Los Angeles, female gangs studied by Quicker (1983) were affiliates of male gangs. Most often the female gang carried as a name the feminized version (in Spanish) of the male gang affiliate. Within the female gangs, decision-making was described as decentralized and democratic, and, for the most part, independent from direct influence by the male affiliate gangs or their members. Quicker observed female members' preference for the designation "homegirls" and suggested that the female gang members saw themselves and their gangs as full participants in the social life of their barrios.

While Short and Strodbeck (1965) focused most of their attention on the gang experiences of males, their references to females as associates of gang members and as gang members did not display a commitment to an androcentric perspective. Perhaps, just as importantly, a research associate on the Short and Strodbeck project, Laura Fishman (1988; also see this volume) presented a paper at the American Society of Criminology Annual Meeting that summarized her observations of a Chicago female gang called the Vice Queens from her perspective as their field observer from 1960 to 1963. The paper was reviewed in some detail by Chesney-Lind and Shelden (1992, 46-48) and has more recently been published in Klein et al. (1995). The Vice Queens were the African-American female auxiliary to the male Vice Kings. The twin portrayal of stereotypical and more independent female gang behavior makes the study an excellent transition between earlier studies and more recent research on female gang involvement. To a large extent, the Vice Queens' major activities were built around those of the Vice Kings. Members were described in roles that included being available for sex—and even bearing children and working as prostitutes—for the Vice Kings. They were pictured as instigating conflicts between the Vice Kings and other male gangs and serving as weapons bearers and lookouts when conflicts were most intense. At the same time, a number of Vice Queen activities were reported that do not fit stereotypic restrictions. They engaged in property crime activities independently of the Vice Kings. Though the Vice Queens did fight with female auxiliaries of male gangs that were enemies of the Vice Kings, "most of their fighting was against another female gang without the participation of the Vice Kings" (p. 47). A number of the Vice Queens expressed a preference for homosexual relationships with each other as opposed to the continued sexual abuse by the Vice Kings and involvement in prostitution. Chesney-Lind and Shelden (p. 48) suggested that Fishman's account of the 1960s Vice Queens of Chicago made them comparable in a number of ways to the female gang members studied almost two decades later by Campbell in New York.

Without doubt, an essential contribution to contemporary thinking on female involvement in gangs was provided by Anne Campbell (1984/1991) in her *The Girls in the Gang.* Campbell's findings were presented as a trilogy of social biographies of three women involved in three separate female gangs in New York City from 1979 into the early 1980s. Connie, a Puerto Rican mother of four in her early thirties, was the leader of the Sandman Ladies, the female auxiliary gang of the Sandman, a Manhattan drug-selling gang with aspirations of being a motorcycle club. Weeza, also Puerto Rican, in her late twenties and a mother of two, was a member of the Sex Girls (originally the Essex Girls, named after Essex street). The Sex Girls were the female auxiliary gang of the Sex Boys, a street gang in the final stages of disintegration at the time of Campbell's research. Campbell's third subject was Sun-Africa, an African-American teenager whose parents had immigrated to New York City from Panama shortly before she was born. Sun-Africa was a member of the Five Percenters, a self-described religious (Islamic) and cultural movement that was identified by the New York Police Department as a gang with criminal activity dating back to the early 1960s. A member of an independent female gang "the Puma Crew" since she was nine, Sun-Africa had joined the Five Percenters when she was fourteen. Hence, Sun-Africa constituted a dual case study for Campbell—on the one hand as a former member of an all-female independent gang, and on the other as a female member of a mixed-sex gang with rules supporting a hegemonic gender structure of men over women.

From her research, Campbell (1984, 32) arrived at two major conclusions about female gang involvement in the early 1980s. (1) "It is still the male gang that paves the way for the female affiliate and opens the door into many illegitimate opportunities and into areas that serve as proving grounds." With some exceptions, females become involved in gang activity through male relatives or boyfriends. (2) Once involved in gangs, however, "a more visible solidarity or 'sisterhood' within the gang appears. A girl's status depended to a larger extent on her female peers." "Worth" within the gang was also not just a matter of a female's relationships with males or "simple sexual attractiveness."

Other studies specifically concerned with the female view of gang involvement followed Campbell's (at least by publication date). Female participation in gangs was not the primary focus of Ruth Horowitz's (1983) study of "coming of age" in a Chicago Chicano community. Still, her attention to the cultural strains placed on maturing Chicana girls provided a sharp contrast with the greater emphasis on personal liberation found in Campbell. From her years of field work in the "32nd Street" community, Horowitz concluded that gang involvement for males and females could only be interpreted within the cultural order of the community. For females, the development of personal identity was constrained by the prevalent cultural symbols of "motherhood, virginity, and male domination" (13). Horowitz observed female gangs that were both affiliated with male gangs and independent, but in every case, female participation emerged as a form of (largely unsuccessful) struggle against male control (133). In the 32nd Street community, "Aggressive behavior is masculine behavior and is expected only of *men.*" [Emphasis in original.] A minority of community females approved of violence in defense of honor, but most fights between female gang members were characterized as being "over men." When a gang "peace" meeting was called, all young women "disappeared" (p. 8). In another instance, as two female gang members took up a challenge, they were forbidden to fight by their boyfriends and obeyed (133). While male involvement in gang violence was pictured by Horowitz as a central component of personal identity, the role of gang involvement for females was treated as a peripheral concern subordinate to other dilemmas facing young women.

Mary Harris (1988) analyzed the results of in-depth structured interviews conducted in 1981 with 21 Chicana girls aged 13 to 18 who were involved in gangs. The term used to describe these girls, *cholas,* is the female plural form of *cholo,* a term used by Americans and more established Mexican-American residents of southern California for "the poorest of the poor, marginalized immigrants" (Vigil 1990, 116). Its origins can be traced back several hundred years to an Indian word used to "describe an indigenous person who is halfway acculturated to the Spanish ways." The females interviewed were members of multiple gangs from the San Fernando Valley. Harris emphasized that Mexican-American barrio gangs are composed of divisions or cliques *(klikas).* Cliques within each gang are based on gender and age. Harris's findings paralleled those of Campbell in that female members govern their own cliques and gain status through their own behavior within their clique (125-26, 130). She did, however, note instances in which the independence of female cliques was not respected or in which homegirls were viewed and treated as sexual objects by their male counterparts (128-29), but these cases were presented as exceptions rather than the rule.

Survey Research on Female Gang Involvement

Field study designs provided valuable preliminary information for exploring and assessing female gang involvement. Products of field research have always included the generation of hypotheses that can be tested with more systematic designs. An early effort revealing the strength of more structured research designs was Bowker and Klein's (1983) analysis of data collected on gang and non-gang girls from inside and outside the criminal justice system in Los Angeles. Survey results from 78 girls identified within the juvenile justice system were supplemented with official records information. Survey data were also collected from a comparison group of girls residing in the neighborhoods in which gangs were active, but with no record of contact with the juvenile justice system. In all, the study compared 122 gang girls and 100 non-gang girls. The survey data included the results of several batteries of psychological tests. Explicitly comparing psychological and social structural explanations of the etiology of female gang membership, Bowker and Klein concluded that

> the overwhelming impact of racism, sexism, poverty and limited opportunity structures is likely to be so important in determining the gang membership and juvenile delinquency of women and girls in urban ghettos that personality variables,

relations with parents, and problems associated with heterosexual behavior play a relatively minor role. (pp. 750-51)

More recently, large systematic surveys designed to measure levels of delinquency in general populations of juveniles have included female respondents and items on gang involvement. Jeffrey Fagan (1989, 1990) constructed cluster samples of 500 high school students and snowball samples of 50 high school dropouts from each of three cities: Chicago, Los Angeles, and San Diego. Each sample was predominantly African-American and Hispanic. Gang members were identified by a self-report item. The prevalence of twelve self-reported delinquent behaviors was found to be higher for male gang members than for female members, but the prevalence rates for female gang members exceeded those of non-gang males for all twelve types of delinquency. Fagan (1990, 213) concluded:

> Females in gangs appear to be involved extensively in versatile patterns of illegal behaviors. Their involvement may indicate the changing status of girls within gangs, within illegal markets, within communities where male gang members frequently are incarcerated, or the evolution of female gangs within changing social and economic contexts.

Two longitudinal surveys on at-risk populations of juveniles funded by the Office of Juvenile Justice and Delinquency Prevention have provided insight into general patterns of self-reported female gang involvement in two cities. Finn Esbensen and his coauthors (Esbensen and Huizinga 1993; Esbensen, Huizinga, and Wieher 1993) used the Denver Youth Survey to identify factors that differentiate gang and non-gang youths, the involvement of gang members in delinquent activity, and the temporal relationship between criminal offending and gang membership. As in Fagan's surveys, gang membership was measured by respondent self-report. While gang membership was observed to be a rare and transient phenomenon among the Denver respondents, Esbensen and Huizinga (1993) found that gang members reported two or three times as much delinquency as non-gang members. That approximately 25% of the gang members found in the Denver survey were females led Esbensen and Huizinga to suggest that the participation of females in gangs may be underestimated by field studies and studies of law enforcement records. From longitudinal survey results on a representative sample of Rochester youth, Thornberry and his colleagues (1993) also concluded that gang-involved youths were significantly more likely to report involvement in violence and other delinquency. By following youths over time, their analysis showed gang involvement to be a transitional process with delinquent activity increasing during gang involvement and declining afterward. Bjerregaard and Smith (1993), also using the Rochester data set, systematically examined gender differences in gang involvement. Increased involvement in delinquency and substance abuse was observed for both male and female gang members, but they found surprisingly little difference in the factors that explained male and female gang involvement. The only major difference observed was that failure in school was a stronger explanatory variable for females than males.

Deschenes et al. (1996) analyzed survey data on 5,935 eighth grade students from 42 schools in eleven cities. They found significant differences between females and males in the neutralization of violence. Males were more likely than females to feel that violence was justified. Gang members regardless of gender were more likely to accept violence than non-gang members. Among gang members, differences between males and females, though not as pronounced, were still observed. In multivariate logistic regression analysis, these attitudinal differences were shown to be statistically significant predictors of levels of violent offending for the total population, for males, and for females.

And Then the "Bad News" on Female Gang Involvement

In 1991, Joan Moore published a study based on followup interviews with a random sample of male and female gang members from two barrio gangs located respectively in the Maravilla and White Fence communities. Of her 156 study participants, Moore (p. 8) reported that "a full third of the sample were females." All were interviewed in 1985, when they were adults. The former gang members of each gender were also categorized by age paralleling the gender-age structure of the cliques that made up the gangs involved. Approximately 40% of the respondents are identified as "older" or having joined the gangs in the late 1940s and early 1950s. The remainder or "younger" group joined their gangs in the 1960s and 1970s. To some extent, Moore's results supported those of Campbell and Harris, with females having some level of autonomy within their cliques. By no means, however, were sexist images of female gang members universal among the males or females studied by Moore, but she chose to distance herself from one of Campbell's conclusions. As Moore (p. 55) noted, "Campbell argues that gang girls have outgrown their sexist image, but we found no indication of change in the quality of sexism between older and younger cliques." In fact, perception of females as sexual objects was 56% among younger men and 41% among older men (p. 53).

In a study that combined official records and survey techniques, Karen Joe and Meda Chesney-Lind (1993) analyzed the offense records and conducted in-depth interviews with male and female gang members in Hawaii. They pursued the theoretical goal of accounting for female gang membership "in its own terms rather than as a comparative footnote to the male gang," while comparing the experiences of female gang members with their male counterparts. Joe and Chesney-Lind found the most common arrest category for girl gang members was larceny theft and for boys, "other assaults" ("most likely fighting," 10). The authors of the Hawaii study rejected what they labeled the "liberation hypothesis" as an explanation for female gang involvement. For them, gang involvement was not an act of rebellion, but an attempt of "young women to cope with a bleak and harsh present as well as a dismal future" (p. 28).

From her ethnographic research with girl gang members in Columbus, Ohio, and St. Louis, Jody Miller (1996) has greatly enhanced our understanding of the relationships between gender, violence, and victimization within the gang. Like Campbell, Moore, Joe and Chesney-Lind before her, Miller found female gang members were less likely than male gang member peers to initiate or experience violence with members of rival gangs. However, girls who reaped this gender advantage of diminished violence from rival gangs were more likely to be subjected to disproportionate levels of violent victimization from the members of their own gang. Miller suggested that girls in male-dominated gangs strike a "patriarchal bargain" in which they participate in the victimization and denigration of female peers. These findings provide additional support for the negative images of female gang involvement offered by Moore and Chesney-Lind.

"Liberated Female Crooks": Sightings

Two research teams in two different cities have published results that carry the "women's-liberation-by-gang-participation" hypothesis beyond any of Campbell's comparatively cautious suggestions. A team affiliated with the long-term research projects of Dan Waldorf in the Bay area was extending its data on an all-female crack-dealing posse (Lauderback et al. 1992), while Carl Taylor (1993) was leading a research team studying female involvement in gangs and drug sales in the Detroit area.

The object of Lauderback and his colleagues (1992, 57) was the Potrero Hill Posse, "a strictly independent group of young African-American women." From a larger study of 65 female gang members, the ten posse members were selected for additional research. The evolution of the Potrero Hill Posse paralleled Anne Campbell's two major conclusions. The five posse founders learned drug selling from their boyfriends during the proliferation of crack sales in San Francisco in the late 1980s. Reportedly the posse founders broke off on their own because they perceived the distribution of drug profits in the operation in which they were involved to be unfair. At the time of the study, the Potrero Hill Posse included 22 to 23 members. To be admitted to the group, young women had to grow up in the area where the group operated and be known to the group. Initiation into membership required proof of worthiness by a demonstration of shop-lifting or crack-selling ability. Once in, relationships within the gang were described as those of a family. The major profit-making activity of the gang was a well-organized operation dealing in crack cocaine. An interesting social byproduct of the crack operation as administered by the posse was the recurring exploitation of non-posse females as "toss ups," women used for sex in crack houses, and as heads of household in residences used as temporary "crack houses."

A similar image of female involvement in gangs and drug sales was offered by Carl Taylor (1993) from his series of case studies of female gang members in Detroit. Taylor characterized the "definitions and analysis" of gangs used by prior researchers as a methodological approach that was "rudimentary" and one by which "our perception (of) females in gangs in the 1990s cannot and should not be limited." As his definition of a gang, Taylor (p. 9) chose "transfamilial social organizations that could include ethnic families, groups, and clans, but are not exclusive to these entities." From his analysis of gang types and infrastructure based on "structure, function, and motivation," Taylor (10) concluded, "Women are participating in gangs in crime as never before in urban America. And, this is not exclusive to Detroit." For Taylor (p. 23), "A new attitude of female criminal independence is emerging. The male-female gang relationship is also being altered." Crucial to this change has been the involvement of female gang members in the drug trade. According to Taylor (p. 9), "The dope business has empowered young and old, female and male, in many major cities."

Two issues arise from this overview of research on female gang involvement. First, how can we reconcile what I (Curry 1998) have elsewhere labeled the "social injury hypothesis" with what Meda Chesney-Lind (this volume) labeled the "liberation hypothesis"? Second, what is the relationship between research and the other two categories of response to female gang involvement examined in this chapter? I will return to each of these questions in the "implications" section at the end of this chapter.

Law Enforcement Response

The primary goal of police and other law enforcement agencies in dealing with gangs or any other "threat to public order" is ensuring the safety of community residents (Spergel 1995). Law enforcement agencies have been primarily identified with that inventory of strategies that Spergel and Curry (1993) identified as suppression. From their 1988 survey of "promising gang response programs," these authors reported that suppression strategies were used by all law enforcement agencies as the primary, and more often, only approach to dealing with gang problems. By 1992, self-reported strategies from law enforcement agencies had undergone a substantial shift. While suppression strategies continued to be reported universally by these agencies, some kinds of what Spergel and Curry labeled "community organization strategies" were also reported by all law enforcement agencies surveyed. This increased commitment to community organization strategies by law enforcement agencies may have grown out of local level re-evaluations of what kinds of programs were working or not working.

It is just as likely, though, that this new attention to community organization strategies in dealing with gangs was correlated with the growing interest of policing professional associations and federal funding agencies in community-oriented policing as an approach to dealing with crime in general.

In addition to providing official policy preferences for responding to gangs, national-level surveys of law enforcement agencies have provided us with estimates of changing levels of law enforcement interest and have served as the most frequent source of estimates of the magnitude of the U.S. gang crime problem. The estimates from such surveys have steadily increased over the twenty years that they have been conducted. These increases may represent increases in female gang involvement, or they may represent increased suppression of females under the justification of reducing gang-related crime. First, let's briefly review the numbers as they have been published.

Walter Miller (1975, 23) offered a questionable approximation of the gang crime problem by gender that is still frequently cited when he noted, "A general estimate that gang members are 90% or more male probably obtains for all gang cities." In fact, Miller's estimate represented only an upper boundary for his own findings in the study from which he generated it. Looking at Chicago statistics, he noted that female gang-related crimes are less than 10% of those recorded annually by police. In New York City, where half of the gangs identified by police were reported to have female auxiliaries, only 6% of gang membership was estimated to be females.

The Office of Juvenile Justice and Delinquency Prevention (OJJDP) and the University of Chicago conducted a 1988 survey of 254 agencies involved in community-level gang programs in 45 sites (Spergel and Curry 1990, 1993). From law enforcement agencies in 34 of their sites, Spergel and Curry (1990, 61) reported a total of 120,636 gang members. These numbers taken from only a subset of U.S. cities exceeded the estimate of 97,940 gang members estimated for 286 cities by Miller (1982) and the 100,000 gang members nationwide suggested by Dolan and Finney (1984). Though no estimate of female gang participation has been published from the OJJDP/University of Chicago survey data, each respondent was asked to report "(w)hat percentage of gang offenders who come to your organization's attention in 1987 were female?" (Spergel and Curry 1990, 223e) Using the data (Inter-university Consortium for Political and Social Research 1993) from the answers to this survey item and the reported numbers of gang members for each jurisdiction from law enforcement respondents, the estimated number of female gang members for each of the 34 law enforcement jurisdictions can be calculated and from these an estimated total of 4,803 female gang members can be computed. Rather than the 10% estimate of Miller, this number represents only 3.98% of the total number of gang members from the sites included in the 1988 study.

In 1992, the National Institute of Justice (NIJ) funded a survey of law enforcement agencies in the nation's 79 largest cities and 42 smaller cities that had been included in the OJJDP/University of Chicago national survey. The 1992 NIJ assessment survey (Curry et al. 1994) specifically requested available official record data on females involved in gang-related criminal activity. Responses revealed that policy decisions by law enforcement agencies were a major factor in the construction of the statistics on female participation in gang-related crime as measured by law enforcement agencies. In a number of cities, females were as a matter of policy never classified as gang members. In other jurisdictions, females are relegated statistically to the status of "associate" members. In all, 23 (31.9%) of the largest city police departments with reported gang crime problems did not provide statistics on female gang members, and 9 (12.5%) more reported no female gang members. The statistics from 40 large city police departments reporting numbers of female gang members total 7,205 female gang members. Including numbers from the selected smaller city and county jurisdictions in the study brings the total to 9,092 female gang members in 61 law enforcement jurisdictions across the nation. As a percentage of the total number of gang members reported to the study, this comes to only 3.65%. If, in an effort to control for law enforcement policies that officially exclude female gang members, gang members are only counted from cities reporting some number of both male and female gang members, this percentage increases to only 5.7%, still well below Miller's 10% estimate.

In addition to requests for numbers of gang members by gender, the 1992 NIJ survey also requested available statistics on gang-related crimes by gender and type of crime. Though a number of law enforcement agencies were not able to report annual statistics for gang-related crimes, 59 (large and smaller cities and selected counties) did report the most commonly available gang-related crime statistic—the number of gang-related homicides. Annual statistics for other types of gang-related crimes were reported by smaller numbers of cities. (Among those departments reporting no records on female gang members, Aurora, CO, attributed two drive-by shootings to females.) Proportionally almost twice as many female gang-related crimes are homicides (4.5% for females and 2.4% for males). This could simply be a matter of a tendency on the part of law enforcement agencies to record more carefully the specific characteristics of homicide offenders than of other types of offenders. Violent offenses not resulting in a homicide are proportionally much more common for the male gang offenders. Gang-related crimes by females are significantly (almost three times as likely) to be identified by law enforcement officials as property crimes.

Looking at raw national totals, only the percentage of gang-related property crimes (1.1% or 75 of 6,880) attributed to females exceeds 1% of the total number for any type of crime. Only 8 (0.7%) of the total 1,072 gang-related homicides are attributed to female perpetrators. If we eliminate jurisdictions where no female gang-related crimes are reported, the percentages attributed to females for each type of crime increase substantially. They exceed Miller's 10% estimate for every type of crime except for violent crimes other than homicide. The respective percentages for each type of crime are 11.4% for females for gang-related homicides, 3.3% for other violent crimes, 13.6% for property crimes, 12.7% for drug-related crimes, and 16.7% for "other" crimes.

An imaginable result of increasing female autonomy in gang activity would be the emergence of independent or autonomous female gangs. Miller (1975, 23) argued that such gangs are without doubt the most rare of gangs in which females become involved. The OJJDP/University of Chicago national survey received reports of the existence of 22 "independent" female gangs from their sample of communities with organized responses to gang crime problems. The 1992 NIJ national assessment survey received reports of 99 independent female gangs spread over 35 law enforcement jurisdictions in 1991. (Among those departments reporting no records on female gang members, Birmingham, AL, reported 2 independent female gangs; Portland, OR, 1; St. Paul, MN, 3; and Wichita, KS, 3.) None were reported for Alaska or Hawaii.

When changes in policy in defining and identifying gangs and differences in survey methodology across national surveys are considered, the increases in female participation in gang-related crime perceived by law enforcement agencies become more problematic to accept. Only 23 of the 34 law enforcement agencies offering 1987 estimates to the OJJDP/University of Chicago survey provided official annual statistics on the number of female gang members in their jurisdictions to the 1992 NIJ survey. The total for 1991 records of 4,971 female gang members for this subset of the OJJDP/University of Chicago sample reported to the 1992 survey barely exceeded the 1987 estimate of 4,803 obtained from that survey. Still though, an indicator of an increase in officially perceived female activity in gangs was the 772 female gang members reported for 1991 by nine of the law enforcement jurisdictions that the OJJDP/University of Chicago reported as not having a gang problem in 1988.

Two issues arise from examining the changing statistics on levels of female gang involvement produced by law enforcement. The first concern is the accuracy of these kind of statistics, and the second question concerns the degree to which law enforcement interest in female gang members has been correlated with the increased interest in the women and girls by researchers, both academic and journalistic.

Social Service Programs

Law enforcement policy makers and practitioners were not alone in consuming the evolving literature on female gang involvement. Also doing so were policy makers with the potential to shape program guidelines, especially through the federal funding process. While programs had not been especially concerned with female gang members, there had been major programs designed to intervene in gang involvement and delinquency through a number of strategies. Joan Moore (1991, 35-39) sketched an outline of intervention programs for Mexican-American gang members dating from the 1940s. In her perception, the most important programs were those that were community-based and empowered residents to have control over their social worlds. She summed up her account as follows:

> From the perspective of most of our respondents, programs directed at normaliz-
> ing gang members were of real use. They rarely transformed either the gang or any
> gang member, but they provided important links to conventionality—links that
> were missing for increasing proportions of the young gang members. (p. 39)

Such community-based programs began to disappear in the early 1970s usually due to the diminishing availability of funds. By the late 1970s and the early 1980s, gang intervention efforts had largely passed from social service providers to law enforcement, where the major strategy was suppression (Spergel 1995).

A major shift in this trend occurred in 1989, when Congress allocated funds for new social programs to prevent the involvement of "at-risk" youth in gang and drug-related criminal activity. The newly created programs were administratively located in the Department of Health and Human Services Family Youth Services Bureau (FYSB). Almost immediately after the decision by Congress, staff members at FYSB convened a small invited conference of selected researchers and practitioners in the area of youth gangs in order to seek input on how the new programs should be structured. In terms of what the program would mean for female gang members, Joan Moore played the most influential role at this preliminary planning level. Moore recounted her evidence (now a part of her 1991 book) that females suffer greater long-term hardships as a result of their adolescent gang involvement than males. She insisted that there be a place in any overall program strategy for specialized programs dedicated to the needs of females.

As the program moved from planning to implementation, one administrator at FYSB, Maria Theresa Candamil, played the major role in ensuring that programs for females involved in gangs were a part of the FYSB effort. Candamil also insisted that Moore's recommendations become defining requirements for which programs should be developed and funded. In 1990, FYSB solicited programs for the prevention and intervention of female gang involvement. By the end of the proposal review process, seven gang prevention and intervention programs specifically designed for at-risk females were funded. Throughout the design of solicitations for proposals, awards to sites, and monitoring the component projects of the FYSB Female Gang Prevention and Intervention Program, Candamil played a central role.

The 1990 projects were located in Boston (MA), Denver (CO), Hartford (CT),

Minneapolis (MN), St. Louis (MO), Seattle (WA), and Stockton (CA). Four more female gang prevention programs were funded in 1992. Two were expansions of programs in 1990 sites in Boston and Seattle, and entirely new programs were initiated in Pueblo (CO) and Washington (DC). Service populations that were the target of these programs were almost entirely Latino (predominantly Mexican-American) and African-American except for programs in Minneapolis, aimed at Native American females; Boston, where a mixed client population included a respectable proportion of white girls living in public housing; and Seattle, where an Asian-American minority population was included in the service population.

The projects included under the umbrella of the FYSB Female Gang Prevention and Intervention Program varied greatly in organization and strategy. Issues of concern were how effective were the programs at reaching girl gang members or even those girls most at risk for gang involvement and what kinds of programs were most effective. Case studies and evaluations of three of the projects were conducted by Katherine Williams and Marcia Cohen of the Development Services Group. I served as a statistical analyst and literature reviewer on this project. Of the three projects, Boston's FORCE program was located in the city's public housing projects. Few of the girls served identified themselves as gang members and comparatively few had juvenile records. The program focused on building self-esteem and providing girls living in public housing access to structured social activities and recreation. Another program in Seattle served a very small population of girls almost all of whom had been referred to the project by the juvenile court. Slightly more than 40% of the girls in the Seattle program were former gang members. (Active gang members were not allowed to participate in the program.) The Seattle program placed a heavy emphasis on individual and group counseling and help with completing school and finding employment. Of the girls participating in a third project in Pueblo, Colorado, half were current or former gang members. Their levels of contact with the juvenile court fell in between that of the girls from the other two projects. The Pueblo project offered a wider, more balanced range of services than the other two projects. Mentoring and one-on-one ties with community adults was central to the Pueblo program. There was some emphasis on self-esteem building, but there were also major program components on awareness of Mexican-American culture and conflict resolution. All three programs have been held up as models by their respective communities, and all have received national attention. Still, only the project in Pueblo maintained records suitable for evaluating the impact of specific kinds of program on specific kinds of girls. (An impact evaluation of this nature for the Pueblo site is currently underway.)

A separate evaluation of the entire range of community-based programs funded during the first round of the overall FYSB effort was conducted using survey data collected for program participants and staff. The final report of this evaluation (Cohen et al. 1995) concluded that while the programs may have had some effect on reducing delinquency and drug-use, actual reductions in gang activity associated with program efforts could not be identified. With growing disfavor for non-law-enforcement-based programs in Congress and the unenthusiastic evaluation results, the focus on gang involvement as a program concern by FYSB was steadily phased out. By 1995, the gang prevention and intervention components of the program (for girls or boys) were discontinued. By 1998, FYSB's remaining programs to reduce and intervene in youth violence had had funding withdrawn, for many agencies, well before the end of the initially proposed program funding periods. Of the responses to gang problems, social service programs have been the least common. The components of the FYSB program discussed above constituted the only federal effort ever to address the problems of female gang involvement specifically. The emergence and decline of one agency's interest in female gang involvement again brings us to the issue of the interrelationships between research, policy, and practice in responding to behaviors perceived to be significant social problems. This will be one of three remaining concerns that will be explored in the final section of this article.

Implications

In this article, I have attempted to review what can be learned about female gang involvement by examining responses to it. I have ordered my discussion under the categories of research, law enforcement strategies, and social service programs. Below, I extend my discussion of two issues that emerged in this review. In utilizing a dialectical approach to seek understanding of female gang involvement, I stress ways that identifying contradictions at both the idealistic level (Simmel) and at the material level (Marx) can facilitate an enhanced understanding of a nexus of behaviors.

The Dialectic of the Social Problem and Social Response

As reviewed above, female involvement in gangs has generated a varying range of response from researchers, policy makers, criminal justice practitioners, and social service practitioners. I join a number of other researchers (Klein 1971; Moore 1978; Hagedorn 1988; Spergel 1990) in my assumption that gang activity and the response to gang behavior are parts of a single social process. Ideally, programmatic response to gangs should be conditioned by levels of gang activity. However, as Hagedorn discovered in Milwaukee (1988) and Huff (1989) discovered in Ohio, gang response may be more sensitive to dramatic, sensational events (such as a highly publicized murder or robbery where the perpetrator is identified as a gang member) than to any empirical or experiential understanding of the severity of a community's gang problem. Gang activity is as much shaped by the kinds of response as by any other factors in the unique community context.

Two observations from the review of responses to female gang involvement conducted above may be helpful in understanding the pattern of influences across the three sectors used to frame the analysis above. First, levels of activity under each the three response sectors has varied over time. Generally these patterns of variation have been attributed to variations in gang activity alone. For example, Walter Miller (1982, 7) has described fluctuations in gang activity over time as being similar to a wave—"a wave that strikes with great fury at one part of the shore, recedes, strikes again at another, ebbs away, strikes once more, and so on." Just as Miller spoke of "waves" of gang violence, I feel that it is just as easy to identify waves of gang response. Hagedorn (1988) identified the elements of such a hypothetical cycle in the pattern of denial, recognition, and repression that he found in Milwaukee. Using Hagedorn's model as one of their guidelines, Curry et al. (1994b) developed a more comprehensive model of cyclical response to gang problems that linked theory, policy, and action. Once such cycles in response are recognized, it becomes difficult to attribute changes in gang activity and gang response to either set of social processes in isolation from the other.

Across all three response sectors examined in this article, such cycles are evident. For example, research on female gang involvement remained at a consistently low level for several decades. Then, following a few exceptional studies, with Campbell's study identified by many as pivotal, research interest in female gang involvement exponentially increased over less than a decade and a half. Law enforcement attention to female gang involvement, as reflected by official statistics collected at the local level and compiled by the Justice Department, has increased steadily over the same period. A different pattern was found for social service programs focused on female gang involvement. Programs designed for providing gang prevention and intervention services to females were part of the community mobilization and social intervention approach to gangs that emerged in 1989, peaked in the early nineties, and may already be in the final stages of a rapid decline.

Second, the patterns of response across sectors suggest reasonable evidence of relationships between sectors. As noted above, a distinctive feature of research on female gang involvement has been a continuum of perspectives ranging from the androcentric interpretation of the nature of female gang participation to the ultra-liberationist perspectives of those who would have us recognize women's gang involvement as a path to freedom, self-actualization, and sisterhood. For a majority of the decades since Thrasher did his ground-breaking work on Chicago gangs, researchers sustained and found empirical support for his conclusions that the social world of gangs reflected the correspondingly male-centered social worlds of those times in big business and war. Females as the proponents of marriage and family and the encouragers of stable employment were depicted as anathema to gang life. In the cases where females were reported to have ventured into the world of gangs, researchers most often assigned them the roles of willing or unwilling tools (or even prizes) of the males who dominated gang life. Researchers and practitioners reinforced each other in their perceptions of the nature of gang activity and the kinds of gang policies justified by these perceptions. During this period, law enforcement reported little or no gang involvement by females, and what social service programs existed were tailored for male gang members.

As noted above, law enforcement estimates of female gang involvement in any jurisdiction have rarely reached the 10% level suggested by Walter Miller (1982). In addition, national surveys of available gang statistics have found that local law enforcement policies in many jurisdictions restricted gang membership to only males or regulated all females to the status of "associate" membership. "In a number of cities females, as a matter of policy, were never classified as gang members" (Curry et al. 1994, 8).

The perception that law enforcement agencies have undercounted female gang members also has support from comparisons of statistics obtained across response sectors and research methodologies. Chesney-Lind et al. (1996) specifically identified several of these inconsistencies between law enforcement and other kinds of data. As noted above, Esbensen and Huizinga (1993), in their longitudinal survey of Denver respondents, found that approximately 25% of youth self-reporting gang membership were females. From her fieldwork with gangs, Moore (1991) estimated that females accounted for a third of all gang members. Chesney-Lind et al. (1996, 194) have concluded that given the "gendered habits" of many gang researchers, gang involvement by females could easily have been undercounted in the past.

One alternative to law enforcement's ignoring female gang involvement may be an even more unsatisfactory outcome. As noted above, Karen Joe and Meda Chesney-Lind (1995) suggest that the criminalization of gang involvement for female gang members may constitute an unnecessary exercise in suppression. In my opinion, it is essential that those of us who contend that female gang involvement is a form of behavior worthy of research study not be misunderstood to be advocating increased criminal justice suppression of girls involved in gangs.

In addition to changing perceptions of the levels of female gang involvement generated by researchers, descriptions of the nature of such involvement can have important implications for policy responses to male and female gangs. As noted by Joan Moore (1991, 136-37), the stereotypes that gained currency from the androcentric view of the gang served as a tool for those who would isolate and separate gang-involved youths from the rest of society. Picturing gang members as non-white minorities has contributed to the creation of a "social cleavage" that separates them from the mainstream of white, middle class America. In the same way, picturing gangs as "quintessentially male" through an act of "cognitive purification" was likewise part of the process of social cleavage. As all-male, violent social entities, gangs could be perceived as fundamentally different from the dual-gendered society in which they existed. Moore (p. 39) has suggested, "Perhaps for the image of 'gang' to include girls as well as boys would be to humanize the gang too much, to force the audience to think of domestic relationships as well as pure male brute force."

The Dialectic of the Gang Experience for Females

Central to the development of theoretically grounded policies for responding to female gang involvement has been the debate between researchers led by Campbell, who have emphasized the positive aspects of gang involvement for women, and researchers led by Moore, who have emphasized the social injury associated with gang involvement for women. Elsewhere, I (Curry 1998) have suggested that there may be truth in both sets of conclusions—liberation and social injury. On one hand, neither Campbell nor Moore are as one-sided as their respective critics would like us to believe. A careful reading of Campbell's works show her to be less committed to a completely positive image of life in the gang for females. Despite their sense of sisterhood and mutual respect shared with other women, the three females who were the subject of *The Girls in the Gang* experienced personal physical injury, threats to their children, prolonged fear, loss of spouses, and complete loss of personal and political freedom (at least, in the case of Sun Africa). Similarly, while Moore specifically distances herself from those who would characterize gang involvement as liberating for men or women, she has continued to refine her gender-sensitive theories of gang involvement. In a recent personal communication, Moore told me that she thinks that certain aspects of gang involvement may be "enabling" for women. Joan clarified her use of the term "enabling" by making reference to the use of the term in the literature on female heroin addicts. With deference to Joan Moore for sharing the term with me, I have no problem asserting that female gang involvement can be both enabling and socially injurious to the same individuals. On the level of day-to-day coping with a milieu characterized by diminished access to opportunities, economic resources, and social capital and increased risks of a diversity of kinds of victimization, this conceptualization is very much in keeping with Joe and Chesney-Lind's (this volume) designation of female gang involvement as a method of "coping." Applying such complementary, yet oppositional, concepts as "enabling" and "injurious" to a single form of social behavior corresponds to the traditions of dialectical theory. From such a dialectical perspective, there is no insurmountable contradiction in simultaneously identifying a social activity as rewarding and destructive. In fact, it is the contradiction itself that is fundamental to understanding the social behavior and an underlying tension of opposing forces that makes social change and instability inevitable. For young women, gang involvement simultaneously offers promising solutions to the threat of violence and social isolation while generating new risks for violent victimization (Miller 1996) and new potentially more enduring forms of social ostracism (Chesney-Lind et al. 1996; Moore 1991). The same analytic interpretation can be informatively applied to the wife in a paternalistic family structure, the worker in a capitalist economy, and the volunteer in military service (Foucault 1979). This approach has the capacity to reconcile such opposing images of male gang members as the "deviant individualist" gang member (Sanchez Jankowski 1991) and the minority gang member alienated from his community realistically concerned with the absence of legitimate employment possibilities (Hagedorn 1988).

The largest study of promising gang programs to date (Spergel and Curry 1993) assessed programs on the basis of agency representatives' perceived effectiveness of their agency's strategies. An irony of that study (funded by OJJDP) was that representatives of program agencies did not universally identify their own agency's strategy as being the most effective. Practitioners responding to the National Youth Gang Suppression and Intervention Program's survey offered candid assessments of which strategies they felt to be working and those which they felt were not. The most commonly reported strategies were suppression and social intervention. On the other hand, the strategies perceived as most effective were community organization and creating life opportunities for those youth for whom gangs remain the only other alternative. With this discord between perceived knowledge and actual program practice at the agency-level, it is not surprising that the patterns of national response to female gang involvement reviewed here fall short in terms of systematic program development and coordination.

3 "Doing Gender" in Times of Economic and Social Change

Introduction: "Doing Gender" and Economic Restructuring

The last decade has seen an exciting new scholarship exploring the role of gender in gangs. Even a cursory reading of this research will reveal that girls in gangs, like their male counterparts, vary considerably (see for example, in addition to the pieces reprinted here, J. Miller 1996; Lauderback et al. 1992; Laidler and Hunt 1998). To further explicate this, we offer an array of current articles in this section which explore the many dimensions of current female gang scholarship. All these articles discuss, in some manner, how female gang members in poor, minority communities "do gender" in times of economic and social change. These authors, however, illustrate not just variation in female gangs, but also flesh out, in a rich, descriptive, manner, important functions of the gang for girls. The sexist notion that female gangs ought to be studied only in their relationship to male gangs has been thoroughly discredited—at least in the works reprinted here.

There is less unanimity, however, on the nature of female gangs today, given massive economic changes facing our cities. Some of the disagreements you will find in the following pieces are due to variation in the nature and functions of female gangs in different cities, of different ethnicities, different ages, and at different times. It is unlikely, for example, that female gangs in ethnically diverse Honolulu would look like African American female gangs in segregated and economically devastated Detroit. Still, real differences of interpretation remain and we think that is a good thing. The reader is encouraged to sort things out for her- or himself.

Joan Moore's article on gang families from her book, *Going Down to the Barrio*, is significant for at least three reasons. First, Moore studies females as well as males, in the context of their neighborhoods. We agree with her stark conclusion: "such even-handed treatment is virtually unknown in the literature on gangs" (136). Second, Moore focuses on families (in the chapter we reprint), an often discussed, but seldom studied aspect of gang life. Third, Moore's careful representative sampling of rosters of *klikas* of male and female gang members from over three decades is a standard that no other study, of male or female gangs, has yet attained. *Going Down to the Barrio* is a virtuoso performance in a gang literature that is seldom longitudinal, and most often made up of cross-sectional, non-randomly selected samples of self-proclaimed gang members. Her collaborative methodology, which she taught to her student, John Hagedorn, adds validity to her data. As a result, she is able to scientifically assess the ways changes in the economy of the area affected the lives of the families in two Chicano barrios over this period, and how these changes in turn affected the gangs she and her colleagues interviewed.

In the chapter reprinted here, Moore details the different ways stresses in the family impact male and female gang members. To start with the obvious, for the girl in a gang, incest is a serious problem not faced by many boys. The girls also reported their parents were more strict than the boys', especially in the earlier cliques. Moore cites a "litany of traditionalism" of problems with fathers calling girls "tramps" and behaving in a patriarchal manner. Girls, Moore finds, were almost twice as likely to run away than boys. It is clear that for girls from such families, the gang will become more of an alternative family, refuge, or source of support. For the boys, on the other hand, the gang will be seen by kids and parents alike as more of a way for the wilder boys to "sow their wild oats." Moore's work stands in contrast to those who find few differences in explanatory variables for males and females (Bjerregaard and Smith 1993).

In the conclusion of her study, not reprinted here, Moore sums up the impact of changes in the economy on East Los Angeles gangs. She finds that gangs today are more deviant, and that fewer good jobs exist for both male and female adults. This limits the ability of gang members to "mature out" of their gang. While Moore finds that little has changed for the *tecato,* or drug addicts, for those gang members who in the past had settled down and been able to lead a conventional life, things may be changing for the worse.

Those changes are documented further when Moore and Hagedorn compare East Los Angeles and Milwaukee female gangs. We are shown differences between Los Angeles and Milwaukee gangs, but also differences between African American and Latina gangs in Milwaukee. We begin to note both profound ethnic differences in the way that gangs work in the lives of young women and the impact of gang membership on young women.

Importantly, the traditional gender norms that haunt the lives of most Latinas were far less evident in the lives of most African American women. Due to the legacy of slavery, African American women have for centuries faced a more advantageous economic position in relation to their male counterparts. Problematic relations with men haunt the girls and women from both ethnic groups, as does the responsibility for children. What differs is the degree to which the women are cynical about male intentions: far more African American women reject the notion that "all a woman needs to straighten out her life is to find a good man." Things are not really much better for their Latina sisters, many of whom report long histories of abuse, but the general distrust of men, for most Latinas, is not as profound.

The main theme of the Moore and Hagedorn piece is to ask an often neglected question: What happens to gang girls as they become adults? While "gender counts" in understanding the life course of female gang members, almost all of whom were mothers, so, too, they argue, does opportunity. There was a greater involvement of Latinas with drug sales, even though most Latinas were more traditional and less independent than African Americans. Moore and Hagedorn argue firmly that while times are changing, gender oppression persists, and girls' and women's lives will be strongly influenced by class, ethnicity, and gender.

Finally, in this article, Moore and Hagedorn return to Fishman's theme of survival. We see the first mention that welfare "reform" may have far-reaching implications for girls' ability to "mature out" of adolescent gangs. Whether economic hardships will lead to major changes in the familiar form of the female gang is an open question.

Carl Taylor answers that question in the affirmative in this selection from his book, *Girls, Gangs, Women, and Drugs,* the only book published to date in the 1990s devoted solely to female gangs. Taylor argues persuasively that the devastating economic changes in Detroit over the past decades have played a significant part in shaping female roles and attitudes. Using interviews with current and former gang members, he shows the changes that have taken place in female gangs. Only Joan Moore's work matches the historical sweep of Taylor's narrative.

Taylor's conclusions, however, are contested by others in this volume. Taylor finds that female gangs in the 1940s were traditional auxiliaries, and in the 1960s gangs were an avenue of participation by some in the civil rights movement. By the 1990s, Taylor controversially finds, a new form of female gang has formed as an equal partner with males in the drug game. Similar to other social scientists (see Baskin and Sommers 1998), Taylor claims the breakup of male drug gangs provided opportunities for females to play a more active role in drug sales. Taylor believes this status for African American women holds true across American cities, but he offers no evidence on this point.

Support for Taylor's views come from one widely read article from San Francisco by Lauderback, Hansen, and Waldorf (1992), not reprinted here (for further analysis from the same data, see Brotherton 1996). These researchers dispute the traditional notions of female gang members as "maladjusted, violent tomboys" and sex objects completely dependent upon the favor of male gang members. They found an independent girl gang who engaged in crack sales and organized "boosting" to support themselves and their young children. Looking past the gang's economic role in their lives, Lauderback and his associates noted that the gang fills a void in the lives of its members, since their own family ties were weak at best prior to their involvement in the group. Studies in Milwaukee and elsewhere have also located all-female drug-selling cliques, but it is unclear how many such groups exist, and if they are becoming more prevalent.

There is no question that contemporary gangs are much affected by class and economic marginalization. Girls, as well as boys, may use the gang or gang connections to survive economically in their neighborhoods. But how gang activities of all types are carried out are profoundly influenced by gender. There has long been considerable support for the notion that gangs, particularly male gangs, are sites for "doing gender" in marginalized communities (see Messerschmidt, this volume). Joe and Chesney-Lind's interviews with youth gang members in Hawaii shows how both male and female gang members "do gender" as they attempt to find meaning and support.

Joe and Chesney-Lind argue that everyday life in marginalized and chaotic neighborhoods sets the stage for group solidarity in two distinct ways. First, the boredom, lack of resources, and high visibility of crime in their neglected communities create the conditions for turning to others who are similarly situated, and, consequently, it is the group that realistically offers a social outlet. At another level, the stress on the family from living in marginalized areas combined with financial struggles creates heated tension, and, in many cases, violence in the home. They found, like Moore, high levels of sexual and physical abuse in the girls' lives; 62% of the girls had been either sexually abused or assaulted. Three-fourths of the girls and over half of the boys reported physical abuse. Also like both Moore's Los Angeles and Hagedorn's Milwaukee findings, Hawaiian gang members come from different kinds of families; i.e., they did not all come from very poor families. For example, in both East Los Angeles and Milwaukee, one-third of all parents of male and female gang members owned their own homes (see Esbensen and Deschenes 1998).

In Hawaii there were critical differences in how girls and boys, Samoans, Filipinos, and Hawaiians express and respond to the problems of everyday life. For the boys, fighting—even looking for fights—was a major activity of the gang. For the girls, however, fighting and violence was a part of life in the gang, but not something they necessarily sought out, similar to the picture of female gangs and aggression painted by Anne Campbell (see also Campbell 1993 and later in this volume). The adolescent gangs studied by Joe and Chesney-Lind are concerned with boredom and other teenage issues—survival is not yet a central concern. The boys sold drugs in a petty way, while girls did not.

This is a much different picture of the female gang than Lauderbach's or Taylor's. While the theoretical issues raised by Joe and Chesney-Lind on differences in how boys and girls "do gender" are crucial, it also could be that lives for girls and young women in Detroit, San Francisco, and Honolulu differ greatly. Small or unknown samples in all these studies, as well as possible differences in age, however, caution against generalization.

A further explication of the role of gender, both in terms of doing gender and in terms of the injuries of gender, can be found in Portillos's interviews with Chicano/a and Mexicano/a gang members in the Phoenix area. Portillos consciously applies Messerschmidt's paradigm, and we are pleased to print it here for the first time. First, like Moore, Portillos notes the pervasive influence of patriarchy in the construction of Chicana/Mexicana youth, with men being granted considerable liberty compared to girls. The Phoenix gang is an undisputed site for *cholo* masculinity, and this is largely unproblematic for boys—gangs provide opportunities to fight as well as to engage in and brag about sexual conquest.

"Doing femininity," however, in these relatively traditional cultures, provides gang girls with a more complex experience. As with other studies in this section, the female gang can provide the girls an escape from the constraint in their homes, but this is a freedom bought at some cost. Portillos comments that the gang in these cultural settings "simultaneously liberates and oppresses women." Gang girls are rarely given leadership roles in the group (or credit for leadership and bravery), and they cannot seem to escape the sexual landscape that so completely defines young women in these neighborhoods. Oppositional femininity, in the form of wearing gang attire, for example, is mediated by settings where more sexual attire are expected and displayed. The sexual double standard continues to operate in the lives of girls in gangs, and much worse, there is considerable sexual victimization of girls by gang members (see also Moore and Hagedorn in this section).

All these pieces together present a rich texture of emerging contemporary scholarship on female gangs. They appear to have set the agenda for theoretical debate and raised substantial questions that only can be answered by more high-quality empirical work. For men, economic restructuring appears to have substantially impacted the nature of gangs—as gang boys become men, many have found their gang to be useful in organizing for survival. Will the female gang undergo a similar transformation, as Taylor implies, especially as the reality of welfare reform sets in, and women face the choice of hustling to feed their children or watching them go hungry? Or will women play less risky and more traditional roles in their own survival and the welfare of their families? Only time will tell.

Gang Members' Families

*by Joan W. Moore**

Most boys and girls in East Los Angeles never became involved with gangs. Because the community has so many problems, over the years researchers have been tempted to search for the roots of gang involvement in some special characteristics of the members' families. After all, *something* must make these particular young people susceptible to the attractions of this most rowdy of youth groups. Where better to search than in the family?

This search has taken three major approaches. The oldest emphasized some structural feature: thus it is said that immigration and poverty causes family stress, and family stress weakens controls. Thrasher noted the general fragility of social controls in immigrant neighborhoods of 1920s Chicago, and the particular "failure of the immigrant [family] to control [its] children" (1927, 489). This concern with immigrant family problems was regularly applied to Chicano gangs (see Griffith 1948). Most recently Vigil (1988), in his concept of "multiple marginality," broadened it. He maintained that large segments of the Mexican-origin population suffered from economic and ecological marginality and from culture conflict, as well. Under these circumstances, family controls often lost out to street socialization. People who could not adapt began to generate a marginalized cholo subculture. Gangs express the essence of this cholo subculture, and youngsters from troubled families are particularly likely to join them. A similar general approach is taken by researchers who argue that stresses suffered by poverty-stricken parents combine with the constraints imposed by limited resources to create "maladaptive parenting" (Garbarino, Schellenbach, and Sebes 1986).

A second approach searches for a subcultural foundation for gang involvement. One of the early contentions was that family socialization to a special working-class subculture generates and sustains male gang activity (Miller 1958). And more recently Moore and Vigil (1987) suggest that once cholos marry and have children of their own, whole families are embedded in the cholo subculture.

A third approach emphasizes psychological problems stemming from the family. A Freudian stance pervaded much of the early literature on juvenile delinquency (see Aichhorn 1935), and when it was applied to gangs, broken homes began to receive considerable attention (Shaw and McKay 1931; Slawson 1926; Glueck and Glueck 1934).[1] This psychological tradition has consistently asserted that delinquency is largely a reaction to frustrating and emotionally disturbing conditions at home (Healy and Bronner 1936; Reckless, Dinitz, and Kay 1957). In fact, one leading scholar contended that a poor self-concept, generated in the family, creates the critical psychological vulnerability to delinquent solutions (Dinitz, Scarpitti, and Reckless 1962). Vigil (1988) echoes much

**Reprinted by permission from Joan Moore,* Going Down to the Barrio: Homeboys and Homegirls in Change. *Philadelphia: Temple University Press. Copyright 1991.*

the same argument with specific reference to Chicano gangs. Gang membership in adolescence reinforces delinquent tendencies that have their roots in family stress during childhood.[2] Several researchers have explored factors in the family that insulate poverty-stricken youngsters from delinquency, and they repeatedly note the importance of the quality of family relationships—the emotional climate (see Werner 1983).

In short, a concern with gang members' families has a long history. There is no question that most recent theorizing about juvenile delinquency—and gangs—has tended to emphasize the influence of larger systems, and thus to de-emphasize the intimate interactions within face-to-face groups. But families play a role in these broader approaches as well. Hagedorn (1988) claims that the recent appearance of gangs in a midwestern minority community is largely the result of economic changes that deprived minority workers of decent jobs and their communities of viable institutions. In particular, he notes that gang members' parents generally held decent jobs of the kind that the members themselves cannot obtain. This view contrasts sharply with the traditional view that gangs come from perennially poverty-stricken or marginalized families. Instead, Hagedorn posits a pattern of communitywide downward mobility—with all its attendant family stresses—in neighborhoods that are already hard-pressed.

In this chapter I deal with each of the major themes relating to the family—questions relating to immigration and ethnicity and to parental economic status, and questions about the emotional climate in the household during respondents' childhoods. The approach is descriptive, and our major interest is in the extent to which families of the earlier clique members reflect more—or fewer—features that have been defined as problems than families of more recent cliques. If one follows Thrasher's reasoning, one might expect that older—largely immigrant—families would have more problems. But if one follows Vigil's reasoning, one might expect that more recent families, increasingly "choloized," would have more problems.

Ethnicity and Poverty in the Families

Mexicanness

Whether "Mexicanness" can be seen as a problem depends on whether one expects strains to be associated with immigrant status and acculturation. We expected the families of members of earlier cliques to be far more "Mexican" than those of the recent ones, and they were, on all measures.

The first aspect was nativity. More than two-thirds of the parents of male members of earlier cliques were born in Mexico, compared with only a third or fewer of the parents of members of more recent cliques. Interestingly, the women gang members—even the ones from earlier cliques—were notably less likely to have Mexican-born parents. The women in more recent cliques were even less Mexican, with a minuscule 9% of parents born in Mexico.[3] About a third of the parents of more recent clique members—both men and women—were born in Los Angeles itself.

The second aspect was cultural. Of course, Spanish was the habitual language in many of the homes. In about 60% of the boys' families and 44% of the girls' families it was the language spoken every day, by both parents and children. (Households in the earlier cliques were no more or less likely than those in recent cliques to rely on Spanish, oddly enough.) In many of the homes, parents spoke in Spanish and children answered in English. English was the everyday language in only a small fraction of the households of earlier clique members, but in the more recent cliques, it was the normal language in 42% of the boys' homes and 61% of the girls' homes. Many of the parents, particularly of recent clique members, actively encouraged the use of Spanish.

We also asked a series of questions designed to give some indication about traditionalism in the family. Did the father set himself up as the head of the household, with no questions asked, in the traditional Mexican pattern? Did he let his wife drive the family car? Did he restrict his wife's visitors? Did he let his wife handle the money?

Generally speaking, households in the earlier cliques were more patriarchal and, generally speaking (not surprisingly, given the nativity patterns) boys' households were more patriarchal than girls'. The majority of boys' fathers in the earlier cliques made claims to patriarchal control and to exclusive use of the family car (if there was one), and a small minority (20 percent) attempted to control their wives' visitors. Ironically, more fathers in the earlier cliques ceded control over money matters to their wives.

The pattern was not quite so patriarchal in the women gang members' households. Only about half of the women's fathers tried to establish themselves as unequivocal heads of the household, and none tried to restrict their wives' visitors. They were also more likely to let their wives drive the family car. Many of the differences in perceived patriarchy between men's fathers in earlier and more recent cliques can be explained by nativity: Mexican-born fathers, both earlier and more recent, acted more like patriarchs.

These differences between girls' and boys' household traditionalism and Mexicanness are somewhat surprising.[4] It may simply be that the more culturally Mexican girls simply didn't join the gangs. Traditional Mexican families are intensely opposed to any kind of street involvement for girls. Many of the girls who joined the earlier cliques came from traditional Mexican households, but they tended to be sisters of the boys who were centrally involved, and we have discussed earlier the ways in which such girls were controlled by their families even if they were members of a gang.

Despite the fact that virtually all of these boys and girls were born in the United States, the family and community combined to make most of them feel Mexican when they were growing up. Not Mexican American, but Mexican. A woman from a recent clique traced the feelings to her family: "Mexican, I felt Mexican. Because both of my parents spoke in Spanish and I had an older sister that wasn't born from here. She was born in Mexico. I grew up knowing English but my mom and dad did speak Spanish in the household and she did tell us what our race was as we were growing up." A woman from one of the earlier cliques explained that her feelings about ethnicity had deeper roots in discrimination than in family processes: "I felt Mexican because [laugh] at a very tender age the white people let me know that my skin color was brown. Which was in Texas and they discriminated against me. And I knew I was Mexican, and after that I was very proud about it. That's why I had so many fights with the white people in San Fernando High and in junior high school because I refused to be put down because I was brown."

Ethnic identity confusion has been identified as a problem for Chicanos in all kinds of communities, and it is by no means confined to youngsters who join gangs or have other kinds of problems. A small minority—about 11% of the gang members from earlier cliques and 5% of those from recent cliques—admitted to feeling "confused" about their ethnic identity when they were growing up. It is more than likely that most people who said they felt Mexican actually experienced many of the feelings that were articulated well by one man from an earlier clique who acknowledged his ethnic identity confusion: "I was confused when I was growing up. [?] Well, because I couldn't speak English properly, the way I thought I should, the way they tried to teach me at school. I couldn't pick it up. And I was eating different food. I was taking tacos and everybody had sandwiches. And at that time in Marianna [school] they used to prohibit you from speaking Spanish. And that was my language." However, it is easy to make too much of such identity confusion. It was undoubtedly shared by other youngsters in the barrios: these gang members were by no means unusually Mexican for their times. In fact, given recent increases in immigration to East Los Angeles, the recent cliques of the gangs may actually be *less* Mexican than the general run of adolescents in these communities. Certainly, there is no indication in these data that Mexicanness or identity confusion led these youngsters into the gang.

Poverty: Household Composition and Mobility during Childhood

We developed several indicators of poverty in the household. Our respondents listed all household members and their jobs, and gave us other information about the household, in five-year intervals for their entire lifetimes. During their childhood, households in this sample were quite large, averaging 6 or 7 people (Table 1). Usually this meant that there were several brothers or sisters, but occasionally a grandparent or—rarely—a cousin or other relative was present. There was substantial variation in household size. Nine percent had only 3 people, including the respondent, while in 17% there were 10 or more people. Very few of the respondents (15 percent) could have a bedroom all to themselves: Most shared with same-sex siblings.

Most of the boys and girls in the earlier cliques grew up with both parents in the household, although fathers tended to disappear as the young people entered adolescence (Table 1). In the recent cliques, it was far more common for these homes to be hit by divorce or desertion when the respondents were quite young. This was particularly the case for the women's families. By their mid-teens, a sizable number—more than a third—of gang boys and girls were living in homes headed by their mothers. However, the majority had both parents, and, if we take seriously the data on patriarchy just presented, the households were not dominated by mothers, either.

There were not very many three-generation households. Occasionally a grandparent lived with the family, and very occasionally grandparents (or some other family member) took charge of the respondent, replacing absent or abusive parents. In sum, these households have more of the characteristics associated with poverty than with the traditional Mexican extended family.

Poverty: The Household Economy during Childhood

The parents of these gang members were generally poorly educated. Only about half of the respondents knew their parents' educational level, but in the earlier cliques, only about 10% of the fathers had completed high school, and in the more recent cliques the proportion was still lower than one-third. Fathers and mothers who were born in Mexico tended to be particularly poorly educated—especially in the earlier cliques, where more than half of the Mexican-born parents were functionally illiterate (with less than four years of school). Even in the more recent cliques, Mexican-born parents had little schooling. Twenty percent of the fathers and 14% of the mothers had no school at all. On the other end, 19% of the fathers and 22% of the mothers had completed high school.

And, generally, although fathers did not hold very good jobs, the jobs were better for fathers of the more recent clique members than of the earlier ones. More fathers of earlier clique members were unskilled (33% compared with 9% in recent cliques), reflecting the higher proportion of Mexican-born workers. In the recent cliques there were more semiskilled factory workers (53% compared with 36% in the earlier cliques) or skilled workers (35% compared with 29% in the earlier cliques). There were few differences between boys' fathers and girls' fathers.

There were, however, interesting gender differences in whether the mothers stayed at home, following traditional role prescriptions, or whether they worked. For both boys and girls, mothers in the earlier cliques were distinctly more likely to be housewives. But in both earlier and more recent cliques, the boys' mothers were much more likely to be at home and the girls' mothers to be working as a matter of course. Specifically, in the earlier cliques 19% of the boys' mothers and 44% of the girls' mothers were working, and in the recent cliques 37% of the boys' mothers and 56% of the girls' mothers were working. Mothers' jobs were strictly for cash—and largely factory work.

Were these gang members from desperately poor families? Probably so, by middle-class standards. However, subjectively, most respondents (61 percent) felt they were no poorer than most other people in the barrio, while 15% felt that their families were "better off," and only 24% felt that they were poorer than most people. Though these were generally poor barrios, most of the gang members did not feel that they were among the poorest of the poor. Slightly more than a third (37%) owned their own homes. A quarter lived in very small homes, with four rooms or less, but 10% grew up in homes with eight or more rooms, even though (judging by local housing characteristics) the rooms probably were very small.

Perhaps even more important than poverty per se, it is important to realize that gang members—especially in the earlier cliques—grew up in households in which at least one and often more than one person worked. In only a handful of male members' households was nobody working. When fathers were present, it was fathers who worked. In more recent cliques, mothers entered the work force in significant numbers as the respondents grew older even when fathers were present. Brothers and sisters contributed to the family income in a quarter of the homes, and in about 8% grandparents also worked. Girls' homes were more frequently broken than boys'. There were higher proportions of girls' homes with no workers (up to 24% in the more recent cliques) and fewer fathers and more mothers worked.

Table 1

Household Composition During Childhood
Earlier Cliques Compared With Recent Cliques

	When Female Respondent Was Aged:			When Male Respondent Was Aged:		
	0-5	6-10	11-15	0-5	6-10	11-15
Median Household Size						
Earlier Cliques	6.0	7.0	7.0	6.0	7.5[a]	7.0
Recent Cliques	6.0	7.0	7.0	5.0	6.0[a]	7.0
Father Was Present						
Earlier Cliques	77.8%	83.3%	61.1%	82.6%	82.6%	71.7%
Recent Cliques	57.6	69.7	63.6	73.3	76.7	63.3
Mother Was Present						
Earlier Cliques	94.4%	94.4%	94.4%	93.5%	91.3%	87.0%
Recent Cliques	97.0	87.9	87.9	95.0	95.0	88.3
Grandfather Was Present						
Earlier Cliques	5.6%	5.6%	5.6%	6.5%	8.7%	6.5%
Recent Cliques	9.1	6.1	9.1	8.3	8.3	8.3
Grandmother Was Present						
Earlier Cliques	22.2%	22.2%	22.2%	6.5%	13.0%	8.7%
Recent Cliques	9.1	9.1	9.1	18.3	15.0	13.3

[a] Kendall's tau significant > .05

Even though wages were the principal source of income in most of these households, respondents noted additional sources, as well. Nine percent of the men and 20% of the women recalled some other sources of income coming into the family when they were between the ages of 6 and 10. These include welfare, odd jobs, pensions and—rarely mentioned—illicit income (in 3% of the households). In their early teens, 30% of the men and 23% of the women listed other sources of income. Importantly, only 9% of the men and 6% of the women listed welfare. Increased proportions recorded their own income from illegal activities (9% of the boys in their early teens, rising to 27% in the later teens).

In most of these respects, these families probably differed very little from their neighbors. They were Mexican, they were large, they were working, they were poor. Occasionally the fathers departed, but the overall profile is not desperately poor, and there is a lot of variation. There is really very little support in these data for the notion that gang membership is generated by the strains of poverty and immigrant life. It is when we turn to the emotional climate of the family during childhood that problems begin to be evident.

Emotional Climate in the Family

Many of these families were not particularly happy, and in some cases they were acutely unhappy—at least in the reminiscences of these former gang members. Retrospective data about family relationships are tricky at best, and here we are dealing with men and women who may have been the family's "bad" boy or girl. Many still harbor unresolved feelings of bitterness toward their parents. However, whether the data we report here reflect the reality of family life or just the projections of unhappy men and women, these perceptions had an effect.

Relations between Parents

Our first set of questions asked about whether the parents were generally cheerful—or grouchy—and about how well the parents got along with each other. Slightly less than half of the men, but two-thirds of the women, said that their fathers were reasonably happy. (Ten percent said that they didn't know their fathers well enough to say.) Respondents from earlier and more recent cliques saw their fathers pretty much the same way. "Happy" fathers were not much discussed. Most of the descriptions of "grouchy" fathers (and even some of the "happy" ones) reflect both the pressures and insecurities of hard manual labor and also the Mexican masculine value of emotional reserve. Here are some of the men from earlier cliques talking about their parents:

> My father was worn down and grouchy. [How about your mother?] Just worn down.
>
> My father was more or less grouchy; that would fit him. My dad wouldn't say too

much, especially when he was sober. He was one of those persons that wouldn't say nothing. He'd say it all when he was drunk.... [How did your parents get along?] Well it all depended how things were going. If things were going all right, they'd get along good. If things were bad financially, there was problems.

My father was grouchy. [Why was that?] Ignorance [laugh]. Because you know at that time men were ignorant. They never played with us or they never took us out or they never sat down and talked to us....You know that—the father is always working. He comes home tired and he has no time for the kids. [I know, just work and come home; just provide. Try and provide and that's it, right?] That's it, just provide.

And some from recent cliques echo the same themes: One member said, "My father was pretty much for working and quiet. He wasn't—[You don't think he was grouchy? Or was he happy?] I'd say my dad was pretty much happy. He was—you know, he'd let my mother take care of the household." Another said, "My father was serious. He hardly ever showed any kind of emotion." A woman from a recent clique recalled her father with undisguised bitterness: "He was mean, selfish, tight. He didn't know anything about understanding the way he had us living.... When I was just 11, he used to come home and hit us when he would come home drunk. We were always afraid. [Did he ever beat up on your mother?] Yeah. I would say about four, five times a month. We would cry or try to defend her, fight back with my father."

A higher proportion of the respondents said that their mothers were happy—two-thirds of the men and 60% of the women, with no differences between respondents from earlier and more recent cliques. Again, the descriptions conform to traditional Mexican family role expectations, emphasizing the joys of motherhood and family security. An older man responded, "Oh, my mother was always happy. [Why was that?] Well, bringing us up, the family." A younger man commented, "My mother was happy. [Why was that?] Well my dad provided for her, you know. That was their main concern, you know." Another young man's response was "She was always happy. She was content to stay at home and look after our needs. For everything that we wanted she was always there."

Only about half of these men and women said that their parents got along well together. A fairly high proportion—especially in the recent cliques—saw their fathers beat their mothers occasionally. Twenty percent of the men and women in the earlier cliques witnessed such battery, as did a third of the men and 40% of the women from recent cliques.) Only a small minority experienced this as a routine feature of their home life. This older man's story is fairly typical:

Yeah, that happened—ah, once in a while. Sometimes when things were not going right for him, you know. It didn't happen every week, but it happened at least once a month. Like I say, he never talked too much, so I didn't know when things were right or when things were bad, but that's when he beat up, or tried to beat up on her, and that's when we knew that things weren't going right for him, you know. [What did you do during those times?] Well, as a youngster, I couldn't do too much, because my dad was a big man. [So you just walked out of the house?] Well, we had to sleep outside of the house, and, you know, stay away from him as much as possible.

This younger woman's parents had been divorced, and the violence occurred when the estranged father tried to come back: "He would usually come in the middle of the night because he was drunk and because he wanted to spend that time with us. My mom would throw him out and he would push her out of the way so he could enter the house. And that's when the fight would start. We would all jump in. We would pull them apart. It was like a nightmare all the time."

How did these people react when they saw their fathers beat their mothers? The two people just quoted represent the range: Almost two-thirds of the men and about half of the women withdrew in fear. More of the women (54 percent) tried to intervene, either to stop the battery or to fight the father themselves.

Much of the paternal violence—toward the kids as well as toward the mothers— appears to have been associated with heavy drinking. In more than 40% of these homes there was somebody that the respondent defined as an "alcoholic"—most often the father. The definition, of course, is not clinical, but seems to refer to a persistent pattern of heavy drinking, especially on weekends. The man just quoted describes his father's behavior when drunk and when sober:

Whenever he got drunk, which was, uh, you know, at least once a week, he was totally two persons, you know, one when he was sober and another person when he was drinking, you know. [In other words when he was sober, he would just let things ride?] Yeah, yeah. [And when he drank, it came back to him and he thought he had something to say?] Yeah, or he would say it, or he'd have the—not the energy, but the guts, like the guts, pues, you know, the drinking would give him the power. That's when he became the mean bad wolf in the house, you know....As a youngster I was very afraid of him, you know. He used to get real drunk and he would try to take it out on whoever was home, and usually I was at home as a youngster.

Relations with Parents

Whatever the source of paternal violence, more than half of these gang members were clearly afraid of their fathers when they were kids. For the boys, it was those in the earlier cliques, with more traditional parents, who were more likely to be afraid (66% as compared with 53% of the men from recent cliques). For the girls, women from earlier cliques were *less* likely to be afraid of their fathers (28% as compared with 68% of the women from more recent cliques).

Often there was good reason for fear: These were anything but ideal children. A man from an earlier clique and a man from a recent clique both describe much the same pattern. A third man from a recent clique experienced rather a bizarre punishment pattern.

> [Were you ever afraid of your father?] Oh yes, because anything that he had in his hand, you know where it went—straight at me. Oh yes, I was scared of that man.
>
> You know they used to really lay it on the line, you know what I mean. He says, "Hey, you blow it, you got to deal with me," you know what I mean. And take it to the fullest extent, you know. Ah man, one day I just took some money from him, and boy, man! And I smoked a cigarette, and ah, man, he made me smoke the whole carton, and it made me sick. He used to use an extension cord. He'd hit us with the closest thing to him. Whatever he could get his hands on. Extension cords, we had extension cords all over the house.
>
> I'd either be spanked or hit with one of those—what do you call them, *mimbrino* branches? [A switch?] Yeah. I'd be spanked and tied. [Spanked and tied?] They would put a chain on me. [Is that right?] Yeah. Outside in the driveway. They used to tie me up with a chain, to a tree. [How long would they keep you tied up?] Oh, an hour or two.

Mothers were almost as fear-inspiring. Girls were more likely to be afraid of their mothers than were boys (55% as compared with 42 percent). Even though many men said that they were afraid of their mothers, they expressed more ambivalence than fear about their mothers. A man from an earlier clique recalled his Mexican-born mother: "I was afraid of my mother. I had more respect for her in a way. I would say, uh, I didn't want to hurt her, but when I hurt—when I knew that I hurt her, I was afraid of her in a sense that I knew she was angry and that hurt me, and that made me afraid of her." Girls were often in real fear of physical violence, like this woman from an earlier clique: "She would hit me, pinch me, and pull my hair, and then she'd have my brother—the oldest one—get a whip, and whip me, and then I'd have stripes all over my body like a zebra, and then I went to school like that." A younger woman, age 26 at the time of the interview, reflected on her violent relationship with her mother, which was still unresolved when she was interviewed:

> Yeah, I was afraid. Because she used to beat me. But not no more. When I was 16 I got her, and I got her on the floor and I pulled her down and I cussed her and I said you never hit me again as long as I live. Never. And to this day she'll never raise a hand to me.... She would call me a whore, all kinds of bad names. I was gonna sleep

with men early. I was gonna get pregnant early. I was gonna work in a potato factory. I was gonna have my house dirty. I told her, "Yeah, come and see my house now!"

And another young woman had an even worse experience:

Yeah, she used to spank a lot, and then it got to where after a while she wasn't spanking, she was hitting, and I was just afraid of her. [?] Yeah, with the fist, and at times she threw things at me. One day she threw a Sparkletts water bottle and one time she hit me in the eye with it, or on the top of my head with a wine bottle, and it cracked my head open. Just various things like that. Even got to a point where at the age of 12 years old I tried to commit suicide because of the problems my mother was giving me.

Girls were generally much more restricted than boys—especially girls in the earlier cliques. We asked whether parents had been "strict or easy" and whether they really enforced the rules or "just let things ride." About 60% of the men said their parents were strict, and more than 80% said that they really did enforce the rules. Men from earlier cliques were no more likely than ones from more recent cliques to say that their parents had been strict. But 94% of the older women, and 72% of the younger ones said that their parents were strict, and almost all of the older women (though only half of the younger ones) said that their parents really enforced the rules. The limitations placed on girls sound like a litany of traditionalism, of parents trying to keep their daughters from being "bad" girls (compare the "good girl-bad girl" syndrome, described in Williams 1989). For example, the young woman just quoted talks about her father's attitude: "I couldn't even wear shorts. I always had to be covered up, because he would just start calling us—me and my sisters—that we were tramps. [How old were you then?] OK, you know, when I started developing—I was about 12, until I was 23. He never stopped until the day he died." A woman from an earlier clique recalled: "I could hardly go out. Cause when I went out I had to go with my brother. He had to take me or else I couldn't go anywhere. Then after we'd get to the dance we'd separate and then we'd get together and come home. I wouldn't be able to get out of the house. Period."

These kinds of restrictions were common among families of the younger women as well. One young woman came from a cholo family; her mother and stepfather were both heroin addicts, but they continued to impose traditional norms on their daughter: "I couldn't have a boyfriend, you know. I had to come home early, straight from school, cook, and you know. [Did they really enforce the rules?] Yeah, yes. We'd get ready for school and my mother and stepfather would say 'You better come straight home from school.' We couldn't watch TV; we couldn't go out with nobody." Recall that these women were teenagers in the 1970s. Here is another one. "I was about, let's see, about

15, 14, around there. I was always—I couldn't—they wouldn't let me go out. I mean I couldn't go to the store by myself, that's how strict they were. So I'd tell my mom I'm going to the store, just to the store and back, and she would make me take one of my brothers with me." Sometimes parental strictness escalated, in futile reaction to the girls' adventures on the streets with the gang boys, as this older woman described: "I got pregnant and she got stricter, beat me up. She called my brother to beat me up. He didn't know why he was hitting me, though, until after. He asked her and she said because I was pregnant. I was only 14. I've been on my own since I was 14. I had two kids by the age of 15."

A number of men reported a pattern of increased tolerance as they moved into adolescence. "Boys will be boys" seems to have been the attitude. This man from a recent clique was raised by his mother and his grandparents: "Ah, they let things ride. When I started ditching, getting drunk at maybe 12 or 13 they thought it was part of growing up. They didn't feel that by restricting me that I was gonna stop. My grandfather had been through that too with his son. [How about your mother?] Oh, she would hit me or ground me, but she couldn't control me. I was too wild for her to control me." A man from an earlier clique reflects the same kind of age-related pattern: "OK let's go back to when I was younger. We couldn't step out of the front yard. Ever since I can remember to the age of 9 years old, there's no way that we could go out that we weren't restricted.... Up until the age that I was about 13, and then everything went wrong [laugh]. Everything. No more paying attention; I'd get whipped [laugh]."

Incest

People who study or treat women drug addicts often speculate that their drug use might be a means of coping with the long-range psychological traumas of incest. It also seems plausible that if family problems in general drive children to increased reliance on their friends and on the gang, incest would be the most extreme family problem for girls. Accordingly, we asked our respondents, "Did anybody in your family ever make any sexual advances to you when you were growing up?"

Twenty-nine percent of the women reported that some member of the family did so. This figure does not differ too much from estimates of incestuous experiences in the society in general. Our interviewers reported that there were a fair number of respondents who answered the question "no," but who hesitated enough before they answered to give the impression that they were not telling the truth. Thus this 29% probably understates the actual occurrence of incest in this sample. (Three men also reported sexual advances, but none seemed to treat the incident as a problem.)

As one would expect from the greater traditionalism of families in the earlier cliques, incest was more common in the older women's families than in the younger women's (39% compared with 24% of the younger women), even though the difference is not statistically significant. However, incest was not more common in homes with Mexican-born or poorly educated fathers.

Incest is generally associated with patriarchy, and there are indications that the more patriarchal homes were in fact more likely to be incestuous. Fathers of incest victims were more likely to beat their wives, and they were more likely to be strict with and depreciatory of their daughters. Incest victims were also more likely to see their fathers as alcoholics, but they were not significantly more likely to feel that their fathers were trying to set themselves up unequivocally as heads of the household or to control their mothers' visitors—other indicators of patriarchy.

In most cases the assailant was the father, but uncles, brothers, and grandfathers were among the culprits. And the experiences occurred at all ages, ranging from 5 to 17, with a median age of about $11^{1/2}$. In about 40% of the cases, only one approach was made, but the remainder reported repeated sexual encounters. There were comparatively few long-term incestuous relationships like the ones described by these two women from earlier cliques, one of whom makes explicit reference to the gang as a refuge from an intolerable home situation:

> Yeah, my brother. I was 14 at the time, I think. [How long did it go on?] Ah, it went on a year, I think. And I didn't want—ah, I couldn't tell—ah, there was nobody to tell. My mother was never there and my father was always drunk. My sister had gotten married and left, and my other brother was too small. [?] He was 15. [?] Well, I would be asleep, and they would all get up and leave, you know, and like I was ditching school, and all that, you know. He would come and I'd wake up—and someone was staring at me, and it was him, over me on the couch, you know. And so, he'd attack me, you know, and I'd try to fight him, and, ah, the second time he did it I just—that's why I used to go to White Fence, see, and stay all the time.

> My grandfather, you know the things he did. He molested me. My dad, too. [Your dad, too, and he left you at a young age! How old were you when all this started?] I was like 7, or 6, and then with my dad I was like 9.... I had to keep all that to myself, you know, because I couldn't tell my grandma because that would hurt her, you know, so, ah, and I couldn't tell my father because he was doing the same thing, and then who could I tell, right? And then my, ah, my father's brother, too. I would sleep with my aunts. He would come to me when my aunts were asleep. And I don't know how he would wake me up, and he'd go like that, and I was afraid of him, right, and so I would have to go to him, you know, and he went all the way, too.... [How long did it go on with your grandfather?] Around four or five years. [And your dad?] About two years. [And the only times was when your father would babysit you? And your uncle only when he would come around?] Well, he lived there too, for a while. Ah, I think that went on for around a year and a half.

In both of these cases, the girl ultimately left the abusive home: the first girl ran away to live with her uncle and aunt and returned home only after her brother had been institutionalized, and the second girl went to live with her mother. Both households were highly traditional: the first girl, for example, was one of seventeen children, and the second girl's grandparents were very "Mexican." However, a note of family deviancy also enters: The second girl's father had been a gang member. Deviancy was specifically adduced by another woman in order to explain her father's behavior:

> Yeah, my father. When he came out of the joint. He must have been in his 40s. Well he went in when he was 28 and came out after 11 years. I was 12 then. It happened twice. [?] Dirty, I felt very dirty. [?] My mother at that time was sick and dying, and I couldn't tell my sisters, and I couldn't tell my brother. I couldn't tell nobody. [And it happened when he came out of the joint?] Yeah. [He was locked up so much—] Yeah, that's what I clean it up with too, that he done a lot of years, and he had just come out, and I was young, but I developed very early.

In a majority of cases, the girl told nobody about the approach and received no help. In a couple of instances, interviewers were the first to hear the story. Several women, like this older woman, mentioned the gang as a major source of support, and several fought back:

> [Did anybody in your family ever make sexual advances to you when you were growing up?] No, not in the family, but yes, my brother-in-law. [?] I was turning 11. He didn't get away with it though. [Did anybody help you with it?] No, I kept it all to myself, yeah, and he tried again when I was working, and I put him in his right-eous place. I told him, "You better cool it, because I'm gonna get after you." Which was me and my friends from the barrio. See I used to turn to my friends in the bar-rio [i.e., the gang], you know, for help a lot of times because I couldn't get it at home, you know.

Girls who effectively resisted were often those who had been approached by someone other than their fathers, like this older woman:

> I was 12 or maybe 13. [Who was that, your stepfather?] Yes. See I would feel that the covers would be coming off me and I thought I was dreaming, but once I caught him doing it to me. And another time was that I was going to take a bath and we had like wooden floors and I happened to look down and I seen a hole and an eye looking up, so I went to tell my mother and she went and threw water so he came up all wet. But I was like a tomboy, and I wouldn't let myself—or else if I would have been another type I would have been seduced. [So he never got—] No.

Running Away

Not surprisingly, given the restrictions placed on girls in general and the high incidence of incest, girls were notably more likely to have run away from home than boys. Almost a third of the boys ran away at least once, and boys from recent cliques were significantly more likely to have done so (38% compared with 20% of the boys from earlier cliques). By contrast, three-quarters of the girls ran away at least once, with no significant difference between girls from earlier and more recent cliques.

Sometimes the runaway incident was specifically related to incest. The girl just quoted, for example, ran away twice: "First time I was 16. I couldn't take it any more. My stepfather was getting to me. One time he tried to do something and I told him something so he got the belt and hit me and left me all marked up. So I had to get out of there." Other women ran from family assaults. This woman from an earlier clique found that running away was the only way that she could communicate with her mother:

I was about 13. I ran away because my brother—my older brother—used to come home drunk and he used to try and hit me all the time. And my mother wasn't there, and I had to jump out the window and go hide down my girlfriend's house. So I got tired, tired, and when I got a little older I just ran away, just stood down Timber's house [homegirl]. And then I'd tell my little brother where I was, and I'd tell him, "Don't tell my mother cause I'm gonna let her get scared, so when she gets scared that something happened to me then she'll do something about it." I'd tell her and I'd tell her and she wouldn't do nothing, so I ran away for two weeks, and then my mom was really scared and she did something about it. Otherwise I couldn't get nothing done.

A slight majority (58 percent) of the girls who ran away did so only once, but many did so repeatedly. A younger woman clearly preferred living on the streets to living at home:

First time I was 10. At that time I wasn't very—my family wasn't a very happy family, so I found happiness out in the streets more. They were sharing that free love, and all that. So I went out to get some. It was the fighting at home, I guess, that they used to have. They were always fighting. I felt I didn't want that because I wasn't part of it. From the age of 10 on I was running away. Till I married at 15. Usually when they would find me I would be getting busted for something or getting loaded somewhere so I'd end up in juvenile hall.

And another younger woman, who ran away a total of five times, explained: "I seen my mom. I seen what she was doing. She was always using [heroin], and there was always no food in the house, and they were constantly fighting, and everything, you know."

In several cases, girls could better to be said to have left home than to have run away.

I was 13. I couldn't take it no more, I just couldn't get along with my dad. [How long did you stay away?] When I ran away I only ran away two blocks, and I stayed two years. [?] Well, I lived with my aunt for two years. From there I moved with my mom because she wasn't living with my dad. She was already separated.

I ran away [from an abusive mother] when I was 12 until I was about 15 years old. [?] I never went back home with my mother, no. After I was 12 I ran away to my older sister's house, and she got guardianship of me. She was just wonderful to me. She just took the mother role.

Other Family Problems

Some researchers (see Werner 1983) suggest that stress is generated in a family when a member's problems begin to be a burden to the rest of the family. These families show a rather high incidence of such problems. I have mentioned "alcoholism." In addition, in a quarter of the men's homes and in 46% of the women's homes somebody was physically handicapped or chronically ill. Most often this was a parent. In 47% of the men's homes and 69% of the women's homes, some member died when the respondent was growing up. Most often this was a grandparent (in a third of the cases) but quite often it was a parent (a father in 30% of the homes and a mother in 11 percent) or a sibling (in 26% of the homes).

In addition to these traumas, which tended to involve older members of the household, siblings' deviance also generated family strains. Thus 20% of the men and 45% of the women grew up with a heroin addict in the home—most often a brother. And, finally, 57% of the men and 82% of the women saw somebody in their homes arrested when they were children. In 56% of these homes, it was a brother that was arrested. (The gender differences reflect the fact that gang girls were more likely than boys to have a gang-member brother at home.) In 28% of the homes, it was the respondent's father; these tended to be the cholo families. In 17% of the cases, respondents reported their own arrests during early adolescence. Even though most of these families seem reasonably conventional and hard-working, there seem to be a large number of families with troubles.

There are a couple of inferences that can be drawn from these rather dry statistics.

First, it is important to note that there are no statistically significant differences between earlier and more recent cliques in the incidence of these problems. We might have expected families in more recent times to have more problems, but that is clearly not the case.

The second point is that *clearly* more women than men came from troubled families. They were more likely to have been living with a chronically sick relative, one who died, one who was a heroin addict, or one who was arrested. In fact, a large majority of the women had a relative die or be arrested. This seems on the face of it to imply that the gang represents a different kind of peer-group outlet to its female members than to its male members, and that for girls it may in fact be more of a refuge from family problems, as some of the women quoted earlier say.

Conclusions

This review of family functioning has been guided by a literature that calls for a search for problems. In addition, we have tried to find whether problems might be greater or lesser among more recent gang cliques.

There is no doubt that we found problems, sometimes severe, in many of these families. But the findings do not cast much light on the broader question about how family problems affect gang membership. For example, we have no way of telling whether these families had more problems than their neighbors in the barrios. Further, the search for problems may itself be misleading: it assumes that there are just two kinds of families—good and bad. Most families, of course, are a mixture of the two. Thus many of our respondents were reared in highly conventional families in which they were the "black sheep," like this man from one of the recent cliques, who was asked how his folks reacted to the gang: "Negative because my family's never been in a gang. I'm the black sheep of my family. There aren't any relatives that are gang members. All my relatives are pretty successful in my family. They're always workers and never criminals." This was a "good" family that could not control one of its members. On the other extreme, there were clearly some "bad" families: Some were riddled with abusiveness; a few were headed by parents who themselves were cholos, and unable to order their own lives, let alone those of their children (see Chapter Seven of *Going Down to the Barrio* on "inheritance" of gang membership).

But what do we say about those in-between, mixed families? Striking a balance is difficult. Maladaptive parenting may affect one sibling more than another. Thus an incestuous father may deeply damage a girl—and send her directly to the gang—while her brother may emerge unscathed. And an overburdened parent may rear his or her first few children with effective controls but just "give up," as some of our respondents said, on the youngest children in the family. Some female-headed households may be extremely effective in controlling their children, while others, in essence, simply collapse (see Moore and Vigil 1987, for a typology of families).[5]

Nor is there any easy answer about an increase or decrease in family problems. Some problems—notably those that theory tells us might be associated with traditionalism and patriarchy—have declined. Thus fewer of the younger men were afraid of their fathers, and fewer of the younger women were incest victims. But other problems— those that might be associated with choloization—were more frequent among families of more recent clique members: There were more female-headed households among the recent clique members, there was more spousal battery, and the men (but not women) were more likely to have run away from home. And, allowing for a bit of anachronism, Thrasher's (1927) worries about immigrant families gain some support from these data. But again, one must be cautious. Girls were particularly likely to chafe under the pressures of traditional role restrictions, for example, but this was almost as common among Los Angeles-born parents, acting in the 1970s, as among the Mexican-born parents acting in the 1950s.

Perhaps the most significant finding is that there are so few differences between families in earlier and more recent cliques—apart from the obvious and expected differences in immigrant status, that is. There were problems in many of these families, but any notion that the passing generations either diminished or exacerbated such problems is generally not borne out by the data. Perhaps the strongest lesson is that then, as now, gang members come from troubled families.

What Happens to Girls in the Gang?

Joan W. Moore and John M. Hagedorn *

Anne Campbell (1984/1991) laid the groundwork for the study of gang women in her classic *The Girls in the Gang*. She argued convincingly that gang girls have rarely been studied as seriously as have gang boys. Instead, they have been stereotyped as promiscuous sex objects—segregated in "ladies' auxiliary" gangs—or as socially maladjusted tomboys, vainly trying to be "one of the boys." The stereotypes appeared in the social work literature and were also strongly embedded in much of the research literature.[1]

Both stereotypes—tomboy and slut—rest on the contrast between gang girls' behavior and that of "decent" girls. The implicit scenario is straight out of the 1950s— that adolescent girls who fail to conform to gender norms will jeopardize their futures. The premise is that marriage is the only serious career option for women and that improper behavior will alienate the kind of man who could be a good husband and provider. This is in sharp contrast with admonitions for boys. Even though gang membership also jeopardizes boys' futures, it's not because they are sexually promiscuous and fight but because they risk acquiring criminal records.

Most recent researchers on gang girls find that the stereotypes are greatly exaggerated. There is substantial variation both between gangs and within gangs in the ways in which girls behave, and girls are considerably more oriented to their gang girlfriends than the male-oriented early literature suggested. What, then, does happen to gang girls? How do their adult careers reflect the gang experience? Is the gang a temporary career diversion or a major turning point?

There is no single answer to these questions. One study showed that gang membership stigmatizes women on several levels and may seriously interfere with their later-life options—depending on how they come into and how they act in the gang, and on what kind of community they live in. Another study suggested that gang membership opens up opportunities for careers in drug dealing. Much of the answer depends on the time, the place, and the local culture of the community. And beyond this is the micro-culture of the particular gang and the initiative of the individual girl.

Time and Place: Variations in What Happens to Gang Girls
Levels of Labeling In Los Angeles

In an effort to understand the later lives of Los Angeles gang women, we analyzed interviews with random samples of 51 females and 106 male members of two long-standing Chicano gangs. All were adults when they were interviewed in 1986-1987. As teenagers,

* *Reprinted from C. Ronald Huff (Ed.),* Gangs in America. *Second Edition, pp. 204-18. Copyright © 1996 by Sage Publications, Inc. Reprinted by permission of Sage Publications.*

half had been active in the gangs in the 1950s and half in the 1970s.[2] The gangs were well established in very poor Mexican and Mexican American communities. Those communities, at that time, held very conservative values, particularly about how young women should behave. (See Moore 1991, and cf. Campbell 1990, for Latina gang members in New York; and Horowitz 1983, for Latinas in a Mexican community in Chicago).

Earlier we had found that gang members exhibited three major adult adaptations: (a) about 40% of the men and fewer of the women matured out of the gang into a "square" lifestyle; (b) more than a quarter of the men and fewer of the women became deeply involved with the lifestyle surrounding heroin—the climax drug in those communities at the time; and (c) the remainder followed an unstable, street-oriented lifestyle (Moore 1991, 125ff.). Although many gang girls did become "square" when they grew up, they were more likely than gang boys to fall into the third, street-oriented lifestyle—"just hanging out."

We were primarily interested in exploring the careers of women who had become at all involved with heroin. Forty-one percent of the gang women had used heroin at one time or another, as compared with 70% of the men. Whether or not they became addicted to the drug, any use of heroin represented extremely risky behavior for these women. We examined several points in their lives: their families of origin, their behavior in the gang, and their behavior in adulthood. It became evident that gang women who became involved with heroin had been largely confined to a street-oriented world throughout their lives. The gang was part and parcel of that life experience. (See Moore 1994, for details.)

To begin with, girls who joined the gangs tended to come from different kinds of families than boys. Because it was more acceptable for boys to be "out on the streets," boys were more likely to come from conventional working-class families, whereas girls were more likely to come from "underclass" families and also from abusive families. Thus, if we take running away from home as some measure of problems in the family, we find that almost a third of the gang boys ran away from home—but fully three quarters of the girls ran away at least once. To put it succinctly, there was a self-selection process in gang recruitment that revolved around gender.

This selectivity was exaggerated for girls who wound up using heroin. Their families were even unhappier and more violent than those of other female gang members. Family members made sexual advances to a third of the girls who became heroin users and more than a quarter of those who did not, whereas such experiences were almost unknown among men. Girls were also more likely to have alcoholic or heroin-using parents.[3]

"Bad" families—including the children—were stigmatized in these communities, and respectable families would not allow their children to play with such children. In addition, street-oriented families may have been more likely than conventional families to be permissive with their daughters and to provide street-oriented opportunities and role models (Giordano, Cernkovich, and Pugh 1978; Moore 1990). In effect, many of the girls may have been propelled by community and family dynamics to join a gang: this was a group that could sympathize with them, welcome them, and in some cases shelter them.

This initial selectivity is fateful, because membership in the heavily stigmatized gang further narrows a young woman's horizons and social opportunities, especially if she turns to heroin.[4] Traditional Mexican American gender norms tend to differentiate between "bad" and "good" girls, and *any* girl who joins a gang is defined as bad, no matter what her family is like. Labeling of boys in gangs is much less harsh.

Labeling happened even within the gang: Gang boys usually didn't consider themselves to be deviant just because they were in a gang, but many of them did consider the girls who joined a gang to be deviant. This was particularly true for the rowdier girls who fought, drank, or used drugs heavily. Not surprising, women who used heroin were more likely to have indulged in those behaviors. This meant that the more conventional boys wanted nothing to do with them and the girls were confined largely to the wilder boys in the gang—those who used heroin and often wound up in prison.

The experience in the gang was pivotal, channeling these girls' "deviant" careers ever more narrowly. The influence of the gang persisted into the heroin-using women's adult lives. Women heroin users were more likely to live with a male gang member at a very early age (16 or under), they were less likely to have been married formally, and they were less likely to work.

Milwaukee: Another Time, Other Ethnic Groups

In the early 1990s, we mounted a study of gangs in Milwaukee, Wisconsin, a large Rust-belt city that like many others in the East and Midwest began to experience serious gang problems in its inner-city neighborhoods as factory jobs faded from the scene.[5] We interviewed both African American and Latino (predominantly Puerto Rican) gang members—90 males and 64 females—when they were in their middle 20s. How did women's gang experiences relate to their later-life adaptations in Milwaukee? In many ways, they were very different from those of women in Los Angeles.

In contrast to the gangs in Los Angeles, which had long-standing, quasi-institutionalized traditions, the Milwaukee gangs were new. All of the men and women had been among the founding members of the gangs when they developed in the 1980s. The gangs adopted symbols and traditions from Chicago gangs (Hagedorn 1988), which were very meaningful for the men, but for the women members—especially the African Americans—had little relevance. This meant that for the women—but not for the men—the gang was almost completely an adolescent experience. None of the African American women were involved in any way with the gang as adults, and fewer than 10% of the Latinas had any involvement. Almost all of the African American members, male and female, had moved out of the gang's old neighborhood, whereas a third of the Latinas still lived in the old neighborhood and the rest lived nearby.

The fact that the women had no gang ties in adulthood doesn't mean that gang membership had been a casual matter to these women when they were teenagers. Like the gang women studied in Los Angeles, female gang members in Milwaukee generally came from more troubled families than male gang members, and sexual abuse was far more prevalent. Thus, for many, the gang represented an alternative family.

Ethnic differences between Latina and African American gangs were important. Drug use differed dramatically, largely for historical reasons. Cocaine, the climax drug in these gangs, had been prevalent in the Latino neighborhood five to ten years before it became popular in the African American neighborhoods, even though the neighborhoods were separated by only a mile. This meant that cocaine use was widespread among Latina gang members during their teens (with 89% using the drug), but nonexistent among the African Americans at the same age. In adulthood, though few were directly involved with the gang, a majority of the Latinas continued to use cocaine, and a third were reported to be heavy users. Cocaine use among African American women was much lower.

Drug dealing also differed. Many more of the Latinas (72% of the women and 81% of the men) than of the African Americans (31% of the women and 69% of the men) reportedly sold cocaine at some time in their lives. In at least one African American neighborhood two drug houses were run independently by women whose brothers or cousins were in the gang, and independent female-run drug houses were found elsewhere as well. At the time of the interview, however, none of the gang women was reported as supporting herself by selling drugs.

Several factors explain why Latinas were more active in the drug trade than African Americans. Of primary importance was the fact that the Latino drug markets were much more lucrative than the African American markets. Latino dealers served an affluent Anglo clientele from the adjacent downtown area, as well as a set of local customers, whereas most customers for African American dealers were also African American and many were from the local community (Hagedorn 1994). One Latina described the first male and the first female in her gang to sell drugs, and her account shows how the work was divided by gender:

> Bobby was the leader. Armida was a runner. She went places to go pick up large quantities. She'd go out of state for the dope and she'd bring it back. Yes, she was part of the group. She was a runner, a pick-up person.

At times, gang drug dealing led to severe sexual exploitation. One Latina explained that although the gang was a source of great support for her from a troubled family life, she was also ashamed of certain things. She nervously told the interviewer how she was offered to drug distributors to induce them to lower their wholesale price to a local gang dealer:

> He used me, to, you know... even thinking about it disgusts me, but it was, you know, I had to do it just to prove myself... [it was] prostitution... do extra favors, you know, starting the guys. You know, their drugs would be a lot cheaper [for the gang dealer].

Thus, comparing the Milwaukee women with the Los Angeles women suggests that ethnicity counts, but so do opportunities. For Latinas in both cities, gang membership tended to have a significant influence on their later lives, but for African American women in Milwaukee, the gang tended to be an episode. There is much less sense in Milwaukee that gang girls of any ethnicity were as heavily labeled in their community as were Chicana gang girls in Los Angeles. For Latinas in both cities, gangs tended more to be a family matter than they were for African Americans. In Milwaukee, Latinas tended to continue living in or near the gang neighborhood, cocaine tended to be more widely available, and there were better opportunities in drug marketing than there were for Latinas in Los Angeles or African Americans in Milwaukee.

Having Children: A Constant for Women

No matter what the cultural context, and no matter what the economic opportunity structure, there seems to be one constant in the later life of women in gangs. Most of them have children, and children have more effect on women's lives than on men's.

Gang men also have children, but for women the consequences are very much stronger. For women, but rarely for men, new responsibilities associated with child rearing may speed up the process of maturing out of the gang.

Part of this process has to do with reputation. Horowitz (1983) argues that a Chicana who has been labeled as "loose" has a chance to retrieve her reputation when she bears a child. If she becomes a "good mother," staying away from gang hangouts, her past is forgiven, but if she neglects her children and continues to hang out with her buddies, her bad reputation is simply confirmed. More important, perhaps, is that her relationship with her parents changes. Teenaged gang mothers usually find that they get more deeply involved with their parents, who may exert "ownership" rights over the children if they don't approve of their daughters' lifestyle (cf. Moore and Devitt 1989).

But childbearing also generates internalized identity changes. For example, when we asked Mexican American gang members in Los Angeles what had been the major turning points in their lives, the differences between males and females were striking. In their teens, the most significant turning points for males usually had something to do with the gang, with drugs, and with being arrested and going to jail—all "tough-guy" stuff. For females, the significant turning points had to do with marriage and childbearing, with parents, and—a distant third—drugs.

Most of these women were primarily responsible for raising their children, often on their own, without the help of either stable husbands or their parents. Only a minority of the men, by contrast, raised their own children. (Differences between males and females are shown in Table 1.) Furthermore, because of the handicaps that gang girls in these communities faced in the marriage market, they were more likely to be encumbered with an alcoholic or heroin-using spouse. On the positive side, women with children have been able to secure income through the welfare system, and this source of income has helped keep many of them from extensive involvement in drug selling. Drug dealing is a dangerous business with an ever-present hazard of prison. Women may be less willing to risk the violence or the chance of being separated from—or losing—their children through incarceration.

The Careers of Female Addicts

Gang members usually use a wide variety of drugs, in addition to alcohol. Heroin and cocaine are "climax" drugs—the "hard" drugs—which take a greater toll on their users. What are the lives of heroin- and cocaine-using gang women like?

The Los Angeles Chicana heroin addicts who were active a generation ago tended to take one of three routes (Moore 1990). More than a third (39%) became "street people," completely and degradingly immersed in the heroin lifestyle. As one woman put it,

> We were, like, in a separate group of people. We were using, ripping, running. People didn't let us go in their houses that knew us…. My family… I was considered like dead to them…. My friends… they didn't consider me like a human being any more.

Table 1
Who Raised Your Children?
Gang Women and Gang Men in Los Angeles

	Female	Male
Respondent alone	50 %	2 %
Respondent with spouse	23	38
Respondent and other relative	12	2
"The children's mothers"	n/a	50
Other relative	15	7
Total N (= 100%)	(48) *	(86) *

Note: *These numbers include only those gang members with children. In the total sample of gang members, 94% of the women and 84% of the men had children.

More of the women—approximately half—were less intensely involved with the street lifestyle. They tended to alternate between dependence on a man—for their heroin supply and for protection, as well as for daily sustenance—or on their gang homeboys and homegirls. Some were able to conceal their addiction from their parents, and many were able to avoid involvement with the police; they were sheltered, at home.

A much smaller proportion of the women—perhaps 10%—fell into a third category. They grew up in families that were established in the drug trade. These women had much less stressful access to heroin, because they got it through family-member dealers, and they tended to be more restrained in their heroin use. They were less likely to become hog-wild addicts. Ironically, even though their families may have introduced them to this dangerous drug in the first place, their families had also given them a head start in coping with some of the most serious dangers of heroin.

The introduction of crack cocaine in the 1980s has often been portrayed in the media as leading to the ultimate in women's degradation. "Crack whores," trading sex for drugs, mothers deserting their children for cocaine—all of these are part of the new stereotype about women and drugs that echoes the old "slut" stereotype of the past. We found no support for this stereotype. Although male gang members in Milwaukee talked about the ease with which drug house workers could exchange cocaine for sex, nearly every female gang member we interviewed was indignant when we asked her whether she had "dope dated." Gang women in Milwaukee were not the primary customers of gang drug dealers and were not selling themselves for crack. Thus, they did not match the stereotype of the crack whore, nor were they regularly involved in prostitution.

Getting Into Dealing

Drug dealing is probably the most important illicit income-generating activity of male gang members. (Some also become sporadically involved in robberies or property crimes, but few rely on such work for a steady source of income in the way they rely on drug dealing.) Drug dealing, as a group enterprise, has been assumed to be particularly easy for gang members because the gang already provides established networks with proven mutual loyalty, willingness to use violence, and a degree of secrecy (Padilla 1992; Steffensmeier 1983).

Is that also true for gang women? After all (unlike many conventional girls), they have the same kind of opportunities as gang boys to establish reputations in networks that would "qualify" them for more responsible roles. Many of them fight, stand up for the gang, and form intense loyalties to the gang as a whole. Some have argued that the intense sexism of the male underworld severely limits women's chances to rise above very narrow roles that emphasize their gender (Steffensmeier 1983). Miller (1973) found that gang girls knew "their place," "actively" sought dependency on a male, and, moreover, that they "gloried in it" (p. 35). They were accomplices in their own dependency, and this accommodation may make the whole system of male domination work more smoothly.

It would thus seem that gang women's chances for a career in dealing drugs are limited by the intragang labeling of women and their reactions to it. Some data from Los Angeles corroborate this view. Even though almost half of a sample of Chicana heroin addicts "had the bag" (i.e., did some heroin dealing) at some time during their careers in the 1970s, most of these women were "employees," rather than entrepreneurs.[6] Only a small minority (perhaps 10%) were career dealers. But not every woman accepted a subordinate status—even then (Moore and Mata 1981).[7]

Several authors argue that times have changed since the 1970s. Carl Taylor (1993), studying African American women in Detroit in the 1990s, asserted that "females have moved beyond the status quo of gender repression" (118), and he went on to describe women's penetration into drug-dealing "corporate" gangs, some of which are independent of male domination altogether. Lauderback and his colleagues in San Francisco found that although in the late 1980s Latina gang members played a wide range of roles, very similar to those found in Los Angeles among Chicanas in the 1970s, at least one gang of African American women, resentful because they were not getting enough of the profits, had broken away from male-dominated selling activities altogether. Their gang was completely independent, operating out of several crack houses (Lauderback, Hanson, and Waldorf 1992).

We have presented ample evidence from Milwaukee that gender repression has not disappeared, however. In all studies comparing male and female gangs, the level of women's dealing is reported as being lower than that of the men. The Milwaukee data show how much women's participation in drug dealing depends on opportunities (which were much greater for Latinas than for African American gang women), but also how much gender norms continue to shape most women's participation. Times may have changed, but gender exploitation persists. Cities may vary, and in each city, there are exceptional women who attain independent status as drug dealers of substance. But the norm is for a lower level of dealing, and for a general pattern of subordination to men.

Conclusion

In this chapter, we have focused on the variety of ways in which girls in gangs grow up in different ethnic communities and at different times. At the beginning, we asked whether the experience in the gang is a major turning point. What happens to girls in the gang does depend on time, place, ethnicity, the local culture, and economic opportunities. But girls who get into gangs are even more likely than gang boys to come from families in trouble, and this means that joining a gang does not necessarily result in their lives taking a sharp U-turn for the worse: They are not leaving the Brady Bunch for the Hell's Angels. Nonetheless, for most women, being in a gang does have a real impact on later life.

What about differences in time and place? What, in particular, has changed? Most of the changes occurred at the level of the broader society.

Changes Over Time and Place. First, and perhaps most important, the 1950s scenario that held out marriage and family as the ultimate ideals is much more difficult to obtain. Most gangs live in the nation's inner cities. The economies of these communities have been seriously damaged in the past generation. Even when a city has generally recovered from the crisis of deindustrialization, inner cities often continue to suffer critically high unemployment rates.

This means that most young males no longer have much of a future to look forward to, and it is much more difficult for women in most gang neighborhoods to look forward to marriage as a predictable aspect of their future. For example, Robin Jarett (1994) cites one young African American woman in Chicago who sadly commented that marriage has become "a little white girl's dream." And in Milwaukee, a young Latina, marginal to a gang, in 1995 expressed the problem when she said she really wanted "a good husband." But then she added, "'Course if they are like the rest of these jerks right now, well I don't want one. I'll take care of myself and my kids" (Thomsen 1996).

Second, there have been changes in gender ideologies corresponding to changes in opportunities for men and for women. Young women like the ones just quoted are now considerably more likely to see themselves as potentially independent, and young men's attitudes have also changed. In poorer neighborhoods, young males are likely to take on what Majors and Billson (1992) call the "cool pose," a facade of aloofness and control, which "counters the... damaged pride [and] shattered confidence... that come from living on the edge of society" (p. 8). The cool pose inhibits the formation of nurturant relationships with women and children. As those who listen to some rap music know, it can be very disparaging of women.

Third, the economy of many inner-city communities has become informalized, with a heavy illicit component. In Milwaukee's gang neighborhoods we found a drug-dealing business operating in virtually every other block of gang neighborhoods. The drug economy is much more important in the 1990s than it was in the 1970s, and immeasurably more important than in the 1950s.

There are also differences by place. Special traditions and patterns develop in particular communities. Los Angeles gangs will never be quite like those in Detroit or Milwaukee. The gang traditions are different and the cities are different in too many ways to be reduced to a few pat statements.

Difference by Ethnicity. In addition to changes over time, there are clearly differences between ethnic communities, largely having to do with the expected role of females. Women in Latino—especially Mexican American—communities are subject to more traditional expectations than those in African American communities, where for generations more women have been forced to assume independent roles, both economically and in the family. For example, when we asked Milwaukee gang women what they thought of the following statement: "The way men are today, I'd rather raise my kids by myself," we found sharp ethnic differences. Seventy-five percent of the African American but only 43% of the Latina gang members in Milwaukee agreed with that sentiment. In a similar vein, 29% of the Latinas—but *none* of the African Americans—believed that "All a woman needs to straighten out her life is to find a good man." And two thirds of the African American women thought that women should have as much sexual freedom as men, whereas only 39% of the Latinas agreed.

Both in Los Angeles and in Milwaukee, we found that when women were asked to assess their gang experiences, they were more negative than the men, but there were interesting ethnic differences, as well. When we asked what they thought of the statement that "Gangs are not all bad," we found that 8% of the African Americans *dis*agreed—meaning that they thoroughly rejected the thought that there was any good in gangs. A much larger proportion of Latinas—57%—disagreed. This supports the notion that, at least in Milwaukee, the gang may well have more long-range effects on Latinas than on African American women.

Unfortunately, the future prospects for women at the bottom of the economic heap are not very promising. Gangs have been proliferating throughout the country, accurately reflecting a declining economy and a growing sense in many inner-city communities that there is no worthwhile future for most adolescents. More young women may now be involved in gangs than at any time in the past. Programs directed at gangs rarely consider the special needs of female members, and the media continue to be fascinated by these women's sexual experiences and to perpetuate the myth of the "new violence" of women's gangs. Ironically, the most important influence on gang women's future may be the dismantling of the nation's welfare system in the 1990s. This system has supported women with children who want to stay out of the drug marketing system and in addition has provided a significant amount of cash to their communities.[8] Its disappearance will deepen poverty and make the fate of gang women ever more problematic.

Female Gangs: An Historical Perspective

*by Carl S. Taylor**

Research regarding African American female involvement in gangs has been very limited. While there have been numerous works on their participation in the criminal justice system, there is nothing of great length or substance on the subject of their role as gang members. Historically, female involvement in gangs and other criminal activities has been defined as subordinate and secondary to their male counterparts. The illegal activity of females was limited to a set of preconceived crimes, with a distinct concept of what females did and did not do.

There are studies that theorize about the female participation in crime. *The Class Structure of Gender and Delinquent Behavior: Toward a Power Control Theory of Common Delinquent Behavior* examined the social basis of gender-delinquency. This theory rejects the contention that gender is a factor in delinquency.[1] Anne Campbell underlined this notion as one of several myths in female gang research.[2] The power control theory implies that gender is of reduced importance as class is factored into juvenile delinquency.[3] However, some researchers argue that traditional models, such as the power control theory, are not sufficient for examining female crime or delinquency because they ignore gender as a major factor.[4]

In 1977, W. K. Brown did research on an autonomous, female African American gang in Philadelphia.[5] Research to date speaks of females participating in gang activity within one of two roles. One identifies them in sexual terms as the "girlfriend" of a male gang member. The other as "tomboys"—rough women or girls displaying unfeminine characteristics who are seldom accepted by other women.

Yet, in a recent study of African American gangs by John Hagedorn, researchers found the same traditional relationship between female and male gangs. The female gangs, with related names, existed only because of male gangs.[6] Professor C. Ron Huff found several female gangs during a late 1980s study of Cleveland and Columbus, Ohio. These female gangs, however, were similar to what Hagedorn found from his work in Milwaukee. These females actually were similar to groupies whose identity was closely tied to that of their male gang allies.[7]

The 1927 classic study of Chicago gangs by researcher Frederic Thrasher underlined these gender roles in his text, *The Gang*.[8] The underlying assertion of Thrasher's study was that female gangs existed only in association with some type of male gang. In 1943, another researcher, W. F. Whyte, supported Thrasher's findings, suggesting that the formation of female adjuncts/gangs was based solely on the notion of females as sex objects.[9] It should be noted however that both Thrasher's and Whyte's findings were

*Reprinted by permission from Girls, Gangs, Women, and Drugs, by Carl S. Taylor *(East Lansing: Michigan State University Press, 1993).*

derived almost exclusively from the male gang members' points of view. This kind of approach has given the research community limited and often erroneous data.[10] The structure of female gangs, aside from an auxiliary relationship with male gangs, has rarely been observed directly. The defining characteristics of female African American gangs are often blurred when interwoven with those of the more visible gangs.

In response, some female researchers have presented arguments for a more comprehensive perspective on female gang research. Anne Campbell presented a balanced study of female gang life in her 1984 work *The Girls in the Gang: A Report from New York City*. Campbell showed that there is a great need for future research in the area of female gang study. As far back as the 1800s, Campbell points out serious flaws in the historical perspective of female gang evolution and in the preconceived notions of females and females in gangs.[11]

According to Agnes Baro, a criminal justices professor at Grand Valley State University:

> We know very little about African American female gangs or about female criminality in general… much of what we do know comes from a suspect knowledge base not just because it was developed with considerable male bias but also because so much of it lacks reference to the actual feelings, socioeconomic circumstances, or daily lives of the women who were studied. The task then is one of gleaning as much as we can from older and mainly ethnographic studies before we construct a new and, hopefully, more accurate perspective.

Criminologist Georgette Bennett, in her book *Crime Warps*, addresses the issue of females and crime. In the chapter "Women Alone," Bennett focuses on what she calls the "feminization of poverty," and the fact is that women, in particular African American women, will head single-parent families in the 1990s at alarming rates.[12] Detroit is one of the cities in America that has an extremely high number of families that are not only headed by females but are also living below the poverty line. The national median income for all female-headed families is between one-third and one-half of the income for all other family arrangements. For African American and Hispanic female-headed families alone, the median income is $2,000 below the poverty line.[13] By 1980, more than 80% of African American families in Detroit, with incomes below $4,000, were headed by single women.[14] The economic realities of Detroit are representative of other rustbelt cities in the Midwest.

Deborah Prothrow-Stith, in her provocative book, *Deadly Consequence*, explains how violence is plaguing the lives of women, men, and youth.[15] While her text addresses young adult violence, it also sheds light on the impact of violence, crime, and drugs. Females, children, and families are suffering severely from these social ills—and this is not unique to Detroit. Her book discusses how violence is intertwined with substance abuse, child abuse, and overall the role of brutality in destroying neighborhoods and communities.

The research thus far on female crime has had mixed results—from theories that support gender as a determinant—to theories that support race as a determinant.[16] One of the more relevant studies pertaining to the study of female gangs was conducted by researcher Darrell J. Steffensmejer. His 1983 work found that the structural and operational properties of crime groups affect the degree and existence of sex-segregated criminal organizations. Some females revealed a traditional, auxiliary relationship with male gangs.[17] One female gang supported recent research, showing females in autonomous gangs involved in organized criminal activities.[18] As our study discloses, a new attitude of female criminal independence is emerging. The male-female gang relationship is also being altered.

Female gang members and non-members are beginning to display attitudes that are diametrically opposed to earlier theories about female participation in gangs.[19] The social structure and economic plight of Detroit and other cities play a significant part in shaping female roles and attitudes presented in this book. As previously discussed, the infrastructure of the inner city has produced many single, female-headed families that are prime candidates for being dysfunctional, largely because of their poverty and isolation.[20] These families are part of a continuous chain of poverty that has produced fourth and fifth generation welfare families.[21]

L. T. Fishman, who studied an African American female gang in Chicago during the 1960s, asserted that there were profound changes in the type of female gangs in Chicago and in the crimes that their members committed.[22] Fishman maintained that "black female gangs today have become more entrenched, more violent, and more and more oriented to 'male' crime." Like other criminologists, Fishman rejected the "women's liberation hypothesis" as a satisfactory explanation of the changes she has observed. Instead, Fishman referred to a "forced 'emancipation'" that stems from economic crisis within the black community."

Our study of Detroit also includes serious consideration of the deterioration of an inner city's economy and the impact that such a situation can have on the opportunities, circumstances, and values of young African American women. Thus, although there is agreement that much of the earlier research on females and gangs has suffered from a male bias, it is also clear that some of it may have been relevant at the time it was written.

Inner City Detroit

In 1920, Michigan had the largest membership of the Ku Klux Klan in the United States, by 1924, 32,000 men were in Detroit.[23] Detroit's growing automobile industry and Henry Ford's five-dollar-a-day wage lured southern whites and blacks northward in droves; the climate was fertile for the Klan. In 1924, the mayor of Detroit was elected with the full support of the KKK.[24] There were countless acts of terrorism during the twenties, including the burning of crosses and intimidation of blacks, Jews, and

Catholics. The Klan as a gang was violent, oppressive, and omnipresent in Detroit. By the 1930s, the infamous Black Legion, another version of the Klan, was responsible for fifty murders in Michigan.[25] Subsequently, the KKK has been implicated in race riots and in fomenting problems between ethnic groups in the central city.[26] The role of women within the Klan structure has never really been researched.[27]

In June 1943, Detroit had the worst race riot in the history of this nation to date. The segregation of Detroit at that time kept blacks in certain areas almost exclusively, while Detroit's other ethnic groups, the Irish, Jews, Italians, Sicilians, and Hungarians, were spread throughout the city. White gangs roamed Detroit; black gangs, on the defensive, fought back. The Detroit Police were slow in restoring peace; and, worse, some blacks felt that the white police (known as confederates of the Klan) were more than accommodating to the white gangs during their offensive into the black neighborhoods.[28] The white gangs were from local neighborhoods and, in some cases, joined their white ethnic rivals to form confederations which attacked the black community at large.[29] Regarding gangs during the race riot, it is unclear if these gangs formed only for the riot; that is, a group of neighborhood residents not usually in any gang that collected themselves to protect the race or neighborhood from the enemy. The distinction between gang and mob is vague. The same is true for female involvement. Definitions hamper any study of clear-cut roles of females in Detroit gangs at this time. Detroit was extremely rough for black females. There is no suggestion that females did not participate in the violence of the black or white gangs during the 1943 Race Riot nor that they did.[30]

In the early 1940s there were African American gangs in the section of town known as Black Bottom, on the Eastside of Detroit. These gangs were formed in much the same way as those Thrasher reported on in Chicago and were divided into compatriot and delinquent gangs. There were no specific commercial or territorial gangs within the black experience at that time.

Segregation kept black gangs in the black ghetto, paralleling other ethnic gangs in the early 1940s.[31] Another factor in shaping the nature of gangs was the presence of a black police officer, Ben Turpin, a detective who ruled Black Bottom. Earl Van Dyke, a renowned Motown Musician, grew up in Black Bottom. Van Dyke attested to the power that Turpin demanded and received from the black community.

> Everyone in Black Bottom knew Mr. Ben was the man in charge. He simply didn't take nothing off the blacks or whites. You had your young gangs, but these young boys knew how far they could go, and with Mr. Ben that wasn't very far. Girls? Gangs? Naw, the neighborhood had boys, and some were bad and some were just young boys growing up with their neighborhood buddies. But, you got to remember, the community kept girls under a watchful eye. Unless you were messing with some fast girls, girls had to follow a strict order from families, and the church was

right there. Mr. Ben was real sensitive about young girls, he didn't tolerate no messing with young girls, he wouldn't let no pimp or no man ever beat any woman in his neighborhood. Now, don't think some fool wouldn't try it, maybe he was drunk or went crazy for a bit. But, you could rest assured that Mr. Ben would make him real sorry.

Ben Turpin was the law in Black Bottom. He loved kids, you hear all this talk about him being so tough, and he was tough. But this man would let kids come to his house and feed them, pay for their baseball team, his wife would cook a full Sunday dinner of turkey with oyster dressing, every Sunday he would have kids, poor kids eat at his house. There was two sides to Mr. Ben, you wanted to stay on his good side. He took the second floor of his home for young kids, put in a ping pong table. I know because I lived around the block from him, he lived on Jay Street.

There was serious drug use by black youth in Black Bottom. Van Dyke spoke of the gangs in the neighborhood prior to the 1943 riot. The Feather Merchants and The Bar Twenties were two Black Bottom gangs.

I can remember young fellas in the neighborhood on heroin as young as 14 years old; when the fellas couldn't get horse [heroin] they would go to the local drugstore and purchase paregoric and mix it with benzene and get high. If they couldn't get that they would get a fifth of gin and get high. You had your little gangs that never got in any trouble because they were just buddies, pals, kids that grew up together and did kid things, nothing to it. But, you didn't see no girls in those kinda street gangs, that was just fellas hanging out on Hasting in the early '40s.

Hastings Street was a rough place for young kids to play. There were problems, however; youths involved in drugs and delinquency were a minority. For females, as Van Dyke said, it was taboo to be out at night or at spots such as the famed Flame nightclub. It was easy for a young girl to get a bad reputation. The only women in the night life were those dating men in entertainment or illicit professions and party-goers. The position for black females was clearly defined in the 1940s. This does not mean that there were no female gangs; it simply means they were not very important.

A former doorman at one of the nightclubs in downtown Detroit talked about the women who were fancy-free and who ran with the Purple Gang.[32]

These gals were having a ball, living high on the hog in those days. You didn't see no women folks driving no big Caddies unless they were married to some doctor, Duke Ellington or Walter Briggs. Women in those days didn't have a lot of choices as to what they could do. The gangster girlfriend could live real good. But they were ladies and they didn't have nothing to do with the crime stuff. Nope, they just spent the money in those days. Ladies were ladies and they didn't talk trashy like women today. Now, mind you, girls who gambled or drank with men, they talked like sailors, but those women were not like regular women, like your wife, or mother. The only women criminals I knew were the ones that worked for pimps, the ones that boosted, sold their bodies for money, or women who worked the flim flam. In the club you see everything, maybe they weren't gangsters but some of them gals were more than just some floozies. The problem is that in those days, you didn't think of women as being able to be tough guys, you didn't think about women like that... tough women, tough maybe like Mae West, tough and sexy. But, tough like killing people, naw, it never crossed my mind.

Detroit was growing and ethnic diversity began to penetrate the suburbs. There were gangs in most neighborhoods in Detroit. The distinguishing factor was if the gang was criminal or compatriot. Compatriot gangs were not involved in criminal behavior. Good-natured pranks might result in scoldings from those in social control, but these gangs were not considered menaces to the community. Many in the neighborhood did not even regard these compatriot gangs as real gangs. The delinquent gang, however, was considered a problem. There were delinquent gangs in the general Detroit area by the 1980s. In fact, there were problems with black delinquent gangs in the 1940s before the riot of 1943.[33] Young white gangs were on the offensive during the race riot of 1943. Delinquent gangs made their presence felt in the late 1940s; in the 1950s there were Italian, Hispanic, Polish, and other ethnic gangs, but they stayed in their territorial neighborhoods. While there were problems with the various gangs, the police and other social controls dealt with them.

The historical role of female gangs in Detroit is identical to other cities in large urban centers. The first visible signs of females in gangs could be seen in the 1950s. Women and girls were involved from the very outset in the early days of boomtown Detroit. In the 1950s, the infamous African American male gang, the Shakers, had the traditional auxiliary female gang found by Campbell in her research on early New York. Without The Shakers, there were no Shakerettes. Francine Norton, a former Shakerette, shared her views:

Girls were the sister gang. Without boys there wasn't anything. Our lives were involved with these bad boys. We got reputations in the neighborhood 'cause we were fast girls. Lots of girls were so scared to get a reputation in those days because it was so easy to become a bad girl or boy. If you kept the wrong company, you were labeled real quick. The fast girls would skip school, smoke cigarettes, curse like the Shakers, and have sex. The good girls didn't skip school, curse, and they went to Cass [High School] if they could. Me and most of the girls in the gang lived in the projects.

If you were with the boys, bad boys, it was just the thing to do on my street. Being with the Shakers was big time. Today, the Shakers would probably be into selling dope like everybody else. My sons are in the streets and it's really hard. I have three girls and the only thing they talk 'bout is the boys who got money. In my day it was pimps, but today it's these dope boys who get all the attention.

The Shakers had a fierce reputation for fighting. Their reputation, like that of other Eastside gangs, was city-wide. Linda J. Folmar, a public relations executive, spoke of her memories growing up as a young woman on the Westside of Detroit in the 1950s.

Everybody knew about the Shakers, and their sister gang, the Shakerettes. As a student at Central High, I can recall how they had been known to invade the school grounds to fight… football games were a favorite of theirs to show up at and beat up someone. Even the tough girls at our school didn't want any part of the Shakerettes. This gang was definitely from the lower class of the city. The middle class kids had their own gangs, they called them clubs, or organizations. But the reality was we had the Gamma Petites, and lower class kids had the Shakers. We didn't fight, because we had nothing to fight about. Middle class and upper middle class kids were happy with the things they had in Detroit. Our gangs were giving dances, and entering into debutante balls. Our parents were teaching us about society, going to college and those sorta things.

The class distinction that Folmar mentions is important. Women in gangs would fight over boys, or to support their brother gang. The activities of female gangs in Detroit in the 1950s were not much different than gang activities in earlier days and other cities. Laura Thaks, 48, and Mary Thaks, 44, former members of the Shakerettes, addressed their gang days.

Well, it's really lots different today, you can't compare our gangs with these young jits today. In the Shakerettes we knew the gang boys as brothers, boyfriends, cousins, friends, before the gang. Were we sexually active? Yeah, some girls were with the boys in the gangs, others had boyfriends outside of the Shakers. See, girls in a way belong to the gang, we all hung out together or knew everybody from your street. The gang, as far as the girls, was our own thing under the boys. We carry things for 'em… things like cigarettes, weapons, wine, or when they stole something and we had to walk or go a long way and they think they might get caught, we would carry or hide their things. We just help any way the boys would need us. Now, sometimes girls would fight each other over boyfriends, that happened a lot. Me and Mary would always stick together, no matter what. My first child was by one of the Shakers, he never gave me shit for the little crumb snatcher. But, back then I was in love, so I got pregnant by this bum. Lots of us got messed over by the Shakers, lots of fights with our gang were over Shakers. When the boys would fight, we usually go for the hell of it, we find somebody to scare, we didn't care if they was a boy or girl. I couldn't fight a lot cause I was expecting my first child. Once you had a baby your whole life changed in a way. My mother was mad as hell at me for getting pregnant. But girls in the gang was my real family. Me and Mary would just love to skip school and hang out.

Do I think we were paid much attention as a gang? Not like the boys, we would do all kinds of shit and the boys would get all the blame. Shakerettes could beat lots of boys' ass, but all you really ever heard about was the Shakers. The police didn't bother with us like they did the boys. When they thought the Shakers did something you'd know cause they come looking for us first. Now, we would be laughing 'bout how dumb the cops would be asking us shit 'bout the boys, like we would tell 'em. We be doing lots of the same shit as the Shakers, nobody even thought we could do the same shit [laughing, they both agreed that they at least tried to do the same things that the Shakers did, maybe after no one was around]… but, now, the boys in the Shakers would get real mad if they saw us getting all the attention. We were the same as the Shakers, we got drunk, smoked, had sex, and would kick your ass if needed and that's the truth… but nobody paid us no mind. Girls would sometimes kick the shit out of another girl and maybe somebody like their momma or something would call the police. That would get taken care of, but it wasn't the same as the Shakers. But the main reason I joined the Shakerettes was 'cause my cousin, it was five boys, they was all Shakers. That's who we were with all the time, they was our boys and we was their girls. That's the way most of the gangs I remember used to be, if you live in the neighborhood, went to school and grew up with those people, then you usually stay with 'em. If you jumped one, you had better get ready, 'cause we all was gonna jump you… we stuck together, no matter what.

Dennis Payne, a criminal justice professor at Michigan State University, remembers his Detroit childhood in a neighborhood where youth gangs prevailed. Females in the area were considered the property of the territorial gang. "The guys in those neighborhoods didn't want outsiders dating or socializing with their girls… the girls were their property, even if they didn't personally have any relationship with the young women."

The Shakers were in the scavenger gang mode; simply a group of young toughs on the Eastside of Detroit. The role and name of their female counterpart gang is similar to those seen in other urban environments. Anne Campbell points out that female gangs in early New York carried names complementary to the names of their male counterpart gang.[34]

If a male gang had street notoriety, more than likely there would be a sister gang. One consequence of this was the labeling of young females within the black community. Traditionally there were the good girls and the bad girls. These labels were considered serious; and because of segregation, the black middle class had emerged as the powerful class within the black community. The black church was the cornerstone of socialization for black residents. Mary Smith, 80, moved to Detroit at the age of ten. Ms. Smith spoke of how black females were labeled in the 1950s.

> Just a different time, folks knew everyone, and everyone went to church. If you didn't go to church on Sunday, well you were labeled as a worthless kinda person. The church was where all the children went to have fun, besides learning 'bout God. There were always picnics, social programs, the choir, you just stayed in church all day...girls that didn't go to church, I don't remember that many. The same was true for boys, children that didn't go to church, I don't remember seeing that many, if any, really. But if you talking 'bout bad girls, fast girls and boys, well er, if you got known as a bad boy or, it was worse for girls, it meant you was not with the other folks, regular folks. Bad girls were treated different from other girls, folks. There were certain things bad girls would wear, say, or just do and that would make them different, and that was bad. Now don't get me wrong, childrens would be with fast kids, I would when I was a child, and my children would also. But, you better not get caught, specially on Sunday you stayed away from those folks 'cause you know they was trouble. Especially for girls, if you got pregnant back then it was the end. Girls just went away. If you got yourself pregnant back then you had better get married. If you didn't get married you were known as that fast hussy; yes it was different in those days. I can't say I remember no girl gangs in our neighborhood, but you sure knew the bad girls and boys.

Good paying jobs in the auto industry provided a certain economic power base for the segregated black community. The middle class that emerged was a direct result of black professionals providing services to blacks who had money that segregated white Detroit would not accept. It was this middle class that shaped its social image into a proud, bourgeois, elitist, caste system. Ted Smith, a lifelong resident, spoke of elitism.

> Without any question there was a caste system. Blacks were very aware of their own presence and worth. Doctors, lawyers, store owners, some were elitist thinking, yet they were connected to the community. A strong community sense of order regulated the members in those days. It was how one went about life in those days. Whites would frequent the same clubs also. During the day, people were very conscious of where they went and who they did it with... without question there were night life people who didn't see the world in the daytime. There was mutual understanding between people in the fast lane and everyday citizens. The church people

controlled the community in the day. The sporting life, the fast lane, controlled the night life in the city. Somewhere in between good girls knew where not to be on Friday and Saturday nights. Young men in the fast lane, young gangs of toughs had their female companions. Now, if they were calling themselves anything particular, like a gang or name, I don't know. But, you knew the girls that hung out with the guys in the fast life. They definitely were not church girls. Any young, or old, woman, for that matter, that smoked, drank, or cursed was considered and labeled as being something of a Jezebel....

Detroit was growing fast in the 1940s and 1950s. Blacks fresh from the south were greeted with inferior and limited housing. Everyone coming north was after a good job. The fact that a person could get a solid job that paid well and did not require any skills or education made school a secondary concern for many ethnic families. The lure of a good paying job in the auto industry was tremendous for many who had never had this opportunity.[35] It encouraged youngsters of all ethnic backgrounds to abandon their education and enter the plants. There were many high school dropouts. Urban cities, the centers of industrialization, shifted their skills to materiel production, and during World War II, Detroit had become the "Arsenal for Democracy." The void left by men leaving the factories to fight the war was filled by women. The image of women in the factory was promoted with popular songs such as "Rosie the Riveter." Women became the backbone of the wartime industry, and Detroit played a significant role in the wartime economy. However, opportunities for African American women were different.

According to Dominic J. Capeci in *Layered Violence,* black women were not part of that "Rosie the Riveter" force.

Actually, black women fared the worst of all workers throughout the war. They remained the last hired, both because white workers insisted on segregated facilities for supposedly unsanitary, diseased females and because federal officials gave their equal treatment a very low priority. They also suffered from the emphasis that both black and white societies placed on male employment, and society's habitual relegating of black females to unskilled, non-industrial jobs.... There were few black Rosie the Riveters, however. Black women made only token inroads, mostly as matrons, sweepers, and stock handlers, though a minuscule number did set precedent by advancing to production lines. In January 1943, they comprised merely 1.5% or 990 of 66,000 females working in the fifty leading war plants, automobile or otherwise; in fact, black females found work in only nineteen of these factories. By spring, small gains occurred in several area industries, but one month after the riot, 28,000 black women constituted the "largest neglected source of labor" in metropolitan Detroit. Their long history as bread winners and contributors to the economic survival of

Afro-America notwithstanding, black women in the Motor City encountered unyielding race, gender, and class discrimination amid the wartime boom.[36]

In the 1950s female gangs were auxiliaries to male gangs. There were basically two distinct types, scavengers and territorial. Commercial female gangs seemingly did not exist, or if they did, they did nothing significant. The role of auxiliary female gangs seems to follow the traditional history of female gangs. The females were property of their male "brother" gang; some were rough and physically capable of fighting or willing to fight with other girl gangs or for the "brother" gang and were sexually active with the "brother" gang or with someone. Most of the female gangs during this time were criminally active. Their activity may have been simple petty crime. Female gangs at this time never received equal billing. Compatriot type gangs during this time were not criminal, and had strong support from the community in some manner.

Black females had few choices outside of the middle class. Gangs represented acceptance in something that was theirs. Meg Stoveall, social worker in the 1950s, explained the plight of girls who were victimized in her opinion,

> Poor girls were getting used by boys in the gangs, they weren't bad girls. They needed someone to help them with life. Their mothers were young and some didn't know what was going on in their own lives. I spent lots of time with young girls trying to explain the difference between love and sex. They were no different from the black girls from the middle class home or out in the suburbs. Their little gangs were just girlfriends getting together like school kids would do. Sure, they did things, they fought and got in trouble. But they were always remembered for one thing, getting pregnant, that is what everyone dwelled on, no one ever wanted to look at the reasons of why they got pregnant. Society says they're bad. Forget them, poor and bad, and let's forget them. Their mistake was not knowing, and trusting some older boy with lines like some smooth movie star. Sure, they got into trouble, but it takes two to tangle. Nobody talked about what the boys did and didn't do. Why did no one talk about boys having sex? Blame the girls all the time. Gang boys were not the same as boys from good homes who knew what a shotgun marriage was…you had bad boys, you had bad girls, although I always said there are no bad girls.

Delinquent female and male gangs were caught within the distinct class lines within the black community. Lower class youth were left out of the social networks of the organizations dedicated to self-improvement. Even when recruitment efforts were made in the lower class there would be friction that further alienated the lower class from the middle class.

Ronald Roosevelt Lockett, director of Wayne County Youth Services, was socially active in the movement for African American justice during the 1960s. Lockett began his activism in high school on the Eastside of Detroit. Speaking of the role of females, he pinpointed a sense of how the street culture had a certain chemistry with social consciousness.

In our quest to name our school [Eastern High] after Dr. King, it was in the conventional sense a team effort; that team included bright students, both male and female. Sisters pushed for strong brothers in the street culture to support our school spirit from the streets and school. Everybody wanted the change. When I say everybody I mean students…even the brothers who didn't necessarily support higher education in the same vein as the college-bound students. My sense of black females and their community involvement became acutely sensitive and more aware because of the kindred spirit forged during that time. The period in which we took up our cause in high school was followed by our protest at Wayne State. There was a great deal of community interest and women played various roles. There were a number of organizations such as the All African People's Union, the Black Panthers, the Shrine, and that doesn't include the traditional organizations like the Urban League, and the NAACP grassroots programs. Females were in all these experiences and the other factors like women's liberation, escalating drunks in our community, Viet Nam, shaped the black community into a constant conduit of action. It certainly would be a mistake to look at females in lieu of those changes and gangs and not look at those facts. When you look at what is taking place today, it's easy to trace where things started over the years.

The 1960s represent a period during which Detroit cultivated Black Power; this dimension was important in relation to other movements in the black community. Gangs were one of several avenues through which people could participate. Political movements such as the Black Panther party and the All African People's Union, along with the Nation of Islam, provided different levels of activism. In July 1967, the worst civil riot in the history of the United States broke out at the intersection of Clairmont and 12th Street (Rosa Parks).

Escalating black consciousness in Detroit was propelled forward by the 1967 riot. White flight from the city now proceeded at a record pace. Political networks formed and expanded throughout the city. Some females began to cultivate a new way of thinking and joined various organization which reflected these new views. The common bond was black consciousness; the *lumpenproletariat* were lured by different black political-labor groups. Gangs who had been empowered through criminality were now being challenged to work for the community. This was a time of change. Many of the gangs were in a state of confusion. Gangs were challenged by the rising social and political thinking of the Black Power movement. Black females now had choices beyond the limited ones of the early 1960s. The church was being challenged by the Shrine of the

Black Madonna, and Christianity was under siege from the Nation of Islam and their fiery spokesperson, Malcolm X. Female gangs were changing along with male gangs during the 1960s. Women were suddenly thrust into the arena of black consciousness.

Ronald Hunt, a community activist and lifelong native of Detroit, who is today a human services administrator, belonged in the late 1960s to the African People's Union, a community organization on the Eastside of Detroit. Hunt spoke of the change within the community and in the streets, particularly with troubled youth who were in neighborhood gangs.

> There were lots of changes during that period for everyone in the neighborhoods. Some kids exposed to political issues and became part of the movement and others continued in the criminal activities. The big change was that they had choices they hadn't seen before. I don't think gangs disappeared, it was that they were no longer the only thing to do. The sense of brotherhood and a unified community was spreading and that made doing the old things not as popular. Getting drunk, or high, was challenged and some kids met the challenge. In the late '60s, our streets were losing lots of young boys to Viet Nam, so girls were active in the movement in different roles. Remember that some of the high school students had already taken political stands in the schools. There was an attitude about treating our women as our sisters. It was different for the young boys and girls. Girls were taking leadership roles and demanding to be heard within our organization. Sisters were growing Afros, identifying with positive things like tutoring younger kids, helping set up food co-ops and protesting against racism. There were lots of young and older sisters and brothers in the grassroots movement against the injustice of police brutality, sisters were out there against things like STRESS.[37] People were participating in helping the community. Times were changing in both good and bad ways for neighborhood gangs. The good was that young people were becoming responsible in the community. The bad was that the drug problem was taking off. We started experiencing junkies, heroin, that was the ugly change, the heroin junkies started to escalate in our neighborhoods. The dope thing was hard to take, people, men and women you knew, suddenly became strung out and some of the gang kids fell into the slavery. Then the problems just went crazy, stealing from the neighborhoods, people stealing to keep up their habits. After the riot in 1967, heroin was the new enemy.

Eleanor, 45, mother of five, talks about her life in a gang:

> I got pregnant when I was thirteen. This counselor at school, a Mrs. Jenkins, tried to steer me right, but it was useless. She told me that William was too old and experienced for me. But I wouldn't listen and just said she was stupid. Me, my sisters and

cousins, were the Jackie Girls. We called ourselves that after Jackie Wilson...he was so fine, the man was like nothing else, we loved us some Jackie Wilson. Mrs. Jenkins tried to tell me that Willie had babies all over town, but I was in love. My momma couldn't do shit with me. Now, my grandmother was strict, but I just used my momma to overrule her. If my grandma had been in charge, well, things would have been different. I really thought that William was in love with me, we was gonna get married, right, married. That fool left me the day I told him that I was pregnant. I cried and my girls cried, I listen to "Lonely Tear Drops" by Jackie and would cry more.

It was ten of us in the Jackies, we would kick girls' ass who lived across Linwood, or who looked cute and acted like they were scared or acted better than us. My brothers and his boys were in their gang and they would just hang out on Linwood all day. The boys would be beating up other boys from 'round Northwestern or trying to screw all the girls from the other schools. My mother was taking care my little boy, until she got mad or if she had a new boyfriend. My dad was in prison until I was sixteen, we get along real good, and that makes my momma mad 'cause she hates him. When I turned seventeen I had stopped going to school. We were still the Jackies and lots of kids from school and the neighborhood knew 'bout us, we had our reputation, I liked that.

Today, it's different with these young kids. My girls is tough, and my boys are gangsters. I don't like it, but what can you do? My daughters would never take the shit I took off men. These girls are more ready to get what they want. You ask if I am proud of my girls and their posse? Yeah, it's nice to see 'em so sure of themselves, and it's nice to know that they ain't gonna make the same mistakes. They don't smoke, drink, and they ain't on no drugs. My girls don't want no welfare, they just like the boy gangster. They're ready to make it on their own terms, they know what welfare and white people got waiting for them.... Nothing but shit and grief, that's all.

Black females had a choice of three lifestyles. They could follow the path of the good girl which consisted of school, church, and the American Dream in the traditional sense. The bad girl's path was the antithesis of the traditional girl. The Shakerettes were a symbol of the time, bad girls with bad boys, with the ending certain to be bad; this was the life of living young on the wrong side of the street. Or as a third alternative, there was street life; prostitution, gambling, drinking, and whatever else the fast life offered in the 1960s.

The mid-1960s brought change. The Shakerettes grew up and got married; the Shakers, as a group, disappeared—some went into the military, some were incarcerated, and some found employment in the auto industry. The Black Power movement brought the street culture into Black Nationalism. The social structure of the black community was ripe for change. Organizations such as the Cotillion Club, the National Urban

League, the National Association for the Advancement of Colored People, the black Greek organizations, the Masons, the Elks, and strong black political action caucuses in unions like the United Auto Workers contributed, along with the black Christian church, in creating social networks for youth. There were numerous activities in the city in which everyone, including youth, could participate.

In many neighborhoods, street gangs became part of the recruits educated in the new order of thinking. Middle class youths were targeted by the various social controls in the community. The lower class youth population had the YMCA, Boys Club, West-side Cubs, Brewster Center, and other recreational centers. Yet, there was no attempt to bring lower class youth into the mainstream cultural events like the Cotillion Ball or the Nellie Watts concerts.

In June 1971 however, the city had its first gangland-style mass killing on the Westside. The Hazelwood Massacre (which was not gang-related) marked the beginning of an era of murder and drug-related crime.[38] Seven people were murdered over heroin business. This event also marked the resurgence of territorial gangs. Eastside gangs, like the Errol Flynns and the BKs, became infamous in the early 1970s. The Errol Flynns, who at times called themselves the Earl Flynns, originated on the east side of the city, but their power and reputation reached far beyond. The BKs, also known as the Black Killers, were no less famous, but their territory was exclusively the Eastside and mem-bership never matched that of the Flynns.

The presence of hard drugs was being felt for the first time in many Detroit lives. Roy James, 46, an auto worker on the Westside, recalls the changing times.

> My brother was involved in the streets, belonged to a small gang called the Richton Boys, they did everything. Don't know where they are today. My brother died from drinking and living in the streets in 1976. They wasn't nothing like those Shakers when we lived over on the Eastside. These here boys would get high and do all kinds of crazy things back then. I remember when they was, in 1966, they all was chew-ing gum with Robitussin cough syrup on a stick of gum. They sniff glue, drink Wild Irish Rose with lemon juice or [laughing] they would get Thunderbird wine and mix it with Kool Aid. I went to the army, got lucky, didn't go to Nam. I came back in 1970, my brother and all his friends were strung out on heroin. All I can say is that when I left, dope was no problem in Detroit, and when I got back we had junkies everywhere. Things just got bad when the riot hit, when I got back the plants weren't in good shape and that blew my mind. When my brother wasn't getting high on the smack, he was drinking hisself to death. Girls in gangs? Don't remem-ber nothing but lots of girls on junk, junkies everywhere on the Eastside. It seemed like the Westside didn't have the same type of problems before I went into the army.

All of the rough customers lived on the Eastside. Today, it's everywhere, the Westside
is messup and so is the east, south, north, wherever you go, it's the same.

The Eastside gangs were ruling the underground. Illegal commerce involving
gambling, property crimes, car theft and other criminal activities included gang members both individually and collectively. The BKs and Flynns were well known, and in the
early 1970s they teetered between commercial and territorial status. These gangs were
similar in several ways. Like traditional African American gangs in the city, they began
along friendship and family lines in their respective neighborhoods. In both of these
gangs there were brothers and cousins; their leadership varied. They did not have the
capital to invest in narcotics, so drug-selling was minor. Willie Jackson, 33, a former
Flynn and chief enforcer for the gang, addressed their status in the 1970s:

> There was no gang as big or bad as us. The BKs weren't near us…we were the kings
> of the hood, the Flynns, the first ones in charge. Later, you started getting Little Fly-
> nns, younger guys from our streets would call themselves Flynns, I mean they was,
> but they wasn't the ones calling the shots, we was…you had the Dirty Flynns, and
> lots of niggahs from other streets who was down with us, but they still wasn't the
> Flynns for real to me. Girls, girls, what are you saying, girls was in the Flynns? [laugh-
> ing] Well, now, that's ummm, ummm, that's a hard one…we had friends, you know,
> girls who were friends or were sisters, cousins, or girls you knew all your life. Girls
> from the hood, girls that hung out with us. Some say they was, they was the Flynn
> Girls, me, I didn't pay that kinda shit much attention. If you went to war with us,
> girls or guys, it would be better if your ass was on the Flynn's side.

Mike Jones, 28, a member of the Black Gloves, discussed the farm team under the
Flynns and the Flynn Girls.

> We was the younger fellas on the block or from the hood, and the Flynns was the
> shit. I remember being proud of the Flynns, we called ourselves the Black Gloves,
> and we all knew that the little fellas had the blessing of the Flynns. The Black Gloves
> was some fighting fools [laughing] and we knew that the Flynns had our backs. We
> would look out for the big fellas, the Flynns, tell 'em if there was anything that was-
> n't straight or if they was getting watched by the hook. We was in elementary and
> middle school, we learned how to fight from the Flynns. The Flynn Girls were in
> there, they were some of the sisters, cousins or friends of the Flynns. The girls were
> serious and they would beat you down. They was always beating other girls down,
> they could get crazy just like the fellas. Trust me, the girls would make you sorry real
> quick if you thought they was some little soft hos.

During this period, these gangs were delinquent, scavenger, commercial, and territorial. The emergence of females at this time demonstrates the change in attitude by males and females toward female abilities in relation to gangs. This period is also a time when compatriot gangs existed, but were, as usual, not controversial. The evolution of the Flynns during this time is comparable to what is described in Thrasher's study.

> It does not become a gang...until it begins to excite disapproval and opposition. It discovers a rival or an enemy in the gang in the next block; its baseball or football team is pitted against some other team; parents or neighbors look upon it with suspicion or hostility...the store keeper or the cops begin to give it shags [chase it]; or some representative of the community steps in and tries to break it up. This is the real beginning of the gang, for now it starts to draw itself more closely together. It becomes a conflict group.[39]

The Flynn Girls testify to the existence of female gangs in the 1970s. Their relationship to the Flynns is not the simple female extension of a male gang witnessed in earlier decades. Yes, they did exist because of and were born of the infamous Errol Flynns, but their actual incubation had glimmers of autonomy. Female gangs were, in fact, in the scavenger-territorial-commercial stages in the 1970s. The historical quandary for female gangs in Detroit was their invisible status; there was no focus on them and they were discernible to only a few.

Teresa Boner, 26, is a former Flynn Girl. While reluctant to talk about her specific involvement, she agreed to explain their general presence as a gang in the city.

> Yes, there were Flynn Girls, we were gangsters [smiling]. People just don't respect girls, they think we're playthings. Me and the girls would be into lots of things, most of us was kicking it with somebody in the Flynns or we grew up with the fellas in the Flynns. It was the same with the girls in the BK-ettes, they was all from their hood, and we would beef with them. Today, the girls is wilder in a way. Now I knew girls in our crew that were just as wild as today, just as cold and ready to throw. But, most of us was down [in a gang] before the Flynns even was down. I used to belong to this gang called the Mack-Babies, we were just 'round thirteen, we hung out, did things girls wasn't suppose to be doing, [laughing] sometimes we just jump on somebody, just to see them run, and then we start something else and get the fellas in the hood in the shit. We was known, and even today, people see me that went to school with me and they look, 'cause they remember, specially people from school or the hood. They know we was the girls...yeah, the girls was in there.... Now, today I am straight, got bigger things to do, like my boy here, Mike, he knows lots of fellas and girls knew I was a star, me and the girls was doing it, we didn't need the boys like everybody always think.

Field Investigator Clyde Sherrod has lived on the Eastside all his life. Sherrod, 35, spoke of the changing attitudes of women in the 1970s as typified by the Flynn Girls and the BK-ettes.

> The girls have been overlooked to a large degree within the historical overview. The girls in the big gangs were certainly more than groupies, they were the first wave of what we're looking at in 1991. My memory of the Flynn Girls going up to South-eastern High School and robbing some females in the lavatory is very vivid because it hit the street so fast and spread like wildfire. You should remember this act was sep-arate from the male gang. This had nothing to do with the Flynns, this was their own independent act, no males involved in any manner. It was a big statement at that time. Those girls were raw, hardcore, just like their male cohorts. We have inter-viewed several young women who were Flynn Girls. Some have disavowed any membership as of now; a few will talk in the general sense. Some are the parents of the new wave girl gangs and boy gangs. It's scary in relation to what is taking place out in the street; the girls are just as capable and deadly, regardless of age.

The 1970s were pivotal to female gang development; during this decade, females began participating in different types of gangs. Organizational structures differed, but generally they were still in the embryonic stages. Other groups, networks, and compa-triot gangs were in existence; but, only the criminal and delinquent gangs attracted public attention. Women were not considered in conjunction with gangs and gang activities, simply because of gender prejudices, although there has been some limited research on Hispanic female gangs.[40] However, in Detroit in the 1970s black female gangs did exist. In some ways, they were typical of traditional female gangs of the time; yet they were beginning to set their own tone, establish their own goals, and make their own decisions. While our understanding of their organization and structure is still ambiguous, they did exist.

The 1980s marked a new era in the evolution of African American gangs in Detroit. The rise of the notorious corporate gang Young Boys, Inc., initiated the merger of juveniles and an illegal narcotics trade. *The* corporate gang of the 1920s and 1930s in Detroit was comprised of young Jewish gangsters and was known as the Purple Gang. Some sixty years later, the corporate criminal enterprise evolved and black gangsters are firmly in control in Detroit. As illegal alcohol empowered the Purples, so heroin empowered YBI. The 1980s also marked a change in thinking about juvenile and serious crime. Prior to YBI, the Eastside gangs such as the BKs and Errol Flynns worked com-mercial operation at times, but rarely if ever on any large scale that would have included the entire gang membership. The YBI model was the first of its kind. This highly orga-nized youth gang grossed $7.5 million weekly and $400 million annually in 1982, according to two federal indictments.[41] Following on the coattails of YBI's success, in 1988 the Chambers Brothers controlled half of the crack houses in Detroit. They ran their organization like a Fortune 500 company, grossing up to $3 million a day.[42]

Some females were impressed, as were some males, with the fruits of these successful corporate gangs. The introduction of illegal dope and its acceptance as a valuable commodity, along with organized gangs beginning a commercial practice, launched a new day for Detroit. Although females were invisible, as usual, this era was crucial in the evolving development of a female persona. Black women, while not identifying in the same way with white feminist "women's liberation," had grown up in the 1970s with the kind of strong black women symbolized by activist Angela Davis. In the 1980s, black females played a different role in gangs than in the 1970s. The 1980s brought about radical change for females in Detroit.

Notwithstanding the dramatic successes of corporate gangs, scavenger gangs continued in the 1980s with no distinct change in structure or motivation. The status of females in gangs was still territorial and still attached to male gangs and hence, not detected by authorities in the criminal justice system. What was unprecedented was the involvement and integration of females into corporate gangs, beginning with the YBI. Initially, the roles of females in corporate gangs appeared to be the traditional ones of girlfriend, friend, or relative of the gang. There was no media coverage nor did anything suggest to the police, the school, or other community officials that something out of the ordinary was occurring regarding girls and their relationships to gangs.

While females were not actually members of corporate gangs, they carried weapons, participated in transporting drugs, and learned the chemistry necessary to process dope. They were educated through affiliation with corporate drug gangs. There were field observations that females were in scavenger gangs and territorial gangs, both integrated and all-female. Yet, none of these gangs proved unusual or outstanding. The turning point for traditional black female gangs came with the creation of YBI. Corporate gangs are willing to focus on members and the merits of their work. This may not be women's liberation in the fullest sense, but it is pivotal. The mixture of gender, youth, and high technology introduced a different corporate methodology than the Purple Gang employed six decades previously. Females did not become high profile members of YBI; in reality they were more like secondary employees or freelancers. However, they became students of the criminal corporate enterprise of selling and distributing illegal narcotics in Detroit.

Melinda Jay, 24, is currently working in a legitimate job. She agreed to explain her role while working for a corporate gang in the 1980s and into the 1990s. She is concerned that her identity be kept entirely secret.

> I grew up on the Westside near the X neighborhood. The fellas in X were my neighbors and my brother's friends. I was impressed with the fellas when I was as young as ten years old. Me and my girls were always trying to be around Tyrone and his boys. You didn't really know what they did, but it looked large, it looked like they were

stars, they were stars in our hood. All I remember is that my brothers were scared and wanted to be like them. Tyrone always had money and he acted like he was important. We weren't a gang, we were just the girls in the neighborhood. It's hard to explain what you feel when you see the fellas driving their new cars, wearing the booming clothes. And the paper is wacked, it's what moves ya, it's the paper, the money, that makes little kids, yo momma, yo older sisters and brothers look at 'em, the paper says it all. They were large, and you just want to be down with 'em. Tyrone is the one that got my brother into working for 'em. My brother worked just long enough to get a little paper and he joined the army to get away when his friend got wacked, he wasn't made for their thang, he was kinda soft. See, people don't know it's hard being down in that dope thang. I always liked school, me and my girls, it's four of us, we all kinda liked school. I was too young to be going with Will, and my father was drugged about me running around, but he didn't know what to say to Will, he was really scared in a way. My mother was upset at my brother until he went into the army, he lives out west now, got a nice job and says he ain't coming back, it's too wacked, he says. My sister is in one of those college sororities and she won't even say hello to a dope boy. Tyrone and his friends used to laugh at her friends when they come over in their little college clothes. That was in 1983; Tyrone got killed in '87, and lots of the fellas are still in the game, but it's their own little crews.

I was working for X in 1982, the year they got popped and I was only 'bout fifteen, I didn't know shit, I just counted the bundles of dope. There are girls like me that got their own crew separate from X, or whatever the big crew is called. We worked for the crew, we weren't a part of their gang, we just worked for them, provided them with our services. Me and the girls would make 'bout $500 a week doing little counting things. But all of us was seeing some dope boy and your allowance could be as much as you could spend if you was with the money crew, or one of the fellas that was rolling hard. It was twelve girls and everybody at school called us the X Girls, we were their girls and we called ourselves the Getting Paid Bitches. There were some real hard girls who worked in the crews after the X bust. These babes were real hard and they worked just like the fellas. That's what's happening today, girls is in their own crews or they work with a big crew. I knew how to run dope thangs, 'cause my man taught me, and I had been 'round the shit since I was little. I thought it was straight until 1990 and Pappie and three fellas I knew got slayed and that made me think how close I was playing it. Then my girls got beat down like dogs by some other fellas 'cause they thought that they had the paper. They was kidnapping the girls who were with certain fellas or crews, they was getting it on. Then I came to this house right after some fellas had taken this fella out, blood was everywhere. I got sick, something scared me to get out, I mean I knew this fella, it was real fucked up, this was too close. I went back to school and started community college. This counselor helped me get my head right, and my aunt got me this real good job, it pay $11.28 a hour and has benefits. I got a little cute fella, he's in community college like me, and he ain't near that rolling madness. I know this female crew right now, they getting it on, they is out there. These girls is making paper and living large. They use to be down in the Eastside, they was with some of the people in the Chambers Brothers. The Chambers wasn't all that shit they hyped in the papers. These girls is down with the right connects, and they ain't showing off, but they getting kinda large and that's bad, that's what made it bad for the fellas in X. There are crews and some is making it and others are talking about making it. Like, I got out, lots of girls stay in, it's just business. Girls can make it if they want to take the chance. Me, I got out when I saw the killing shit happen too close to me. One of my girls, who is still down with her crew, check me, and say you might get taken out just going out to the store, and she's right.

In the 1980s commercial and corporate gangs were established as the dominant forces in the city. Commercial dope gangs were formed from smaller gangs, some of which were integrated. There were females like Melinda working in lower status positions that required little knowledge of the gang's operation. In the crack houses, younger females were assembly line workers, packaging and making cocaine into crack for organizations like the Chambers Brothers. This practice of using juveniles and females was part of the YBI model from the early 1980s. The dismantling of YBI by law enforcement forced commercial gangs to redefine their method of operation. So, females who had been restricted to lower positions within the drug gangs moved on to the next stage.

The new stage was ideal for young women. The covert nature of commercial gangs demanded smaller groups of members or supporters. The term Covert Entrepreneur Organization is used to distinguish them from past commercial gangs. The success in attacking corporate gangs in Detroit was made possible partially because of their visibility. Like the more famous Los Angeles gangs, with their colors, it was easier for law enforcers to identify the hundreds of members in YBI because of their known moniker, dress, and lifestyle. Reflecting on how quickly their demise came about, Mickey Franklin, 31, spoke of how the community at large knew his gang, YBI.

> Everybody knew us, if you messed with us they knew it would be real trouble. Little kids, stores, car salespeople, Burger King, White Castle, girlies, police, everybody knew us and that was just the way it was…in the end that's what caused us problems, we was too well known. It was easy for the police to stay up on us.

In the 1990s, there is another dimension to females gangs besides that of commercial and corporate. Women's independence means taking power and territory and that means fighting over what is deemed important. This is similar to what Anne Campbell described in her studies of female gangs. There were battles over boys, and yet the focus was not primarily boyfriends but the issue of respect.

Police reports and school records in the early 1990s give little indication of female gangs or females in male gangs. Territorial battles, at times by younger crews, have gone unnoticed. This ignorance of female activity sometimes simply means that authorities are following the practice of traditional ignorance of female gangs. At other times the media has been misled, creating gangs of females when, in essence, there is simply female criminal behavior. One classic example is that of a young woman from a troubled background who, at seventeen, was the leader of a group of three young black males who were convicted of the first degree murder of seven people in the worst massacre in the city since the Hazelwood Massacre in 1971. The St. Aubin Street Massacre, like the one at Hazelwood, was drug-related. There was no gang; while the young woman was the instigator of these murders, the events were not gang-related; they were no different than drug robberies. The young woman had some personal contact with some of those murdered; but allegations of jealousy have no relevance to any gang theory. This case is a reminder of women's changing roles in major crime in America. In the 1990s it was revealed that Detroit had African American females in many disparate gang types. Women in the city were involved in non-gang activity that supported the nationalism of African Americans in both social and political advocacy networks. The gangs in which females participated ranged from compatriots to corporate. Territorial gangs were conducting on-going battles in different parts of the city. The 1990s disclosed varied experiences for African American females.

There are female criminal and non-criminal gangs in Detroit in the 1990s. Theorist Walter Miller named three ways in which females appear in relation to gangs. These are as independently functioning units, coed gangs, and female auxiliaries to male gangs.[43] This only begins to define the current status of female gangs in Detroit in the 1990s. The common denominator for commercial and corporate gangs is money. Within the sphere of commerce women either function or falter. In the gangs that have become competent it is apparent that gender is irrelevant. There may not be equal opportunity all the time, but the opportunity for women is there. Where women have entered the corporate arena and proven their worth, the gang generally does not differentiate between the sexes. They may not have the same level of participation, but females are included in the subculture of crime.

Black female gangs are part of the new era of commercial gangs. They are participants within the various gang types. The scavenger, delinquent, criminal, compatriot, territorial, and corporate types are all part of the transfamilial social organizations in Detroit. Gang types are not limited to particular parameters because they are constantly redefining themselves. It is necessary to include females in the history of Detroit gangs because the city has not acknowledged that female gangs exist nor that they are a problem. This study does not claim that they are dominant or growing. This study declares their presence both in the past and at present.[44]

The complex issues involved in defining how girls were part of the gang culture in Detroit is displayed in the contrast between the 1960s and the 1990s. The evolution of a young female engaging in delinquent acts, and, eventually, criminal acts as an adult, is summarized by a paroled, 40-year-old, African American woman, Johnnie Gladstone:

I was in trouble in grade school. I knew I was gonna stay in trouble because I got kicked out of school all the time. Me and my girlfriend Delores would smoke in the girls' bathroom on purpose.

We called our gang the Dexter Girls. The boys didn't have no name. They didn't need one. Everyone at school knew they were the baddest in our school, the neighborhood. We all wanted to be with these young niggahs. They were all out of school and most of 'em was older, like sixteen or seventeen, and we was twelve or thirteen at best. I lost my cherry when I was in the sixth grade. Most of the girls I knew were screwing by the time they were in the sixth grade. I remember we all had Angel blouses and black tight skirts. I had to sneak my blouse cause my girlfriend Delores' grandmother was watching us, or trying to. By the time I was sixteen, I had my first child. The gang shit stopped in one way, but it just kept going on 'cause we got knocked up at the same time. So you just talked to your girls, 'cause they were the only ones you could talk with. You would just stay in the house. In those days people would just act like you was a tramp if you got knocked up. My momma kept me in the house and my life was just messed up from that day on. I got mixed up with some pimping niggahs and later learned how to steal real good. I was boosting real strong by the time I was twenty one. This niggah named James tried to get me to ho for him, but boosting was easier, and I looked real good so if I got caught the police would always let me go most of the time.

Our gang was real small. After we all had babies it just meant you had to change your way of getting action with the men. Today, it's different in the street. Girls can make it without men, and my boys are making money in the streets. It's just different for women today. I wish I was young and fine as I was. I would have had me anything I wanted. In the 60s, girls had to do what the man said or get her ass kicked, but today, it's different, these young girls ain't taking no shit.

"Just Every Mother's Angel":
An Analysis of Gender and Ethnic Variations in Youth Gang Membership

*Karen Joe and Meda Chesney-Lind**

Few studies of gangs have explored both ethnic and gender variations in the experience of gang membership. Based on an analysis of interviews with 48 youth from a number of ethnic gangs in Hawaii, this paper explores boys' and girls' reasons for joining gangs. The results suggest that while gang members faced common problems, they deal with these in ways that are uniquely informed by gender and ethnicity. The interviews also confirm that extensive concern about violent, criminal activities in boy's gangs has distracted researchers from exploring the wide range of activities and experiences gangs provide their members. Girls and boys growing up in poor and violent neighborhoods turn to the gangs for many reasons, and the gangs themselves take on a variety of forms in response to the diverse challenges facing their members. Most important, the interviews reveal that girls and boys, even those in the same ethnic groups, inhabit worlds that are heavily influenced by gender. As a result, male and female gangs tend to provide different sets of experiences, skills, and opportunities to their members.

Introduction

Official estimates of the number of youth involved in gangs have increased dramatically over the past decade. Currently, over 90% of the nation's largest cities report youth gang problems, up from about half in 1983. Police estimates now put the number of gangs at 4,881 and the number of gang members at approximately 249,324 (Curry et al. 1992). As a result, public concern about the involvement of young men in gang activity, and the perceived violence associated with this lifestyle, has soared. The role of young men of color in these official estimates of gang activity, to say nothing of the public stereotypes of gangs, can hardly be overstated. Indeed, with nearly half (47%) of African-American males between the ages of 21 and 24 finding their way into the police gang database in Los Angeles (Reiner 1992), *gang* has become a code word for race in the United States (Muwakkil 1993).

But what of girls and young women? The stereotype of the delinquent is so indisputably male that the police, the general public, and even those in criminology who study delinquency, rarely, if ever, consider girls and their problems with the law. Connell (1987) describes this process as the "cognitive purification" of social cleavages. Moore (1991), writing about the impact of this process on the public perception of gang

Reprinted from Gender and Society *9:4, pp. 408-30. Copyright © 1995 by Sage Publications. Reprinted by permission of Sage Publications, Inc.*

activity, notes that media images of gangs "sharpen and simplify" middle class notions of what constitutes lower class maleness (137).

Occasionally, girls and women do surface in media discussions of gangs and delinquency, but only when their acts are defined as either very bad or profoundly evil. The media's intense interest in "girls in gangs" (see Chesney-Lind 1993), which actually revisits earlier efforts to discover the liberated "female crook" (Adler 1975b, 42), is lodged within the larger silence about the situation of young women of color on the economic, political and judicial margins. The absence of any sustained research on these girls means there is often little with which to refute sensationalistic claims about their involvement in violence and gangs, as well as very little understanding of why they are in gangs.

There is a clear need, then, to balance, sharpen, and focus our analytical lenses on gender and ethnic variations in youth gang participation. Toward this end, this paper first examines the place of gender in theoretical discussions on gangs and delinquency, and suggests that the most immediate task is to understand the role of masculinities and femininities in gang involvement. We then provide a general overview of the geographical setting of our current gang study, particularly in relation to ethnicity, economy, and crime. Next we report the findings from our in-depth interviews with 48 boys and girls from a number of ethnic gangs in Hawaii. We found that while boy and girl members faced common problems, they deal with these in ways that are uniquely informed by both gender and ethnicity; moreover, consistent with previous ethnographic research, we found that delinquent and criminal activities in boys' gangs have been so exaggerated that it has prevented an understanding of the many ways that the gang assists young women and men in coping with their lives in chaotic, violent, and economically marginalized communities.

Masculinity and Gangs

Historically, the gang phenomenon and its association with youth violence has been defined and understood as a quintessentially male problem. This analytical focus first emerged in the pioneering work of Thrasher (1927) and continued in the same fashion with subsequent generations of gang researchers. During the second wave of research on gangs in the 1950's and early 1960's, the "gang problem" as "male" was even more clearly articulated (Cohen 1955; Miller 1958; Cloward and Ohlin 1960). The only point of difference between these researchers was found in their explanation as to why such delinquent peer groups and their distinctive subculture emerged among boys living in poor communities.

According to Cohen (1955), boys in lower class communities suffer from "status frustration" because of their inability to succeed by middle class standards. Ill-equipped to compete in school with their middle class counterparts, they reject middle class values and develop a delinquent subculture that emphasizes nonutilitarianism, malice, and negativism. These alternative values justify their manly aggression and hostility and become the basis for group solidarity. Miller (1958) contends, however, that the value gang boys place on "toughness, smartness, excitement, and cunning" is part of lower class culture where boys and men are constantly struggling to maintain their autonomy in households dominated by women. Cloward and Ohlin (1960) countered this "culture of poverty" explanation and adopted a structural framework for understanding gang subculture in lower class communities. lower class boys are blocked from legitimate, and in some cases, illegitimate opportunities, and as a result, rationally choose from among their limited options to engage in particular types of crime. Again, though, all these researchers assume gangs to be a uniquely young man's response to the pressures and strains of poverty.

After this work, research on the gang phenomena fell out of fashion, even though the few studies done during that period document the fact that gangs continued to be a feature of life in poor, minority communities (Moore 1978; Quicker 1983). The economic dislocation of these communities during those decades of silence meant that gang cliques gradually found a place in the underclass (Hagedorn 1988; Moore 1991). In this context, a number of researchers attribute the involvement of young men in gangs and crime (as in organized drug sales) primarily to the material advantages a collective can bring in an environment with fewer and fewer legitimate options (Taylor 1990a; Sanchez-Jankowski 1991; Skolnick et al. 1989). Others (Hagedorn 1988; Waldorf 1993; Moore 1991) however, have found little evidence to support the notion that gangs are lucrative business enterprises. In other words, the reasons for membership are far more complex and varied because gangs flourish while clearly failing to provide their members with a ticket out of poverty.

In this connection, how are we to interpret the role of violence and the subcultural emphasis on toughness and bravado in boys' gangs described by earlier as well as later generations of researchers? Jankowski (1991) believes that gang violence and the defiant attitude of these young men is connected with the competitive struggle in poor communities.

> The violence associated with members of gangs emerges from low income communities where limited resources are aggressively sought by all, and where the residents view violence as a natural state of affairs. There the defiant individualist gang member, being a product of his environment, adopts a Hobbesian view of life in which violence is an integral part of the state of nature." (1991, 139)

In the end, Jankowski's argument is actually little more than a revisiting of the "culture of poverty" arguments of the late 1950's, with all of the flaws associated with that perspective (Ryan 1972). Of greater concern, though, is the fact that such characterizations "totalize" a range of orientations toward violence found among gang youth (Hagedorn 1994b). Such generalizations are not only insensitive to the critical differences among individuals and groups, but they also result in a one-sided, unidimensional understanding of the lives of gang members; moreover, policy-makers, the police, and the media are likely to interpret these findings precisely in that way, and the notion that "one bad ass is just like the next" becomes a justification for repressive, and ultimately racist, social control policies.

A far more promising theoretical avenue is found in recent discussions about masculinities and crime that examine the "varieties of real men" in relation to their differential access to power and resources (Messerschmidt 1986,1993; Connell 1987). These authors move beyond the "culture of poverty" thesis, recognizing that manly displays of "toughness" are not a rebellious reaction to "the female-headed household" nor an inherent value of lower class culture (Miller 1958). Instead, they have widened the lenses by adopting a structural approach which locates such acts of manliness within the broader economic and social class context. Specifically, Messerschmidt (1993) argues that social structures situate young men in relation to similar others so that collectively they experience the world from a specific position and differentially construct cultural ideas of hegemonic masculinity—that is dominance, control, and independence. In the case of young minority males living in economically dislocated communities, [they] "are typically denied masculine status in the educational and occupational spheres, which are the major sources of masculine status available to men in white middle class communities and white working class communities" (Messerschmidt 1993, 112).This denial of access to legitimate resources creates the context for heightened public and private forms of aggressive masculinity.

As Katz (1988) calls it, "street elite posturing" (e.g., displays of essential toughness, parading), represents one cultural form of public aggressiveness and is a gender resource for young minority men to accomplish masculinity. Similarly, acts of intimidation and gang violence by marginalized young men are not simply an expression of the competitive struggle in dislocated neighborhoods, but a means for affirming self respect and status.These are cultural forms which celebrate manhood, and "solve the gender problem of accountability" in increasingly isolated poor communities (Messerschmidt 1993, 111). The "street," then, becomes both a battleground and a theater dominated by young minority men doing gender (Connell 1987).

Girls, Femininity, and Gangs

Gang research generally has assumed that delinquency among marginalized young men is somehow an understandable, if not "normal," response to their situations. How are we to understand the experience of girls who share the same social and cultural milieu as delinquent boys? Despite seven decades of research on boys' gangs and crime, there has been no parallel trend in research on girls' involvement in gang activity. As Campbell (1990) correctly points out, the general tendency to minimize and distort the motivations and roles of girl gang members is the result of the gender bias on the part of male gang researchers, who describe the girls' experience from the boy gang member's viewpoint. The long-standing "gendered habits" of researchers have meant that girls' involvement with gangs has been neglected, sexualized, and oversimplified.[1] Girl members typically are portrayed as maladjusted tomboys or sexual chattel who, in either case, are no more than mere appendages to boy members of the gang. Collectively they are perceived as an "auxiliary" or "satellite" of the boys' group, and their participation in delinquent activities (e.g., carrying weapons) is explained in relation to the boys (see Miller 1975b, 1980; Rice 1963; Brown 1977; Flowers 1987).

This pattern was undoubtedly set by Thrasher (1927), who spent about one page out of 600, discussing the five or six female gangs he found.[2] A more recent example of the androcentrism of gang researchers comes from Jankowski's (1991) widely cited *Islands in the Streets,* which contains the following entries in his index under "Women":

- "and codes of conduct"
- individual violence over
- as "property"
- and urban gangs

One might be tempted to believe that the last entry might refer to girl gangs, but the "and" in the sentence is not a mistake. Girls are simply treated as the sexual chattel of male gang members or as an "incentive" for boys to join the gang (since "women look up to gang members") (Jankowski 1991, 53). Jankowski's work, as well as other current discussions of gang delinquency actually represent a sad revisiting of the sexism that characterized the initial efforts to understand visible lower class boy delinquency decades earlier.

Taylor's (1993) work *Girls, Gangs, Women and Drugs* goes a step further to provide a veneer of academic support for the media's definition of the girl gang member as a junior version of the liberated female crook of the 1970s. It is not clear exactly how many girls and women he interviewed for his book, but the introduction clearly sets the tone for his work: "We have found that females are just as capable as males of being ruthless in so far as their life opportunities are presented. This study indicates that females have moved beyond the status quo of gender repression." (Taylor 1993, 8). His work then goes on to stress the similarities between boys' and girls' involvement in gangs, despite the fact that when the girls and women he interviews speak, it becomes clear that such a view is oversimplified. Listen, for example, to Pat in answer to a question about "problems facing girls in gangs":

> If you got a all girls crew, um, they think you're "soft" and in the streets if you soft, it's all over. Fellas think girls is soft, like Rob, he think he got it better in his shit

'cause he's a fella, a man. It's wild, but fellas really hate seeing girls getting off. Now, some fellas respect the power of girls, but most just want us in the sack (Taylor 1993, 118).

Presently there are a small but important number of studies which move beyond stereotypical notions about these girls as simply the auxiliaries of boy gangs to more careful assessments of the lives of these girls (Campbell 1984/1991; Fishman 1988; Harris 1988; Moore 1991; Quicker 1983; Lauderback, Hansen, and Waldorf 1992). Of particular significance are those elements of girl gangs that provide them with the skills to survive in their harsh communities while also allowing them to escape, at least for a while, from the dismal future that awaits them.

These ethnographies document the impact of poverty, unemployment, deterioration, and violence in the communities where these young women live. The girls share with the boys in their neighborhoods, the powerlessness and hopelessness of the urban underclass. As Campbell (1990) notes in her ethnography of Hispanic girl gang members in the New York area, they exist in an environment that has little to offer young women of color. The possibility of a decent career, outside of "domestic servant," is practically nonexistent. Many come from distressed families held together by their mothers who are subsisting on welfare. Most have dropped out of school and have no marketable skills. Future aspirations are both gendered and unrealistic with the girls often expressing the desire to be rock stars or professional models when they are older.

Their situation is further aggravated by the patriarchal power structure of their bleak communities. They find themselves in a highly gendered community where the men in their lives, while not traditional breadwinners, still act in ways that dramatically circumscribe the possibilities open to them. The Portrero Hill Posse, an African American girls' group in Northern California, found themselves hanging together after having been abandoned by the fathers of their children and abused and controlled by other men (Lauderback, Hansen, and Waldorf 1992). Their involvement in selling crack and organized "boosting" (i.e., shoplifting) were among the few available resources for supporting themselves and their children.

Campbell (1990) describes much the same abandonment among young Hispanic women of New York who, constrained by being young mothers and raising children alone, spent their time "hanging out" and "doing nothing." In addition to the burdens of early motherhood, Moore (1991) also found significant problems with sexual victimization in her interviews with Chicana gang members in East Los Angeles. Faced with problems like these, it is clear that girls are drawn to gangs as much or more for the familialism and support they provide than the possible economic advantages associated with gang membership.

These ethnographies also clearly establish the multifaceted nature of girls' experiences in gangs. Importantly, there is no one type of gang girl. Some girl gang members did bear out the stereotypes. The Cholas, a Latino gang in the San Fernando Valley, rejected the traditional image of the Latino woman as "wife and mother," supporting instead a more "macho" homegirl image (Harris 1988). Moore (1991) found a similar pattern among some of the Chicana gang members in East Los Angeles, but also notes the price paid for rejecting the cultural norms of "being a woman." In documenting the sexual double standard of boy gang members as well as barrio residents, Moore notes that girl gang members were labeled as "tramps" and symbolized as "no good," despite the girls' vigorous rejection of these labels; further, some boy gang members, even those who had relationships with girl gang members felt that "square girls were their future" (p. 75).

For the Vice Queens, an auxiliary to the Chicago Vice Lords of the early 1960s, toughness and independence was less an issue of rejecting cultural gender norms, and more a necessity to demonstrate "greater flexibility in roles" (Fishman 1988, 26-27). Growing up in rough neighborhoods provided this loosely knit group of about 30 teenage African American girls "with opportunities to learn such traditional male skills as fighting and taking care of themselves on the streets," particularly since it was expected that the girls learn to defend themselves against "abusive men" and "attacks on their integrity" (Fishman 1988,15). Given the further deterioration of the African American community since the 1960s, these young women face an even bleaker future. In this context, Fishman speculates that "black female gangs today have become more entrenched, more violent, and more oriented [toward] 'male crime'" (Fishman 1988, 28). These changes, she adds, are unrelated to the women's movement, but are instead the "forced 'emancipation' which stems from the economic crisis within the Black community" (Fishman 1988, 28-29; see also this volume).

None of these accounts confirm the stereotype of the hyper-violent, amoral girls found in media accounts of girls in gangs. Certainly they confirm the fact that girls do commit a wider range of delinquent behavior than is stereotypically recognized, but these offenses appear to be part of a complex fabric of "hanging out," "partying," and the occasional fight in defending one's friends or territory. These ethnographies also underscore that while the "streets" may be dominated by young men, girls and young women do not necessarily avoid the "streets," as Connell (1987) suggests. The "streets" reflect the strained interplay between race, class, and gender.

For those with the conventional criminological perspective on gender, girls engaged in what are defined as "male" activities such as violent crime or gang delinquency are seen as seeking "equality" with their boy counterparts (see Daly and Chesney-Lind 1988). Is that what is going on? A complete answer to that question requires a more careful inquiry into the lives of these girls and the ways in which the gang facilitates survival in their world. Their lives are more complex than simple rebellion against traditional notions of femininity, and heavily shaped by an array of economic, educational, familial and social conditions and constraints. A focus on the meaning of the gang in girls' lives also means that comparisons with the experiences of the young men in their neighborhoods who are also being drawn to gangs will be possible. Our intent, then, is to move beyond the traditional, gender-specific analyses of contemporary gangs to a more nuanced understanding of the ways in which gender, race, and class shape the gang phenomenon.

Social Setting
Ethnicity
Hawaii is probably the most ethnically diverse state. The largest population groups are Japanese American (25 percent), European American (33 percent), Filipino American (13.9 percent), and Hawaiian/part-Hawaiian (17 percent); other non-Caucasian ethnic groups comprise the rest of the population (Department of Business and Economic Development and Tourism 1993). Although Hawaii is ethnically diverse, it is not without racial or ethnic tensions. Class and ethnic divisions tend to reflect the economic and political power struggles of the state's past as a plantation society and as well as its current economic dependence on mass tourism. In this mix, recent immigrants as well as the descendants of the island's original inhabitants are among the most dispossessed; consequently, youth actively involved in gangs are drawn predominantly from groups that have recently immigrated to the state (Samoans and Filipinos) or from the increasingly marginalized Native Hawaiian population.

Crime in Hawaii
Despite its image, Hawaii has many of the same crime problems as other states. In 1991, Hawaii ranked fortieth out of the fifty states in overall crime, but eighth in terms of property crime victimization. In the city and county of Honolulu, the nation's eleventh largest city (Federal Bureau of Investigation 1992, 79-106), where three quarters of the state's population lives and the state's capital of Honolulu is located, the pattern is much the same. Oahu's total crime rate is slightly more than half the national average for cities between 500,000 and 1 million (6,193 per 100,000 versus 9,535.1 per 100,000 nationally), but the state's property crime rate is considerably closer to the national average (Crime Prevention Division 1993). Previous research (Chesney-Lind and Lind 1986) has linked part of the property crime problem in the state to the presence of tourists.

Like other major cities, Honolulu has witnessed a rapid growth in police estimates of gang activity and gang membership. In 1988, the Honolulu police (HPD) estimated that there were 22 gangs with 450 members. In 1991, the number of gangs climbed to 45 with an estimated membership of 1,020. By 1993, the number of gangs reached 171 with 1,267 members (Office of Youth Services 1993).

Methodology

Hawaii policy-makers, concerned about the trends in gang membership reported by the HPD, enacted legislation to develop a statewide response to youth gangs. Previous evaluations of this system included a quantitative assessment of the youth in HPD's gang database, and it also compared arrest patterns among officially labeled gang members with those of non-gang members. The results of that study, which are reported elsewhere (Chesney-Lind et al. 1992), suggest that stereotypes regarding gang members' involvement in serious criminal behavior are just that. Both boys and girls labeled by police as gang members are chronic, but not necessarily violent, offenders; moreover, the research raised serious questions about the assumed criminogenic character of gangs and underscored the need for a more qualitative understanding of gang membership among boys and girls.

Toward this end, in-depth interviews with 48 self-identified gang members were conducted from August 1992 through May 1993. The sample includes interviews with 35 boys and 13 girls. Respondents were recruited through a snowball sampling technique (Watters and Biernacki 1989) from referrals provided by the interviewers' personal contacts as well as agency and school staff who work closely with high-risk youngsters. Four young people refused to be interviewed. Interviews were conducted in a wide variety of locations, and none were held in closed institutions. Interviewers were selected based on their knowledge about local culture and the "streets" and, when possible, matched according to gender.

The interview instrument was derived from similar research efforts in San Francisco (Waldorf 1993) and modified for use in Hawaii. The interview consisted of two parts in which the youth first responded to social survey questions regarding personal and familial characteristics, self-reported delinquency, and contact with the juvenile justice system. The second half of the interview was more qualitative in nature. Here, the informant responded to a series of open-ended questions regarding their gang's history, its organization, activities, membership roles, and his or her involvement with the group, and their interaction with family, the community, and police.

Gangs, Ethnicity, and Culture in Hawaii

The respondents are predominantly male (although we specifically sought out female gang members), and they are from "have-not" ethnic groups: the males are largely of Filipino (60 percent) or Samoan (23 percent) background. Slightly under half of the boys were born in another country. The majority of the girls are Samoan (61 percent) or Filipino (25 percent), and born in the United States. The boys in the interview sample are slightly older than the girls; the mean age for the boys interviewed is 16.7 years of age and 15.3 years of age for the girls. The average age of our sample is younger than the young adults found in HPD's gang database, partially because of our reliance on agency and school-based referrals. Most of the boys (94 percent) and all of the girls said they were attending school.

The majority of boys (60 percent) and girls (69 percent) live with both parents, and are dependent on them for money—though about a third of the boys also work. About one fourth of the boys and girls report stealing to obtain money. Their family lives are not without problems—over half (55% of the boys and three quarters of the girls report physical abuse. In addition, 62% of the girls state that they have been sexually abused or sexually assaulted.

Over 90% of the boys and three quarters of the girls were arrested, some many times. Indeed, over a quarter of the boys and the same proportion (23 percent) of girls report being arrested 10 or more times. Boys committed a wider range of offenses than girls, with the most frequent being property offenses, vandalism, violent offenses, and weapons offenses. Girls were as likely to report status offense arrests as criminal offenses, but about a third of the girls were arrested for a violent crime. Both boys and girls say peer pressure was a major reason for their involvement in criminal activities, but boys were more likely than girls to mention needing money as a reason for their illegal activities.

All respondents described the visible presence of gangs in their neighborhoods, and in most cases, a family member could provide them with firsthand knowledge about gangs. Virtually all of the girls (90 percent) and boys (80 percent) had a family member, usually a sibling, who belonged to a gang. In terms of their own experiences with the gang, boys tended to be slightly older than the girls when they joined (respectively, 14 compared to 12), and despite popular conceptions, few respondents said that "joining" involved "initiation" or "jumping in." The boys' gangs were larger than the girls' groups, with 45% of the boys indicating that their group included 30 or more members. By contrast, almost half of the girls said their gangs had between 10 and 20 members, compared to only 23% of the boys.

Although the interviews were done of individual gang members, it is important to know that gangs in the Islands tend to be ethnically organized and generally exclusively male or female. Filipino youth and Samoan youth tend to share the stresses of immigration; these include language difficulties, parentalization, and economic marginality. Beyond this, though, the cultures are very different. Samoan culture is heavily influenced by the Polynesian value system of collective living, communalism, and social control through family and village ties. In Samoa, although contact with the West has been present for a considerable period, there is still a clear and distinct Samoan culture to be found (unlike Hawaii). Samoan adults drawn from this traditional, communal society experience cultural shock upon immigration when poverty forces isolation, frustration, and accommodation to a materialistic, individualistic society. As their children begin to feel caught between two very different systems of values, and as the village system of social controls weakens, the pressures and problems in

Samoan families multiply. Gender relations in traditional Samoan families are heavily regulated by Polynesian traditions of separation, obligation, and male dominance, while girls and women have always found ways to circumvent the most onerous of these regulations (Linnekin 1990).

In contrast, Filipino immigrants come from a culture that has already been affected by centuries of colonialism. As a consequence, the Philippines is a myriad of discrete ethnic cultures that have been reshaped by Spanish and U.S. conquest and occupation. Of the many costs attending colonialism, one of the most insidious is that many Filipinos feel ambivalent about the value of their own culture. In addition, although pre-Hispanic women in the Philippines were dynamic and vital members of their ethnic groups, girls in modern Filipino families are impacted by colonial cultural and religious (largely Catholic) norms that stress the secondary status of women, girls' responsibility to their families, and a concern for regulating female sexual experimentation (Aquino 1994; Lebra 1991). Boys, on the other hand, are given considerable freedom to roam, though they are expected to work hard, do well in school, and obey their parents. The downward mobility, over-employment, and cultural shock experienced by many adult Filipinos put special pressure on the cultural values of filial obligation and strain relationships with both sons and daughters.

Native Hawaiians have much in common with other Native American groups as well as African Americans. Their culture was severely challenged by the death and disease that attended contact with the West in the late eighteenth century. Until very recently, Hawaiian was a dying language, and many Hawaiians were losing touch with anything that resembled Hawaiian culture. Hawaiians, like urbanized Native Americans and low-income African Americans, have accommodated to poverty by normalizing early motherhood, high rates of high school dropout; and welfare dependency for girls and high rates of drug dependency, crime, and physical injury for Hawaiian boys.

Living in Chaotic Neighborhoods: Common Themes in Gang Membership

A number of interrelated themes surfaced in the interviews with our respondents, which provide a framework for understanding youth involvement in gangs. The following discussion focuses on how everyday life in marginalized and chaotic neighborhoods sets the stage for group solidarity. At one level, the boredom, lack of resources, and high visibility of crime in their neglected communities create the conditions for turning to others who are similarly situated, and consequently, it is the group that realistically offers a social outlet. At another level, the stress on the family from living in marginalized areas combined with financial struggles creates heated tension, and in many cases, violence in the home. It is the group that provides our respondents with a safe refuge and a surrogate family, though the theme of marginality cuts across gender and ethnicity, there were critical differences in how girls and boys, and Samoans, Filipinos, and Hawaiians express and respond to the problems of everyday life.

The "Hood"

One distinctive geographical factor about Hawaii is that many neighborhoods are class stratified rather than class/ethnic stratified. This is partly related to the history of the state's political economy (i.e., plantation, tourism) and the limited space of the island. These factors mean that a variety of low-income ethnic groups will live in close proximity to each other.

Our respondents reside in lower-middle and working class neighborhoods. About a third (29 percent) of our respondents live in the central urban area of Oahu in the Kalihi district. This is a congested, densely populated area with a large Filipino population. It is filled with single family residences, housing projects, local small businesses, hospitals, and churches. Hawaiians and Samoans live along the fringes of the central district of Kalihi-Palama. This is an area that the police have targeted as being a high-crime neighborhood, particularly for drug sales, and this impression confirmed through the observations and experiences of our respondents. Given law enforcement interest in this area, it is not surprising that several of our interviewees reported being tagged, harassed, and stopped by patrol units.

By contrast, similar ethnic groups are concentrated on the west end of the island, in what local residents refer to as the "plantation areas" and the "country." In some pockets of these rural neighborhoods, crime and drug transactions are visible as our respondents reported. Overall, however, neighborhoods in these rural areas are less crowded and relatively quiet; consequently, law enforcement surveillance operates differently in these areas than in the central district. Several of our respondents indicated that they were treated fairly by the police. In a few instances when the youth were caught for a crime, the police sternly issued a warning and returned them home.

Despite differences in the density of and police attitudes toward these communities, these areas are similar to those described in recent gang ethnographies where the ongoing presence of crime combined with high rates of unemployment have resulted in a bleak and distressed environment (Rockhill et al. 1993). Not surprisingly, some of our respondents recognize that there has been little government investment in their neighborhoods, and all of them are quick to point out that there are few resources available for young people in their communities. They describe their lives in their neighborhoods as "boring." Simply put, being poor means being bored; there are few organized recreational activities, no jobs, no vocational training opportunities, no money to pay for entertainment, nowhere to go, and nothing happening for long stretches of time. Boys and girls alike echo this view: "there is nothing to do." How then do they cope on a daily level with having no money, no employment opportunities, and little to occupy their time?

Gang Provides a Social Outlet

Generally boys and girls have found the gang to be the most realistic solution to boredom. Our respondents uniformly state that their group provides a meaningful social outlet in an environment which has little else to offer. A sense of solidarity develops among those who face a similar plight, and as our respondents describe, their group provides a network of reliable friends who can be "counted on"; consequently, a large number of hours in school and outside of school are spent "hanging out" together and "wanting to have fun." How do they define "hanging out and having fun?" Much of their time together is spent in social activities, particularly sports. Both boys and girls indicate that they routinely engage in a variety of sports ranging from basketball to football to volleyball (mostly girls), and understandably, given the state's beaches, swimming, boogie boarding, and body surfing. Because program resources are either limited or nonexistent in their communities, our respondents are left on their own to organize their own activities. In many instances, they develop makeshift strategies to fill the time void. Because the local community center's hours are restricted, the girls from a Samoan group in the Kalihi area find themselves waiting for nightfall when they can climb the fence unseen, and swim in the center's pool.

Beyond sports, however, the social dimension of the group and the specific solutions to boredom operate differently in the lives of the girls as compared with the boys and, in many ways, is tied to traditional and cultural gender roles. For example, several of our female respondents, particularly our Samoan girls, indicate that they spend a great deal of their time together "harmonizing, going to dances and competitions and all that." Singing, dancing, and learning hula from family members are time-honored activities within Pacific cultures, and the integration of these activities into gang life signifies an interface between traditional culture and the culture of the streets.

By contrast, the boys relieve the boredom and find camaraderie in the traditional sport of "cruising." Cruising in an automobile is a regular part of their life with the group, allowing them more mobility than our girl respondents, who are largely confined to the gym or park in their neighborhood or who ride with boys or take the bus to other areas. For those girls who live in the more rural areas of the island, mobility is simply not an option. Not surprisingly, cruising for the boys is often accompanied by other expressions of masculinity, specifically "drinking," "fighting," and "petty thieving" including "ripping off tourists." All our male respondents state that they drink, usually beer, and the majority report regular use. The combination of boredom along with the limited avenues to express their manliness cuts across ethnic and community lines. Trip, an 18 year old Samoan from Waipahu, describes his daily routine:

> After school there is nothing to do. A lot of my friends like to lift weights, if there was someplace to lift weights. A lot of my friends don't know how to read, they try to read, but say they can't, and they don't have programs or places for them to go.... There are no activities, so now we hang around and drink beer. We hang around, roam the streets.... Yesterday we went to a pool hall and got into a fight over there.

A 14-year old Filipino boy from the Kalihi area recounts a similar experience to Trip's:

Get up at 1:00 in the afternoon. Then take a shower, then at 3:00 o'clock, go with my friend to Pearlridge [shopping mall], look for girls, and then cruise in Tantalus, and we almost got into a fight. We was gonna drop off the girls and go back but they had too many guys so we turned around. We had four guys and they had 20.

Interestingly, while cruising is also connected for many of the boys with "looking for girls," girls responded that while they sometimes talk about boys in their gangs, they do not see the group as a vehicle for "looking" for boys.

This is not to say that girls are not involved in drinking or fighting like their boy counterparts; however, fighting and drinking are less frequent among the girls, with a few indicating that when they party, "they don't drink, smoke or nothing," and "can't stand that stuff." Significantly fewer girls talked explicitly about getting into fights. Their fights usually have been due to "rumors" as Quente, whose group The Meanest Crew consists of a group of girls living in one of the city's largest and most densely populated housing projects in Oahu, explains:

Yes, they say rumors they saw this person. The first day of school, they say my sister wanted to beat up this girl, but my sister never knew who this girl was.... Then my other sister, they was fighting, and then my sister her nose was bleeding, and my sister and my cousin started fighting, and I came and beat up this eighth grade girl. She was big and fat. She was taller than me. Then after that we went to the office, and they say my sister and I gang up on that girl. Those Kuhio girls they say my sister wanted to fight but my sister didn't know them.... Those SOK started it.

We are told that members of The Meanest Crew and the SOK live in the same neighborhood, attend the same high school, and consider themselves rivals. SOK member, Anna Marie, who is also from Kalihi and 15 years of age, reports that her group too gets in fights. Her first arrest for assault occurred three years ago when she was "mobbed" by another group, and has since been arrested six to seven times for assault. All 16 of the members have been picked up for assault, fighting, stealing, and running away.

As our girls suggest, their involvement in fights has less to do with an attempt to gain an egalitarian position to their male counterparts, but, instead, is directly related to the desperate boredom they experience. In this way, their situation is similar to their male counterparts. One 17-year-old Samoan girl explained her group's attempts to deal with boredom in the Kalihi district:

Before it got worse? [Then] after school everybody would meet at Brother Brian's Bar, drink, dance, talk story, then when the sun was going down that's when all the drug dealing started. And then [later] couple times we would go out and look for trouble. Some of us just felt hyped and would go out and beat up people. We went up to this park and had this one couple, and so for nothing we just went beat em up.

Gang Serves as an Alternative Family

The impact of distressed communities is felt not only by young people but their families as well. Our respondents come from several different types of family situations. In many cases their parents are "overemployed," holding two jobs in working class and service industry occupations. They are, for example, laundry workers, hotel maids, and construction workers. Given the high cost of living in Hawaii, this is a common practice among working class families. Unfortunately, when both parents are struggling to stay afloat in this economy, supervision is absent in the home. A few youth indicate that they are essentially on their own because their single parent, who is consumed by his or her job, is rarely home to supervise. In some instances, parents have difficulty keeping a steady job and are either unemployed or underemployed for periods of time. As their children recognize and describe to us, supervision may be present, but filled with tension as parents try to cope with financial problems. In a small but important number of cases, the cultural and familial ties of parents required either the mother or the father to remain in their native land. This was true among a few of our Samoan and Filipino respondents.

In light of family financial pressures and limited time for parental involvement or supervision, it is not surprising that these young people feel a sense of isolation and consequently find support and solace among members of their group. As one Samoan girl plainly puts it:

> [It's] good to just kick back and relax and have fun, but not get into trouble. We tell each other our problems.... I don't like to be a loner or feel isolated.

In sharing their problems at home with each other, the members of the group take on the role of a surrogate family. A common theme in the lives of our female and male respondents is that the gang serves as an alternative family. As Tina, a 15-year-old Samoan explains, "We all like sistas all taking care of each other." The symbolic kinship of the group is even reflected in the name of one female Samoan group called "JEMA," which stands for Just Every Mother's Angel. Seventeen-year-old Daniella recounts the origins of her group's name.

> We chose that because all the girls I hang out with, yeah, all their mothers passed away, and during elementary days, we all used to hang out and all our mothers were close yeah, so that's how we came up with that name.

The males express similar views to the "sistas." Kevin, a 17-year-old Hawaiian, likens the leader of his group to "like the father of the house." On meeting the leader, he reports that "[the] first time I saw him I felt like bowing. I didn't though. He said if I respected him, he would respect me." Or as Ricky, a 17-year-old Filipino states, "the gang is a closer family than my parents because they are there to help me everyday... unlike my parents."

The tension on the family is amplified by other factors. As noted earlier, among Samoan and Filipino families, the immigrant experience is frequently one of alienation due to differences in language and culture. The marginalization of the native Hawaiian people and their culture has a long history and has left them in an ambiguous cultural position. These ethnically diverse pressures on the family heighten the conflict at home, and, in many instances, erupt into violence.

In this way, the group's surrogate family role takes on an even greater significance for the young people who report physical, emotional, and sexual abuse by a family member. As indicated earlier, 75% of the girls (6 out of 8 who were asked) and 57% of the boys (12 out of 21 who were asked) report "lickings" by one or both of their parents. In the midst of financial tension, physical abuse appears to be connected to the violation of cultural and gender role expectations. The girls, for example, indicate that their lickings were due to violations of traditional sexual double standard: "not calling home," "coming home late," and "not coming home for the night." Staying out all night is interpreted differently for girls than for boys. When girls engage in these behaviors, this is "running away" and is often connected with "promiscuity." When boys don't come home for the night, this is normal adolescent behavior for working-class boys.

By comparison, all four of the Hawaiian boys and four of the nine Samoan boys reported that they were physically struck by one of their parents for delinquent behaviors such as "fighting," "stealing," and "smoking pakalolo [marijuana]." Kevin, a 17-year-old Hawaiian boy, described how his mother threw him down the stairs, cracking his ribs and bruising his spinal disc when she found a bag of marijuana in his room. For two boys and one Samoan girl, their father's beatings were aggravated by alcohol and drug use respectively. The experience of the four (out of eight) Filipino boys who stated that they received lickings differed from the South Pacific Islanders. According to the Filipino boys, the beatings were related to a wider range of behavior which their parents believed to be intolerable, such as a "bad attitude" and "poor grades." Dwane, a 17-year-old Filipino, recalled that his lickings stopped as he got older.

These young people's response to the abuse is usually one of reluctance and resistance to report the abuse, and must be viewed in a cultural context. Family loyalty is important among Filipino youth, where strong cultural pressures, language problems, and an understandable reticence to involve external agencies (and perhaps jeopardize immigration status) depress reporting of abuse. The Hawaiian and Samoan boys and girls who reported being physically abused also refused to call or permit official intervention (unless detected by school authorities). Despite child abuse education in the classrooms at all age levels, these young people viewed their loyalty to their parents as paramount. One 17-year-old Samoan male's loyalty to his father took precedence over his own victimization:

> Since my grandma passed away, I don't get along with my father. He comes home drunk and beat us up. He beats us up with those weight-lifting belts. The police never come, I don't tell nobody. I don't want nobody that's why, I don't want nobody butting in now. I run away when I can't stand it.

Family is the core of the Pacific Island culture. Traditionally social and economic activities took place within the context of the family. This familial arrangement, however, is severely ruptured in the Western economic context. In Samoa and other Pacific Islands, families live in open fales[3] where behavior is clearly visible and hence, children's behavior can be directly controlled. When a child is unruly, he/she can be sent to stay with relatives, given the extended sense of family there. Hawaii's "hanai" system provides a similar extended family arrangement for caring for troublesome children. Anna Maria, a 15-year-old Samoan girl, was taken out of her parents' home, spent two weeks in a shelter, and now lives with her auntie and uncle who also physically abuse her, but states that "it was far worse with my parents, that's why I stay with my auntie and uncle."

Although the "sistas" and "brothers" of the gang offer some level of support, it is understandably difficult for many to cope with everyday life. One 18-year-old Samoan girl who has been severely abused, physically and emotionally, by her parents finds that her group provides "someone to talk to." In this particular case, the group has been especially important as she is fiercely loyal to her parents and rationalizes the beatings as a feature of the Samoan ways. "My parents aren't understanding. They are Samoan, and everything you do you get lickings"; moreover, she refuses to tell school and child protective services authorities because they will intervene. She must consequently contend with "wanting to kill myself because I'm tired of getting beat up." Many of them view their lives as "hopeless" and their future as being "jammed up." Their options seem limited as nearly half of them had contemplated suicide. Suicidal thoughts were more prevalent among the girls (71% or 5 of the 7 females asked) compared to the boys (33.3% or 6 of 18 males asked).

Differences in Crime and Delinquency

Boy and girl gang members differ in the area of crime and delinquent behavior. Although girls commit more crime and engage in more fights than their stereotype would support, they are certainly less involved in this behavior than the boys. They are also far less involved in drug selling, robbery, and other types of criminal behavior.

As noted earlier, for boys, fighting—even looking for fights—is a major activity within the gang. If anything, the presence of girls around gang members depresses violence. As one 14-year-old Filipino put it, "if we not with the girls, we fighting. If we not fighting, we with the girls." Many of the boys' activities involved drinking, cruising, and "looking for trouble." Looking for trouble also meant being prepared for trouble—though guns are somewhat available, most of the boys we interviewed used bats or their hands to fight. Some of this is cultural—as one respondent explained:

> My friend had a gun, one of our boys had a gun, but one of our gang members said put it somewhere else, cause we're Samoans and Samoans fight with hands.

Another Samoan youth who lives in the country adds, "down here we no more guns, just fist fight." Some of this may also be strategic, since some respondents mentioned knowing where to get their hands on guns, but not carrying them regularly. The hiding of guns and carrying of baseball bats, for example, avoids arrest for possession of an illegal firearm, since a bat can always be a piece of sporting equipment.

Another major difference between the girls and the boys was involvement in drug dealing. Although girls drink and use drugs in the gang, a number (though not all) of male gangs are involved in selling drugs. As a 17-year-old Filipino male who was in a leadership position with his gang noted, the gang is important because it provides "opportunities to make money and use drugs." The gang helps you "find drugs faster… [and] buy and sell drugs faster."

The boys' gangs did demonstrate a range of orientations to drug use and selling. Some only sold drugs ("Guys in my group don't do drugs, sell yea, but only weed"); other groups did not use drugs ("We don't sell no drugs, we cruise, we used to paint graffiti, but not any more"). For most of the boys, though, the gang was the site of drinking and doing drugs in a social way, "We do sports together, parties, we party every day, some guys do drugs and shit." One or two gang members belonged to groups that focused exclusively on drug selling. Logically, those most seriously involved in drug selling had moved to Waikiki and were selling to tourists. These gang members "sit on the wall and talk, look for vices,[4] if a deal comes up, go and make the deal. [We] don't get into that much trouble, most people in Waikiki know us." This variation in delinquent and criminal involvement of different gangs is consistent with other male gang studies (Fagan 1989)

As alluded to earlier, the violence associated with boys' gang life is largely an outgrowth of the violence in their neighborhoods, which explains why in many of the boys' interviews, protection was mentioned as a major reason to join the gang. As one young man put it, the gang gives you "protection for when you go to school, some guys tough and that's your power… the gang's that power… you don't get picked on or beat up."

The violence that fuels membership in gangs, though, spills over into more general "trouble" as groups of young men begin to hang out, "Yeah, we have fights with other groups, sometimes when it is getting close to the weekend, there are fights.

Sometimes one on one fights or the whole group against another group… [we] just collide into each other and fight."

Experience with this kind of violence and drug use combined with the fact that almost all of these youth had relatives in gangs occasionally produces a reflective voice:

Sometimes when my friends are in trouble, we go help my friends… that is how we get into fights and stuff. We play sports together, party, look for women, go to concerts, when we party sometimes my friends drink, but me I only drink a little… chill out… cruise… cause one of my uncles he used to drink and smoke a lot he died last year… when I think of him I think it is going to happen to me.

Only infrequently are non-gang members the targets of violence; when they are, they are tourists assaulted to get their money. As one fourteen-year-old Hawaiian youth puts it, "When we no more money, me and my friends walking around and get hungry, the first Jap[anese tourist] we see, we knock and take his money and go to McDonalds lidat [like that], eat and go home after." This behavior, though, was the exception. Most of the youths who engaged in gang behavior did drugs, sold drugs, and engaged in petty thefts—again chiefly as a group activity. As one 17-year-old Filipino puts it, "if one person go steal car, we all go steal car… they don't have to, but everybody go for watch." Another 17-year-old Samoan youth says, "I've been gang banging since I was fifth grade, I've been hitting [stealing?] cars and all kinds of shit."[5]

For girls, fighting and violence is a part of their life in the gang—but not something they necessarily seek out. Instead, protection from neighborhood and family violence is a major theme in girls' interviews. One girl simply states that she belongs to the gang to provide "some protection from her father." Through the group she has learned ways to defend herself physically and emotionally. "He used to beat me up, but now I hit back and he doesn't beat me much now." Another 14-year-old Samoan put it, "You gotta be part of the gang or else you're the one who's gonna get beat up." Though this young woman said that members of her gang had to "have total attitude and can fight." She went on to say, "We want to be a friendly gang. I don't know why people are afraid of us. We're not that violent." Fights do come up in the lives of these girls, "We only wen mob this girl 'cause she was getting wise, she was saying 'what, slut' so I wen crack her and all my friends wen jump in." Later this young women explained that the gang and its orientation to violence changed:

At first [I] thought of the gang as a friendship thing, but as I grew into the gang, it just started to change. I started seeing it as, I guess, I don't know, I guess as trying to survive in the streets and everything, and that about it… protection, cause at the time I was scared, cause my sister and cousin used to beat me up and before I even joined the gang, you know how you would threaten your sister… my sister stole my mom's car and her money and my cousin use to steal her dad's money, and I knew all these things, and my sister would say, "we're going to beat you up if you tell dad."

In general, the girls talk about the trouble the gang gets into as tonic for boredom. "Sometimes we like cause trouble yeah cause boring, so boring. So we like make trouble ah, for make scene, so we just call anybody, if they looking at us." Girls rarely carry weapons ("No, I don't carry weapons, but I can get it if I want to."). In fact, one girl said in answer to a question about knives, "I have knives, but only for food." This same 13-year-old girl saw some of the pointlessness of their violence:

> I think the girls and boys that don't join gangs are smart, but girls like me who are in gangs are stupid, they are just wasting their time cause dumb fighting over color, just for a stupid color.

Girls are also less involved in drug selling than boys. Arrests for running away from home and problems with status offenses are more commonly mentioned by girls, as are other problems on the streets. Also mentioned are problems with parents who insist on the double standard ("I couldn't handle, cause my parents always telling me do the things around the house, they never let me go out"), and the stereotypes of bad or wild girls: "I'm pretty sure a lot of people think we are prostitutes on the road, we just hang out with the mahus [transvestites] who crack us up."[6]

Conclusion

This paper has stressed the need to explore gangs in their social context and to avoid totalizing notions of either boys' or girls' gangs. Previous research as well as our own interviews clearly suggest that such an approach is needed. One of the major conclusions one draws from listening to these young women and men is that the gang is a haven for coping with the many problems they encounter in their everyday life in marginalized communities. Paradoxically, the sense of solidarity achieved from sharing everyday life with similarly situated others has the unintended effect of drawing many gang youth—both boys and girls—into behaviors that ultimately create new problems for them.

On the broadest level, both the girls and boys are growing up in communities racked by poverty, racism, and rapid population growth. The gang is a clearly a product of these forces. Shaped by the ethnicity, race, and gender of its participants, the gang takes on different shapes depending on its composition. Clearly, for both males and females, the gang provides a needed social outlet and tonic for the boredom of low-income life. The gang provides friends and activities in communities where such recreational outlets are pitifully slim. Gender, though, shapes these activities. For girls, the list of pro-social activities is longer than boys. For boys, getting together in groups quickly moves into cruising instead of hanging out and that, in turn, leads to fights and confrontations with other groups of boys.

The violence that characterizes their family lives and their communities is another prod into the gang for most of these youth. Gangs provide protection for both girls and boys. Many youth are drawn from families that are abusive, and particularly for girls, the gang provides the skills to fight back against the violence in their families. In a few cases, the violence the girls learn begins to express itself in relations with other girls. As Anne Campbell (this volume, p. 255) notes, in reflecting on the meaning of this in her research: "If we are willing to allow young women to be exploited by poverty and crime—if we can offer them no way out of victimization—then we can hardly be surprised if they respond by nurturing a self-protective reputation for craziness." The violation of traditional notions of femininity then, particularly the "unacceptable" displays of toughness and independence, are hardly a reflection of their liberation from patriarchal controls. The costs of having been born female are not only clear in their lives, but are, in fact, attenuated by the economic dislocation of their communities.

The marginalization of working and lower working class communities has specific meaning for young men as well. The displays of toughness and risk taking described by the boys in our study are a source for respect and status in an environment that is structurally unable to affirm their masculinity. Their acts of intimidation and fighting are rooted in the need for protection as well as the need to validate their manliness. Police harassment of gangs, particularly in the cities, further strengthens their group solidarity and, at the same time, increases their alienation from conventional others (like store owners) in their neighborhoods.

Abuse and neglect shape experiences with their families as well, but here there are rather stark ethnic differences in the ways both the boys and girls experience abuse. First, girls are more likely to experience abuse as girls, with problems of sexual victimization and sexual abuse appearing in their accounts of family life. For boys, the violence is further mediated by culture. Filipino boys report that they are more likely to be physically abused for failing to attend school, not getting good grades, and so on. Abuse also appears earlier in their lives. For Samoan and Hawaiian boys, the abuse appears later and is directly tied to delinquent and criminal behavior. Virtually no youth report such behavior to officials, and some go out of their way to hide the bruises and normalize the incidents. Samoan life is profoundly family centered; as a consequence, the youth rely on cultural strategies to deal with their problems—such as moving in with relatives. Filipino youth employ their own cultural tradition of *barkada* which encourages the social grouping of young men and women thereby facilitating the creation of a surrogate family system.

Gangs, though, do produce opportunities for involvement in criminal activity. Especially for boys from poor families, stealing and small time drug dealing make up for a lack of money. These activities are not nearly so common among the girl respondents. Instead, their problems with the law originate with more traditional forms of girl delinquency, such as running away from home. Their families still attempt to hold them to a double standard, which results in tensions and disputes with parents that have no parallel among the boys.

Media constructions of gang behavior, then, which stress the violence done by gang members, need to be countered by far richer assessments of the role played by gangs in the lives of these young people. Gang participation and gang structure is clearly shaped by both gender and race. Products of distressed neighborhoods, the gangs emerge to meet many needs that established institutions—schools, families, communities—do not address. Many of the impulses that propel youth into gangs are prosocial and understandable—the need for safety, security, and a sense of purpose and belonging.

For boys, violence is certainly a theme in gang life, but it is as much a product of violent neighborhoods as it is a cause of the phenomena. Boys' experiences of violence and abuse within the family, while kept from official agencies by cultural norms stressing the centrality of the family, certainly provide an additional and powerful perspective on the violence of boys. For girls, violence (gang or otherwise) is not celebrated and normative; it is instead more directly a consequence of and a response to the abuse, both physical and sexual, that characterizes their lives at home.

Girls' participation in gangs, which has been the subject of intense media interest, certainly needs to be placed within the context of the lives of girls, particularly young women of color on the economic and political margins. Girl gang life is certainly not an expression of "liberation," but instead reflects the attempts of young women to cope with a bleak and harsh present as well as a dismal future. One 15-year-old Samoan girl captured this sense of despair, when in response to our question about whether she was doing well in school said "No, I wish I was, I need a future. [My life] is jammed up."

Attempts to totalize these youth as amoral and violent must be seen as part of a larger attempt to blame them for their own problems in a culture where gang has become synonymous with race. As young women are demonized by the media, their genuine problems can be marginalized and then ignored. Indeed, they and their boy counterparts have become the problem. The challenge to those concerned about these youth is, then, twofold. First, responsible work on gangs must make the dynamics of this victim blaming clear. Second, research must continue to build an understanding of gangs that is sensitive to the contexts within which they arise. In an era that is increasingly concerned about the intersection of class, race, and gender, such work seems long overdue.

Women, Men and Gangs:
The Social Construction of Gender in the Barrio

Edwardo Luis Portillos ★

What do you know about us other than fear? People see me and my friends walking down the street and they quietly move out of our way. Nothing slips out of their mouths but their stares speak a thousand words. Do they fear my tattoos, my baggy pants, or the color of my skin? Obviously, they dread each of those things. Yes, I know how to hurt people, and I have! I am ready to do whatever I have to, even if they call me violent. Some people would rather we stay in the house than join our partners on the streets, including our family and the community in which I live. The funny thing is that people in my gang don't really understand us either. In one hand they expect us to carry hate and violence, and in the other love and a baby.

This short narrative is a fictional account based on interviews with gang members in Phoenix. It expresses views held by young women and men in gangs. In part, it draws attention to the way in which young Chicanas/os and Mexicanas/os[1] are viewed as criminals because of the color of their skin, the clothes they choose to wear, and the neighborhoods in which they reside. Interestingly, the mostly white youths in the suburbs who dress in baggy pants and long t-shirts are seen as less dangerous than young people of color who dress in a similar way.

This fictional account also directs our attention to the tensions felt by young women as they dance between fighting and nurturing norms and expectations. This very tension lies at the heart of this analysis. The community and family expect young women in gangs to "act like women." Women are not supposed to be in the streets involved in criminal gang behavior. A dominant view holds that they should be in their houses studying in the hopes that they will have a meaningful future. Some women resist such notions, realizing that the educational system has failed them. If they are not studying, however, it is expected that their mothers will equip them with the skills necessary for a life of care-giving by teaching them to cook and clean. Yet, many young women observe their brothers lounging on the couch. They may rebel against this double standard and then may suffer beatings if their form of insurgence means not doing their chores. Hoping to escape the gendered and marginalized experiences in their homes and schools, some young women move into the gangs where they can maintain a sense of control over their lives.

In the gang, the ideal female gangbanger is ready to resort to violence and, when

★*This essay was presented at the American Society of Criminology meetings, San Diego, November, 1997, and is published here for the first time.*

called upon, to display a veil of toughness. Yet women's experiences in the gang are paradoxical because the gang is not, ultimately, a place where they can escape gendered expectations. Women's positions in these social groups in some ways reflect presuppositions held by their parents and society. The gendered expectations found in the gang are different than in the family because in the gang women are allowed to use drugs, have sex, and become involved in delinquent and antisocial behavior. Nevertheless, this behavior is subordinated for young women in a way that it is not for young men. To understand these gender differences in the gang we will focus on how gender is constructed distinctly for men and women (Messerschmidt 1993, and this volume).

Young Women and Gangs

In November of 1997, *Primetime Live* aired a segment on Chicanas involved in gangs entitled, "Girls in the Hood." Two young women were asked to carry cameras in their barrio for four months. They show a young woman with a large tattoo on her belly, youths carrying weapons, young teenagers having babies, and people dying at parties. Although the segment presented the harsh realities of life in a barrio, at the same time it trivialized their lives. This was especially evident when the reporter who interviewed the youths stared at them in shock and shook her head as she heard their life stories. The reporter's response to these young women reflected the ease with which the larger society can look down upon women in gangs and the way in which poor women of color are condemned. It is easy to blame and disdain; it takes much more work to understand how women find themselves involved in gangs.

Today, the number of women in gangs has increased. They are involved in female-only gangs and in gangs with both male and female members. The number of women involved in these gangs varies across geographical regions, cities, and types of gangs. Racial differences also exist, with women involved in biker gangs tending to be white (Hopper and Moore 1990), while street gangs are made up primarily by people of color. Street gangs also vary in terms of ethnic composition. They tend to be mostly racialized so that African-American females join black gangs and Latinas join Latino gangs.

Despite the growing number of women in gangs, social science research reveals that women in gangs are nothing new to our society (Campbell 1984; Thrasher 1927). The problem may not be that increasing numbers of women are involved in gangs but that they are deviating from expected gender norms. Our chivalrous society shivers at the thought that women are placing themselves in such vulnerable positions. Hanging out with a crowd of male gang members implies that they can be raped, physically beaten, or involved in consensual sex. In part, these beliefs stem from patriarchal notions of protecting women. Also, most research on gangs and juvenile delinquency has been conducted by men and its focus has been primarily concerned with boys and young men involved in crime. When researchers did consider women, they tended to reinforce

femininity accepted by her peers. It was different than the femininity found in the family. At home, she was not viewed as an independent woman with valid thoughts and concerns, instead she had to fulfill the gendered expectations of her family. When she did not live up to the family expectations of a woman, she was degraded and beaten.

Sixty percent of the young women interviewed have experienced sexual or physical abuse within their family. Young girls growing up in abusive households in the barrio learn that they must manage and guard their sexuality, even from their own relatives. They use these experiences to help construct an oppositional femininity. The gang helps to make the transition from violence in the family to violence in the their peer group, where it is among equals and respected by the gang. The physical mistreatment allows abused young women to thrive in the gang since it has hardened them. One young woman describes how she was beaten when she joined the gang. For her, the beating she endured when she was jumped into the gang was nothing compared to what she experienced at home:

Susan: Because they call me Little Loca and they were like, "Oh yeah, you're Little Loca," and the guys just start hitting me. Oh my gosh, they hit me with a bat and I had an asthma attack. I didn't cry or nothing, I was use to it.

[You were used to what?]

Susan: Getting hit like that from my grandma. When I use to live with my grandma she would, when we would cry, she would hit us. She would hit us for everything so I got use to it. When I got "jumped-in," it was no big thing. My grandma would hit me harder.[3]

Joining the Gang

Research with Phoenix gangs shows the complexities inherent in situationally constructing gender. This construction is based on how an individual enters the gang and how members prove and assess loyalty to their peers. Most males in this research project reported that they entered the gang between the ages of 9 and 13. Most females reported that they entered the gang between the ages of 12 and 13, although one female reported entering at the age of 9.5.

Initiation rites are one means of establishing commitment and loyalty to the gang. The different mechanisms for entering the gang vary according to gender, and help to situationally produce femininities. The three mechanisms for entering the gang are being "jumped-in," "born-in," and "trained-in."

The primary means by which male gang members enter the gang is called "jumping-in." Typically, "jumping-in" occurs when between four and six gang members physically beat a youth, and the youth must fight back to show strength and valor. The initiation rite allows youths to gain respect from fellow gang members and creates a sense of prestige from his peers (Campbell 1984; Messerschmidt 1995; Padilla 1992; Rodriguez 1993; Vigil 1988; Zatz and Portillos, n.d.). While boys may also be born into a gang's territory they typically "jump-in" to gain respect and demonstrate their toughness.

Females, similar to males, gain respect depending on how they enter the gang. For young women, however, the way in which they enter the gang may also result in a lack of respect. The type of respect gained from their friends depends on the situation at the time she joins the gang. Therefore, how she enters the gang greatly affects later perceptions of her. The gang allows young women several means by which to enter the gang.

Young women "born-into" a gang were born or have resided in the neighborhood since a very young age. As they grow, they come to know future homeboys and homegirls through play groups that form in their neighborhoods. Participation in these play groups established strong fictive kin relationships between the young people. One ideal of the gang is to protect the barrio, and this includes future members who may become part of the gang family. Older male gang members come to view these young women in the neighborhood as sisters. It is their responsibility to protect and defend them. The young women "born-in" gained respect by being part of the barrio. They grew up in the neighborhood, and so do not have to establish trust or loyalty for the barrio or the gang. Female gang members who are not part of the neighborhood must prove their loyalty to the gang through other means. Those not born into the neighborhood must gain respect through "jumping-in."

Similar to young men, four to six gang members "jump" a young woman into the gang. Research revealed "jumping-in" was situational, based on who was around at the time the decision was made to "jump" the person in. The ideal situation for the gang was to have females beat other females into the gang. In some cases there were not enough young women available, meaning that some males had to participate. Despite the fact that male respondents have stated they are reluctant to hit females, they would do so as part of the formalized rite of "jumping-in." Young women who are "jumped-in" have gained respect by displaying their toughness in fighting.

In contrast, young women "trained" into the gang are not respected by either male or female gang members. Research reveals the numbers can be as low as three, and in one case which seemed an exaggeration, as high as sixty participants. Females who are "trained-in" demonstrate subservience to the gang by surrendering their bodies to each member who wishes to participate. A majority of respondents did not acknowledge their participation in this form of initiation, defining it as lewd and "nasty." "Train-ins" usually occurred during what gang members refer to as "kicking it" (hanging out, partying). In most cases they were at a party. Respondents described several gang members drinking, including the females who will later become the center of sexual activity. Often the decision to "train" women into the gang is made by the young men. For example, male gang members described situations where young men decided to "train-in"

Chicanas and Mexicanas who were drunk or high:

> My whole barrio was suppose to be there but a lot of people weren't there and this girl she wanted to get "jumped" into my barrio. I don't know, I guess she looked good because my homeboys wanted to train her in. My homeboy was like, 'Man she looks good, let's train her in.' My homeboys were all like, 'Fuck it,' they were all high anyway you know, 'Yeah lets train her in,' this and that. We voted on it, to get her "jumped-in" or "trained-in." Training her was the wrong question, all my homeboys trained her in.

Many Chicana/o and Mexicana/o gang members viewed women who were "trained-in" as desiring to have sex with gang members to enter the gang, even if they were drunk.

> Most of them that do it want it. That's because they want to be in and they don't want to be "jumped in" so they get slept in. But they don't have to be in a gang, they just want to because they think it's cool. So they go ahead and sleep with all the guys. Most of them like it so they do it with all the guys anyway. Some of them slept with half of them anyway, so they think all they got to do is sleep with a couple more, that's it.

The decision to "train-in" has a lasting influence on how the young woman is viewed by both male and female members. Once a young woman is "trained-in," it is difficult to shake the label. She is unlikely to gain respect and male members will continue to treat her like a sexual object. In some cases, gangs who "train-in" females will not accept them as true members. The woman is led to believe that she will become a members of the gang, but after the initiation she may be told mockingly that she is not really in the gang.

The term "hood rat" is used to demonstrate the lack of respect for these young women. A "hood rat" is a derogatory term for females who have been "trained-in," as well as females who sleep with many males in the gang. The gang uses "hood rats" for sex, money, and transportation.

Both males and females indicated their lack of respect for "hood rats." The general perception is that young women should control their sexuality even when they are drunk. There is a sense that males in the gangs will try to sleep with young women. It is the female's responsibility to prove her virtue by refusing such attempts, even when intoxicated. Gang members appear to value the attribute of fending off the homeboys because it demonstrates that she will not allow males to treat her as a sexual toy. The homeboys involved in the rapes were not viewed, however, with less respect. Rather they gained some prestige, at the expense of the females, because of their sexual exploits. Messerschmidt views violent sexual group rapes as a means to help maintain and reinforce an alliance among the males by humiliating and devaluing women (Messerschmidt

1993, 114), thereby validating their masculinity. "Train-ins" have a similar affect in that they also help maintain and reinforce alliances within the gang.

Gender Differences in the Gang

Although the gang provides an escape from traditional notions of femininity and abuse, it cannot be described as a site of gender equality. Rather, it simultaneously liberates and oppresses women. For example, young women are encouraged by young men around them to become sexually involved with only one male. Other males constantly test her by propositioning her, but she must maintain an image of monogamy. Therefore, the men dictate accepted dating and sexual behavior while at the same time controlling and establishing criteria that are obviously double standards.

Nevertheless, female gang members will discuss the various men that they have dated on the side with their homegirls, even if they have a boyfriend. Sharing information only with other women is a form of oppositional femininity for young women in the gang because it goes against what the young men impose. Men in gangs are aware that these secrets are carefully guarded by the young women, who don't seem to brag like the men. Two male gang members discuss how they perceive this difference between young men and women.

Tony: Man, you let her go with somebody by herself, *ese,* and you know that girl she is going with macks [dates] with other people. You know she ain't going to tell you nothing.

Gustavo: I know, girls are smart dude. You don't know what girls do. They can hide their secrets, dude. Guys, they be, like, I macked on [tried to pick up] this girl, aay. Then it goes here and there, then you are like fuck, what happened? Then it gets to your girlfriend.

Young men's masculinity is constructed through interactions with men and women in the barrio. Beyond a demonstrated ability to fight, one way of constructing a masculinity is through sexual conquests of women. Young men are encouraged at an early age to become sexually involved. This helps to construct a masculinity that is similar to heterosexual expectations in the larger society. They develop a macho image by detailing their sexual conquests to the older men or friends in the neighborhood. During interviews, young gang members did not hesitate to relate their stories to another Chicano. For example, Miguel discusses his relationships with one of his girlfriends:

[So you haven't been faithful?]

Miguel: Nah, I've been trying to and shit. I been here (in detention) so…

[What did your girlfriend tell you when you were unfaithful?]

Miguel: I told her the truth and stuff because I didn't want to hurt her and shit. I told her the truth, I told her I was seeing someone else and she didn't want to talk to me. I just gave her a kiss on the cheek and I left. I didn't talk to her for about a month and shit. I think I got locked up. I got out, my cousin gave her my phone number and we started talking again. We got back together and she found out I was going out on her again. I got locked up again and I started going out with somebody else. We went to get something for my *tía* [aunt] and she saw me with some hickies on my neck. A little while after I got out, she found out I was going out with somebody else, she didn't do nothing. I told her, me and that girl aren't seeing each other no more and then I broke up with the other girl.

In the barrio, displays of sexual conquest are a way to show you are a man. The hickies displayed on gang members' necks and phone number collected from a night of partying are often worn as medals or displayed as trophies to highlight their sexual conquests. Even having children can be badges of honor for some young Chicano gang members. Not all young gang members are fathers or mothers, but they seem avidly to support heterosexual sex. If a young man does not pursue women, he is considered less than a man. For example, Frank states the following when he discusses how he meets young women: "I try sometimes, sometimes a girl likes me, you know. I ain't going to look like a punk, sitting right there when a girl likes me and my other homeboys have girls too. You do whatever happens."

During interviews in which they described their relationships with the opposite sex, homosexual activity was not discussed except in reference to young women who were assumed to be lesbians. These young women were respected for their fighting abilities similar to heterosexual men and women in the gang. For example, one youth stated the following about some of the tough young women in his gang:

Manuel: No, they're all the same way, all the same. They like girls too, ha, ha, ha. They like girls, half the girls in my gang like other girls.

[Why do you say that?]

Manuel: They are dykes, ha, ha, ha.

Young male gang members openly discussed their sexual experiences. They often suggested that they were sexually involved or that they intended to have sex with the young women they were discussing at the time of the interview. One male gang member illustrates this as he describes a night of partying:

My cousin invited me, she goes, 'Come over, you know you barely got out.' I said, 'I can't, my parole officer is going to fuck me up' [get him in trouble], she goes, 'All right then'.... I talked to her again, she said, 'Are you going to come this time?'

I said, 'Well hold on, pick me up at nine because at 8:30 p.m. is when my Keys officer [parole officer] comes to check up on me.' So I told him, 'Is it all right that I go
anywhere?' He goes, 'Yeah you better be back by twelve.' Boom, I took off, she came
to pick me up, her and a whole bunch of girlfriends. They got a Nissan truck, I
jumped in the back. I was checking them out, you know I barely got out. I had to
get me some stuff [sex]. I came out and I was checking it out you know, they had a
DJ, kegs but I didn't get drunk because I had to take UA's and stuff.[4]

Gender differences are also found in the way young people dress in the barrio. At
this period in the young women's lives, dress is an important feature in how they construct their femininity. In the home, they dress respectably, in conformity with their parents' expectations of femininity. Similarly, another, more revealing, style of dress is
apparent for their boyfriends or for various activities in the community where the
opposite sex will be found. This may include tight and short shorts called "daisy dukes"
and snug shirts that these young women wear to express their femininity. A sexy style of
dress is oppositional to parents' expectations but at the same time it implies for some
men one notion of femininity—sexual submissiveness. Young women also wear the traditional Chicano gang attire on the streets, which aids them in constructing an oppositional femininity. Interestingly, young men only wear gang clothes as they move from
the gang, to community outings, to the family setting.

Male and female gang members use their style of dress to create an image of fear.
They present themselves as heavily involved in parties, some criminal activity, and as
people who will use violence to retaliate for any insults. Young Chicanas present themselves as similar to males when they demonstrate that they will fight, use drugs, and retaliate for the community. Yet they also show their femininity by protecting and helping
other community members (such as fellow gang members' relatives) in difficult situations. One young woman illustrates how she was pressured to conform to those ideals:

Once you're in a gang and they give you a name, label, they have your respect and
they look at you because of your actions, judge you. They have that opinion forever.
Once someone knows you are a *chola,* right away they have an opinion of you, that's
like kind of bad because you grow out of it. You're still a *chola* but you're sophisticated. Like when your homeboy asks you to go do something. Or when your
homegirls are with you and you've got to do a crime or something. And you back
away from it, you're weak. You get labeled as a weak ass ranker. You know, you're not
down [loyal to the gang] anymore and you can't get that feeling of respect from the
neighborhood.

For young Chicanas and Mexicanas the gang also becomes an arena to prove that
they, too, can be loyal to the gang through violence. Notions of protecting your homeboys,

not backing down from a fight, and enacting revenge against those who have challenged you become the ideals of the marginalized Chicana and Mexicana gang members, as well as their male peers. Chicano/a and Mexicano/a gang members positively sanction these ideals, which are passed down from older, respected gang members known as *veteranos*.[5]

Although Chicanas and Mexicanas can construct their femininity by conforming to violent gang ideals, they also use aspects of their sexuality in a way that men do not. Chicanos/as and Mexicanos/as involved in gangs realize that rival gang members strive for the heterosexual ideal of using women for sex to show that they are a man. Young Chicanas are used to lure rival gang members to isolated locations, where their home-boys will jump the rival men. Depending on the individual and her situation, females are both willing participants and coerced into these actions. For example:

Carlos: I tell her what's up, I'll tell her, 'Nay, nay.' I'll tell her, 'Set that guy up, take him by himself, so we can beat him up.'

[What if she doesn't want to?]

Carlos: Then I'll tell her 'We'll kick your ass out.' I don't know because we did that a couple of times. Because when a southside girl goes to a eastside party and then my homegirls take him to a place real quick and we beat his ass.

The following quote illustrates that some young women take an active part in luring rival gangs members. They use their sexuality, as well as their ability to fight, as resources for constructing their femininity. This excerpt also illustrates how young women accomplish gender by using their sexuality as they wish, not just as men demand:

We did that before, you know what I mean. You know how they are real pretty and this and that. This is how it is for guys from other gangs. They don't have problems with girls from different gangs because you know they are all pretty. They don't look at the gang. They look, you know, because of the sex and they want to do them because of that. We did that once, setup some guys. And so she was acting like she was going to do nasties with them. She started taking off her shirt in the room and she had the window open. We all jumped in through the window and started beating him. She goes, 'You thought, you thought wrong,' and she put on her shirt. She boom, she starting kicking, pop, pop. I was like dang, ha, ha, ha.

Despite their willingness to fight, the gang rarely acknowledges the contributions of women. In fact, the gang replicates the larger society's devaluation of the contributions of women to the family, to the workforce, and to society. For example, when both male and female gang members were asked whom they respected, they all named male *veterano* gang members. Not once was a *veterana* mentioned as a person who is respected. It may be that young Chicana and Mexicana gang members are not respected because they are expected to construct their gender based on traditional notions of femininity.

Unlike male gang members, young women are expected to care for children as they grow older. Though the gang becomes a site to construct an oppositional femininity, they cannot resist the cultural expectations to care for children. This unequal view of Chicanas and Mexicanas was exemplified when male gang members were asked if the young women were as strong as the men. Often, women were viewed as weaker members of the gang because they did not display loyalty and did not "have the heart to kill." Some young men did fear particular Chicanas and Mexicanas because of their size and ability to fight. Young women sometimes agreed that the male gang members were more loyal to the gang. Nevertheless, Chicanas and Mexicanas felt many males were not loyal and believed women showed more dedication to the gang. For example, one young woman states,

Susana: I feel like female gang members are more down than guys.

[Why do you say that?]

Susana: Because we don't hesitate and I think some of my homeboys do. Me and Precious, we were walking and some guys pulled a gun out on us and all our homeboys started running. We started laughing. Shoot us, shoot us, we don't show fear.

Another young women states similar feelings,

[Are there ways that female gang members are stronger than male gang members?]

Norma: Yes. We are a lot braver than men. When I use to be banging, we'd be a lot braver than men. I mean we would have a rumble against another gang and shit, and the girls would usually stay in back. There was a couple of us that would stand in front of the fucking men and yell 'NSM motherfuckers, NSM [North Side Mafia] what's up,' and 'Fuck all you *putos.*' And we would be boxing [fighting].

[What other ways?]

Norma: We were just stronger, we never snitched. We would stand up to the boys, even our homeboys. They would tell us not to do this and to do that. We would do it anyway, and like when cops got on our asses, we would take our blame for the homeboys because they were too fucking pussied out to do what we had to do, you know. They'd rather blame it on the girls so they wouldn't go to jail, and we would be *pendeja* [stupid] enough to just say, okay.

Conclusions

My research shows that gender in the barrio is constructed differently for men and women. In most social situations young women are expected to control their sexuality. They are expected and permitted to have sex with one gang member at a time, as long as they are clearly in a romantic relationship. In other social situations young women are expected to construct a femininity that serve the purposes of the gang. Therefore, women must construct their femininity very carefully. For example, Chicano and Mexicano gangs revolve around the notion of masculinity based on sexual conquest of females. Accordingly the women must limit their sexual experiences. If they do not control their involvement in sexual activity, or at least the appearance of such involvement, both male and female gang members degrade them. These young women are sometimes called "hood rats," that is, young women whom male gang members use for sexual pleasure. Thus, even this oppositional femininity is subordinated to gang masculinity.

Chicana and Mexicana gang members are expected to protect themselves from situations that allow males to use them for sexual purposes. The "train-ins" (group rape) described by gang members illustrate this view. Moreover, "train-ins" prove to fellow gang members the masculine ideal that they are men because they adequately engage in sex (Messerschmidt 1993; Portillos et al. 1996). This notion of masculinity oppresses young Chicanas and Mexicanas and creates standards of appropriate sexual activity.

Nevertheless, the women who have been raped in do not believe these violent actions were necessary. For example, one young woman stated that her friend became angry at her because she did not stop the rape even though she knew that her friend was drunk and their homeboys were going to take advantage of her. The decision not to help out her friend who was being raped illustrates how young women are pressured to go along with group activities. Allowing the men to display their masculinity is a way to construct their femininity because the men expect and demand loyalty from young Chicana and Mexicana gang members in all social situations. Thus, to understand women's position in gangs we cannot view them simply as a new breed of violent women involved in masculine crimes. Nor can we view them as mere sex toys or tomboys. Their lives and the decisions they face each day are far more complex than such labels suggest.

4 Girls, Gangs, and Violence

Introduction: Femininities and Aggression

Construction of girls' delinquency and gang membership has always been affected by societal concerns about femininity and girlhood. For most of this century, the regulation of girls' sexuality was dominant, and those activities that did not involve girls' expression of their sexuality, including girls' violence, were largely ignored by those in authority (Shacklady-Smith 1978; see also Bernard, Fishman, and Quicker in this volume).

Early ethnographies, including many reprinted here, indicate that girls have long been involved in violent behavior as a part of gang life, but this violence tended to be ignored or trivialized. Girls' gang experience has always been looked at as less important than boys', somehow not genuine, and defined by the male experience. More recently, it has been the subject of sensationalized media accounts that generally feature young women of color. In general, girls' and women's violence tends either to be completely denied or demonized (see Chesney-Lind 1997). Usually, these constructions are deployed with an eye toward the social control of all women, rather than in the search of a true understanding of the ways in which violence works in the lives of girls on the economic and racial margins.

This section aims to take a far more nuanced look at the role of violence and the gang in the lives of these young women. The four articles explain the ways in which girls and young women "do gender," sometimes violently, in poor communities. They provide a context to understand the use of violence by marginalized girls faced with difficult choices on today's mean streets. The section concludes with a broadside against sensationalized media misrepresentations of female gangs and a plea for greater understanding. That, of course, is one purpose of this volume.

Campbell, in an important piece published here for the first time, contrasts the aggression and violence of middle class girls and women with that of the girls she interviewed who were in gangs. While, in general, Campbell found that female violence was *expressive* as opposed to *instrumental*, such a clear differentiation was not found in her analysis of the violence of girl gang members. Indeed, Campbell is struck by the instrumental language employed by her gang girls about their violent encounters. Campbell sees the instrumental violence of the gang girls she studied to be functional for an everyday life that is full of danger.

But, for Campbell, that does not mean that gang girls are "tomboys" or pretending to be men. She argues that such instrumental violence by her female gang informants were fundamentally different from how men "do gender." First, she supports the theme we have been demonstrating in this volume that aggression is normative for men, but oppositional for women. Second, boys are, on the whole, physically larger and stronger than girls. Girls, reasonably, thus, have relatively more to fear. Finally, violence is instrumental for men, not only in protection and status, but in making money. Gang women are much less involved with robbery or drug sales than gang men, two activities where violence is exceptionally functional.

These basic differences between male and female gangs are taken up by Hagedorn and Devitt. The title of their article, "Fighting Female," conveys the dual notion that female gang members not only fight others, but fight the stereotyped female role itself. They begin by demonstrating that the very idea of the female gang as a male auxiliary, mixed gender, or independent gang, may not be so much an objective truth as a reflection of different conceptions of gender held by different female gang members.

Hagedorn and Devitt demonstrate that there is substantial variation not only between female gangs, but also within them. This fact should alert readers to be cautious when reading studies based on small samples. Second, the authors of this piece demonstrate that whether the female gang was seen as being led by women or by men, whether the girls met together by themselves or not, and whether girls or guys "called the shots" varied according to the conception of gender held by each female gang member within each gang. Those girls who were more traditional saw the gang as a male auxiliary, while those girls who were more independent saw the gang as the girls' own group. This surprising finding has important implications for gang research.

Finally, the gang girls studied in Milwaukee, as a whole, "loved to fight." Hagedorn and Devitt write about a virtual "celebration" of fighting. Girls' gangs may even have fought more than the boys, but they fought differently, with fewer weapons and with less lethal consequences. In a nutshell, those who most loved to fight had a less male-centered outlook, and those who fought with less relish had more traditional notions of gender. Fighting, in other words, was as much about rebelling against being a stereotyped female as it was to "kick ass."

Deschenes and Esbensen's article takes us to the national level and reinforces the case study evidence of the violence in female gangs. They show that female gang members are more violent than male non-gang members, even in their sample drawn from middle schools with a sizable proportion of middle class students. Still, 8 % of the girls in these middle schools reported they had joined gangs, and a fifth of that number reported they had shot a gun at someone. Female gang violence nationally, this study confirms, is not to be ignored.

Chesney-Lind's piece completes this section, noting that traditional schools of criminology have assumed that for males, delinquency, even in its most violent forms, was somehow an understandable if not "normal" response to their situations. This same "understanding" is not, however, extended to girls who live in violent neighborhoods. If they engage in even minor violence, they are somehow perceived as more vicious than their male counterparts. In this fashion, the construction of an artificial, passive femininity lays the foundation for the demonization of young girls of color, as has been the case in the media treatment of girl gang members.

These sensationalistic accounts tend to suggest to an uncritical public that girls in gangs are seeking "equality" with their male counterparts by the use of violence. These journalistic notions really are little more than the old chestnut that girls are worse than boys, more devious, more cruel, and depraved. Chesney-Lind argues that such constructions bear little resemblance to reality, and links them to a backlash against girls and women, particularly girls and women of color.

All these papers show that girls' gang membership is complex and varied and that we need to seek ways of describing girls' groups without mechanically tying them to boys' groups. Curry (1988) argues that the discussion of girls' involvement with gangs has tended to go to one extreme or the other. Either girls in gangs are portrayed as victims of injury, or they have been portrayed as "liberated," de-gendered gangbangers. The truth is that both perspectives are partially correct and incomplete without the other.

Careful inquiry into the lives of these girls documents the ways in which the gang facilitates survival in their world. This volume is our small contribution to furthering that careful inquiry.

Female Gang Members' Social Representations of Aggression

*Anne Campbell**

In 1984, I reported my research on girl gang members in New York City (Campbell 1984). Generations of gang members have passed from the streets since that time, and when I left them I returned to the relative safety of studying non-criminal men and women. But the memories of gang members' lives stayed with me, and I have continued to reflect on them as a kind of testing ground for my more recent ideas. For the last few years, I have been examining gender differences in the way in which men and women understand, interpret and explain their own anger and aggression (Campbell 1993). First I will briefly outline some of these findings before seeing what they have to say about the accounts that gang girls offer of their street violence.

Female aggression differs from that of men—and not only in terms of its frequency of occurrence. Meta-analytic and narrative reviews (Bettencourt and Miller 1996; Eagly and Steffen 1986; Frodi, Macauley, and Thome 1977; Harris 1996; Hyde 1986; Knight, Fabes and Higgins 1996) indicate that women's aggression is less likely to escalate from verbal to physical; is more likely to involve crying and throwing things rather than hitting; occurs in private and with fewer observers; is directed at cross-sex (more than same-sex) targets; results in more guilt and anxiety than in men and is viewed more negatively on attitudinal inventories. The challenge is to understand not simply women's relative desistance from violence but, when it occurs, the particular pattern of emotional, behavioral, and attitudinal differences between the sexes.

To do this, I have been using the concept of social representations. These representations are everyday, lay person's theories or models about mundane but opaque phenomenon such as the causes of aggression. They are social in the sense that they are socially transmitted in a given culture rather than being devised individually by each member. Serge Moscovici (1984), who revised Durkheim's original notion of collective representations, suggested that when social groups differ in their behavior, a difference in social representation may lie at the heart of it. My first study used discourse analysis to examine how men and women talk about their experiences of aggression in spontaneous same-sex conversations (Campbell and Muncer 1987). Two distinct gender-linked models were implicit in the texts.

Men spoke of aggression in a rhetorical framework of interpersonal control. Aggression was seen as a means of social coercion when another person threatened the speaker's right to autonomy and self-esteem. Though anger (in the form of righteous indignation) was present, the chief aim of the aggression was to cause the other person

This essay is published here for the first time.

to back down and withdraw. I call this the *instrumental* representation, and it finds parallels in a number of academic theories of aggression, such as Bandura's (1973) social learning theory; Tedeschi's (Tedeschi, Smith, and Brown 1974) model of aggression as social influence; Black's (1983) view of crime as a form of social control; and in the impression management perspective, including Toch (1969), Felson (1982), and Luckenbill (1977). The key principle which unites these writers is the idea of aggression as a functional interpersonal tool for controlling others and thereby meeting personal needs which may be material, emotional or social. The accounts that men gave were characterized by a sense of challenge, excitement and even enjoyment:

> You don't want to fight the guy. I want that guy to know I'm going to beat him and I want him to back down. I don't want to hit him. I want that guy to be the guy to say, "OK, we're not going to fight." I want to maintain my self-respect. That's the kind of person I am. I just want to get one-up on him and then walk away and go "He-ha." It doesn't work that way most of the time. This is the problem. You take that one extra step, you can't walk off. It's the fear that's exciting. You're wired. Psyched.

Women used quite a different rhetorical framework—one of *expressive* aggression. Here the emphasis was upon self-control rather than interpersonal control. Women spoke at length about the psychological tension between anger and behavioral restraint and saw aggression as a failure to hold back the internal frustration—even fury—that they were feeling. The aim of the aggression was cathartic—to release the unbearable anger that they could no longer suppress. Their aggression served not to dominate their antagonist but to elicit some acknowledgement of their frustration. This expressive representation finds its academic correspondence in the hydraulic drive and instinct theories of Lorenz (1971) and Freud (1950) as well as in the frustration-aggression hypothesis (Dollard, Doob, Miller, Mowrer and Sears 1939), Berkowitz's (1989) reformulation in terms of instinctual response to negative affect, Eysenck's (1964) theory of individual differences in behavioral inhibition, Gottfredson and Hirschi's (1990) emphasis upon the restraining influence of self, as well as social, control and Bernard's (1990) view of underclass life stresses as subverting the regulation of anger expression. The critical features of the expressive representation are a focus on intrapsychic dynamics, on the accretion of stress and on aggression as dysfunctional and (in normally socialized individuals) guilt-inducing.

> We had a really terrible fight. It probably was about nothing important. I can't remember what it was about. But it did terminate with him going in and taking a shower, and I was furious. I just sort of whirled round and I tried to pick up the phone. I don't know if I wanted to throw it, but I knew it wasn't going to go far enough. So I picked up the frying pan that was right there and I tossed it right through the curtain. I didn't even think about it and then he came out dripping

holding the frying pan. And he said, "You could have killed me, do you know that?" I still didn't realize I could have killed him because I didn't feel like I wanted to kill him. It wasn't even in my head at the time that I was throwing it. I could have flung it against the wall. I just threw it at him. I really have a very blind kind of rage sometimes when I seem to get really crazy.

In a number of subsequent quantitative studies this gender difference has been confirmed in over 800 subjects (Archer and Haigh 1997a,b; Archer and Parker 1994; Campbell, Muncer and Coyle 1992; Campbell, Muncer, and Gorman 1993; Campbell and Muncer 1994; Campbell, Muncer, Guy, and Banim 1996; Campbell, Sapochnik and Muncer 1997). The effect size over these studies is large (d = .50 -1.00). I believe that women's view of their own aggression can help to account for its critical distinctive features: tears rather than blows, private rather than public location, male rather than female targets, stronger feelings of guilt, and a negative evaluation of aggression generally.

But the subjects in my own research and those of others have been predominantly middle class. When I reread the transcripts of gang girls talking about aggression, I was struck by the clear instrumental rhetoric that they used. In relating accounts of fights, the texts produced by male and female gang members were virtually interchangeable. Listen to a member of the Sex Girls in Brooklyn discussing a routine antagonistic encounter.

This girl tells me, "You'd better get out of here. This is my block." I say, "If you consider this much your block, why don't you take me out? I'm staying right here, baby." Then she sees me getting pissed off. She kept on talking to me. She got to the building, then she ran upstairs. She wouldn't come down.

This is an instrumental interpretation which emphasizes the classic features of challenge, threat, the opponent's intimidated withdrawal, and the speaker's ritual triumph. Why do young women in gangs sound so much like their male counterparts and so radically different from middle-class women?

Although representations of aggression are associated with sex, they are not determined by it. Social representations must be functional within the context of people's lived experience. Men's instrumental view fits well with the male role and the culture of masculinity contained in the social psychological literature on agency and instrumentality (Bakan 1966; Messerschmidt 1993; Spence 1985). Men's lifestyles emphasize autonomy, independence, and competition in a social world organized in terms of hierarchical power structures (Weisfeld 1980). Techniques of interpersonal control including aggression are vital where power relations are negotiated daily and where powerlessness means vulnerability (Katz 1988). Women's expressive view, in which aggression is about unendurable stress rather than interpersonal control, fits well in the more communally organized world of women. Gilligan (1982) and Tannen (1990), among many others, have described women's social world as anchored in reciprocity and interdependence and marked by an absence of hierarchical relations. Here aggression is feared as it breaks interpersonal bonds and threatens relationships.

But women's expressive view with its emphasis on self-control is only functional in a world where others also contain and curb their aggression and where interpersonal bonds are sufficiently highly valued to make aggression an undesirable option. The lives of most middle-class women fulfill these criteria. But where the bonds that bind a woman tightly to others are broken, she has no reason to desist from aggression. And where self-control is not valued but seen as a sign of weakness or cowardice, then it becomes only an avenue for her own exploitation and victimization. These are the factors that I believe are relevant in understanding why gang girls reject an expressive interpretation of aggression.

The fear and mistrust that propels them away from an expressive view of aggression begins early for gang girls. Moore's (1988) data from Chicana gang members suggests that one-third had seen their mother beaten and abused. Weeza was in her early twenties and a founding member of the Sex Girls in Brooklyn. She recalled her early years growing up in Puerto Rico.

> My father, he was always in the street—never bring money to the house. He used to work with smoke [marijuana]. He went to jail and everything, when we were small. When we got to about six or seven, he used to be going out, stay out, hit my mother. We always got to be moving, hiding, you know, late in the night and everything. Sometimes I had to be running. Hiding. I say, "Shit, what kind of life is that?

Later she found herself on the receiving end of her fathers' violence. Weeza vividly recalled her father's anger when one of her friends refused his sexual advances.

> My father, he was drunk, and it was my girlfriend here. When he's sober, he's straight, but when he's drunk, he gets a little bit nasty. She don't want to pay no attention to him because she don't like him, so he just came to her and smack her. And I tell him, "You don't do that." That was in the street. Then she came up, and he came up knocking on the door. My kid was here and he came to the living room and he start saying, "You're a whore," in Spanish, and I tell him, "Look, stop that. This is my house. You don't do that in my house. She's in my house. You want to say that, you wait for her to go outside. Don't say that in my house because my kids are here." He told me, "You're another one".... But then he came in with a gun. He shot—he almost killed me.

Moore's data suggest that sexual advances are not restricted to the daughter's friends. Twenty-nine percent of gang girls reported experiencing sexual advances from a family member (see also Chesney-Lind 1997). Even those girls who escape downright brutality, may experience emotional rejection. Connie, the leader of the Sandman Ladies, saw her father die from heroin addiction when she was two. (Forty-five percent of Moore's Chicana girls grew up in a household that contained a heroin addict.) Her mother, in bad health and desperately poor, moved between New York and Puerto Rico living with relatives or in rundown apartments. When her mother moved in with a man Connie hated, it was clear that either she or he would have to go. At eleven, Connie was sent to live permanently with her aunt. The loss of her father (experienced by more gang girls than boys) and then her mother, the constant moves and disruption left Connie with the feeling that no one cared about her. When the earliest and most fundamental relationship of trust between a parent and a child is marred by violence, it becomes harder to believe in the safety of any relationship. These unhappy and brutal childhoods led not only to a profound sense of rejection, but to an inability to give love to anyone else. As Weeza explains it:

> I never think I was in love. Never. I say inside me, "I want to find out what love means. I really don't know how to feel it. A lot of my girlfriends tell me they're in love and it feels good. But you know, I say, "I want to find out." I never feel like that. A lot of guys say they love me and you could see they love you. But for me, I never love nobody. Only my kids, I love them. But that's a different love.

Their love for their children remains constant in an emotional world that is largely empty of affection. Moore's data indicate that about 94% of gang girls have children and three-quarters are raising them. The bonds with their children are especially strong for gang girls. Because of the hardships they have known, they are extremely protective. And children provide a friend for girls who have come to distrust the world of adults. As one girl described her relationship with her baby daughter: "I think of her like a little sister in a way. And I say, 'Come on, you're little. You ain't got nobody else neither. You hang out with me and we'll learn these things together.'"

Though most vow not to tolerate the beatings that they witnessed their own mothers suffer, history has a way of repeating itself. Physical abuse is so much part of their romantic relationships that it is sometimes rationalized as a demonstration of love. And threats come from outside as well as inside the home. The neighborhoods in which gangs thrive are amongst the poorest and most crime-ridden in the city. Rapes, burglaries and robberies are frequent. Assaults in bars and on the streets are commonplace. Drug dealers and pimps own the sidewalks. No one is safe, not even gang girls when they are alone.

Girls As Crazy Women

The gang offers solutions to their two most fundamental needs: acceptance and safety. The two are intimately connected. Because they are so often victimized by those who purport to love them, the gang offers a sisterhood of like-minded others and an escape from victimization by force of numbers and the gang's tough reputation. Initiation guarantees exclusiveness. The gang will not accept just anyone, and this fact alone augments their self-esteem, which has taken hard knocks from teachers, social workers, police, and families. It also guarantees that members are willing and able to fight in support of one another. This give-and-take of protection and support is what initiation is all about. The gang rejects "prospects" whose aim is merely to avail themselves of the gang's fighting ability for their own ends—they must contribute as well as benefit from it.

Once in the gang, the girls work as hard as the boys on their reputation as fighters. The demonstration of "heart" or courage in the public forum of intergang feuds is a requirement for the image-promoting talk which the girls enjoy. Once a girl has proved that she is capable of handling herself in a fight, she is licensed to proclaim herself to be a "crazy bitch." This mutually endorsed bragging is a process by which specific acts of daring are crystallized, elaborated, and offered as incontrovertible evidence of toughness. Stories are told and retold; each time the fear is minimized and the cold instrumentality exaggerated until the girls persuade their listeners and themselves that they are invulnerable. When they have persuaded themselves of their own fearlessness, they begin to use aggression as a response to any potential threat. Aggression becomes preemptive rather than reactive.

So hard do the girls work on their crazy reputations, that it is easy to miss the small voice of fear and vulnerability that runs as a counterpoint to the brave talk. Booby's description of the value of toughness reflects the fear of its opposite. Openness and trust become weakness, and to be weak is to be exploited.

> Let's say you're a new jack round here, right? You be going to the store, they be taking your money. Now if you ain't going to kick their ass, they're going to keep picking on you. So before they wind up kicking your ass, you got to get tough on them. If not, you can't even walk the streets by yourself. They're going to wind up hurting you or killing you or whatever they feel. You have to be tough out here.

The transformation from fear to belligerence is essentially a shift from an expressive to an instrumental representation of aggression. Self-control and the containment of anger do nothing to prevent victimization. So they begin to see aggression as a way of controlling other people. It becomes instrumental. The uses of a tough reputation—of being considered crazy or *loco*—was succinctly explained by a member of the Turban Queens in Brooklyn:

> I'm glad I got a reputation. That way nobody will start with me, you know. Nobody will fuck with me—they know, you know. They're going to come out losing. Like all of us, we got a reputation. We're crazy, nobody wants to fight with us for that reason, you know. They say, "No, man. That girl might stab me or cut my face or something like that.

Fear and loneliness in their families, their communities, their schools, and their homes are the forces that drive young women from an expressive to an instrumental view of their aggression. They live in circumstances of poverty and disorganization that have eroded the old taboos against attacking and exploiting women. For these girls, aggression as a line of last resort is no longer a tenable viewpoint. To survive, force must be met with more than unspoken anger or frustrated tears. Less physically strong and more sexually vulnerable, the best line of defense is not attack but the threat of attack. The key to this is the development of a reputation for violence which will ward off opponents. There is nothing so effective as being in a street gang to keep the message blaring out: "Don't mess with me—I'm a crazy woman."

Some will object that the scenario I have described is equally true for male gang members—that they also become "hardmen" in an attempt to protect themselves from victimization. But I believe that there is a fundamental difference between the sexes. First, boys are part of a masculine subculture that prescribes instrumental aggression as a gender-affirming response to threat or challenge. Developmental psychologists have amply demonstrated the power of the male peer group from the age of three to support aggressive coercion as an index of status (Boulton 1996; Fagot 1985; Weisfeld 1980). The cut-and-thrust ethos of competition and dominance is part and parcel of male development. So the nurturing of a tough reputation is normative in young men, while in young women it is less common because most girls are protected from the masculine maelstrom of attack and counter-attack. Second, as boys develop into men they are physically better able to deal with physical attack because of their size and strength, whereas, even as adults, women face a situation in which half the population is stronger than they are. Third, men in gangs, having established a reputation for instrumental violence, are willing to use it not just to preempt attack, but as a means of systematic financial gain (Fagan 1990; Taylor 1990).

Young women in gangs are much less likely to be involved in robbery, protection rackets, rape, and extortion—all of which involve the use of instrumental aggression in the service of economic or sexual gain. Aggression as a means of protection is distinct from aggression as a source of income. Women certainly commit economic crimes, but they are more likely to shoplift, write bad checks, use stolen credit cards, and defraud welfare than to engage in robbery or extortion (Daly 1989; Steffensmeier and Allan 1996).

It is tempting to gloss my remarks as implying that gang girls are more masculine than their non-gang counterparts, and I want to make it very clear that this is not what I am saying. We have traveled down that road before and found it to be a dead-end. Gang girls are not to be pathologized as pseudo-males. My point is that when young women lose their trust in others, the idea of mutual dependence is the first casualty. When they are victimized and exploited the idea of expressive aggression—the middle-class feminine idea of aggression as a breakdown of self-control—is no longer tenable. It cannot compete with the ethos of instrumental aggression without becoming self-destructive. Instrumental aggression is the lowest common denominator. If we are willing to allow young women to be exploited by poverty and crime—if we can offer them no way out of victimization—then we can hardly be surprised if they respond by nurturing a self-protective reputation for craziness. If women like men are forced to see trust as weakness and vulnerability, the attraction of being a "hardwoman" is easy to see.

Fighting Female:
The Social Construction of Female Gangs

John M. Hagedorn and Mary L. Devitt[*]

> *In short, people do not simply want to excel; they want to excel as a man or as a woman...*
> *in seeking solutions to their problems of adjustment, they seek solutions that will not endanger*
> *their identification as essentially male or female.*
> —*Albert Cohen*

> *Q: When you were active in the gang, how did you personally feel about fighting?*
> *A: I loved it.*
> *Q: Why?*
> *A: 'Cause I used to kick ass!*
> —*Milwaukee female gang member*

There is a growing interest in female gangs, hopefully not all of it due to the inducement of federal research money on the topic (Curry this volume). Historically, female gangs have been generally dismissed as too few to bother with (Thrasher 1927) and have been neglected in theoretical work (e.g., Cloward and Ohlin 1960). Even today, female gangs have been ignored by some (e.g., Sanchez-Jankowski 1991) or characterized as little more than "pale imitations" of male gangs (Spergel 1995). In the last few years there have been a few important, if contradictory studies (e.g., Joe and Chesney-Lind this volume; J. Miller 1996; Moore 1991; Taylor 1993). However, we are still short on both facts and theory.

Contemporary conceptualizations of female gangs can be divided into those which follow the "liberation hypothesis" (Taylor 1993) and those which advocate "the social injury hypothesis" (Joe and Chesney-Lind 1995). Basically, the liberation view suggests that changing female gender roles have had a major influence on gang girls, increasing the number of female gangs, and inducing young women to become more violent and more involved with male activities, like drug sales. The contrary view questions the extent of those changes and points to the more serious harm the gang causes for women, who, these researchers argue, come from more troubled families than gang men. Curry in this volume suggests that the two viewpoints can be reconciled.

What this promising but still small literature may lack is a full appreciation of variation. It also may lack understanding of the different ways the female gang can be socially constructed. This paper looks at variation between Milwaukee female gangs as well as within them. We argue that female gangs vary as much as male gangs, and on many of the same criteria. We also find that the nature and structure of both male and

*This essay is published here for the first time.

female gangs is not a simple, objective fact, but socially constructed by gang members, among others. We question the validity and utility of the long-standing typology of female gangs as mixed gender, autonomous, or male auxiliary (W. Miller 1973). The paper concludes with an exploration of how the Milwaukee female gang member is "fighting female."

The Nature of Female Gangs

There have been many recent critiques of the failure of the gang literature to address the nature of female gangs (Campbell 1990; Curry 1995; Moore 1991). Suffice it to say, female gangs have not been a high priority for gang research. One reason for the lack of academic attention may be that female gangs are less violent and cause less trouble than male gangs. Therefore female gangs are of less interest to gang research, which is strongly influenced by the needs of law enforcement. This possibility is not a flattering one for social science.

Another less than complimentary reason for the neglect of female gangs may be criminology's historically male perspective. In their classic article on feminism and criminology, Daly and Chesney-Lind (1988, 508) point out that criminology has two different problems when it comes to women. First is the generalizability problem: the assumption that male theories of gangs can be generalized to women. Second is the problem of how to explain the fact that women commit fewer and less violent offenses than males, or the gender ratio problem.

The Generalizability Problem

Most gang researchers have spent little time studying female gangs. The first author of this article (Hagedorn 1988) is not innocent of this sin of omission. This overall lack of attention, we think, is based on three different assumptions. The first is that there just aren't that many female gangs, so there is little reason to generalize. Like all gang research, this idea started with Thrasher (1927/1966, 161) who flatly said: "Gangs composed entirely of girls are exceedingly rare."

Thrasher found only five or six female gangs out of 1,313 gangs he studied. Cloward and Ohlin (1960), in their classic statement of differential opportunity theory, did not mention female gangs, and Spergel's (1964) version mainly saw girls as instigators of fights or subverters of the male gang through marriage. The gang, for most earlier researchers, was a male phenomenon, and gender sometimes completely disappeared as a variable. Many reports of female gangs conceptualized them solely as ladies auxiliaries, composed of "sex objects" and "tomboys" who did not have any independent role or life. Campbell (1990) pointed out that much of what we know about earlier female gangs was provided by male gang members, male outreach workers, or male gang researchers. And as Moore (1991, 53-57) showed, gang men may have very different ideas about the relationship of females in the gang to males than do gang women. Other studies questioned the absence of girls in gangs or disputed that they played solely a passive role (see Bowker and Klein 1983; Brown 1977; M. G. Harris 1988; Quicker 1983).

Some recent surveys of gangs suggest that the relative paucity of female gangs may be changing and prompt us to question the accuracy of past estimates. While Miller (1975) found that about 10% of gang members were female, as did Campbell (1984), Esbensen and Huizinga (1993) found a quarter of Denver gang members were girls and Moore (1991) and Fagan (1990) estimated that about a third of gang members were women. Data from the Rochester Youth Survey found that more females than males claimed to be participating in gangs (Bjerregaard and Smith 1993). Curry et al. (1996), however, found that at most 5% of all gang members identified by law enforcement were females. Even if lower estimates are more accurate, we are still looking at no less than 25,000 active female gang members with perhaps 100,000 girls and young women who recently have been involved with gangs in the U.S. (see Chesney-Lind et al. 1996).

A second assumption which has led us away from the need to study female gangs is that "female gangs are mostly alike." Earlier studies of gangs, like Thrasher's, found the few female gangs to be mainly male auxiliaries, and concluded that there was little need to look for further variation. Most contemporary researchers (e.g., Swart 1991) follow Miller (1975), who categorized female gangs primarily by their relationship to male gangs—as auxiliaries, mixed, or autonomous. One female gang Miller (1973) studied, the Molls, were mainly concerned with currying favor with men. More recent studies, however, have found many more types of girl gangs. Moore (1991) finds many significant differences among East Los Angeles female gangs, as does Brotherton (1996) in San Francisco. Klein (1995, 65-66), though not spending many pages of his latest book on girls in the gang, summarizes a more contemporary understanding of female gangs:

> Another thing to note about the girl gangs, just as with the boys, is that they came in a wide variety of sizes, structures, age ranges, and levels of criminal involvement. The best generalization is not that they had a particular character but that they showed considerable variation on just about all dimensions of interest.

The final reason often given for not studying female gangs is the view that data from male gangs can be easily generalized to female gangs. Cohen (1955, 140) has been widely noted for dismissing women as delinquents, arguing, from anomie theory, that "the delinquent is a rogue male." Likewise Spergel (1995, 90), citing Anne Campbell, claims that female gangs are "pale imitations" of male gangs. For this reason, he says, "The emphasis…is on the male gang member." This implies rather blatantly that we don't need to study female gangs, since we can simply generalize from male gangs and water down our findings (e.g., Bjerregaard and Smith 1993).

Feminist criminology has taken issue with the notion of the generalizability of male delinquency theories to females. Noting that most classic theories of crime are based on the notion that masculinity is at the core of delinquency (e.g., Cohen above), Chesney-Lind and Shelden (1992, 67) conclude:

> In carefully reading these influential works, one reaches the unavoidable conclusion that uncritical constructions of traditional gender roles found their way into the core of these theories…it is unclear how such theories would address the situation of girls in poor neighborhoods.

Other scholarship has pointed out that female peer groups are not just "boy-centered" and are as influential to their members as male groups (Bowker and Klein 1983; Giordano this volume). What may differ may not be the ecological processes which lead both boys and girls to form gangs, but rather the different kinds of experiences within the gang and different reactions of parents and authorities (Bowker and Klein 1983; Moore 1991). The social injury hypothesis is based on an understanding that the gang experience may in fact be more harmful for women than for men. In that regard, while Cohen's *Delinquent Boys* was based on stereotypes of female behavior, some of his comments may ring true to "difference" or cultural feminists (e.g., Gilligan 1982; Johnson 1988):

> It follows from all this that the problems of adjustment of men and women…rise out of quite different circumstances and press for quite different solutions. (Cohen 1955, 139)

William Swart (1991) has argued that females in gangs are striving to be "acceptably deviant." His research is based on male auxiliary gangs whose members are struggling to moderate their sexuality, drug use, and violent behavior in order to maintain contrasting gender roles to male gang members. For Swart, female gang behavior is "deviant either way." If gang girls act liberated, they are chastised by traditional male gang members. If they act traditionally, they are chained to live out the devalued status accorded females by society. Swart's notion of moderate drug use by females is contradicted by data from Moore (1991) and others. Swart's argument needs to take into account a greater variability in female gang behavior than he supposed. He also narrowly defines girls' deviance primarily in terms of their relationship to men and ignores variation by ethnicity. Still, his attention to the different ways in which female gang members conceive their gender roles effectively questions the generalizability of studies of male gangs.

It can be concluded that in order to generalize from male theories and data to female gangs, researchers need to take into account differences in how gender is acted out. This leads directly to the gender ratio problem.

The Gender Ratio Problem

Simply stated, there is a considerable body of evidence that gang girls compared to gang boys, like women generally compared to men, commit less crime and especially less violent crime. We've argued that this may be one reason for the lack of attention to female gangs. But we need to briefly consider the evidence for and against this proposition and the rationales behind the competing points of view.

Thrasher did not find it difficult to understand why girls did not form gangs and were less criminally inclined. As a control theorist, he saw that girls were more tightly supervised in their adolescent lives than boys, and girls are more influenced by family and tradition, and apparently more content with their lives. Zones of transition where gangs were found were only disorganized for less supervised males, Thrasher contended. Those few girls who did join gangs, the father of gang research said, were tomboys playing the role of the male.

Addressing the gender ratio issue directly, Cloward and Piven (1979) agree with Thrasher that adolescent males tend to hang out more together, and much of their deviance is thus collective and rebellious. They argue that women, on the other hand, are more likely to be socially isolated and this leads to more individual, as opposed to group, deviance. As a result, female deviance is more individual and self-destructive than males' and women deviate much less in aggregate.

However, Cloward and Piven directly challenge Thrasher's explanation for the absence of girl gangs. They argue that there is no reason to conclude that women have lower levels of stress than males, but rather choices of how to confront stress are gendered and vary by placement in the social structure. Women's relative lack of involvement in collective deviance is attributed to two factors: (1) the absence of ideological traditions which define stresses experienced by woman as wrong and mutable, and (2) the gendered patriarchal reality that women are simply denied the capacity to make some types of responses to oppression (1979, 661-64).

> We suggest, in short, that given the disabling and killing character of the deviant options open to them, women simply choose to endure stress...stress not only fails to lead to particular deviant adaptations; it may lead to none at all.

This view however, has been strongly challenged by criminologists who claim that "women's liberation" and the changing occupational structure are influencing women to become more like men—and more criminally inclined. The liberation hypothesis is based on a notion that changes in the economic and social structure are equalizing gender roles (Adler 1975b). It is consistent with the views of "second wave" or liberal feminists who argue that woman's equality means being given the opportunity to "act like men" (see Daly and Chesney-Lind 1988, 509-12).

The influence of economic changes on gangs has been widely noted, and is a standard variable with "underclass" theories of male gangs (e.g., Hagedorn 1988). Carl Taylor (1993) argues that changes in economic and social conditions have spawned the creation of corporate gangs who are concerned only about money (see also Lauderback, Hansen, and Waldorf 1992). Tracing the history of male and female African American gangs over the past sixty years in Detroit, in an historical account rivaled only by Moore's (1978; 1991), Taylor (this volume, p. 197) also sees a developmental process in female gangs.

> In the 1950s female gangs were auxiliaries to male gangs....The females were the property of their male "brother" gangs…

The urban riots of the 1960s brought with them a new nationalist consciousness and this politicization deeply impacted black females. But the promise of the sixties and seventies gave way to the more depressing realities of the eighties and nineties. Drug dealing and violence took over the world of gangs, and from the less organized scavenger and territorial gangs, corporate gangs emerged with a focus on getting rich through drug sales. Taylor (this volume 205, 208) concludes with a forthright synopsis of the liberation hypothesis, brilliantly applied to African Americans:

> Black women, while not identifying in the same way with white feminist "women's liberation," had grown up in the 1970s with the kind of strong black women symbolized by Angela Davis. In the 1980s, black females played a different role in gangs than in the 1970s. The 1980s brought radical changes for females in Detroit… *Where women have entered the corporate arena and proven their worth, the gang generally does not differentiate between the sexes.* [Emphasis added.]

This view has come under strong attack on empirical as well as theoretical grounds. Statistically, there does not seem to be much proof that women are becoming more violent or much more involved with serious criminal activities (Steffensmeier and Steffensmeier 1980; Chesney-Lind and Sheldon 1992). For example, one Chicago study found that while gang-motivated murders of women had increased in the 1990s, the risk of a woman becoming an offender has remained stable for more than thirty years (Block et al. 1996). If crime by women has not seriously increased, why so much attention to it by the media and some academics?

Meda Chesney-Lind (this volume, p. 309), for one, argues forcefully that the media and academics like Taylor sensationalize female participation in gangs and fuel a "backlash" against women's advancement into male occupations: "As young women are demonized by the media, their genuine problems can be marginalized and then ignored. Indeed, they have become the problem."

Understanding why women are less violent than men is one factor at the heart of the "difference" school of feminism (e.g., Gilligan 1982; Johnson 1988; Lorber 1994) and carries over into the gang literature. For Anne Campbell (1993, 8), in her underappreciated study of female violence, male and female violence are fundamentally different.

> In the normal course of growing up, girls learn to respond to aggression not with a sense of being purified and calmed but with a sense of shame. Aggression feels good to men but not to women.

Female violence, according to Campbell, is expressive of their inner rage (50), while for men violence is instrumental toward dominating others (see also Klein 1995, 111). Gang girls don't like to fight, they get forced into a corner, and then explode. Joe and Chesney-Lind (1995, 425) concur:

> For girls, fighting and violence are part of life in the gang—but not something they necessarily seek out.

Female peer groups, Johnson (1988) finds, are less competitive and less hierarchical than male groups. Male peer groups are also based on a devalued status of women, an outlook which carries over into female peer groups. Girls, however, Campbell (1984) argues, are in gangs for different reasons than boys. While both boys and girls see the gang as a temporary antidote to a future of powerlessness in the underclass, girls are also struggling to escape a bleak future of domestic labor, the responsibility for children, subordination to men, and the social isolation of the housewife. Women seek an escape in the gang, but find the patriarchal and status seeking nature of society reproduced by boys acting out their masculine fantasies of power and domination. This leads to disillusionment and more oppression.

> In understanding the fundamentally conservative structure and values of the gang, the position of girls becomes more explicable. Females must accept the range of roles within the gang that might be available to them in society at large…. The traditional structure of the nuclear family is firmly duplicated in the gangs. (Campbell 1993, 242)

For Campbell, feminine gender roles are reproduced even in youth gangs. Campbell argues that gang girls adopt a male "instrumental" perspective on violence in order to keep themselves from becoming victims (1984/1991, 87; see also Messerschmidt 1986, 44). Indeed, for Campbell (1993, 136), the gang is

> a sisterhood of like-minded others and an escape from victimization by sheer force of numbers and a tough reputation.

Unfortunately, we have too few studies of gang girls as they grow up to be able to confidently generalize. Most studies do not explore variation within the gang and draw conclusions based on the observations of a few female gang members in convenience samples. Daly and Chesney-Lind (1988, 519) point out that the only way to develop theory is to get our "hands dirty" and do research on young girls' lives. This inductive perspective has been fundamental to our on-going Milwaukee gang study (Hagedorn 1990). It is past time for us to apply it to female gangs.

Methods and Description of the Sample

The patterns described here are based on quantitative and qualitative analysis of data from a study of founding members of Milwaukee female gangs, collected in 1995. As in previous studies, the research follows an inductive and collaborative model (see Moore 1978), in which gang members cooperate with academic staff to focus the research design, construct interview schedules, conduct interviews, and interpret the findings.

For this study, 72 women, core members present when their gangs took names, were interviewed by former female gang members on our staff, using an interview schedule consisting of over 500 questions, and 12 information grids. Information was also collected on an additional 176 women who were identified as having been members of the eight gangs to which the interviewed members had belonged. Interviews generally lasted from one and a half to four hours, were conducted face-to-face, generally in the respondent's home, and were audio-taped and transcribed. Respondents were paid $50, and a finder's fee of $50 was paid to those who identified eligible others willing to be interviewed. A Certificate of Confidentiality was obtained from the National Institute on Drug Abuse.

This study built on extensive field work and observation with Milwaukee gangs and gang members over a number of years. During the early 1980s, the principal author directed the first gang diversion program in the city, and became acquainted with many leaders and other founders of these groups. He has maintained a privileged relationship with many of them. Previous studies focused primarily on male gang members.

To better understand variation between and within the gangs, we interviewed nearly the entire rosters of two female gangs and sampled from rosters made up of the original founding members from six other female gangs in three different types of neighborhoods. Only five (7%) of the women said that they considered themselves still members of their gang. Founders are likely to be representative of "hard core" gang members, and not of peripheral members or "wannabes." As time has passed, the exploits of the gang founders have been handed down and they have been looked up to by younger Milwaukee gang members as street "role models." Our research design does not enable us to conclude how representative our sample is of succeeding groups of gang members.

Twenty-five percent of the women interviewed were African American, and 75% Latina. Among the Latinas, 19 (35.2%) were Mexican; 33 (61.1%) were Puerto Rican; and two others (3.7%) were mixed. Their median age was 28 years, with 80% between 25 and 29 years old. The interview had the women recount their gang experiences in the early and mid-1980s and reflect on their personal lives. Extensive detail was elicited concerning the women's experiences of violence, drugs and drug-dealing in and outside of the gang, family of origin and adult family. The women were also asked about current employment and income, future goals, and attitudes related to gender and gang life.

Milwaukee female gangs were not made up exclusively of extremely poor underclass women. Twenty-six (36.1%) of the women said their family had "never" had a really rough time with the basics of food, housing and clothes when they were growing up; twenty-six (36.1%) answered in the middle, indicating some of the time, and only nine (12.5%) said "all the time." The mean response to this item was 3.49, on a scale of 1 (all the time) to 5 (never). Twenty-six (36.1%) of the women said that the family they grew up with had at some time owned their own home.

Still most female gang members experienced considerable trouble growing up. Thirty-eight (52.8%) of the women had either run away, or been kicked out of the house at some point in their youth. Of these, 19 (26.3%) had run away but had not been kicked out and 4 (5.5%) had been kicked out, but had not run away. Fifty-one (70.8%) of the women interviewed had not completed high school at the time of our interview.

Of the twenty-one who had finished high school, 6 (8.3%) said they had some further schooling. Sixteen (22.2 %) of the women were married; 2 (2.7 %) were divorced; fifty two (72.2 %) had never been married and 23 (31.9 %) said they had a steady man. Sixty-two (86.1%) of the women had kids, with the number of children ranging from 1 to 8 (mean 2.52). The ages of these gang women's children ranged from infant to 29 years. One quarter of the women had children two or younger at the time of the interview. Three-quarters had children 6 years of age or younger. These women became mothers at ages ranging from 13 to 27. One quarter had had their first baby by age 17; half by age 19.5; three-quarters by age 22.

The Social Construction of the Female Gang

Q: In some gangs, the girls say that the guys treat them like possessions. How true do you think that is for your gang?

A: Very true. Because they talked about us like bitches. Like bitches, like when they were with you, they'd hug you and then they'd let... well you can have her. And shit like that. They were typical men, they didn't give a shit. Even now they talk [like that].

The dominant typology of female gangs has classified them as male auxiliaries, autonomous female gangs, or mixed gender gangs (W. Miller 1975). This typology assumes that the central characteristic of female gangs is their relationship to male gangs. Male gangs have been historically classified as fighting gangs, criminal gangs, or retreatist gangs (Cloward and Ohlin 1960), or more recently by Klein (1995) as youth gangs versus drug gangs (see also Skolnick 1990). Female gangs, however, are apparently best defined by whether or not they are tied to a male gang.

While a moment's reflection reveals the male bias of this dubious assumption, the question of the relationship of male to female gangs may depend on whom you ask. If you ask men about the female gang, you may get different answers than if you ask the women. And women may differ among themselves. When we asked women how their gang started, most of our respondents from all eight female gangs described for us the classic portrait of the formation of a peer group:

> It's just a group of girls who hung out and hanging out at the playground. I used to
> have a lot of friends, and we used to hang like in big groups. We probably started out
> in like groups of ten and then one day we just came together, we just decided to
> come together as a group.

These are the modal responses from Latina and African American gang members who were in gangs with similar names to male gangs in their neighborhoods. Were these gangs male auxiliaries? For the women who were in African American gangs, the answer was unambiguously "no." Only 1 (6%) of the girls said the guys decided who should be in the gang, while nearly 90% said "the girls decided" and one other said "both" decided.

For Latinas, the situation was different. Only a third of the Latinas answered that they held female-only meetings compared to three quarters of the African Americans. Differences between Latinas and African Americans on "who calls the shots," who decided who joined, and whether girls held meetings on their own were highly significant. Differences also existed among Latinas, even within the same gang. While about half of Latinas said that the girls called the shots, about a quarter said it was the guys, and 15% said both, with the remainder giving an ambiguous answer. Some Latinas saw the gang as being started by the males:

> Well... they, the guys, it was guys ... I guess they decided they needed girls. So all
> the girls that used to hang around they just got them.
>
> Q: How did the female gang get started?
> A: It's just a division of the guys. Guys were the Kings and we were Queens. We
>   went out with some of them so we started calling ourselves Queens.

Some saw the female gang in a way similar to Anne Campbell:

> Well we were part of their gang, the guys' gang. So we were somewhat their property.

Others had a more ambivalent understanding, seeing the girls as the active force, after the guys in the neighborhood had already formed a gang:

> Q: Why did the guys want a female gang?
> A: I don't think they wanted a female gang, I think we were just there. I don't
>   think they ever said, "We're going to get a girl gang together."... I really can't
>   tell you how it started, it was that we were just there.

Contrast this variety of answers to the more stereotyped descriptions of female gangs by male gang members. In the original interviews with 47 gang members (Hagedorn 1988), the guys were asked about the female gangs. Here's one male gang member describing how he saw the role of teenage female gang members:

Females in the projects, we call 'em PJs. PJ Queens, you know. You got a man out here, and you his queen. You sittin' up on his throne.

Most thought very little about the role of girls in the gang. These answers were typical:

Q: Did the girls have their own thing, or was it separate or what?
A: Just like us. We come home from a fight and the girls are waiting for us here. (Laughter).
A: Yeah, we had a few girls that we called the Queens. That was mostly a couple of my cousins and a few odd girlfriends, a few nieces.

When asked whether the women had their own gang, some male gang members said the girls had a separate group, but it was under control of the men:

Q: Did they have their own thing or was it part of the Gangsters?
A: They had their own thing and it was part of the Gangsters. They were like our fillies—our women, you see?

Others denied any autonomy for the girls:

Q: So you don't have a separate group of girls at all?
A: No. It don't look right for girls to be in gangs.

Q: Do the girls have their own separate thing, or are they part of it?
A: They serve us.
Q: Serve us?
A: Serve us men… women supposed to serve, that's how we look at it. They supposed to serve us.

We can easily understand the self-interested reasons behind the men's understanding of the female gang: having a female auxiliary fits in with their view of the dominant position of the male. But why did Latinas from the same gang give contradictory responses to our questions about autonomy? Most—nearly all African Americans, but also most Latinas—experienced their gang as being started by women themselves. Some Latinas (but no African Americans) insisted that the "leader" of the gang was a man. For example, this woman is asked to explain why the guys treated Latinas "like possessions":

I don't think it's got to do with anything, it's just the way that Hispanic guys are.

			Table 1

Gang Structure by Ethnicity

Interview questions	African Americans N=18	Latinas N=54	Signif. Chi Sq.
Who called the shots?			p < .05
Girls on their own	88.2%	46.2%	
Both girls and guys	5.9	15.4	
Guys	5.9	23.1	
Other		15.4	
Who decided who got in?			p < .05
Girls on their own	87.5	44.2	
Both girls & guys		32.7	
Guys	12.5	17.3	
Other		5.8	
Did the girls have meetings on their own?			p <.01
Yes	77.8	31.5	
No	22.2	66.7	
No response		1.9	
Did gang have leaders?			N. S.
Yes	66.7	53.8	
No	33.3	46.2	
How organized was the gang?			N.S. (p <.07)
Very organized	16.7	3.8	
Organized	50.0	71.2	
Not very organized	16.7	21.2	
Not organized at all	16.7	3.8	

One reason for a more traditional view of the gang may be that more Latinas were girl friends of male gang members, which may have influenced their perspective. A few Latinas, we reported earlier (Moore and Hagedorn 1996), were organized as sexual possessions for the gang leader's drug connections' pleasure. These women also surely had a different perspective on the gang than other members, who strongly differentiated themselves from dope fiends, crack whores, sluts, or other kinds of mere "sex objects.

Another source of variation may be the way a woman, particularly a Latina, conceptualizes her gender—whether she saw herself as a traditional deferential female, or as a more independent woman. African Americans were significantly less traditional on most measures than Latinas. However, Latinas who were more traditional in upbringing (Spanish was primarily spoken in their home) and those who felt that "the guys treated them like possessions," were significantly more likely than other Latinas to say that the guys called the shots in the gang. The highest percentage of those who said the gang was

**Gang Structure by Ethnicity:
Latinas Only**

Table 2

Interview questions	Mexican N=19	Puerto Rican N=33	Signif. Chi Sq.
Who called the shots?			N.S.
Girls on their own	63.2%	36.4%	
Both girls and guys, situational	26.3	36.4	
Guys	10.5	27.3	
Who decided who got in?			p < .05
Girls on their own	72.2	31.3	
Both girls and guys	22.2	43.8	
Guys	5.6	21.9	
Other		3.1	
Did the girls have meetings on their own?			p <.001
Yes	68.4	15.2	
No	31.6	84.8	
Did gang have leaders?			N. S.
Yes	61.1	53.1	
No	38.9	46.9	
How organized was the gang?			N.S.
Very organized	5.6	3.1	
Organized	66.7	71.9	
Not very organized	27.8	18.8	
Not organized at all		6.3	

mainly negative (46%) were among those women who said the guys called the shots. Importantly, all of the women (23.7%) who regarded the gang as a positive experience, reported that the girls decided things by themselves. In other words, Latinas who expressed more independent attitudes tended to think the gang was female run and felt better about their experiences. Women who were more traditional were more likely to see themselves within a mixed gender gang, dominated by the men, and look at the gang experience negatively.

For African American women, the gang was socially constructed in a different way. While interviewing the women on the rosters of one female gang, we uncovered an entire "gang" of women who claimed the same name as the gang we were studying, were from the same school, at the same time, but whose existence as "gang members" was unknown to all but one girl from the original gang. These women were dismissed by the female gang members we interviewed as "wannabes," or women who were tricked by the guys into believing they were in a gang so the men could sleep with them. We were only able to interview one of these women (the one who was on our original roster). But for her, those on the second roster were also "real members" whose sexual relationship to the guys legitimated their status. So which gang was real and which was Memorex?

The social construction of the gang experience varied not just between and within ethnic groups, but even within the "same" gang. The boundaries, membership, and structure of the gang itself were socially constructed and this construction was related to various conceptions of gender.

Women were not alone in socially constructing their gangs. The men we interviewed within the same gang differed on such fundamental issues as whether the gang had a leader, who that leader was, and which gang member was the first to sell dope (the modal answer in some gangs was "me").

Thus both males and females socially constructed their gangs. For social scientists, this should lead us at least to doubt the copious allegations by male gang

More Gang Differences by Ethnicity

Table 3

Interview Questions	African Americans N=18	Latinas N=54	Signif. Chi Sq.
The guys treated the girls like possessions.			$p <.001$
True	29.4%	87.0%	
Not true	70.6%	13.0%	
Did the women deal drugs by themselves or were they part of the guys' operation?			N.S. ($p < .06$)
By themselves	8.3%	1.9%	
Part of the guys' operation	8.3%	42.3%	
Not deal, no response	83.3%	55.8%	
Did you ever use cocaine on a daily basis?			$p <.01$
Yes	27.8%	66.7%	
No	72.2%	33.3%	
How often did you go to school high when you were a teenager?			$p <.05$
Never	38.9%	42.0%	
Once in a while	0%	28.0%	
At least once a week	22.2%	10.0%	
Almost every day	38.9%	20.0%	
Was the gang more positive or negative?			$p < .01$
More Positive	3.3%	5.7%	
Mixed	50.0%	58.5%	
More Negative	16.7%	35.8%	
Did you go with anyone in the gang?			N.S. (p<.08)
Yes	61.1%	81.5%	
No	38.9%	18.5%	

members that a female gang is their "auxiliary." For women, the issue of autonomy is likely tied to differing conceptions of gender. Stereotypes of the female auxiliary are often based on interviews with one or two female gang members, often the girl friends of male gang members (e.g., Decker and Van Winkle 1996). Why should we take the men—or their girlfriends—at their word, and not listen to all of the women? Our method in this study of interviewing the entire membership of a gang uncovered a more complex picture.

Differences Between Female Gangs

Q: How did you get started?

A: A fight at a block party.

Q: I'm sure that's not the only fight at block parties that ever happened. Why did this one lead to a gang?

A: Well, there was a family feud and me and my sister didn't lose the fight. It was only me and her against the family.… A lot of the guys [in the male gang], I didn't know them at the time, they were at the block party and they broke up the party cause it wasn't a fair fight.… [the male gang members] started hanging around the house.

The eight female gangs we studied varied as much as the male gangs. For example, female gangs started in many ways, like the one above which began in classic Thrasher-style, integrated by conflict, with a twist of male involvement. There were some female gangs who did not have a companion male gang, and reported they started as a "dancing group" (Hagedorn 1988), or another variant of "just girls hanging out." Some of the girls in these gangs became all-female drug-selling cliques. To these women, our questions about their relationship to male gangs had no relevance whatsoever.

Other women joined pre-existing male neighborhood gangs, as barroom buddies. For these women there was no concept of a female gang at first, but just men and women who hung out together.

There was no female gang, we just hung around with them…like we were friends of theirs, and we just hung around with them. Just hung out.

Later the women in this gang formed an all-women's group entirely composed of girl friends and relatives of the Chicago-affiliated male gang.

Other differences between gangs include ethnicity and whether girls sell drugs or not, a central variable in Klein's (1995) analysis of male gangs. In Milwaukee in the mid 1980s, Latinas sold drugs as part of an on-going cocaine selling operation, while African American women did not. This is related to the earlier appearance of cocaine in Milwaukee Latino neighborhoods than in African American neighborhoods (see Hamid

1992), which explains why Latinas used cocaine as teenagers and African Americans did not (Hagedorn et al., 1998). However, marijuana was commonly used by both groups of teenagers, with African Americans reporting that they were significantly more likely to go to school "high" "nearly every day" than Latinas.

Milwaukee female gangs were also quite unlike Fishman's (this volume) Chicago gangs, which featured prostitution and other gendered deviance. Such behavior was harshly condemned in Milwaukee gangs. Milwaukee gangs varied by age, with the barroom buddy gang made up of women in their mid- to late twenties, while most of the gangs we studied were made up of teenagers who almost all left the gang by the time they left their teen years. Only a few of the women became involved in on-going drug sales.

The point is rather obvious: female gangs vary as much as male gangs, and not merely as "auxiliaries," "independent," or "mixed" gangs. Indeed, we have pointed out the questionable nature of these categories. We can identify significant differences between female gangs in ethnicity, structure, type of criminal activities, drug use, and age, as well as type of relationship to a male gang. Finally, all Milwaukee female gangs were fighting gangs, and they differed sharply from the New York gangs described by Anne Campbell (1984) and the Hawaiian gangs described by Karen Joe and Meda Chesney-Lind (1995). Their notion of being "fighting females" was also tied to their rebellious construction of their gender.

Fighting Females

Q: What was the fight you had the most fun in?
A: All of them.

One major difference between our study and Anne Campbell's is how much Milwaukee female gang members, regardless of ethnicity, loved to fight. When we developed the interview questionnaire, our staff insisted on adding a question: "Which fight did you enjoy the most?" That question received enthusiastic responses, casting a different light on Campbell's wry comment that, for men, the "best moment of a fight is its retelling to an appreciative audience of men" (1993, 66). Milwaukee gang girls, too, loved to tell other women about their fights.

Milwaukee female gang members were "fighting females" and may have fought even more as teenagers than did gang boys, though we can't tell for certain from our data. But gang girls fought differently than the boys. For one thing, they possessed significantly fewer weapons, and seldom used guns in battle. Forty percent never used weapons in a fight and 80% used weapons no more than once. As adults the women were far less likely to have guns in the home, some citing concern for the safety of their children. The adult gang women we interviewed were exposed to significantly less gun fire over the course of their lives than similarly aged gang men and had personally

	Table 4
Lifetime Exposure to Violence by Gender	

	Group total: Number of times shot at	Mean per gang member	Group total: Number of people seen killed	Mean per gang member
Female gang members N=68	23	.33	21	.31
Male gang members N=68	617	9.1	143	2.1

The N=68 of the males represents the fact that many Latinos refused to answer these questions, probably because of their continued involvement with drive-by shootings and other unsolved crimes. Thus our male data probably significantly underestimate male violence and the gulf between male and female exposure to violence.

witnessed many fewer homicides. In the use of lethal violence, female gangs do appear to be "pale imitations" of male gangs.

Consistent with a lower use of weapons and exposure to gunfire and homicides, female gang violence was less about power and domination than about the thrill of fighting, or observing norms of solidarity with their homegirls. In Anne Campbell's (1993) terms, female violence was more expressive than instrumental. For example, in collaboratively coding our transcripts, we read this response:

Q: Did you like to fight?
A: Yeah! You know to see who's the strongest, yeah.

Our female staff, all former gang members, laughed. One joked, "Was that a guy talking?" The conception of fighting as "power" is predominately a masculine notion, and helps explain the aversion to the use of weapons by women. Gang women had three different attitudes toward fighting: The vast majority were evenly divided between those who "liked to fight" and those who fought mainly in solidarity with their homegirls. A small number reported they were "not a fighter." These women were looked down on by others, as violating gang norms.

Those who fought mainly in response to gang norms enjoyed fighting, but their responses were always couched in obligation: one criterion of being in a gang was that one backed up one's homegirls.

Q: When you were active in the gang, how did you personally feel about fighting?
A: I was down for the count. I was down for it. Cause I was... really into what I was doing. I was dedicated to... my friends,... I was dedicated to the gang. And I was there for whatever.

Those who "liked to fight" responded enthusiastically and unconditionally: their modal answer to the question "How did you feel about fighting?" was: "I loved it!" African Americans were more inclined to be in the "liked to fight" category than Latinas. For a few of the Latinas, however, our staff suggested they may have "liked to fight" as one way to win a man's heart, showing the guys "even ladies can fight."

Conception of gender was related to whether a girl "liked to fight" or fought mainly in solidarity. Those who answered they "liked to fight" had significantly less of a male-centered outlook, strongly disagreeing with the statement "all a woman needs to get her life in order is a man." Those women who saw fighting as solidarity were significantly more likely to be in a current relationship with a man. Those who considered themselves "bullies" had significantly less traditional notions of gender and were significantly more likely to have fought often with people other than gang members.

Similarly, those women who reported that they fought a lot outside the gang were significantly more independent than those who reported they did not fight much outside the gang. These always-fighting women strongly agreed that "the way men are today, I'd rather raise kids myself." They tended not to be in an adult relationship with a man and were significantly more likely than other gang women to believe that men don't take enough responsibility at home, and that men are intimidated by strong women. They also were more balanced about the gang experience, strongly agreeing that "gangs are not all bad."

The main reason for fights varied by ethnicity. Most of the fights Latinas participated in were turf battles or caused by the rival gang "representing." For African Americans, gang related fights were slightly less than half of all fights, but battles over "lack of respect" were more than a quarter of all fights. Additionally, for African Americans, "the guys" or "jealousy" were the cause of about a third of all fights, as opposed to a negligible percentage of Latinas' fights. One woman related how, in contrast to the usual stereotype of females instigating fights among males, the men were sometimes the instigators:

Q: What kinds of things did the guys get the girls to do?
A: They used to try to instigate fights. They liked to see the girls fight.

Campbell's gang girls were more ambivalent about fighting, consistent with her general theory of female aggression. Violence for gang girls, Campbell argued, defensively copies men's instrumental notions, as these girls fear victimization. In our study, however, violence by gang girls was much less ambivalent or based on fear. What has to be called a virtual celebration of fighting in our interviews seemed to be close to a liberal feminist position, with our respondents rebelliously insisting that, like men, women can fight. Nearly all of our respondents were mothers in their mid-twenties when interviewed, and looking back to the days of the gang brought back memories of the fun they had, when they were perhaps leading a less constrained life.

Table 5

Gang Fights by Ethnicity

Interview questions	African Americans N=18	Latinas N=54	Signif. Chi Sq.
How often did you use weapons?			N.S.
Never	50.0%	35.8%	
Only once or twice	33.3%	45.3%	
About half of the time	11.1%	17.0%	
Most of the time	5.6%	1.9%	
What was the main reason for gang fights?			p < .01
Respect	23.5%	13.5%	
Representing, turf: gang related	41.2%	78.8%	
Jealousy, the guys	29.4%	3.8%	
Felt like it	5.9%	3.8%	
How did you feel about fighting			N.S. (p <.08)
Not a fighter		5.6%	
Down for it	27.8%	51.9%	
Liked to fight	72.2%	42.6%	
Did you fight a lot with anyone other than the gang?			N.S.
Yes	72.2%	53.7%	
No	27.8%	46.3%	
Did the girls fight alongside of the guys in gang fights?			N.S.
Yes	47.1%	45.3%	
No	52.9%	49.1%	
Other		5.7%	

There is some evidence that one reason why the Milwaukee teenage girls loved to fight came from repressed rage at experiences in the home (Chesney-Lind 1997). Those who "liked to fight" were significantly more likely to have experienced severe strains within their family, though they were not more likely to have suffered sexual abuse. On the whole, family variables predict few differences in female gang member behavior (see Hagedorn et al. 1998). Fighting apparently was mainly tied to adolescent rebellion from home, school, and traditional gender roles.

Finally, one way the violent gang experience was most gendered was the way it ended. Most males maintained some minimal gang involvement as adults, with more than half of all Latino males reporting they are involved "the same" or "more" as adults than they were as teenagers. For all those men who were "winding down" their participation in the gang, slightly less than half (42.6%) said they "matured out" in their early to mid-twenties by getting older and wiser, and about the same (40.6%) said that going to jail, seeing a friend or relative killed, or doing "too many drugs" led to a changed attitude.

Women differed. Nearly all the women (95.7%) reported that by the end of their teens they were "not at all" involved with the gang. Half (43.5%) said they "just stopped," and a sixth (15.9%) said they got pregnant and quit. But nearly a third (31.9%) said the reason they left the gang was that they "moved," meaning in almost every case that their parents left the neighborhood to get them away from the gang. No men said that their gang experience ended or tailed off as a result of moving.

Moving to get out of the gang is strongly related to a more protective attitude of parents toward female gang members. It reflects a parent's fear of the "unladylike" attitudes of their daughters. Those who moved to get out of the gang were significantly more likely to have "liked to fight" as teenagers. This aggressive behavior must have appalled more traditional parents. Parents' attitude toward boys' gang involvement was equally gendered by being less controlling, perhaps accepting the gang as a version of "boys will be boys." Boys' fighting may better fit aggressive conceptions of masculinity than resulting from reactions to stress in the family. As adults, those women who had moved away to get out of the gang demonstrated a more traditional attitude toward gender roles, measured on their attitude toward motherhood.

Discussion

The social construction of gender is an important variable in studying male (Hagedorn 1998a, 1998b) as well as female gangs. How men and women construct their gender influences even the way the structure of the gang is seen. We submit that the female gang, like the male gang, represents, in part, a working out of the notion of gender on the part of rebellious young people (Portillos this volume). It has been long established that gang boys see the gang as reinforcing types of masculinities (e.g., Miller 1958; Messerschmidt 1993). But being in a "gang" is more problematic to a girl: "gangs" or "fighting" and "being female" are usually seen by peers and adults, especially parents, as contradictory. We define gang girls "fighting female" as the variable struggle of young women in the process of constructing their notion of gender. Our study has the following implications for gang research:

(1). We need to develop a non-sexist typology of female gangs. We should stop using Miller's categories of "auxiliary," "independent," and "mixed" as the principal way to categorize female gangs. Female gang structure varies at least by ethnicity, age, drug selling, drug use, type of criminality, and propensity to fight. In fact we have argued that the very structure of the female gang itself is not an unquestioned objective fact, as much as it is socially constructed by both male and female gang members—as well as by neighbors, police, and, yes, even gang researchers. Research needs to move beyond convenience samples in order to appreciate the variation in female gang members' conceptions of their gangs.

(2). We need to better understand the reasons why female gangs are less violent than male gangs. This is a reason to emphasize the study of female gangs, not neglect them. The joy of fighting expressed by our Milwaukee respondents represents an active rebellion from stereotyped female gender roles, as well as from the threat of a bleak future. Fighting in Milwaukee gangs may be quite different, however, than fighting by female gang members elsewhere. We suspect that broader investigation will lead gang researchers to study how differing conceptions of gender interact with various neighborhood and drug market conditions and other factors to produce different levels of violence by female gang members. A more important topic of study than violence by gang women is violence against them. It is also important to study why most young adult women so sharply decrease both fighting and gang involvement (see Moore and Hagedorn this volume).

(3). We need to better understand the different ways female gang members are "fighting female." Girls in gangs do not construct their gender in the same ways, and these constructions of gender are important correlates of how they experience the gang and how the gang influences their later lives. Female roles within gangs vary considerably more than simplistic male notions of girls as either "tomboys" or "sex objects." Just as the exaggeration of the male gender role is a component of the male gang experience, rebellion from traditional gender norms is a significant component of the female gang experience. As with the men, the female gang was rated an important experience for nearly all of the women in our study (see Giordano this volume). However, variation in constructions of gender asserts itself even here. The gang was a more positively valued experience the more the girls felt themselves, and not the guys, were in control. Remember, *all* of the women who regarded the gang as a positive experience reported that the girls decided things by themselves.

The study of female gangs is in its beginning stages. Generalization and typologies await further research. Rather than become preoccupied with sensationalized journalistic accounts of female violence (e.g., Sikes 1997), we social scientists need to get our "hands dirty" and produce more careful studies of the real lives of female gang members.

Violence among girls:
Does gang membership make a difference?

by Elizabeth Piper Deschenes and Finn-Aage Esbensen★

Introduction

Until recently, the nature and extent of female involvement in gangs has been a relatively neglected area of inquiry (Campbell 1991; Chesney-Lind 1993; Chesney-Lind and Brown 1996; Elliott 1988). However, media stories have brought a heightened awareness to this issue. Chesney-Lind, Shelden and Joe (1996) describe a "veritable siege" of news stories in the 1990s. These stories portray girls as more violent than ever before and attribute this behavior to the search for "equality." Using both quantitative and qualitative data, Chesney-Lind et al. (1996) argue that the media picture is distorted. They suggest the choice of gang membership is shaped by economic, educational, familial and social conditions.

Even though the media portrayal may be inaccurate, there is a growing body of research reporting higher rates of female participation in gangs than previously believed (e.g., Bjerregaard and Smith 1993; Esbensen and Huizinga 1993; Fagan 1990; Thornberry, et al. 1993). Whereas official records of arrestees tend to show lower prevalence rates of gang membership among females than males (Howell 1994; Curry et al. 1994), the estimates of the proportion of gang members who are female generally range between 10 and 46% in self-report studies (Campbell 1991; Esbensen, Huizinga and Wieher 1993; Esbensen and Winfree 1996; Fagan 1990; Moore 1991). In a recent study (Bjerregaard and Smith 1993) of a high risk sample of youths in the general population, the prevalence rate of gang membership was slightly higher for females than for males (22 vs. 18 percent). Has there been an increase in female gang membership and is this related to violent crime rates?

Unfortunately, there is a lack of consistent empirical evidence regarding violent crime by female gang members. Ethnographic accounts suggest some female gang members can be as violent and aggressive as their male counterparts (Campbell 1991; Moore 1991; Vigil 1990). However, many of these studies have major flaws. One of the problems is that the majority of prior studies have focused on older populations, not young adolescents. In addition, ethnographies are usually limited to one geographic area. As a consequence, we get varied pictures of the interactive effect of gender and gang membership on violent offending. For example, the picture of Hispanic female gang members in Los Angeles (Harris 1988; Moore 1991) is quite different from the portrait of New York Puerto Rican gang members (Campbell 1991).

★*This essay is published here for the first time. The research was supported under award #94-IJ-CX-0058 from the National Institute of Justice, Office of Justice Programs, U.S. Department of Justice. Points of view in this document are those of the authors and do not necessarily represent the official position of the U.S. Department of Justice.*

Little is known about the nature and extent of differences in gang activity and delinquency among younger females in the general population. Thus, the purpose of this study is to examine differences between gang and non-gang girls using a younger sample of female adolescents. In other research we have examined the differences between male and female gang members (see Esbensen, Deschenes and Winfree, forthcoming, as well as Deschenes and Esbensen 1999) and gender differences between gang and non-gang youth in violence (Deschenes and Esbensen 1998). This chapter looks at differences between gang and non-gang girls in those factors related to gang membership and violent behavior as well as the prevalence and incidence of violent behavior in a multi-site sample of 8th grade students. How different are girl gang members from their non-gang counterparts? Are they really meaner and more violent?

Prior Research

Many of the early studies of gangs (Thrasher 1927; Yablonsky 1962) and even some of the current gang studies (Sanchez-Jankowski 1991; Taylor 1993) tend to downgrade the role of females to that of auxiliaries (Campbell 1991; Chesney-Lind et al. 1996; Moore 1991; Moore and Hagedorn 1996). Because there were few all-female gangs in the 1950s and 1960s (Klein 1995), females were often described either as sex objects who instigated fights between rival gangs, or tomboys (Campbell 1991). In comparison, most modern-day researchers have moved beyond this stereotypical notion (Campbell 1991; Chesney-Lind 1993) and point to other reasons why females join gangs, including social structural and economic factors, weak social bonds to family and school, individual experiences (victimization and sexual activity) or beliefs (self-esteem and social isolation) and peer group influence (Chesney-Lind and Shelden 1992).

Several researchers (Fagan 1996; Hagedorn 1988; Moore 1991; Vigil 1988) have linked the presence and growth of gangs (regardless of gender) to the urban underclass. Individuals living in the inner cities have been subjected to major structural economic changes and are referred to by some (Wilson 1987) as the "truly disadvantaged." These conditions have resulted in a lack of education and employment, and lives of poverty without opportunities (Short 1996). According to Vigil (1988) and Moore (1991), Los Angeles barrio gangs are a product of this economic restructuring and street socialization. Vigil (1988, 9) suggests both male and female gang members experience "multiple marginality." Not only do they live in the ecologically marginal areas and are consequently affected by the pressures of marginal economics, but they also have marginal ethnic and personal identities. Vigil argues that youths who are looking for identity and stability adopt the cholo subculture and engage in alcohol and drug use as well as conflict and violence that are an integral part of gang life. Moore suggests:

Gangs as youth groups develop among the socially marginal adolescents for whom school and family do not work. Agencies of street socialization take on increased importance under changing economic circumstances, and have an increased impact on younger kids (1991, 137-38).

Campbell's (1991) portrayal of Puerto Rican females in New York gangs suggests they become gang members because they are the victims of chronic poverty, marginalization, and unemployment. She believes these women hold unrealistic middle class values and face multiple problems, including subordination to males and the powerlessness of the underclass. She suggests they become gang members because they are trying to escape reality. These girls have watched their mothers become victimized by poverty and culture and know their futures as housewives would entail meaningless domestic labor, responsibility for children, and social isolation. Campbell's description of the life histories of three female gang members reflects the instability in their lives, the exposure to violence in the home, and their fear of abuse. This background makes them desire the attachment and sense of belonging in the gang.

The sociocultural and environmental context of behavior is an important factor in explaining the relationship between gender and violent behavior (Baskin and Sommers 1993). In their study of females' initiation into violent crime, Sommers and Baskin (1994) found juvenile females who engaged in violent street crime were likely to live in "distressed communities"; that is, their childhood communities had high concentrations of poverty and stranger victimization.

Community levels of family dysfunction, economic and social dislocation, as well as the presence of illegitimate opportunity structures provided the landscape for the lifestyles and routine activities that were related to the women's participation in violent street crime (Baskin and Sommers 1998, 126).

Female initiation into violent street crime was related to use of alcohol or marijuana and association with a violent peer group. Life histories of females arrested for violent crimes in New York revealed a background of violent experiences, at home, in school, and on the streets. Baskin and Sommers (1998) indicate that by the age of 10 the majority of the women they interviewed were involved in school fights and associated with peers who were violent. They suggest this pattern of violence was a reinforcement of earlier experiences with siblings and other family members. Similar to males, females' motivation for robbery during adolescence appeared to be related to thrill seeking, excitement and peer pressure, whereas the motivation for assault was the need for respect and honor. These motivations changed as the women got more involved in the world of drugs and alcohol and they needed money to support their addiction.

Several studies have found that girls are in gangs because they want to have a sense of belonging to a peer "familial" group (Giordano 1978; Harris 1988; Joe and Chesney-Lind 1995). For example, in an ethnographic study of Latina gang members in male dominated Latino gangs in the San Fernando Valley of California, Harris (1988) concluded that Latina gang members were lost between two worlds, between Anglo and Mexican American society and culture. The complex social and cultural roles of Latinas, according to Harris, are displayed in Latina gang membership and behavior in which females found peers with whom they could relate. The females would "fight instead of flee, assault instead of articulate, and kill rather than control their aggression" (Harris 1988, 174). Interviews with gang members in Hawaii revealed girls join gangs for protection from family and neighborhood violence (Joe and Chesney-Lind 1995).

In a more recent study of high risk youth in Rochester, New York, Bjerregaard and Smith (1993) tested the contribution of social control theory to explaining female gang participation, delinquency, and substance use. They also included measures of social disorganization, poverty, self-esteem, and sexual activity in the analyses. Few of the factors were significant. For example, parent attachment and supervision were not important factors, nor was self-esteem, but sexual activity and school expectations were significant factors in predicting gang membership for females.

Other studies provide evidence that belonging to a group or gang that approves of violence is a strong predictor of violent behavior (Callaghan and Rivera 1992; Webster et al. 1993). In two separate studies conducted in New Mexico, one involving incarcerated youth (Winfree, Mays and Backstrom 1994) and the other ninth grade students attending public school (Winfree, Backstrom and Mays 1994), Winfree and associates reported that social learning theory variables (differential reinforcers, differential associations, pro-gang definitions and values) were significant in separating youth (males and females combined) according to gang and non-gang status. These researchers found gang membership was relatively unrelated to individual personal violence, whereas group context offending, particularly violent crimes, exhibited ties to gang involvement.

Gang membership and violent crime are seen as almost exclusively male behaviors. Several studies show male gang members have higher rates of delinquency than non-gang members do (Esbensen and Huizinga 1993; Fagan 1990; Thornberry et al. 1993; Tracy and Piper 1982). But is the same true for females? Even though both male and female gang members in the Rochester sample (Bjerregaard and Smith 1993) had higher rates of delinquency than non-gang members, serious delinquency was lower among female than male gang members. And at least one study has indicated a lack of differences between female gang and non-gang members in individual offending rates (Esbensen and Huizinga 1993).

Research has attributed differences between gang and non-gang youth to social bonds (Fagan 1990), attitudinal measures (Esbensen et al. 1993) and social learning variables (Winfree et al. 1994a,b). Increased peer support for female involvement in crime has been linked to the changes in female criminality (Giordano 1978). But are these factors the same for males and females?

The nature of the violent acts by female gang members may be qualitatively different from those engaged in by males. For example, Joe and Chesney-Lind (1995) reported gender differences in gang behavior and violence in Hawaii. Boys were more likely to be involved in drug dealing and other types of criminal behavior, whereas girls were more likely to have arrests for running away or other status offenses. These differences were explained both by the reactions of police (arresting only females for running away) and the nature of the gang activities. Boys were less likely to hang out and more likely to "cruise," which would lead to confrontations with other gangs. Once they join gangs, girls learn how to cope with the hostile environments in which they reside by being involved in fighting, and violence (Chesney-Lind and Shelden 1992; Boyle 1992). An alternative explanation is that there is greater social control of female behavior. Chesney-Lind and Brown suggest, "Being a girl is to be subject to certain constraints and risk factors which distinguish her experience of violence in important ways from that of boys in her neighborhood" (1996, 2).

Based on conversations with female gang members in New York, Campbell (1984) found the majority of fights involved domestic and romantic disputes between partners and some were over personal integrity, rather than fights between gang members. It is suggested that these acts of aggression are not visible to police.

In sum, it is unclear what role gang membership plays in violence by female adolescents. Prior theory and research on violent behavior and gangs has tended to focus on the behavior of males and there are few studies of females. The review of the literature has indicated a lack of consensus on the relationship between gender, gang membership and involvement in violent crime. Most studies attribute the same causes to female and male behaviors. The purpose of this study is to examine differences between non-gang and gang girls' involvement in violent criminal activities and reasons for these differences. The explanatory factors are representative of variables found to be related to gang membership or violent crime in prior studies. These factors are divided into four domains representing family, school, peer, and individual influences. The analyses were designed to answer three questions:

- What is the nature and extent of violent behavior by non-gang and gang girls?
- Do the behavior and attitudes of younger females reflect the known patterns of gang membership and violent offending from prior studies of older females?
- Are there other differences between non-gang and gang girls that might explain the current increase in violent offending?

Research Design and Methods

This investigation of gender differences in violent behavior is part of a larger evaluation of the Gang Resistance Education and Training (G.R.E.A.T.) program, a gang prevention program for youths in middle schools. As such, evaluation objectives dictated many of the design elements, including site selection and sampling procedures. Although not specifically designed for the purposes of this study, the data collected for the evaluation of G.R.E.A.T. provide a rich data set for studying behaviors and attitudes of gang and non-gang youth. One component of the evaluation was a multi-site, multi-state cross-sectional survey of eighth grade students[1] conducted during the Spring of 1995.[2]

Site Selection

Cities in which the G.R.E.A.T. program had been delivered in school year 1993-'94 (when the targeted students were seventh graders) were identified using records provided by the Bureau of Alcohol, Tobacco, and Firearms, the federal agency with oversight of the G.R.E.A.T. program. Prospective sites had to meet two criteria. First, only those agencies with two or more officers trained prior to January 1994 to teach G.R.E.A.T. were considered eligible. Second, in order to enhance the geographic and demographic diversity of the sample, some potential cities were excluded from consideration.[3] Eleven sites that met the requirements for inclusion and agreed to participate[4] were selected for the evaluation: Las Cruces, NM; Omaha, NE; Phoenix, AZ; Philadelphia, PA; Kansas City, MO; Milwaukee, WI; Orlando, FL; Will County, IL; Providence, RI; Pocatello, ID: and Torrance, CA. These sites provide a diverse sample. One or more of the selected sites can be described by the following characteristics: large urban area, small city, racially and ethnically homogeneous, racially and ethnically heterogeneous, east coast, west coast, mid-west, inner-city, working class, middle class.

Within each of the eleven sites, schools that offered G.R.E.A.T. during the past two years were selected.[5] Group administered questionnaires were conducted with all eighth graders in attendance on the specified day.[6] Attendance rates varied from a low of 75% at one Kansas City middle school to a high of 93% at several schools in Will County and Pocatello. This resulted in a final sample of 5,935 eighth grade students from 315 classrooms in 42 different schools. Of these approximately half were females. These 3030 girls are the subjects of the analyses reported in this chapter.

Measures

Measures included in the student questionnaires can be divided into three main categories: demographic, attitudinal, and behavioral. Demographic data include gender, age, parental educational attainment, race/ethnicity, and family composition. In the current study, the attitudinal variables included in the family domain were perceptions of maternal and paternal attachment as well as parental monitoring. Measures of the school domain included perceptions of school violence, attitudes regarding educational opportunities, and school commitment. Peer influence was measured by commitment to negative peers and perceptions of pro-social peer behavior. Within the individual domain were measures of social isolation, self-esteem, impulsivity, risk-seeking, neutralization of violent behavior and perceived guilt for engaging in violent acts. Behavioral measures consist of self-reported delinquency, victimization, and self-reported gang membership. Unless otherwise indicated, the measures were adapted from the National Youth Survey (Elliott et al. 1985) or the Denver Youth Survey (Huizinga et al. 1991).

Self-reported delinquency, victimization and gang affiliation were asked of respondents toward the end of the questionnaire. This self-report technique has been used widely during the past forty years and provides a good measure of actual behavior rather than a reactive measure of police response to behavior (e.g., Hindelang, Hirschi and Weis 1981; Huizinga and Elliott 1987; Huizinga 1991). Respondents were asked if they had ever done each of these things (ever prevalence). Those students indicating that they had engaged in these behaviors were then asked to indicate how many times during the past twelve months they had committed each offense (e.g., frequency).[7]

For the purposes of this study, we defined violent crime to include the following behaviors:

• Hit someone with the idea of hurting him or her.
• Carried a hidden weapon for protection.
• Attacked someone with a weapon.
• Used a weapon or force to get money or things from people.
• Shot at someone because someone else told you to.
• Been involved in gang fights.

While there may be some overlap in some of these behaviors (e.g., gang fighting and hitting someone), these activities cover a broader range than the more traditional definition of person offense.

The same self-report procedure was used to measure being a victim of violent crime. Both measures of ever prevalence of victimization and last year frequency of victimization were obtained. The victimization measure included:

• Been hit by someone trying to hurt you.
• Had someone use a weapon or force to get money or things from you.
• Been attacked by someone with a weapon or by someone trying to seriously hurt or kill you.

Gang membership was determined through self-identification. As with most social phenomena, definitional issues arise.[8] By relying on self-definition, we are adhering to law-enforcement's primary criteria for identifying "official" gang members. In the current research, two filter questions introduced the gang-specific section of the questionnaire: "Have you ever been a gang member?" and "Are you now in a gang?" Given the current sample, with almost all the respondents under the age of 15, even affirmative responses to the first question followed by a negative response to the second may still indicate a recent gang affiliation. In an attempt to limit our sample of gang members to "delinquent gangs," we employed a restrictive definition of gang status. Thus, only those youths who reported ever having been in a gang and who reported that their gangs engaged in at least one type of delinquent behavior (fighting other gangs, stealing cars, stealing in general, or robbing people) were classified as gang members. This strategy resulted in identification of 237 female gang members, representing 7.8% of the females in the sample.

Findings

The demographic characteristics of the female study participants shown in Table 1 are categorized by gang membership. About 40% of the sample reported their race as white, slightly over one quarter replied African-American, nearly 20% were Hispanic, only 6% were Asian-American, and 9% were categorized as Other.[9] The majority of female students

Table 1

Demographic Characteristics of Study Participants by Gang Membership

	Non-gang			Gang			Total	
	N	Row %	Col %	N	Row %	Col %	N	Col %
Gang Membership*	2793	92.2		237	7.8		3030	100.0
Race*								
White	1133	95.6	41.0	52	4.4	22.0	1185	39.5
African-American	738	92.0	26.7	64	8.0	27.1	802	26.8
Hispanic	478	87.7	17.3	67	12.3	28.4	545	18.2
Asian	179	93.7	6.5	12	6.3	5.1	191	6.4
Other	234	85.1	8.5	41	14.9	17.4	275	9.2
	2762			236			2948	
Age* (%)								
13 and under	920	94.9	33.2	49	5.1	21.0	969	32.2
14	1668	91.9	60.2	147	8.1	63.1	1815	60.4
15 and over	184	83.3	6.6	37	16.7	15.9	221	7.4
	2772			233			3005	
Family Structure*								
Single	870	89.9	31.3	98	10.1	41.4	968	32.1
Intact	1702	94.4	61.2	101	5.6	42.6	1803	59.8
Other	210	84.7	7.5	38	15.3	16.0	248	8.2
	2782			237			3019	
Parent's Education*								
< High School	268	87.3	11.0	39	12.7	19.0	307	11.6
High School	602	91.6	24.7	55	8.4	26.8	657	24.9
Some College	1565	93.4	64.3	111	6.6	54.1	1676	63.5
	2435			205			2640	

* Significant difference between gang and non-gang youth, $p < .05$ using a chi-square test.

(60 percent) were age 14 at the time of the survey and reported they lived with both parents. About one third were age 13 or younger and a similar proportion reported they lived with a single parent. Less than 10% of girls were age 15 or over or lived with some other relative. Parents' education was missing for 14% of the students, but among those who reported, very few (less than 15 percent) reported either parent had less than a high school degree.[10] Roughly one quarter of mothers or fathers had completed high school and the majority (64 percent) reported either their mother or father had attended some college.

There were statistically significant differences between the non-gang and gang females, which can be seen in both the row and column percents. For example, gang members were less likely to be white and more likely to be Hispanic. A higher proportion of gang than non-gang females reported their race was "other." Gang members tended to be older than non-gang members. Less than 10% of those age 14 or under reported gang membership, in comparison to 17% of those ages 15 and over. Girls from single parent households and those living with other relatives were more likely to be gang members than those living in an intact household. The proportion of gang members who reported either parent had some college was lower than for non-gang members (54% to 64% respectively). On the other hand, the fact that over half of gang members reported a parent had some college education would seem to challenge the assertion of some gang researchers that gang membership is an underclass phenomenon.[11] Nonetheless, the presence of gangs could be linked to social structural and economic factors. The background characteristics of gang members appear to be similar for both females and males. The only significant difference between male and female gang members found in other research (Esbensen and Deschenes 1998) was related to the age group. A higher proportion of the female gang members were younger in age in comparison to male gang members.

Prevalence and Frequency of Violent Behavior and Victimization

Students were asked if they had ever engaged in various criminal activities and how many times they had done so in the past 12 months. For those items relating to violent behavior, we examined the proportion who reported involvement (prevalence), and the average number of times (frequency) they engaged in the behavior.[12] Similar questions were asked regarding the number of times they had been victimized. Table 2 presents the results of our analysis of differences in ever prevalence and annual frequency rates by gang membership.

For each category there were significant differences between non-gang and gang girls, with a higher proportion of gang members reporting involvement in violent crimes. The most minor form of violent behavior, hitting someone with the idea of hurting him or her, was reported by over 40% of non-gang girls. Twice as many gang

Table 2

Prevalence and Frequency Rates of
Violent Behavior and Weapon Use by Gang Membership

	Non-gang		Gang	
	Ever prev.	Annual freq.	Ever prev.	Annual freq.
SRD Item				
Hit someone with the idea of hurting them?	43.1	2.61	81.1*	8.23*
Carried a hidden weapon for protection?	16.1	0.84	64.7*	7.35*
Attacked someone with a weapon?	7.6	0.23	38.9*	2.48*
Used a weapon or force to get money or things from people?	1.7	0.01	17.4*	1.29*
Shot at someone because you were told to by someone else?	0.8	0.00	21.1*	1.06*
Been involved in gang fights?	9.6	0.27	77.8*	7.67*
Victimization Item				
Been hit by someone	39.4	1.50	64.1*	2.65*
Been robbed	4.2	0.01	10.2*	0.41
Been attacked	5.6	0.01	27.2*	0.83*

* Significant differences between gang and non-gang youth, $p < .05$, using Chi-square measures of association or t-tests of means.

Frequencies for individual items were truncated at 52 times per year prior to calculating means.

members reported they had hit someone and the number of times in the past year was three times as great for gang members. Carrying a hidden weapon was clearly more prevalent among gang girls (65 to 16 percent) and they did so with much greater frequency, almost nine times the rate of non-gang girls.[13] Actual use of a weapon was fairly infrequent among non-gang girls, either for the purpose of assault or robbery. In comparison, 39% of gang girls reported they had used a weapon to attack someone, 21% reported they had shot at someone, and 17% reported they had ever used a weapon to rob someone. The occurrence of two of these behaviors in the past year was relatively low, with gang girls reporting they had robbed or shot someone an average of one time in the past year. The annual frequency for attacking someone with a weapon was somewhat higher, an average of over two times. However, this is not surprising when one notes that 78% of gang girls reported involvement in a gang fight, an average of 8 times in the past year. Even though the prevalence of involvement in gang fighting is certainly higher for those girls who were gang members, it is important to note that almost 10% of non-gang girls reported involvement. In sum, the nature and extent of involvement in violent behavior is evidently connected to gang membership. Over 90% of females who were gang members reported they had engaged in violent behavior.

In addition, being the victim of a violent crime appears to be associated with gang membership, as indicated in the lower panel of Table 2. A majority of gang girls (64 percent) reported they had been hit by someone, in comparison to about 40% of non-gang girls. Moreover, the frequency of this victimization was higher. Very few youths (10% or less) reported they had ever been robbed, and there was no difference between gang and non-gang girls in the annual frequency. Over a quarter of gang girls reported they had been attacked with a weapon, in contrast to 6% of non-gang girls, and the frequency was just less than once in the past year.

These results indicate that experiencing violence and committing crimes of violence are associated with being in a gang, even though non-gang females do report a moderate amount of hitting. But are these findings different for females and males? In other research we have found that there were significant gender differences in violent behavior, even when controlling for gang membership (Deschenes and Esbensen 1999). Do gang girls differ from gang boys? For most types of violent behavior except hitting someone or being hit and the frequency of gang fighting, the rates of ever prevalence and annual frequency were higher for males than females (Esbensen, Deschenes, and Winfree, forthcoming). Why are these gang girls exposed to more violence? In prior studies we found different factors explain both involvement in gangs (Esbensen and Deschenes 1998) and rates of violent crime (Deschenes and Esbensen 1999). In this chapter we examine some of the differences between non-gang and gang girls that might explain involvement in violent behavior and compare the results to earlier studies.

Family Factors

Many researchers suggest gang membership and violent behavior may be caused by weak parental bonds and lack of supervision. Differences between non-gang and gang girls in variables related to the family, e.g., attachment to mother and father and parental monitoring, were examined using t-tests of means. The results presented in Table 3 indicate that gang girls were unlike non-gang girls on every dimension. They reported much lower levels of attachment to mothers than non-gang girls did. For example, non-gang girls were more likely to report they could talk to their mothers. Paternal attachment was even lower than maternal attachment among gang girls and significantly different from non-gang girls. Even though both gang and non-gang girls were likely to agree with most of the statements regarding parental monitoring (i.e., the average score was above the median of 3), there were significant differences between gang and non-gang girls, with gang girls reporting lower levels of monitoring.

School Factors

Outside of the family, the school is perhaps the most important social institution shaping the lives of young adolescents. Baskin and Sommers (1998) reported neighborhood violence and school experiences were factors influencing females' involvement in violent crime. Thus, it is important to measure the influence of school environment and activities. We examined differences between non-gang and gang girls in perceptions of

Table 3

Family Factors by Gang Membership

	Non-gang			Gang		
	N	Mean	s.d.	N	Mean	s.d.
Maternal attachment[a]						
Can talk to mother*	2753	5.04	1.69	231	4.61	2.04
Mother trusts*	2751	5.15	1.69	231	3.94	1.98
Mother knows friends*	2752	4.69	1.74	230	4.07	1.93
Mother understands me*	2752	4.59	1.78	231	3.95	1.89
Ask mother's advice*	2750	4.39	1.95	231	3.68	2.08
Mother praises me*	2751	5.63	1.70	231	4.81	2.17
Paternal attachment[a]						
Can talk to father*	2487	3.85	1.92	213	3.25	2.09
Father trusts me*	2483	5.12	1.82	213	4.15	2.14
Father knows friends*	2489	3.52	1.90	213	2.76	1.73
Father understands me*	2793	4.82	2.36	237	4.13	2.62
Ask father's advice*	2487	3.66	2.05	213	2.81	2.00
Father praises me*	2490	5.39	1.93	213	4.64	2.31
Parental monitoring[b]						
Leave note when go*	2777	4.06	.99	233	3.57	1.19
Parents know where I am*	2774	3.88	1.04	233	3.30	1.25
I know how to contact parents*	2772	3.97	.95	234	3.58	1.19
Parents know who I am with*	2773	3.68	1.07	233	3.10	1.26

[a] Responses given on a scale from 1 to 7 with 7 being a positive statement
[b] Responses given on a scale from (1) strongly disagree to (5) strongly agree
* Significant difference, $p < .05$, between gang and non-gang youth using t-test of means

school violence. As shown in Table 4, all of the items were statistically different, indicating gang girls were more likely to report higher levels of gang activity and students beating up teachers at school. Gang girls were also less likely to feel safe at school or in the surrounding neighborhood, probably due to the higher perceived incidence of racial conflict and gang fights.

Other researchers have found that school expectations explain adolescent female gang membership (Bjerregaard and Smith 1993) and that low academic orientation is predictive of violence (Saner and Ellickson 1996). Another factor related to the underclass and poverty myth is that of limited educational opportunities. Our findings in Table 4 indicate that gang girls perceive their opportunities are more limited than do nongang girls. For example, they were more likely to believe they would not be able to do the type of work they wanted because they would not have enough education. They also were more likely to believe that they wouldn't finish high school and had little chance to go to college. The desire to do well in school in order to go to college is often related to

Table 4
School Factors by Gang Membership

	N	Non-gang mean	s.d.	N	Gang mean	s.d.
School environment[a]						
School gang activity*	2757	2.91	.97	232	3.38	1.09
Students get along well*	2752	2.89	.96	235	2.69	1.14
School fights*	2748	3.33	1.00	235	3.56	1.07
Students beat up teachers*	2763	1.88	.98	235	2.32	1.16
School racial conflict*	2749	2.83	1.17	234	3.19	1.32
Safe at school*	2769	3.30	1.06	234	2.93	1.21
Safe in school neighborhood*	2760	3.40	1.07	234	3.09	1.20
School pressure to join gangs*	2765	2.10	.92	235	2.56	1.18
School gang fights*	2759	2.43	1.03	235	3.03	1.21
Limited educational opportunities[a]						
Won't be able to do work I want to because not enough education*	2764	1.91	1.07	235	2.55	1.30
A person like me has a pretty good chance of going to college*	2774	4.22	.97	236	3.70	1.28
Won't be able to finish high school because family wants me to get job*	2766	1.44	.75	236	1.72	.94
Not enough money for college*	2768	2.11	1.05	235	2.39	1.26
School commitment[a]						
Homework is a waste of time*	2774	2.52	1.17	235	3.02	1.30
I try hard in school*	2774	4.14	.86	236	3.66	1.16
Education important, worth it to put up with what I don't like*	2755	3.99	.98	235	3.49	1.15
I like school*	2773	3.33	1.09	236	2.70	1.25
Grades are very important*	2776	4.21	.91	236	3.69	1.23
I finish my homework*	2770	3.69	1.06	236	2.98	1.18
Choose to go out friends/study*	2771	3.17	1.21	235	2.34	1.23

[a] Responses given on a scale from (1) strongly disagree to (5) strongly agree
* Significant difference, $p < .05$, between gang and non-gang youth using t-test of means

the degree of school commitment. On all measures of school commitment, non-gang girls had higher scores than gang girls. They were more likely to try hard in school, to believe grades are important and to try to finish their homework rather than go out with friends.

Peer Factors
Associating with negative peers is also related to the degree of commitment to the peer group. As shown in Table 5, gang girls reported higher levels of commitment to negative peers than non-gang girls did. They reported they were more likely to still hang out with their friends even if they were getting them into trouble with police.

Table 5
Peer Factors by Gang Membership

	N	Non-gang mean	s.d.	N	Gang mean	s.d.
Commitment to negative peers[a]						
If friends get you into trouble at home						
how likely still hang out with them?*	2760	2.56	1.27	233	3.71	1.30
If friends get you into trouble at school						
how likely still hang out with them?*	2763	2.39	1.26	236	3.50	1.39
If friends get you into trouble with police						
how likely hang out with them?*	2756	1.70	1.11	233	2.97	1.50
Pro-social peers[b]						
Friends in school activities*	2760	3.21	1.08	236	2.86	1.18
Friends get along school adults*	2760	3.35	1.11	233	2.51	1.03
Friends good students*	2756	3.46	1.05	233	2.67	1.07
Friends in community activities*	2734	2.63	1.23	235	2.02	1.16
Friends in religious activities*	2723	2.51	1.16	237	1.93	1.08
Friends in family activities*	2709	3.12	1.14	233	2.57	1.21
Friends honest*	2744	3.07	1.13	236	2.40	1.12
Friends obey school rules*	2751	2.99	1.24	237	1.99	1.00

[a] Responses given on a scale from (1) not at all likely to (5) very likely.
[b] Responses given on a scale from (1) none of them to (5) all of them.
* Significant difference, $p < .05$, between gang and non-gang youth using t-test of means.

Having pro-social peers can be an insulator against delinquency and gang membership. Thus it is no surprise that non-gang girls report that more of their friends were involved in pro-social activities, e.g., school, community, and family (see Table 5). Gang girls were more likely than non-gang girls to report that few of their friends were honest or obeyed school rules or were good students.

Individual Factors

Individual-level variables are important when comparing gang and non-gang youth because they reflect differences in attitudes and beliefs that are shaped by the other domains of social structure, family, school and peers. For example, some criminologists have stated that girls who join gangs are likely to do so because they are socially isolated (Joe and Chesney-Lind 1995; Harris, 1988). These factors are examined in Table 6. Our results indicate no difference between non-gang and gang girls in feelings of social isolation in school or with friends, but significantly greater isolation at home with family. These findings corroborate the earlier results indicating that gang girls had lower levels of attachment to parents. Other research has examined whether girls join gangs for respect and self-esteem (Bjerregaard and Smith 1993) or may engage in violent crime to gain honor and respect (Baskin and Sommers 1998). When individual items measuring self-esteem of gang and

Individual Factors by Gang Membership

Table 6

	Non-gang			Gang		
	N	mean	s.d.	N	mean	s.d.
Social isolation[b]						
Feel lonely at school	2771	2.51	1.19	236	2.56	1.35
Feel lonely with friends	2772	2.44	1.16	236	2.39	1.20
Feel lonely with family*	2772	2.77	1.28	236	3.33	1.31
Self esteem[a]						
I'm a useful person*	2760	3.88	.94	236	3.63	1.17
I'm a person of worth*	2733	4.00	.99	234	3.72	1.18
Good job as a person*	2760	4.01	.90	234	3.46	1.18
Able to do things*	2762	4.11	.91	236	3.84	1.12
Feel good about myself*	2770	3.98	1.15	236	3.55	1.51
When I do a job I do it well*	2769	4.04	.90	236	3.62	1.18
Impulsivity[b]						
Act on the spur of the moment*	2733	3.07	.96	231	3.43	1.08
No effort preparing for future*	2751	2.26	1.10	233	2.61	1.19
Do what brings pleasure now*	2720	2.96	1.07	233	3.41	1.12
More concerned with short run*	2728	2.84	1.08	233	3.26	1.05
Risk seeking[b]						
Test myself by something risky*	2750	3.19	1.10	234	3.68	1.20
Take risk for fun*	2762	3.07	1.17	233	3.76	1.20
Exciting to possibly get in trouble*	2762	2.88	1.20	234	3.69	1.23
Excitement/adventure more important than security*	2753	2.35	1.01	232	3.04	1.26
Neutralization - fighting[b]						
Okay to fight if hit first*	2724	3.64	1.28	236	4.56	.74
Okay to fight if protect rights*	2773	3.79	1.11	235	4.55	.69
Okay to fight if threat to family/friends*	2767	3.72	1.13	236	4.56	.73
Guilt about violent behavior[c]						
Feel guilty about hitting someone*	2758	2.29	.73	236	1.67	.75
Feel guilty attacking with weapon*	2756	2.62	.65	236	1.95	.81
Feel guilty armed robbery*	2754	2.82	.48	234	2.31	.82

[a] Responses given on a scale from (1) almost never to (5) almost always

[b] Responses given on a scale from (1) strongly disagree to (5) strongly agree

[c] Responses given on a scale of (1) not very guilty/badly, (2) somewhat guilty/badly, (3) very guilty/badly

* Significant difference, $p < .05$, between gang and non-gang youth using t-test of means

non-gang girls were examined we found significantly lower levels of self-esteem among the gang girls.

Recent studies have indicated that females who engage in violence as adolescents do so for the same reason as boys—i.e., thrill-seeking. The results shown in Table 6 indicate that gang girls report higher levels of impulsivity and risk seeking than non-gang girls do. They are more likely to act on the spur of the moment or to take a risk for the fun of it.

Few adolescents approve of violence, but many youths accept the use of violent behavior in specific situations and are more likely to do so if they associate with negative peers. Agnew (1994) suggests that adolescents use techniques of neutralization to justify violent behavior. Our findings in Table 6 show there were significant differences between gang and non-gang girls in neutralization of fighting behaviors. Gang girls were more likely than non-gang girls to believe hitting someone is justifiable if (1) one is hit first, (2) it is necessary to protect your rights, or (3) there is a threat to family or friends. Non-gang girls were also more likely to feel guilty about committing crime than gang girls, for all three types of violent offenses (see Table 6). These differences are reflected in the actual behavior of gang girls, which was more violent than that of non-gang girls.

Discussion

The results of this study clearly indicate that adolescent females who report gang membership are significantly different from non-gang girls. They differ in background, behavior, and attitudes. Although not all gang girls grow up in an urban underclass, they do have some disadvantages. They are more likely to be non-white and to come from households without both parents. Girls who are in gangs are not as closely attached to their family members, and they feel more socially isolated. They are not monitored as closely by their parents and thus have the opportunity to engage in gang activities. Female gang members appear to have different perceptions of their future opportunities than those who have not joined gangs. Believing they have limited educational opportunities, they are not committed to school, nor are they associating as often with pro-social peers who might steer them away from criminal activities. Gang girls, like their male counterparts, report a higher degree of commitment to negative peers.

Girls who join gangs are more likely to report they are victims of and are engaged in violent behavior. In this regard they are more similar to boys who join gangs. In other research we have found that the gang girls are more violent than non-gang boys (Deschenes and Esbensen 1999). In many ways the gang boys and gang girls are similar when compared to non-gang youth. Esbensen, Deschenes and Winfree (forthcoming) reported few significant differences between male and female gang members. Both reported similar reasons for joining gangs (fun, protection, get respect, friend in gang), yet more males reported they joined a gang for money. On the other hand, girls' attitudes about gang membership varied from those of boys, indicating a stronger affective attachment. Girls agreed more strongly that being in a gang gave them a feeling of belonging and importance and that the gang was like a family. One reason for this may be that gang girls reported higher levels of social isolation and lower levels of self-esteem than did the boys in the gang. In another study we found that females were more likely to feel guilty about committing a crime than males, even among gang members (Deschenes and Esbensen 1999). On the other hand, males were more likely to neutralize acts of physical violence than females, except there were fewer differences among gang members. In this study we found that girls in the gang had higher levels of neutralization and lower levels of guilt about involvement in violent behavior than non-gang girls.

The results of our study confirm some of the findings of earlier research, even though this is a younger sample of female gang members than found in most studies. Gang girls reported more social isolation along with low parental attachment and joined gangs because they wanted a sense of belonging, as was found in prior research by Joe and Chesney-Lind (1995). These gang girls also reported a high degree of school violence and fighting, similar to the reports by females in the study by Baskin and Sommers (1998). On the other hand, we found gang girls had lower self-esteem than non-gang girls, which would seem to contradict the belief that girls join gangs for honor and respect. As found earlier by Bjerregaard and Smith (1993), girl gang members had lower school expectations as measured by limited educational opportunities and school commitment.

Are these differences between gang and non-gang girls in attitudes related to behavior? In other research we tried to predict both gang membership (Esbensen and Deschenes 1998) and involvement in violent behavior (Deschenes and Esbensen 1999) using many of these explanatory factors. We found significant gender differences that led us to test different models for males and females. Among females, gang membership appeared to be related to low maternal attachment, higher perceived levels of school violence, stronger neutralization of fighting, lack of guilt for violent behavior, and a lower number of pro-social peers. Engaging in violent crime was associated with some of these factors, but not all of them. Higher rates of violence were predicted most strongly by lack of guilt and stronger neutralization, and having been victimized in the past year, and less strongly by a lack of school commitment, few pro-social peers, greater risk-seeking and lower self-esteem. Gang membership was related to violence, but was not as important as other variables in explaining frequency of behavior. Even though the current study shows significant differences between non-gang and gang girls in background and attitudes, our prior research indicates not all of these variables are related to violence. Since both studies were limited to cross-sectional data, it is impossible to determine whether these factors are only *correlates* or whether they could be *causes* of violent behavior.

Knowing that 8% of young adolescent females in various cities across America have joined gangs and that 20% of them have shot at someone because they were told to by somebody else, what should be done to reduce violence? Part of the answer does seem to be to prevent girls from becoming members of gangs. Even so, about 40% of non-gang girls report they have either been hit by someone or have hit someone else. Although they may feel somewhat guilty, a majority of non-gang girls believe it is okay to fight if you are hit first, to protect your rights, or if your family or friends are being threatened. Has the greater equality of males and females made our society more violent by encouraging girls to be more aggressive and fight back? Unfortunately, the current study can not provide an answer to that question. Nonetheless, our findings of significant differences between gang and non-gang girls in attitudes and behaviors do suggest policy makers should target interventions toward family, school and peer influences in order to have a cumulative effect on individual attitudes and peer group affiliations. Efforts should be made to reach out to those girls who lack parental attachment and who feel socially isolated from their families or have low self-esteem. Moreover, there should probably be a renewed emphasis on education and support for pro-social activities. In addition, it might be wise to discourage risk-seeking and impulsive behaviors and encourage more accountability for negative behaviors. Girls and boys need to learn that being in a gang may not protect them from the violence on their streets. Instead, it may lead to an increase in their own violent behavior and their own victimization.

Girls, Gangs, and Violence:
Reinventing the Liberated Female Crook

Meda Chesney-Lind★

Reflexive Statement

I have been working to break the silence about girls and their problems for over twenty years now, so it probably seems odd that I would consider writing a paper that basically attacks journalists for showing an interest in girls. Sadly, that is what I am compelled to do after a siege of media calls to me about the "problem" of girls in gangs. Perhaps the strangest was from a national television series that wanted me to produce a girl robber for their weekend program, but there have been many others. The reporters who call me are almost all young women themselves, but they quickly become aggravated with me when I won't confirm "what everybody knows"—that girls are more violent today.

As their lack of interest in the real problems of girls becomes clear, I find myself becoming increasingly frustrated and angry. I try to appeal to them as women, to establish that they were once girls, and that they, too, have likely suffered as a result of being born female. The damage done by the stories they have culled from the police files about girls a different color than they, living in a part of their city they don't understand, finding themselves in situations they cannot imagine, is hard to undo.

These days there is much talk about the differences between women and the need for many feminisms; that need has been made clear to me in these conversations. The feminism these young women reporters feel close to has addressed issues very different from those of the girls who find gangs a partial answer to the many problems in their lives. Still, I feel compelled to try to define a sisterhood that can stretch that far and to try to pull together an understanding of girl gang members that makes their lives more accessible to others; this paper is part of that effort. It is also an attempt to make clear that the divides between women have been used by the media to demonize young women of color, thereby making them responsible for their own marginalization, while simultaneously warning their more privileged white sisters of the "dark" side of their efforts to seek a better life for women.

Introduction

Generally, the girls who find their way into the juvenile justice system have been invisible. The stereotype of the delinquent is so indisputably male that the general public, as

★*Reprinted from* Humanity and Society *17 (1993), pp. 321-44. Reprinted by permission.*

well as those in criminology who study delinquency, rarely, if ever, consider girls and their problems.

Occasionally girls and women do occupy center stage, but only when their acts are defined as either very bad or profoundly evil. Such visibility was granted women's crime in the mid-nineteen seventies when the liberated "female crook" (Adler 1975a, 42) was discovered, and today a similar pattern is being seen with the media's intense interest in "girls in gangs." In both instances, these media crime waves were lodged within the larger silence about girls, their problems, and their delinquency. For this reason, there is often little with which to refute sensationalistic claims about girls' crime. More importantly, the relative lack of interest in this topic makes it difficult to craft an accurate understanding of girls and their relationship to their gangs.

Research on gangs

Existing theories of crime and delinquency, because they were constructed almost entirely with boys and men in mind, would appear to be fundamentally inadequate to the task of explaining young women's crime. Some contend, though, that despite their flaws, many of these theories can be adapted to explain female as well as male behavior (Canter 1982; Figueria-McDonough and Barton 1985; Giordano 1978; Simons, Miller,, and Aigner 1980; Smith and Paternoster 1987; Sommers and Baskin 1993).

Even these researchers, however, would likely concur that the degree of the androcentric bias found in theories of juvenile gangs is extreme. From the current gang frenzy that has gripped the United States comes a rather clear example of the problem. Martin Sanchez-Jankowski's (1991) widely cited *Islands in the Streets* has the following entries in his index under "Women"

- "and codes of conduct"
- individual violence over
- as "property"
- and urban gangs

One might be tempted to believe that the last entry might refer to girl gangs and the emerging literature on girls in gangs (see Campbell 1984/1991; Quicker 1983; Harris 1988), but the "and" in the sentence is not a mistake. Girls are simply treated as the sexual chattel of male gang members or as an "incentive" for boys to join the gang (since "women look up to gang members") (Sanchez-Jankowski 1991, 53).

Jankowski's work, as well as other current discussions of gang delinquency (see Hagedorn 1988) actually represent a sad revisiting of the sexism that characterized the initial efforts to understand visible lower class, male delinquency in Chicago over half a century earlier. Field work on gangs in Chicago clearly set the stage for decades of delinquency research. Then, too, researchers were only interested in talking to and following the boys. Thrasher (1927) studied over a thousand juvenile gangs in Chicago. He spends approximately one page out of 600 on the five or six female gangs he encountered in his field observation of juvenile gangs.[1]

During roughly the same period Shaw and McKay utilized an ecological approach to the study of juvenile delinquency. Their impressive works (1930, 1933, 1942) set the stage for much of the subcultural research on delinquency. In their eco-logical work, however, Shaw and McKay analyzed only the official arrest data on male delinquents in Chicago and repeatedly referred to these rates as "delinquency rates" (though they occasionally make parenthetical reference to data on female delinquency) (see Shaw and McKay 1942, 356). Similarly, their biographical work traced only male experiences with the law.[2] Another major theoretical approach to gangs and delin-quency focused on the subculture of lower class communities as a generating milieu for delinquent behavior. Here again, noted delinquency researchers concentrated either exclusively or nearly exclusively on male lower class culture. For example, Cohen's work on the subculture of delinquent gangs, which was written nearly twenty years after Thrasher's, deliberately considers only boys' delinquency. His justification for the exclusion of the girls is quite illuminating:

> My skin has nothing of the quality of down or silk, there is nothing limpid or flute-like about my voice, I am a total loss with needle and thread, my posture and car-riage are wholly lacking in grace. These imperfections cause me no distress—if anything, they are gratifying—because I conceive myself to be a man and want peo-ple to recognize me as a full-fledged, unequivocal representative of my sex.... I am reliably informed that many women... often affect ignorance, frailty and emotional instability because to do otherwise would be out of keeping with a reputation for indubitable femininity. In short, people do not simply want to excel; they want to excel as a man or as a woman (Cohen 1955, 138).

From this Cohen concludes that the delinquent response, "however it may be condemned by others on moral grounds, has at least one virtue: it incontestably con-firms, in the eyes of all concerned, his essential masculinity" (Cohen 1955, 140).

Feminist criminologists have faulted these and other theoretical schools of delin-quency for assuming that male delinquency, even in its most violent forms, was some-how an understandable if not "normal" response to their situations. Girls who shared the same social and cultural milieu as delinquent boys but who were not delinquents were somehow abnormal or "over-controlled" (Cain 1989). Essentially, law abiding behavior on the part of at least some boys and men is taken as a sign of character, but when women avoid crime and violence, it is an expression of weakness (Naffine 1987).

For those with this conventional criminological perspective on gender, girls engaged in what are defined as "male" activities such as violent crime or gang delin-quency are seen as seeking "equality" with their male counterparts (see Daly and

Chesney-Lind 1988). Is that what is going on? A complete answer to that question requires a more careful and complex inquiry into the lives of these girls and the role the gang in their world. But understanding has not been a major earmark of the current media interest in girls in gangs. Instead, the media has focused on the nontraditional, non-feminine, and sensationalistic aspects of these girls' behavior. A review of the media construction of the problem of girls in gangs will illustrate this quite clearly. This will be followed up by a summary of ethnographic and quantitative assessments of the girl gangs. Finally, this paper will offer a possible explanation for the intense media interest in this topic at this time.

Media Portraits of Girls in Gangs

On August 6, 1992, a short-subject appeared on a CBS program entitled *Street Stories.* "Girls in the Hood," which was a rebroadcast of a story that appeared first in January, 1992, opened with this voice-over:

> Some of the politicians like to call this the Year of the Woman. The women you are about to meet probably aren't what they had in mind. These women are active, they're independent, and their exercising power in a field dominated by men. In January Harold Dowe first took us to the streets of Las Angeles to meet two uncommon women who are members of street gangs. (CBS 1992)

This story was one of many media accounts to have appeared since the second wave of the "liberation" hypothesis was launched by journalists. Where did this come from? Perhaps the start was an article entitled "You've Come a Long Way, Moll," which appeared in the *Wall Street Journal,* January 25, 1990. This article noted that "between 1978-1988 the number of women arrested for violent crimes went up 41.5%, vs. 23.1% for men. The trend is even starker for teenagers" (Crittenden 1990, A14). But the trend was accelerated by the identification of a new, specific version of this more general revisiting of the liberation hypothesis. "For Gold Earrings and Protection, More Girls Take the Road to Violence," announced the front page of the *New York Times* in an article that opens as follows:

> For Aleysha J., the road to crime has been paved with huge gold earrings and name brand clothes. At Aleysha's high school in the Bronx, popularity comes from looking the part. Aleysha's mother has no money to buy her nice things so the diminutive 15 year old steals them, an act that she feels makes her equal parts bad girl and liberated woman. (Lee 1991, A1)

This is followed by the assertion that "[t]here are more and more girls like Aleysha in troubled neighborhoods in the New York metropolitan areas, people who work with children say. There are more girls in gangs, more girls in the drug trade, more girls carrying guns and knives, more girls in trouble." Whatever the original source, at this point a phenomenon known as "pack journalism" took over. *The Philadelphia Inquirer,* for example, ran a story subtitled, "Troubled Girls, Troubling Violence" on February 23, 1992, that asserted:

> Girls are committing more violent crimes than ever before. Girls used to get in trouble like this mostly as accomplices of boys, but that's no longer true. They don't need the boys. And their attitudes toward their crimes are often as hard as the weapons they wield—as shown in this account based on documents and interviews with participants, parents, police and school officials. While boys still account for the vast majority of juvenile crime, girls are starting to catch up. (Santiago 1992, A1)

This particular story featured a single incident in which an African-American girl attacked another girl (described as "middle class" and appearing white in the picture that accompanies the story) in a subway. The *Washington Post* ran a similar story entitled, "Delinquent Girls Achieving a Violent Equality in D.C." on December 23, 1992 (Lewis 1992).

In virtually all stories on this topic, the issue is framed in a similar fashion. Generally, a specific and egregious example of female violence is described. This is followed by quick review of the Federal Bureau of Investigation's arrest statistics showing what appear to be large increases in the number of girls arrested for violent offenses, and finally there are quotes from "experts," usually police officers, teachers, or other social service workers, but occasionally criminologists, interpreting the events.

Following these print media stories, the number of articles and television shows focused specifically on girls in gangs jumped. Popular talk shows such as *Oprah* (November, 1992), *Geraldo* (January 1993), and *Larry King Live* (March, 1993) did programs on the subject, and most recently *NBC News* had a story broadcast on its nightly news which opened with the same link between women's "equality" and girls' participation in gangs:

> Gone are the days when girls were strictly sidekicks for male gang members, around merely to provide sex and money and run guns and drugs. Now girls also do shooting... the new members, often as young as twelve, are the most violent... Ironic as it is, just as women are becoming more powerful in business and government, the same thing is happening in gangs. (NBC 1993)

For many feminist criminologists, this pattern is more than a little familiar. For example, a 1971 *New York Times* article entitled, "Crime Rate of Women Up Sharply Over Men's" noted that "Women are gaining rapidly in at least one traditional area of male supremacy—crime" (Roberts 1971, 1).

A more expanded version of what would come to be known as the "liberation hypothesis" appeared in Adler's *Sisters in Crime* in a chapter entitled "Minor Girls and Major Crimes":

Girls are involved in more drinking, stealing, gang activity, and fighting—behavior in keeping with their adoption of male roles. We also find increases in the total number of female deviances. The departure from the safety of traditional female roles and the testing of uncertain alternative roles coincide with the turmoil of adolescence creating criminogenic risk factors which are bound to create this increase. These considerations help explain the fact that between 1969 and 1972 national arrests for major crimes show a jump for boys of 82%—for girls, 306% (Adler 1975b, 95).

Of course, the female crime wave described by Adler (1975b) and, to a lesser extent, by Simon (1975) was definitively refuted by subsequent research (see Steffensmeier and Steffensmeier 1980; Gora 1982), but the popularity of this perspective, at least in the public mind, is apparently undiminished. It remains to be seen whether in the 1990s something different might be going on, particularly with reference to girls and gangs. It is to that question, that this paper now turns.

Trends in Girls' Arrests

A review of girls' arrests for violent crime for the last decade (1982-1991) initially seems to provide support for the notion that girls are engaged in more violent crime. Arrests of girls for murder were up 12%, robbery arrests were up 48.7%, and aggravated assault was up 70.3%. Indeed, arrests of girls for all Part One Offenses[3] were up 62.1% (Federal Bureau of Investigation 1992b, 218).

These increases may sound substantial despite the fact that they are actually considerably less dramatic than those that generated the first media version of a female crime wave. Between 1968 and 1977, for example, the total number of young women's arrests was up 61%, arrests of girls for robbery were up 112%, aggravated assault arrests of girls soared by 158.7%, and girls' arrests for Part One violent offenses were up 138.8% (Federal Bureau of Investigation 1978, 175).

To put these increases in perspective, though, only 2% of girls' arrests (4,889 arrests) in 1977 were for serious crimes of violence. By 1991 this figure had climbed to 2.9% (10,194 arrests out of a total of 343,506 arrests). Moreover, girls' share of serious crimes of violence (i.e., the sex ratio for these offenses) has changed very little during the two time periods. In 1977, for example, arrests of girls accounted for 10.6% of all arrests of youth for serious crimes of violence; in 1991, the comparable figure was 11.7% (Federal Bureau of Investigation 1978, 179; Federal Bureau of Investigation 1992, 222). While many questions can be raised about the actual significance of such increases (e.g., the numbers involved are small and quite volatile), such an exploration is probably not salient. Changes in these sorts of official crime statistics failed to signal the rise of youth gangs (of either gender). As a consequence, it might be more useful to examine other sources of information on girls in gangs. Fortunately, there have been some excellent ethnographic studies of individual girls in gangs, and they seem a good starting point for any discussion of major changes in the character of this form of female delinquency.

Girls in Gangs[4]

Girls' involvement in delinquent gangs has never been of the same magnitude as boys. Traditional discussions of gang delinquency, reviewed earlier, stress the image of girls as playing auxiliary roles to boys' gangs, if they are involved in gang activity at all. More recent criminological research seemed to confirm this impression. Miller's nationwide study of gangs, for example, in the mid-1970s, found the existence of fully independent girl gangs to be quite rare, constituting less than 10% of all gangs. He also noted that about half of the male gangs in the New York area had female auxiliary groups, and of all the gangs known to exist in the Bronx and Queens areas of New York City, there were only six independent female gangs. Further, he reported that the crimes committed by the girl gangs were far less serious than crimes by male gangs, and were no more violent than in the past (Miller 1975b).

Miller (1980) also conducted an in-depth analysis on a Boston gang known as The Molls. This gang consisted of a core membership of 11 girls whose age ranged from 13 to 16. They were white and Catholic (mostly Irish). These girls seemed to fit the stereotype of inner-city working class girls, as they spent most of their time "hanging out" around street corners—looking and talking tough. They were known in the neighborhood as "bad girls." Their illegal activities included truancy, theft, drinking, property damage, sex offenses, and assault, in order of frequency. Truancy was by far their most common offense, occurring about three times as often as the next most common offense, which was theft (predominantly shoplifting).

These girls were closely associated with a male gang in the area known as the Hoods. The girls aspired "to become recognized as their girls," which they did by approving, supporting, and abetting the criminal activities of the Hoods (Miller 1980, 243-44). In fact, in order to be accepted by the Hoods the girls had no choice but to go along with their criminal activities. Contrary to popular belief, "the Molls did not flaunt their sexual exploits in order to win esteem," and they believed that to get the boys to like them was to imitate their behavior as much as possible, rather than be sexually accessible to them (Miller 1980, 244).

Rice reported similar findings in his study of a New York gang, the Persian Queens. He noted that the gang was completely controlled by males and was oriented toward male activities. There is very little the gang girls could do to achieve power or prestige in the gang world. He also reported that if these girls fight, then the males will not like them; on the other hand, if they play a more feminine role, they are disregarded by the males, except for sexual gratification. Similar findings have been reported in Philadelphia (Brown 1977) and in New York City (Campbell 1984). In general, while there have been some changes ity of girls who are part of gangs are either the girlfriends of the male members or a "little sisters" subgroup of the male gang (see Bowker 1978b, 184; and Hanson 1964).

There is abundant evidence that girls often join gangs for the same kinds of reasons as males, such as a sense of belonging, whereby the gang becomes a sort of "family." Brown (1977) found that friendships with fellow girl gang members is of utmost importance for girl gang members. Giordano's (1978) study arrived at the same conclusions. Gangs may also provide opportunities for relationships with boys (Flowers 1987, 137). Girls in gangs observed by Campbell very often engage in the same behavior as the boys, such as smoking pot, drinking, fighting, committing theft, and "partying." Also, most of the fights the girls get into arise mostly from domestic or romantic disputes (Campbell 1984, 33). Summarizing these and other studies, Mann concluded that the stereotypical gang role for girls is "to conceal and carry weapons for the boys, to provide sexual favors, and sometimes to fight against girls who were connected with enemy boys' gangs" (Mann 1984, 45).

Other first-hand accounts of girl gangs, while not completely challenging this image, have focused more directly on the race and class issues confronting girls who find themselves in gangs. Quicker's study of female Chicano gang members in East Los Angeles found evidence that these girls, although still somewhat dependent upon their male counterparts, were becoming more independent. These girls identified themselves as "homegirls" and their male counterparts as "homeboys," a common reference to relationships in the "barrio." In an obvious reference to "strain theory," Quicker notes that there are few economic opportunities within the barrio to meet the needs of the family unit. As a result, families are disintegrating and do not have the capability of providing access to culturally emphasized success goals for young people about to enter adulthood. Not surprisingly, almost all their activities occur within the context of gang life, where they learn how to get along in the world and are insulated from the harsh environment of the barrio (Quicker 1983).

Harris's study of the Cholas, a Latino gang in the San Fernando Valley, echoes this theme. She notes that while the Cholas in many respects resembles male gangs, the gang did challenge the girls' traditional destiny within the barrio in two direct ways. First, the girls rejected the traditional image of the Latino woman as "wife and mother" (Harris 1988), supporting, instead, a more "macho" homegirl role. Second, the gang supported the girls in their estrangement from organized religion, substituting instead a form of familialism that "provides a strong substitute for weak family and conventional school ties" (Harris 1988, 172).

One of the most interesting pieces of research on girl gangs comes from a study by Fishman (this volume) of a black gang known as the Vice Queens. This gang was a female auxiliary gang to a boys' gang, the Vice Kings, that existed in Chicago during the early 1960s. Living in a mostly black community characterized by poverty, unemployment, deterioration, and a high crime rate, the gang of about 30 teenage girls was loosely knit (unlike the male gang), and provided the girls with companionship and friends. Failing in school and unable to find work, the bulk of their time was spent "hanging out" on the streets with the Vice Kings, which usually included the consumption of alcohol and sexual activities, and occasional delinquency, most of which was "traditionally female" like prostitution, shoplifting, and running away, but some of which was more serious (e.g., auto theft). They also engaged in fights with other groups of girls, largely to protect their gang's reputation for toughness.

Growing up in rough neighborhoods provided the Vice Queens "with opportunities to learn such traditional male skills as fighting and taking care of themselves on the streets." It was generally expected that the girls had to learn to defend themselves against "abusive men" and "attacks on their integrity" (Fishman 1988, 15). Their relationship to the Vice Kings was primarily sexual, having sexual relations and bearing their children, but with no hope of marriage.

Fishman notes that the Vice Queens were "socialized to be independent, assertive and to take risks with the expectations that these are characteristics that they will need to function effectively within the black low income community…. As a consequence, black girls demonstrate, out of necessity, a greater flexibility in roles" (Fishman 1988, 26-27). She also notes that there has been little improvement in the economic situation of the African American community since the 1960S; indeed, she believes that, if anything they face an even bleaker future than the Vice Queens she interviewed. In this context, she speculates that "black female gangs today have become more entrenched, more violent, and more oriented to 'male' crime" (Fishman 1988, 28). These changes, she goes on to say, are unrelated to the women's movement, but are instead the "forced 'emancipation' which stems from the economic crisis within the black community" (Fishman 1988, 28-29).

Fishman's bleak speculation about the situation of girl gangs in contemporary poverty-stricken neighborhoods has been largely confirmed by more contemporary research by Lauderback, Hansen, and Waldorf on an African American female gang in San Francisco. Disputing the "traditional notions of female gang members in which they are portrayed as maladjusted tomboys and sex objects completely dependent upon the favor of male gang members" (Lauderback, Hansen, and Waldorf 1992, 70), these interviewers found an independent girl gang who engaged in crack sales and organized "boosting" to support themselves and their young children. Looking past the gang's economic role in their lives, Lauderback and his associates noted that the gang "fills a void in the lives of its members," since their own family ties were "weak at best" prior to their involvement in the group (Lauderback, Hansen, and Waldorf 1992, 69). All under 25, abandoned by the fathers of their children, abused and controlled by other men, these young women wish they could be "doing something other than selling drugs and to leave the neighborhood," but "many felt that the circumstances which led them to sell drugs were not going to change" (Lauderback, Hansen and Waldorf 1992, 23).

Campbell's work on Hispanic gangs in the New York area (Campbell 1984/1991) finds much the same pattern. Campbell noted that the girls in her study joined gangs for reasons that are largely explained by their situation in a society that has little to offer young women of color (Campbell 1990, 172-73). First, the possibility of a decent career, outside of "domestic servant," is practically nonexistent. Many have come from female-headed families subsisting on welfare, and most have dropped out of the school and have no marketable skills. Their aspirations for the future were both sex typed and unrealistic, with the girls expressing desires to be rock stars or professional models. Second, they find themselves in a highly gendered community where the men in their lives, while not traditional breadwinners, still make many decisions that circumscribe the possibilities open to young women. Third, the responsibility that young Hispanic women will have as mothers further restricts the options available to her. Campbell cites recent data revealing a very bleak future indeed, as 94% will have children and 84% will have to raise their children without a husband. Most will be dependent upon some form of welfare (1990, 182). Fourth, these young women face a future of isolation as a housewife in the projects. Finally, they share with their male counterparts a future of powerlessness as members of the urban underclass. Their lives, in effect, reflect all the burdens of their triple handicaps of race, class, and gender.

For these girls, Campbell observes, the gang represents "an idealized collective solution to the bleak future that awaits" them. The girls have a tendency to portray the gang to themselves and the outside world in a very idealized and romantic manner (1990, 173). They develop an exaggerated sense of belonging to the gang. Many were loners prior to joining the gang, having been only loosely connected to schoolmates and neighborhood peer groups. Even the gangs' closeness, as well as the "excitement of gang life is more of a fiction than a reality. Their daily "street talk" is filled with exaggerated stories of parties, drugs, alcohol, and other varieties of "fun." However, as Campbell notes (1990, 176):

> These events stand as a bulwark against the loneliness and drudgery of their future lives. They also belie the day to day reality of gang life. The lack of recreational opportunities, the long days unfilled by work or school and the absence of money mean that the hours and days are whiled away on street corners. "Doing nothing" means hang out on the stoop; the hours of "bullshit" punctuated by trips to the store to buy one can of beer at a time. When an expected windfall arrives, marijuana and rum are purchased in bulk and the partying begins. The next day, life returns to normal.

Current research on girl gangs, then, has moved beyond stereotypical notions about them as simply the female auxiliaries of male gangs to more careful assessments of the role played by these groups in girls' lives. Of particular significance are those elements of female gangs that provide the girls with the skills to survive in their harsh communities while also allowing them to escape, at least for a while, from the bleak future that awaits them.

None of these accounts, even the most recent, confirms the stereotype of the hyperviolent, amoral girls found in media accounts of girls in gangs. Certainly, they confirm the fact that girls do commit a wider range of delinquent behavior than is stereotypically recognized, but these offenses appear to be part of a complex fabric of "hanging out," "partying," and the occasional fight defending one's friends or territory.

Historically, though, those activities that did not fit the official stereotype of "girls' delinquency" have been ignored by those in authority. A clear documentation of this pattern is found in Shacklady-Smith's (1978) research on girl gang members conducted in Bristol between 1969 and 1972. She noted that delinquent girls and gang girls—the vast majority of whom were officially charged with the British equivalent of non-criminal, status offenses (like running away from home, being incorrigible, being a truant, etc.)—had committed a wide range of delinquent behaviors, including fighting. Her figures indicated that nearly three quarters (73.3%) of her gang sample as well as 63% of her probation sample said they had "taken part in a fight." Said one girl:

I reckon we fight as seriously as the boys. You know, if anybody comes up to us we'll smack a bottle in their faces. You know we say, "you try it," and they don't think we will use it on them. But we will if they try anything. (Shacklady-Smith 1983, 86)

In the main, though, this behavior was ignored by official authorities, according to her interviews:

It's funny because once when I was down at the cop shop for fighting, this woman saw the swastika on my arm and forgot all about what she was looking for. They never did nothing—just told me to stop fighting. But the woman cop, she kept on about the swastika and Hell's Angels. What a bad lot they were for a girl to go around with, and how I had better stop going round with the Angels or else I'd get a really bad name for myself. Then she kept asking me if I'd had sex with any of 'em or taken drugs." (Shacklady-Smith 1978, 83)

Shacklady-Smith's work, as well as the work of others who studied girls in gangs in earlier decades (Fishman 1988; Quicker 1983), suggests that girls have long been involved in violent behavior as a part of gang life. During earlier periods, however, this occasional violence was ignored by law enforcement officers far more concerned with their sexual behavior or morality. Shacklady-Smith's findings on the relative similarity of delinquent girls' and gang girls' activities also suggests the need to explore the degree to which girls in gangs are actually engaged in significantly different and more violent offending than their non-gang, but delinquent counterparts. A quantitative study of youth gangs in the state of Hawaii permits just such an exploration.

Girls in Gangs in Hawaii

Research on youth gangs in Hawaii has been conducted as part of an ongoing study of the state's youth gang response system (see Chesney-Lind et al. 1992). Data gathered from files maintained by the Honolulu Police Department (HPD), which serves the City and County of Honolulu (on the island of Oahu where over three quarters of the state's population is located), permit a more quantitative assessment of girls' involvement in gang activity.[5]

Like other major cities, Honolulu has experienced a rapid growth in police estimates of gang activity and gang membership. In 1988, the HPD estimated that there were 22 gangs with 450 members; in 1991, the number of gangs has climbed to 45 with an estimated membership of 1,020, and by 1993 the number of gangs stood at 171 with 1,267 members (Office of Youth Services 1993).

Research on the characteristics of youth labeled by HPD as gang members commenced during August, 1991, and a demographic profile on a sample ($N=361$) of these youth was constructed. The sample was drawn randomly from a complete list of identification numbers for each gang youth contained in the HPD GREAT computer system.[6] Subsequent to this, additional information, particularly on prior offenses, was gathered from the HPD juvenile offender and adult offender records. Ultimately, the profile was able to provide the ethnicity, gender, age, neighborhood, school (or previous school), zip code (at time of arrest), and offense history of youth identified as gang members as of August 1991.

The general results of this research have been reported elsewhere (Chesney-Lind, et al. 1992), but these data also permit an examination of gender and gang membership. Only 7% of the suspected gang members on Oahu were female. About 70% of girls and 78% of boys were legally adults. While the bulk of both the men and women in the population of youth gang members were young (between 18 and 21 years of age), this was less true for women and for men. About half of the men (48.4%), but only slightly over a third of the women (37.5%), were in this age group. A third of the women were over 26 compared to only 13.4% of the men. There was, in fact, one woman in the database who was 52 years old. Thus, the median age for women was 24.5 and 21.4 for men. Taken together, these findings make the use of the term "youth gang" somewhat questionable particularly for women labeled by police as gang members.

Virtually all the youth identified as gang members were drawn from low-income ethnic groups in the islands, but ethnic differences were also found between male and female gang members. The men were more likely than the women to have been drawn almost exclusively from immigrant groups (Samoan and Filipino); the women, by contrast, were more likely to be Native Hawaiian and Filipino.

Most importantly, women and girls labeled as gang members committed fewer of most offenses than men (see Table 1) and they also committed less serious offenses (see Table 2).

Offense Patterns
Males and Females Labeled as Gang Members

Table 1

Mean number of	Women N = 337	Men N = 24
Arrests	9.1	11.6
Incidents	5.6	7.6
Drug offenses	2.9	.04
Property offenses	2.0	3.6
Status offenses	2.0	1.6
Violent offenses	0.227	1.4

Rank Order of Most Serious Arrests of Suspected Gang Members by Gender

Table 2

Offenses	Women N = 21	Men N = 328
Larceny theft	38.1	14.0
Status offenses	19.0	—
Drug offenses	9.5	—
Criminal property damage	4.76	—
Motor vehicle	4.76	6.1
Other assaults	4.76	27.0
Robbery	—	12.0
Burglary	—	7.9

Table 1 clearly indicates that while both the males and female in this sample of suspected gang members were chronic but not serious offenders; the rank ordering of the most serious arrest in Table 2 demonstrates that this pattern is particularly clear in the case of women suspected of gang membership. Indeed, this rank ordering reveals, for the girls, a pattern that bears a very close relationship to typical female delinquency. For example, the most common arrest category for girls in 1991 in the U.S was larceny theft (F.B.I. 1992, 218), and the most common arrest category for these girls was larceny theft, followed by status offenses. For boys, the pattern is somewhat more sobering, with "other assaults" (which likely means fighting with other boys) as the most serious arrest for the bulk of these young men. In total, serious violent offenses (murder, sexual assault, robbery, and aggravated assault) accounted for 23% of the most serious offenses of males suspected of gang membership but none of the girls' most serious offenses.

Finally, it is important to note that once police identified a youth as a gang member, they apparently remained in the database regardless of patterns of desistence; for example, 22% of sample had not been arrested in three years and there was no gender difference in this pattern.

These patterns prompted a further exploration of the degree to which young women labeled by police as "suspected gang members" differed from young women who had been arrested for delinquency. To do this, a comparison group was created for those in the Oahu sample that were legally juveniles. Youth suspected of gang membership were matched on ethnicity, age, and gender with youth who were in the juvenile arrest database, but who had not been labeled as gang members. A look at offense patterns of this smaller group indicates no major differences between girls suspected of gang membership and their non-gang counterparts. Indeed, the modal most serious offense for gang girls was status offenses, and for non-gang girls it was other assaults.

While the numbers were very small in this subsample (N=5), girls who were arrested for juvenile delinquency but not identified by the police as youth gang members were generally more seriously delinquent than girls suspected of gang activity. Girls suspected of gang membership had a mean of 5 arrests compared to 6.2 in the delinquent group. This pattern was consistent across all the arrest categories. Girls in the suspected gang group had .2 violent arrests compared to .8 in the delinquent group; they also had more arrests for property offenses (4.6 arrests compared to 3.7), and more arrests for status offenses (4.5 arrests compared to 4.4).

This finding is not totally unexpected. Bowker and Klein (1983), in an examination of data on girls in gangs in Los Angeles in the nineteen sixties, compared both the etiology of delinquent behavior of gang girls and their non-gang counterparts and concluded:

> The overwhelming impact of racism, sexism, poverty and limited opportunity structures is likely to be so important in determining the gang membership and juvenile delinquency of women and girls in urban ghettos that personality variables, relations with parents and problems associated with heterosexual behavior play a relatively minor role in determining gang membership and juvenile delinquency. (Bowker and Klein 1983, 750-51)

In addition, similar studies, using comparison groups in Arizona (Zatz 1985) with Hispanic gangs and in Las Vegas (Shelden, Snodgrass, and Snodgrass 1993) with African American and Hispanic gangs, while not focusing on gender, found little to differentiate gang members from other "delinquent" or criminal youth.

Finally, research on official "careers" of non-white (71% of the non-white girls were African American) and white girls, while not dealing specifically with gang girls, found far less serious and violent delinquency in the non-white girls than would be expected if they were "converging" with their black, male counterparts. In examining a cohort of youth first referred to Clark County in 1980, no difference was found in the types of offenses for which non-white and white girls were referred. Over a quarter of all the offenses resulting in referral to court were status offenses. Examining "personal" or violent offenses, these were found to comprise 6.5% of white girl's referrals and 4.7% of non-white girls referrals. For boys, a sharper and more violent pattern obtained with 8% of the referrals of white males and 18% of non-white males. But about 60% of both groups were referred only once. In short, race plays a major difference in the length and seriousness of delinquent careers, but only for males (Shelden and Chesney Lind 1993).

Taken together, assessments of gang delinquency in girls, whether quantitative or qualitative, suggest that there is little evidence to support the notion of a new, violent female offender. Instead, what emerges is a more complex picture where some girls solve their problems of gender, race, and class through gang membership. Clearly, girls' experiences with gangs cannot be simply framed as "breaking into" a male world. They have long been in gangs and their participation in these gangs, even their violence, is heavily influenced by their gender.

Conclusion

This review of the literature on girls in gangs suggests that girls have long been members of gangs, that their roles in these gangs have been considerably more varied than early stereotypes would have it, and that girls' occasionally violent behavior has, during other decades, been largely ignored. Since there is little evidence of a radical change in girls' behavior in gangs over the past few decades, one must ask why these facts are being used now to construct female crime wave?

A quick comparison of the articles that comprise each surge of media interest in crimes committed by girls and women suggests some answers to this question. While there are many similarities between the two media crime waves, there are some crucial differences. Those who tout both crime waves utilize a crude form of equity feminism to explain the trends observed and, in the process, contribute to the "backlash" against the women's movement (Faludi 1991).

The age and ethnicity of the women in each of the crime waves does differ. In the stories that announced the first crime wave during the 1970s, the liberated "female crook" was a white political activist, a "terrorist," a drug using hippie. For example, one story syndicated by the *New York Times* service had pictures of both Patty Hearst and Friederike Krabbe (Klemesrud 1978). Today's demonized woman is African American or Hispanic, and she is a violent teenager.

In both instances, there was some, small amount of truth in the image found in the articles. As this paper has shown, girls and women have always engaged in more violent behavior than the stereotype of women supports; girls have also been in gangs for decades. The periodic media discovery of these facts, then, must be serving other political purposes.

Yesterday, the goal may have been to discredit the young white women and their invisible, but central African American counterparts (Barnett 1993) who were challenging the racism, sexism, and militarism of that day. Today, as the research on girls and gangs has indicated, young minority youth of both genders face a bleak present and a grim future. Today, it is clear that "gang" has become a code word for race.[7] A review of the media portrayal of girls in gangs suggests that beyond this, media stories on the youth gang problem can create a political climate where the victims of racism and sexism can be blamed for their own problems.

In short, this most recent female crime wave appears to be an attempt to reframe the problems of racism and sexism in society. As young women are demonized by the media, their genuine problems can be marginalized and then ignored. Indeed, they have become the problem. The challenge to those concerned about girls is, then, twofold. First, responsible work on girls in gangs must make the dynamics of this victim blaming clear. Second, it must continue to build an understanding of girls' gangs that is sensitive to the contexts within which they arise. Good ethnographic work is beginning to fill this void and explain the utility and logic of the behavior of girls—including gang participation—as a response to being on the economic and political margins. In an era that is increasingly concerned about the intersection of class, race, and gender, such work seems long overdue.

Notes

Section 1 • Frederic M. Thrasher • Sex in the Gang

1 Manuscript prepared by a former member of the gang.
2 Teacher's interview with a boy.
3 Manuscript prepared by a former member of the gang.
4 Manuscript prepared by a former member of the gang.
5 Manuscript prepared by a former member of the gang.
6 Manuscript prepared by a former member of the gang (the girl in the case).
7 See document 14, p. 51.
8 Interview with a court reporter.
9 Interview with a court reporter.
10 Manuscript prepared by an observer of the gang.
11 See Daniel Russell's forthcoming study of dance halls in Chicago.
12 Louise de Koven Bowen, *The public dance halls of Chicago* (Rev. ed.), from an investigation of the Juvenile Protective Association, 1917. Since prohibition great progress in the direction of better moral conditions in public dancing has been made. The report of the Juvenile Protective Association for 1921-'22 shows a decrease in number of smaller, badly regulated dance halls, and a fine spirit of co-operation from the Association of Ball Room Managers.
13 Stag parties. *Bulletin,* The Juvenile Protective Association, Vol. III, No. 3 (May, 1921).
14 *Chicago Tribune,* March 15, 1923.
15 Ibid ., October 12, 1924.
16 Interview with a physician resident in a social settlement.
17 Interview with a social worker in the district.
18 Interview with a police matron.
19 For an interesting account of Belle Star and her bandit gang see unsigned article, Bobbed-hair bandit of early Texas days, *New York Times* April 13, 1924.
20 Genevieve Forbes, Girl, twenty-one, tells how she ruled holdup gang, *Chicago Tribune,* January 3, 1923. This account in the main has been verified from interviews with members of other gangs and other informants. It seems, however, that Honey was the "brains," not the leader of the gang. The leader was Tom, "a husky bird and a good fighter." The gang was composed of about nine members ranging in delinquency of the gang was burglary, rather than robbery. Honey was given a year's sentence by Judge Caverly, but this was suspended contingent on good behavior.
21 Interview with a physician practicing in the district.
22 See document 188, p. 310.
23 Walter C. Reckless, The natural history of vice areas in Chicago, manuscript in University of Chicago Library, p. 157.
24 J. A. Puffer, *The boy and his gang* (Boston: Houghton-Mifflin Co., 1912), 76

Section 1 • John C. Quicker • The Chicana Gang

1 Jean Strouse writing for *Ms* (August 1972, p. 72) shows that in 1964 the ratio of male to female delinquencies known to the police was 15:1. By 1972 that ratio had narrowed to 3:1. Even in staid old Britain, a *Times* article (October 16, 1972, 33-34) indicates that female gangs are not only increasing but becoming very violent.
2 I have experienced an instance of a group of girls leaving a gang at one time, and not having to "throw" with the remaining girls. In this case the group leaving was sufficiently large that a confrontation with the remaining girls might produce a loss for these latter girls.
3 Girls have told me stories of *veteranas* carving the initials of the gang in the girl's back. Other

stories indicate instances where the girls have required hospitalization due to the beatings. Another girl reported that she had been raped by eight boys from the gang that she had left as part of her ordeal.

4   I have learned of some women in their late 20s to their early 40s who still consider themselves and are considered by the gang to be members.

5   One story that was related to me indicated a clear-cut instance where the homeboy was wrong. In fact, the girl telling me the story stated that if he had done to her what he had done to this other girl, she probably would have reacted similarly. However, the boy was defended, and the girl threatened, and informed that any further acts would be severely dealt with.

6   Henry D. McKay and others have demonstrated the viability of this notion in numerous studies. Specifically McKay (1967, 115) lends support to this notion when he states "rates of delinquency have increased in situations where basic institutional roles are disrupted for large segments of the population."

Section 1 • Laura T. Fishman • Black Female Gang Behavior

1   The role of females in Chicago gangs, described by Short and Strodtbeck (1965) is documented by Keiser (1969) and Dawley (1973) who provided extensive accounts of the Vice Kings' activities during the sixties.

2   According to Fields and Walters (1985) and Valentine (1978), *hustling* refers to a wide variety of conventional, sometimes extra legal or illegal activities designed to produce economic gain.

3   The most comprehensive discussion of the design of this study in found in James F. Short Jr. and Fred L. Strodtbeck, *Group process and gang delinquency* (Chicago: University of Chicago Press, 1965), 1-26.

4   All interviews held with the workers were recorded. The atmosphere created by the male interviewer was one of informality—an old boys' sense of "we-ness" developed between the workers and the interviewers. Within this informal milieu, the workers seldom chose to talk in a middle class vernacular (and all the workers were from lower middle or middle class backgrounds). Instead, they spoke the language of the streets, which tended to be graphic, rough, and crude with a minimum of middle class niceties. Nevertheless, as shown in the text, their observation tended to be reliable.

5   Detached worker's interview, Youth Studies Program, University of Chicago, May, 1962.

6   Detached worker's interview, Youth Studies Program, University of Chicago, June 2, 1962.

7   Detached worker's interview, Youth Studies Program, University of Chicago, June 21, 1962.

8   Detached worker's interview, Youth Studies Program, University of Chicago, March 12, 1962.

9   Detached worker's interview, Youth Studies Program, University of Chicago, June 21, 1962.

10   Detached worker's interview, Youth Studies Program, University of Chicago, May 24, 1962.

11   A similar observation was made by Campbell (1981, 1982) in her study of female gangs in England.

12   Detached worker's interview, Youth Studies Program, University of Chicago, June 21, 1962.

13   Observer's report, Youth Studies Program, University of Chicago, August 21, 1963.

14   Detached worker's report, Youth Studies Program, University of Chicago, November 9, 1961.

15   Observer's report, Youth Studies Program, University of Chicago, February 8, 1962.

16   Observer's report, Youth Studies Program, University of Chicago, August 21, 1963.

17   Detached worker's interview, Youth Studies Program, University of Chicago, July 16, 1962.

18   Observer's report, Youth Studies Program, University of Chicago, March 21, 1962.

19   Ibid.

20   Detached worker's interview, Youth Studies Program, University of Chicago, June 2, 1962.

21   Detached worker's interview, Youth Studies Program, University of Chicago, May 24, 1962.

22   According to feminist criminologists, the literature on female crime, prior to the seventies, has been hampered by a sexist translation insofar as it tended to reduce all female delinquent and criminal

behavior to a fundamentally sexual level (see, for instance Campbell 1981, 1984, 1990; Klein 1973; and Smart 1977).

Section 2 • Peggy Giordano • Girls, Guys and Gangs

1   G. Konopka (1966). *The adolescent girl in conflict*. Englewood Cliffs, NJ: Prentice Hall.

2   G. Barker and Adams. (1962). Comparison of the delinquencies of boys and girls. *Journal of Criminal Law, Criminology and Police Science* 470.

3   A. K. Cohen (1955). *Delinquent boys: The culture of the gang*. Glencoe, IL: Free Press.

4   Two researchers have directly tested this theory, but they found that their delinquent sample actually perceived fewer obstacles to marital goals than the control group. See Sandhu and Allen, Female delinquency: Goal obstruction and anomie, *Canadian Review of Social Anthropology* 107 (1969), 6. And one researcher found that delinquents reported more dates than the non-delinquent sample but attempted to explain the difference by reference to the "quality" of the dates the delinquents were able to obtain or the sexual favors they may have had to "bestow" in order to get the dates. See R. R. Morris, Female delinquency and relational problems, *Social Forces* 82 (1964), 43. Morris also compared the difference in the observers' rating of facial features, figure, and grooming between delinquents and non-delinquents, but found significant differences only in terms of grooming. *Id.* The importance of this finding, however, is tempered when one considers that the inferior degree of cleanliness and neatness reported may simply be a reflection of middle class interviewer standards and the result may have little to do with the criteria by which boys and girls judge each other as acceptable dating partners.

5   Federal Bureau of Investigation Uniform Crime Reports (Table 28) (1973). The problem with official statistics is well known: however, a recent comparison of self-reported delinquency involvement by girls incarcerated at a state institution in 1960, with the level of involvement reported by a comparable 1975 sample, indicates significantly greater involvement in almost every offense category by the 1975 subjects. See P. Giordano and S. Cernkovich, Changing patterns of female delinquency (August 30, 1976) (unpublished paper resented at the Annual Meetings of the Society for the Study of Social Problems in New York.).

6   F. Adler (1975) *Sisters in crime: The rise of the new female criminal*. New York: McGraw-Hill.

7   Id. at 15.

8   P. Giordano and S. Cernkovich (1977). On complicating the relationship between liberation and delinquency. Unpublished paper presented at the annual meeting of the International Sociological Association, Research Committee for the Sociology of Deviance and Social Control, in Dublin, Ireland.

9   See T. Hirschi (1969), *Causes of delinquency*. Berkeley: University of California Press.

10 See T. Parsons (1942), Age and sex in the social structure of the United States. *American Sociological Review* 7, 604.

11 See R. Cloward and L. Ohlin (1960). *Delinquency and opportunity: A theory of delinquent gangs*. New York: The Free Press.

12 See G. J. Jensen and R. Eve (1976), Sex differences in delinquency: an examination of popular sociological explanations. *Criminology* 13, 427.

13 See C. Shaw and H. McKay *Juvenile delinquency in urban areas* (Chicago: University of Chicago Press, 1942); E. Sutherland *Principles of criminology*. (Philadelphia: Lippincott, 1934); F. M. Thrasher *The gang: A study of 1,313 gangs in Chicago* (Chicago: University of Chicago Press; 1927/1966); A. K. Cohen and J. M. Short Research in delinquent subcultures, *Journal of Social Issues* 14 (1958), 20-37.; W. Miller (1958). Lower class culture as a generating milieu of gang delinquency, *Journal of Social Issues* 3 (1958), 5-19.

14 T. Hirschi, supra note 9. See also R. L. Akers, *Deviant behaviors: a social learning approach*. Belmont,

CA: Wadsworth Publishing Co., 1976; R. D. Conger, Social control & social learning models of delinquent behavior, *Criminology (1976)*, 14, 17.

15 In fact, the more general literature on adolescence supports this view. See J. Coleman (1961), *The adolescent society*; R. L. Curtis ,Adolescent orientations toward peer status, *Adolescence (1975)*, 40, 483.

16 F. I. Nye and J. P. Short, Sealing delinquent behavior. *American Sociological Review (1957)*, 22, 326-32.

17 P. Lerman. Gangs, networks, and subculture delinquency, *American Journal of Sociology* (1967), 13, 63.

18 Similar results for these and subsequent tests were also obtained when the social and institutional samples were computed separately.

19 P. Giordano and S. Cernkovich, supra note 8.

20 See e.g., National Institute of Mental Health. (1975). The contemporary woman and crime Public Health Service, Pub. No 161, which suggests, "They have worked under the direction and guidance of men who have been their lovers, husbands, or pimps," Id. 3-4.

21 See H. Blalock (1972). *Social statistics.* New York: McGraw-Hill.

Section 2 • Anne Campbell • Self-Definition by Rejection

1 For a fuller account of these gangs, see Campbell (1984).

2 There is, of course, considerable scholarly debate as to the primacy of each of these factors, and researchers in women's studies, minority studies, and economics would certainly disagree as to the relative influence of gender, race, and class on lifestyles and self-conceptions.

3 It should be born in mind that gang members themselves are not exempt from victimization. When one of the gang girls was the victim of an attempted rape, it was clear to gang members that the perpetrators were "criminals."

4 Personal Communication with Planned Parenthood of New York City, Inc., January 1984.

5 None of the girls I spoke with admitted to prostitution in their past. Where money was accepted from men after a date, it was treated as an unanticipated act of generosity. For example, one girl occasionally met men outside a Manhattan swingers club and went in with them. This lowered the men's admission price. The money they gave her at the end of the evening was considered a gift.

Section 2 • James Messerschmidt • Feminist Theory, Criminology, and the Challenge of Diversity

1 Not all female gangs are connected to male gangs. Independent girl gangs do exist but seem to be rare. A recent notable example of such a gang is the "Potrero Hill Posse" in San Francisco (see Lauderback et al., 1992).

2 Other primary money-making activities by girl gangs are drug dealing and shoplifting (for an example, see Lauderback et al., 1992).

3 This is not to suggest, as is regularly portrayed in the mass media, the emergence of a "new violent female criminal." On the contrary, I agree with Meda Chesney-Lind (1993, 339) who recently documented that "girls have long been members of gangs, that their roles in these gangs have been considerably more varied than early stereotypes would have it, and that girls' occasionally violent behavior has, during other decades, been largely ignored.

4 This raises an important issue that has been ignored in the criminological and feminist literature—intragang cross-gender violence as a form of "family violence."

5 For example, in the 1850s, one Lucy Ann Lobdell left her husband in upstate New York and passed as a man to support herself. "I made up my mind to dress in men's attire to seek labor," she explained, and to earn "men's wages." Later, she became the Reverend Joseph Lobdell and set up house with Maria Perry, living for 10 years as man and wife. (Emilio and Freedman, 1988, 124-25). Similarly, in another case in mid-1800s New York, a woman took the name Murray Hall and began to dress as a man. She opened an employment bureau, settled down with the first of her two wives, and later adopted a daughter. Hall became influential in the Tammany Hall Democratic political

machine and earned a reputation for drinking, playing poker, and being "sweet on women." (D'Emilio and Freedman 1988, 125)

Section 3 • *Joan W. Moore* • *Gang Members' Families*

1   But even the earlier studies concluded that family breakup per se might not be as damaging to a child as endemic family discord. Under certain circumstances breaking up a bad marriage might actually be an improvement for the child. Later studies confirmed this view (Kaplan and Pokorny, 1971).

2   Even researchers less wedded to a personality view of delinquency emphasize the importance of the family. Thus Mancini (1980), adopting a symbolic-interactionist approach, finds "strategic styles" of relating to others to be of great importance in distinguishing delinquent from nondelinquent slum teenagers. These styles, of course, are generated in the family, and reinforced by interactions in both peer group and school.

3   Overall, respondents remember that two-thirds of the Mexican-born parents took on American citizenship. This is a rate considerably higher than the usual rate of naturalization for Mexicans. According to McCarthy and Valdez (1986), only 56% of California's Mexican immigrants entering before 1950 were naturalized by 1980 (1986, 32). Mexican-born parents of younger clique members were significantly more likely than parents of older clique members to be naturalized: 83% of younger men's fathers, for example, compared with 62% of older men's fathers.

4   Seven variables were dichotomized and combined to form a global "Mexican ethnicity" score. These variables were: (1) father was born in Mexico; (2) mother was born in Mexico; (3) Spanish was the normal language at home; (4) use of English in the home was frowned upon; (5) father was considered head of the household with no questions; (6) father controlled mother's visitors; (7) respondent felt "Mexican" (as compared with "Chicano," "Mexican American," "confused," etc.). This global measure showed that younger cliques were significantly less "Mexican," and women were generally less "Mexican" at all ages.

5   Some indication of the long-range effects of the family may also be gleaned from answers to the question, "Which of your brothers and sisters was most successful?" Almost none said that nobody had been successful. A few hinted at a miserable family by singling out as "successful" a brother or sister who had avoided the street life (i.e., were drug-free), while a few were equivocal, citing the successful siblings' kindness and helpfulness. But a good three-quarters—men and women, old and young—used good jobs, money, and material possessions as their indicators of success. And, as I discuss later, many of these respondents, gang members though they were, also turned out reasonably well.

Section 3 • *Joan W. Moore and John M. Hagedorn* • *What Happens to Girls in the Gang?*

1   In the 1990s, the tomboy stereotype was embellished, at least in journalistic accounts, by the notion that female gangs had moved into a new and violent phase, emulating their male counterparts. Chesney-Lind (1993) saw this wave of coverage as exaggerating the evidence for increased violence and continuing the tradition of "demonizing" the young women. (See also Bowker and Klein, 1983, for an early refutation of the maladjustment approach.

2   Research was supported by Grant #DA03114 from the National Institute on Drug Abuse, which bears no responsibility for opinions expressed in this chapter.

3   A quarter of the heroin-using women had an addicted father, and 14% an addicted mother, compared with 3% of the non-using women's fathers and mothers. By contrast, only 7% of the heroin-using men had addicted fathers, and none had an addicted mother. No non-using men had parents who were addicted to heroin.

4   Rosenbaum (1988) developed the concept of 'a career of narrowing options' to understand the lives of women heroin addicts.

5   Research was supported by Grant #DA07128 from the National Institute on Drug Abuse, which bears no responsibility for opinions expressed in this chapter.

6   There were several routes to drug-dealing. A third of the women had established good relationships with their connections, which led the latter to set them up as dealers. Another 16% had a stock of heroin on consignment. Almost 21% first got the bag through relatives, another 12% by dealing for a friend. Only 12% got the bag when their heroin-dealing husband went to prison. Another 9% got the bag by means that were too varied to be categorized. Other studies report that between 15% and 34% of women in gangs as far apart as New York, Los Angeles, and Detroit sold drugs (Fagan 1990; Harris 1988; Taylor 1990a)

7   In Los Angeles, the gang was particularly important for women making connections to obtain drugs for personal use. 32% in the "Heroin" study (Moore & Mata, 1981) said that their connections were homies from the same gang, and an additional 28% connected through their boyfriends (who were often fellow gang members). A smaller—11%—made their connections through relatives outside of these networks. As for dealers, most frequently (in a majority of the cases) they obtained their stock of heroin through their connections. Another 16% first got it on consignment. 21% first got their heroin from relatives, and 12% by selling for a friend. Only 12% got the bag when their dealer-husbands went to prison.

8   Almost a quarter of the income (21%) in Milwaukee's African American communities was provided by welfare.

Section 3 • Carl S. Taylor • Female Gangs

1   J. Hagan, A.R. Gillis, and J. Simpson, The class structure of gender and delinquency: Toward a power-control theory of common delinquent behavior," *American Journal of Sociology* 90, no. 6 (1985): 1151-78.

2   A. Campbell, *Girls in the gang* (New York: Basil Blackwell, 1984).

3   J. Hagan, J. Simpson, and A.R. Gillis, The sexual stratification of social control: A gender-based perspective on crime and delinquency, *British Journal of Sociology* 30 (1979): 25-28.

4   M. Chesney-Lind, Girls' crime and a woman's place: Toward a feminist model," *Crime and Delinquency* 35 (1989): 5-29.

5   W. K. Brown, Black female gangs in Philadelphia, *International Journal of Offender Therapy and Comparative Criminology* 21 (1977), 221-28.

6   J. M. Hagedorn, *People and folks: Gangs, crime, and the underclass in a rustbelt city* (Chicago: Lake View Press, 1988).

7   Ibid.

8   F. M. Thrasher, *The gang: A study of 1,311 gangs in Chicago* (Chicago: University of Chicago Press, 1927).

9   W. F. Whyte, *Street corner society: The social structure of an Italian slum* (Chicago: University of Chicago Press, 1943).

10 Campbell, *Girls in the gang.*

11 Ibid.

12 Georgette Benett, *Crime warps.*

13 Ibid.

14 Report of the Detroit Strategic Planning Project, November 1987, 79.

15 D. Prothrow-Stith with M. Weismann, *Deadly consequences* (New York: Harper Collins, 1991).

16 L. McDermott, Analysis of serious crimes by young black women. *Criminology* 23 (1985): 81-98.

17 D.J. Steffensmeier, Organization properties and sex-segregation in the underworld: Building a sociological theory of sex differences in crime. *Social Forces* 61: 4 (1983): 1010-32.

18 C.S. Taylor, *Dangerous society* (East Lansing: Michigan State University Press, 1990).

19 A. K. Cohen, *Delinquent boys: The culture of the gang* (Glencoe: Free Press, 1955).

20 W. J. Wilson, *The truly disadvantaged: The inner city, the underclass and public policy* (Chicago: University of Chicago Press, 1987).

21 A. Campbell, *The girls in the gang;* J. W. Moore, Changing Chicano gangs: Acculturation, generational changes, evolution of deviance or emerging underclass, in *Proceedings of the Conference on Comparative Ethnicity,* ed by J. H. Johnson Jr. and M. L. Oliver (Los Angeles: Institute for Social Science Research, UCLA, 1988); C. S. Taylor, *Dangerous society.*

22 L. T. Fishman, The Vice Queens: An ethnographic study of black female gang behavior (Paper presented at the annual meeting of the American Society of Criminology, Chicago, 1988).

23 The Report of the Detroit Strategic Planning Committee, Detroit, Michigan, 1988; Nora Faires, Transition and turmoil: social and political development in Michigan, in *Michigan: Visions of Our Past,* ed. by R. Hathaway (East Lansing: Michigan State University Press, 1989) 205.

24 L. Dinnerstein and K. T. Jackson, *American vistas* (New York: Oxford University Press,, 1987).

25 D. Georgakas, *Detroit, I do mind dying: A study in urban revolution* (New York: St. Martin's Press, 1975).

26 D. J. Capeci, *Layered violence: The Detroit rioters of 1943* (Jackson, University of Mississippi, 1991).

27 L. Dinnerstein and K. T. Jackson, *American vistas.*

28 D. J. Capeci, *Layered violence.*

29 Ibid.

30 Ibid.

31 C. S. Taylor, *Dangerous society.*

32 C. Sifakis, *The mafia encyclopedia* (New York: Facts on File, 1987).

33 D. J. Capeci, *Race relations in wartime Detroit: The Sojourner Truth housing controversy of 1942* (Philadelphia: Temple University Press, 1984).

34 C. R. Huff, *Gangs in America* (Newbury Park: Sage Publications, 1990).

35 D. J. Capeci, *Layered violence.*

36 Ibid.

37 STRESS (Stop the Robberies Enjoy Safe Streets) is a decoy unit of the Detroit Police.

38 A. P. Goldstein, *Delinquent gangs* (Champaign: Research Press, 1991).

39 C. S. Taylor, *Dangerous society.*

40 A. Campbell, *Girls in the gang;* J. M. Hagedorn and J. W. Moore, Milwaukee and Los Angeles gangs compared (Paper presented at the annual meetings of the American Anthropological Society, Oaxaca, Mexico, 1987).

41 T. Belknap, Young Boys Inc. ring – 20 plead guilty in dope trial. *Detroit Free Press* 3 April 1983.

42 I. Wilkinson, Detroit crack empire shows all earmarks of big business. *New York Times* 18 December 1988.

43 W. Miller, The Molls. *Society* 11 (1973): 32-35.

44 A. Campbell, *The girls in the gang.*

Section 3 • Karen Joe and Meda Chesney-Lind • "Just Every Mother's Angel"

1 For exceptions see Brown 1977; Bowker and Klein 1983; Campbell 1984/1991; Ostner 1986; Fishman 1988; Moore 1991; Harris 1988; Quicker 1983.

2 Thrasher did mention, in passing, two factors he felt accounted for the lower number of girl gangs: "first, the social patterns for the behavior of girls, powerfully backed by the great weight of tradition and custom, are contrary to the gang and its activities; and secondly, girls, even in urban disorganized areas, are much more closely supervised and guarded than boys and are usually well incorporated into the family groups or some other social structure" (Thrasher 1927, 228).

3 Open-air Samoan dwelling

4 Members of the Honolulu Police Department's vice squad.

5 Gang banging refers to being a part of a gang.

6 Hawaiian culture had an institutionalized role for transvestites. This cultural tradition has meant a

greater acceptance of both cross-dressing and homosexuality in Hawaiian communities.

Section 3 • Edwardo Luis Portillos • The Social Construction of Gender in the Barrio

I wish to thank Marjorie Zatz for helpful comments on drafts of this manuscript and for her valuable suggestions throughout the project. This chapter is an outgrowth of my masters' thesis. I thank my masters' committee members, Marjorie Zatz, Nancy Jurik, and Mary Romero for their helpful suggestions throughout the process.

1 For purposes of this chapter, Chicano/a refers to young men and women of Mexican descent living in the United States. Mexicano/a refers to men and women who were born in Mexico. While the Mexicano and Mexicana youths had to be living in the United States at the time of my interviews to become part of my sample, they may or may not be U.S. citizens or permanent residents.

2 "Get *cholo*," is used by this young woman to illustrate that some members of the family have started to acculturate to the U.S. value system and are becoming involved in gangs.

3 All individual and gang names are pseudonyms.

4 UAs refer to Urine Analysis Tests that help determine if the young person has recently used drugs. Often they are required for some youths considered at risk and on parole or probation.

5 V*eteranos/as* are young men and women who are long time gang members and who are respected for their dedication to the gang. Their actions in defense of the barrio demonstrate their loyalty to the gang (gang youths consider this as one way of "putting work into the barrio").

Section 3 • John M. Hagedorn and Mary L. Devitt • Fighting Female

1 The first study (Hagedorn 1988) interviewed 40 males from 9 gangs, and 7 females from 4 gangs. A follow-up study, funded by NIDA grant DA 07128-01, interviewed 90 males from 9 gangs and 11 females from 5 gangs (Hagedorn 1994). This study continues that NIDA grant as DA 07128-02.

2 Spanish spoken in the home was strongly correlated with two other measures of traditional orientation: birthplace of parents (Puerto Rico and Mexico) and positive answers to our questions: "How important is it for you to stick to your own culture?" The Mexican women were significantly less likely to have foreign-born parents and to speak only Spanish at home.

3 We are mindful that the notion of the social construction of gangs questions the "real" nature of each gang. Differences between gangs here are based on a crude calculus of "majority rules."

Section 4 • Elizabeth Piper Deschenes and Finn-Aage Esbensen • Violence Among Girls

1 This was done to allow for a one-year follow-up, since the G.R.E.A.T. program is taught to seventh grade students, while at the same time guaranteeing that none of the sample was currently enrolled in the program.

2 Another part of the study was a process evaluation of the training and implementation of the program. The third component of the evaluation that includes an experimental design with longitudinal follow-up in six sites is currently underway.

3 With the program's origin in Phoenix, cities in Arizona and New Mexico were overrepresented in the early stages of the G.R.E.A.T. program. Thus, cities such as Albuquerque, Tucson, Scottsdale, and other smaller cities in the southwest were excluded from the eligible pool of potential sites.

4 Reasons for exclusion included the following: a number of the cities had not yet implemented the program; not all the sites had processed enough students through the program the prior year to allow for the retrospective data collection planned; and, in some situations the police had instructed all seventh graders, making it impossible to construct a comparison group of students who had not received the G.R.E.A.T. training.

5 At most sites it was possible to identify schools in which the G.R.E.A.T. program had been taught to

some but not all of the students as seventh graders. In Will County and Milwaukee, it was necessary to select entire schools to serve as the treatment and control groups because G.R.E.A.T. instruction had been delivered to or withheld from all seventh graders in those schools.

6   Passive consent procedures (i.e., a procedure that requires parents to respond only if they do not want their child to participate in a research project) were approved in all but the Torrance site. The number of parental refusals at each school ranged from 0 to 2% at one school. Thus, participation rates (the percent of students in attendance on the day of administration actually completing questionnaires) varied between 98% and 100% at the passive consent sites. Participation rates in Torrance, where active consent procedures were required, ranged from 53% to 75% of all eighth grade students in each of the four schools. With a few exceptions, the student self-report survey was administered in a group setting in individual classrooms during a 50-minute class period. In order to increase the reliability of responses, one researcher read the questions out loud to the students while 1-2 other research staff walked around the room to monitor students and answer any questions. As necessary, Spanish instruments were provided to students.

7   The responses were truncated at 52 times per year in order to reduce the effect of extreme outliers.

8   For further discussion of this definitional issue, see Maxson and Klein (1990) and Winfree et al. (1992).

9   Other includes persons of mixed race, e.g., Hispanic and African-American, as well as persons reporting race as a type of religion or nationality.

10 This is about the same as the national averages from 1977 to 1990 (Smith et al. 1995, 72-73). However, when gang and non-gang youth were compared we found some significant differences, with gang youth more likely than non-gang youth to come from families with less than a high school education and without college, but with similar proportions completing high school.

11 Obviously these data do not actually test the hypotheses since we did not have a direct measure of social class. However, if education can be considered a proxy for social class, it does contradict earlier findings. On the other hand, this was a multisite study and in some of the areas the proportion of parents with a higher education was much lower than the 50% reported here. In Phoenix the proportion of parents with a high school degree was less than 40%. National averages are reported to be about 70%.

12 Individual offending rates were also calculated but were not included in this paper since we were interested in predicting frequency levels of involvement for the complete study group rather than the offending rates for those engaged in a specific behavior.

13 Type of weapon was not specified so it is possible that students reported carrying pen knives or fingernail files as a weapon.

Section 4 • Meda Chesney-Lind • Girls, Gangs and Violence

1   Thrasher did mention, in passing, two factors he felt accounted for the lower number of girl gangs: "first, the social patterns for the behavior of girls, powerfully backed by the great weight of tradition and custom, are contrary to the gang and its activities; and secondly, girls, even in urban disorganized areas, are much more closely supervised and guarded than boys and are usually well incorporated into the family groups or some other social structure" (Thrasher 1927, 228).

2   In *Brothers in crime*, for example, the delinquent and criminal careers of five brothers are followed for fifteen years.

3   Defined by the F.B.I. as murder, forcible rape, robbery, burglary, aggravated assault, larceny theft, auto theft, and arson (added in 1979).

4 A portion of this section is drawn from Chesney-Lind (1995).

5 For purposes of this discussion, it is sufficient to say that if the police in Honolulu are guilty of anything it is overdefinition of what constitutes a gang member. Two other counties, which tended to take a more conservative position about gang membership reported either no girls who met this definition (Kauai County) or so few the data would not be useful (Maui with 3 girls out of 71 suspected gang members).

6 GREAT is an acronym for Gang Reporting Evaluation and Tracking System.

7 Nearly half (47%) of all young black men in Los Angeles between the ages of 21 and 24 made appearances in the Los Angeles Sheriff's Department's gang database (Muwakkil 1993).

References

Acker, J. 1990. Hierarchies, jobs, bodies: A theory of gendered organizations. *Gender & Society* 4:2, 139-58.

———. 1992. Gendering organizational theory. In A. J. Mills and P. Tancred eds., *Gendering organizational analysis*, 248-60. Newbury Park, CA: Sage.

Ackley, E. and B. Fliegel. 1960. A social work approach to street corner girls. *Social Work* 5, 29-31.

Acosta-Belen, E. and E. H. Christenson. 1979. The Puerto Rican woman. New York: Praeger.

Adler, C. 1986. Unemployed women have got it heaps worse: Exploring the implications of female youth unemployment. *Australian and New Zealand Society of Criminology* 29, 210-24.

Adler, F. 1977. The interaction between womens emancipation and female criminality: A cross-cultural perspective. *International Journal of Criminology and Penology* 5:1, 101-12.

———. 1975a.. The rise of the female crook. *Psychology Today* 9, 42-46, 112-114.

———. 1975b. *Sisters in crime: The rise of the new female criminal.* New York: McGraw Hill.

———. 1971. The female offender in Philadelphia. Unpublished doctoral dissertation, University of Pennsylvania.

Agnew, R. 1994. The techniques of neutralization and violence. *Criminology* 32:4, 555-80.

Aichhorn, A. 1935. *Wayward youth.* New York. Meridian Books.

Akers, R. L. 1976. *Deviant behaviors: a social learning approach.* Belmont, CA: Wadsworth Publishing Co.

Allen, J. 1989. Men, crime, and criminology: Recasting the questions. *International Journal of the Sociology of Law* 17:1, 19-39.

Anderson, E. 1994. The code of the streets. *Atlantic Monthly* 81-91.

———. 1992. Seattle team for youth: Adolescent female gang prevention and intervention project. Proposal to Administration for Children, Youth and Families, U.S. Department of Health and Human Services, 90CL1078. Seattle, WA.

Aquino, B. 1994. Filipino women and political engagement. The Office for Womens' Research, working paper series. Vol. 2, 1993-1994 Honolulu: University of Hawaii, Manoa.

Arch, E. C. 1993.. Risk-taking: A motivational basis for sex differences. *Psychological Reports,* 73:2, 3-11.

Archer, J. and A. Haigh. 1997a. Do beliefs about aggression predict self-reported levels of aggression? *British Journal of Social Psychology* 36, 83-105.

———. 1997b. Beliefs about aggression among male and female prisoners. *Aggressive Behavior* 23, 405-15.

Archer, J. and S. Parker. 1994. Social representations of aggression in children. *Aggressive Behavior* 20, 101-14.

Asbury, H. 1927. *The gangs of New York.* New York: Alfred A. Knopf.

Ayers, E. L. 1984. *Vengeance and justice: Crime and punishment in the 19th-century American South.* New York: Oxford University Press.

Bakan, D. 1966. *The Duality of Human Existence.* Chicago: Rand McNally.

Baker, P. 1984. The domestication of politics: Women and American political society, 1780-1920. *American Historical Review* 89 June, 620-47.

Bandura, A. 1973. *Aggression: A Social Learning Analysis.* Englewood Cliffs, NJ: Prentice Hall.

Barnett, B. M. 1993. Invisible southern black women leaders in the civil rights movement: The triple constraints of gender, race, and class. *Gender and Society* 7, 162-82.

Barker, G, and W. T. Adams. 1962. Comparison of the delinquencies of boys and girls. *Journal of Criminal Law, Criminology and Police Science* 53:4, 470-75.

Baskin, D. and L. Sommers. 1998. *Casualties of community disorder: Women's careers in violent crime.* Boulder CO: Westview Press.

———. 1993. Females' initiation into violent street crime. *Justice Quarterly* 10:4, 559-84.

Bedau, H. A. and M. L. Radelet. 1987. Miscarriages of justice in potentially capital cases. *Stanford Law Review* 40:1, 21-98.

Bederman, G. 1995. *Manliness and civilization: A cultural history of gender and race in the United States, 1880-1917.* Chicago: University of Chicago Press.

Beirne, P. and J. W. Messerschmidt. 1995. *Criminology.* 2nd ed. San Diego, CA: Harcourt Brace.

Belknap, T. 1983. Young boys Inc. ring—20 plead guilty in dope trial. Detroit Free Press. April 3.

Bell, R. R. 1971. The related importance of mother and wife roles among black lower class women. In R. Staples, ed., *The black family: Essays and studies,* Belmont, California: Wadsworth Publishing Co.

Benett, G. Crime Warps.

Bennett, J. 1981. *Oral history and delinquency: The rhetoric of criminology.* Chicago: University of Chicago Press.

Berkowitz, L. 1989. Frustration-aggression hypothesis: Examination and reformulation. *Psychological Bulletin* 106, 59-73.

Bernard, W. 1949. *Jailbait.* New York: Greenberg.

Bernard, T. 1990. Angry aggression among the truly disadvantaged. *Criminology* 28, 73-95.

Bettencourt, B. and N. Miller. 1996 Gender differences in aggression as a function of provocation: A meta-analysis. *Psychological Bulletin* 119, 422-47.

Biernacki, P. and D. Waldorf. 1981. Snowball sampling: Problems and techniques of chain referral sampling. *Sociological Methodology* 10:2, 141-63.

Bjerregaard, B. and C. Smith. 1993. Gender differences in gang participation, delinquency, and substance use. *Journal of Quantitative Criminology* 9:4, 329-55.

Black, D. 1983. Crime as social control. *American Sociological Review* 48, 34-55.

Blalock, H. 1972. *Social statistics.* New York. McGraw-Hill.

Block, C. R., A. Christakos, J. Ayad and R. Przybylski. 1996. *Street gangs and crime.* Research Bulletin: Illinois Criminal Justice Information Authority.

Block, J. 1984. *Sex role identity and ego development.* San Francisco: Jossey-Bass.

Bobbed-hair bandit of early Texas days. 1924, April 13. *New York Times.*

Boisjoly, R. M. 1987. Ethical decisions: Morton Thiokol and the space shuttle Challenger disaster. Paper presented at the annual meeting of the American Society of Mechanical Engineers, Boston, MA.

Boujouen, N. 1991. Hispanic health council: Las jovenes. Proposal to Administration for Children, Youth and Families, U.S. Department of Health and Human Services, 90CL1072. Hartford, CT.

Boulton, M. 1996. A comparison of 8- and 11-year-old girls' and boys' participation in specific types of rough-and-tumble play and aggressive fighting: Implications for the functional hypothesis. *Aggressive Behavior* 22, 271-88.

Bowen, L. D.. 1917. *The public dance halls of Chicago.* Rev. ed. Chicago: Juvenile Protective Association.

Bowker, L. H. 1978a. Gangs and prostitutes: Two case studies of female crime. In L.H. Bowker, ed., *Women, crime, and the criminal justice system.* Lexington, MA: Lexington Books, 143-69.

———. 1978b. *Women, crime and the criminal justice system.* Lexington, Mass,: Lexington Books.

Bowker, L.H., H. S. Gross, and M. W. Klein. 1980. Female participation in delinquent gang activities. *Adolescence* 15, 509-19.

Bowker, L H. and M. W. Klein. 1983. The etiology of female juvenile delinquency and gang membership: A test of psychological and social structural explanations. *Adolescence* 18, 739-51.

Boyle, K. 1992. School's a rough place: Youth gangs, drug users, and family life in Los Angeles. Office of Educational Research and Improvement. Washington, DC, May 6, 1992, contract no. 433J47000723.

Brooks, A. B. 1980. The black woman within the program and service delivery systems for battered women: A cultural response. In *Battered women: An effective response,* chapter 2. Minnesota Department of Corrections. June.

Brotherton, D. C. 1996. Smartness, Toughness, and Autonomy: Drug use in the Context of Gang Female Delinquency. *Journal of Drug Issues* 26:1, 261-77.

Brown, R. M. 1975. *Strain of violence: Historical studies of American violence and vigilantism.* New York: Oxford University Press.

Brown, W. K. 1978. Black Gangs as Family Extensions. *International Journal of Offender Therapy and Comparative Criminology* 22, 39-45.

———. 1977. Black female gang members in Philadelphia. *International Journal of Offender Therapy and Comparative Criminology* 21, 221-28.

———. 1976. Gangways: an expressive culture approach to understanding gang delinquency. Unpublished Ph.D. dissertation. University of Pennsylvania.

———. 1974. An expressive culture approach to understanding gang delinquency. *American Journal of Corrections* 36, 44-46.

Brundage, W. F. 1993. *Lynching in the new South: Georgia and Virginia, 1880-1930.* Chicago: University of Illinois Press.

Cain, M., ed. 1989. *Growing up good: Policing the behavior of girls in Europe.* London: Sage.

Callaghan, D. M. and F. P. Rivera. 1992. Urban high school youth and hand-guns. *Journal of the American Medical Association* 267, 3038-42.

Campbell, A. 1993 *Men, Women and Aggression.* New York: Basic Books.

———. 1992. Female gang members' social representations of aggression. Paper presented at the annual meetings of the American Society of Criminology. New Orleans, Louisiana.

———. 1991. The girls in the gang. 2nd ed. Cambridge MA: Basil Blackwell, Inc.

———. 1990. Female participation in gangs. In C. R. Huff, ed., *Gangs in America,* 163-82. Newbury Park, CA: Sage Publications.

———. 1987. Self definition by rejection: The case of gang girls. *Social Problems* 34:5, 451-66.

———. 1986. Self report of fighting by females. *British Journal of Criminology* 26, 28-46.

———. 1984. Girls' talk: The social representation of aggression by female gang members. *Criminal Justice and Behavior* 11:2, 139-56.

———. 1984/1991. *The girls in the gang.* Cambridge, MA: Basil Blackwood.

———. 1981. *Girl delinquents.* Oxford: Basil Blackwood.

Campbell, A. and S. Muncer. 1994. Sex differences in aggression: Social roles and social representations. *British Journal of Social Psychology* 33, 233-40.

———. 1987 Models of anger and aggression in the social talk of women and men. *Journal for the Theory of Social Behaviour* 17, 489-512.

Campbell, A., S. Muncer, S. and E. Coyle. 1992 Social representations of aggression as an explanation of sex differences: A preliminary study. *Aggresive Behavior* 18, 95-108.

Campbell, A., S. Muncer, and B. Gorman. 1993. Sex and social representations of aggression: A communal-agentic analysis. *Aggressive Behavior* 19, 125-35.

Campbell, A., Muncer, S., A. Guy, and M. Banim. 1996. Social representations of aggression: Crossing the sex barrier. *European Journal of Social Psychology* 26, 135-47.

Candamil, M. T. 1992. *Female gangs: The forgotten ones.* Administration for Children, Youth, and Families. Washington, DC: U.S. Department of Health and Human Services.

Canter, R. J. 1982. Sex differences in self-report delinquency. *Criminology* 20, 373-93.

Capeci, D. 1991. *Layered violence: The Detroit rioters of 1943.* Jackson: University of Mississippi.

———. 1984. *Race relations in wartime Detroit: The Sojourner Truth housing controversy of 1942.* Philadelphia: Temple University Press.

Carrington, K. 1993. *Offending girls.* Sydney: Allen and Unwin.

CBS. 1992. *Girls in the hood.* Street Stories. August 6.

Chesney-Lind, M. 1997 *The Female Offender: Girls, Women and Crime.* London: Sage.

———. 1995. Girls, delinquency, and juvenile justice: Toward a feminist theory of young women's crime. In B. Price and N. Sokoloff eds., *The criminal justice system and women,* 2nd ed., 71-88. New York: McGraw-Hill.

———. 1993. Girls, Gangs, and Violence: Reinventing the liberated female crook. *Humanity and Society* 17, 321-44.

———. 1989. Girls' crime and a woman's place: toward a feminist model. *Crime and Delinquency* 35, 5-29.

Chesney-Lind, M. and M. Brown. 1996. Girls and violence: An overview. Paper presented at the annual meetings of the American Society of Criminology.

Chesney-Lind, M. and I. Lind. 1986. Visitors as victims: Crimes against tourists in two Hawaii counties. *Annals of Tourism Research* 13, 167-91.

Chesney-Lind, M. and R. G. Shelden. 1992. *Girls, Delinquency and juvenile justice*. Pacific Grove, CA: Brooks/Cole.

Chesney-Lind, M., R. G. Shelden, and K. A. Joe. 1996. Girls, Delinquency and Gang Membership. In C. R. Huff, ed., *Gangs in America*, 2nd ed., 185-204. Thousand Oaks, CA: Sage Publications.

Chesney-Lind, M., N. Marker, I. Stearns, A. Yap, V. H. Song, Y. Reyes. and A. Rockhill. 1992. Gangs and delinquency in Hawaii. Paper presented at the annual meetings of the American Society of Criminology, New Orleans, LA.

Chibnall, S. 1985. Whistle and zoot: The changing meaning of a suit of clothes. *History Workshop Journal* 20 Fall, 56-81.

Clatterbaugh, K. 1990. *Contemporary perspectives on masculinity*. Boulder, CO: Westview.

Clifford R. Shaw, H. D. McKay and J. F. McDonald. 1938. Brothers in Crime. Chicago: University of Chicago Press.

Cloward, R. and L. Ohlin. 1960. *Delinquency and opportunity: A theory of delinquent gangs*. New York: The Free Press.

Cloward, R. and F. F. Piven. 1979. Hidden Protest: The channeling of female innovation and resistance. *Journal of Women in Culture and Society* 4, 651-69.

Cockburn, C. 1985. *Machinery of dominance: Women, men, and technical knowhow*. London: Pluto.

———. 1983. *Brothers: Male dominance and technological change*. London: Pluto.

Cockburn, C. and S. Ormrod. 1993. *Gender and technology in the making*. Newbury Park, CA: Sage.

Cohen, A. K. 1955. *Delinquent boys: The culture of the gang*. Glencoe, IL: Free Press.

Cohen, A. K. and J. P. Short. 1958. Research in delinquent subcultures. *Journal of Social Issues* 14, 20-37.

Cohn, C. 1995. Wars, wimps, and women: Talking gender and thinking war. In M. S. Kimmel and M. A. Messner eds., *Men's lives*, 131-143. Boston: Allyn and Bacon.

———. 1987. Sex and death in the rational world of defense intellectuals. *Signs* 12:4, 687-718.

Coleman, J. 1961. The adolescent society. New York: The Free Press.

Collins, H. C. 1979. *Street gangs: Profiles for police*. New York: New York City Police Department.

Collins, P. H. 1992. Learning to think for ourselves: Malcom X's black nationalism reconsidered. In J. Wood, ed., *Malcom X: In our own image*, 59-85. New York: St. Martin's.

Conger, R. D. 1976. Social control and social learning models of delinquent behavior. *Criminology* 14, 17.

Connell, R. W. 1995. *Masculinities*. Berkeley: University of California Press.

———. 1995. Masculinity, violence, and war. In M. S. Kimmel and M. A. Messner, eds., *Men's lives*, 125-30. Boston: Allyn and Bacon, .

———. 1987. *Gender and power: Society, the person, and sexual politics*. Stanford, CA: Stanford University Press.

Cosgrove, S. 1984. The zoot suit and style warfare. *Radical America* 18:1, 38-51.

Cosmos Corporation. 1993. Forum on the prevention of adolescent female gang involvement. Washington, DC: ACE-Federal Reporters, Inc.

Cowie, J. C., V. Cowie, and E. Slater. 1960. *Delinquency in girls*. USA: Humanities Press.

Crime Prevention Division. 1993. Crime in Hawaii. Honolulu: Department of the Attorney General.

Crittenden, D. 1990. January 25. You've come a long way, Moll. *Wall Street Journal*.

Cross, T. 1984. The black power imperative: Racial inequality and the politics of nonviolence. New York: Faulkner Books.

Cullen, J. 1992. "I's a man now!": Gender and African American men. In C. Clinton and N. Silber eds., *Divided houses: Gender and the Civil War*, 76-91. New York: Oxford University Press.

Cummings, S. and D. J. Monti, eds. 1993. *Gangs: The origins and impact of contemporary youth gangs in the United States.* Albany: State University of New York Press.

Curry, G. D. 1995. Responding to female gang involvement. Paper presented at American Society of Criminology in Boston.

Currie, G. D., R. J. Box, R. A. Ball, and D. Stone. 1992. National assessment of law enforcement anti-gang information resources. Draft Final Report. West Virginia University: National Assessment Survey 1992.

Curry, G. D. and I. A. Spergel. 1992. Gang involvement and delinquency among Hispanic and African-American adolescent males. *Journal of Research in Crime and Delinquency* 29, 273-91.

———. 1988. Gang homicide, delinquency, and community. *Criminology* 26, 381-405

Curry, G. D., R. A. Ball, and R. J. Fox. Forthcoming. Criminal justice reaction to gang violence. In M. Costanzos and S. Oskamp eds., *Violence and the Law.* Newbury Park: Sage Publications.

———. 1994. Gang crime and law enforcement record keeping. Research in Brief. Washington, DC: U.S. Department of Justice, National Institute of Justice, Office of Justice Programs.

———. 1992. National assessment of law enforcement anti-gang information resources. Draft Final Report. Washington, DC: National Institute of Justice.

Curtis, R. L. 1975. Adolescent Orientations toward peers: variations by sex, age and socioeconomic status. *Adolescence* 40, 483.

D'Emilio, J. and E. B. Freedman. 1988. *Intimate matters: A history of sexuality in America.* New York: Harper and Row.

Daly, K. 1989 Gender and varieties of white collar crime. *Criminology* 27, 769-94.

Daly, K. and M. Chesney-Lind. 1988. Feminism and criminology. *Justice Quarterly* 5, 497-538.

Datesman, S. K., F. R. Scarpitti, and R. M. Stephenson. 1975. Female delinquency: An application of self and opportunities theories. *Journal of Research in Crime and Delinquency* 12, 107-23.

Davis, A. 1983. *Women, race and class.* New York: Vintage.

Davis, D. E. 1962. An inquiry into the phylogeny of gangs. In E. L. Gliss, ed., *Roots of Behavior.* New York: Hafner.

Dawley, D. 1973. *A nation of lords: The autobiography of the Vice Lords.* Garden City, New York: Anchor Books.

Decker, S. H. and B. Van Winkle. 1996. *Life in the gang: Family, friends and violence.* New York: Cambridge University Press.

DeKeresedy, W. S. and M. D. Schwartz. 1993. Male peer support and woman abuse. *Sociological Spectrum* 13:4, 393-413.

Department of Business and Economic Development and Tourism. 1993 Hawaii State Databook, 1992. Honolulu: DBET.

Deschenes, E. P. and F. Esbensen. 1999. Violence and gangs: Gender differences in perceptions and behavior. *Journal of Quantitative Criminology* 15:1, 63-95.

Deschenes, E., F. Bernat, F. Esbensen, and W. D. Osgood. 1996. Gangs and school violence: Gender differences in perceptions and experiences. Paper presented at the annual meetings of the American Society of Criminology, Chicago.

Devor, H. 1987. Gender-blending females: Women and sometimes men. *American Behavioral Scientist* 31:1, 12-40.

Dill, B. T. and D. C. Hine, ed. 1990. *Race, class, and gender: Prospects for an all-inclusive sisterhood.* Brooklyn, New York: Carlson Publishing Inc.

Dinitz, Simon, Frank Scarpitti, and Walter Reckless. 1962. Delinquency vulnerability: A cross group and longitudinal analysis. *American Sociological Review* 17, 515-17.

Dinnerstein, L. and K. Jackson. 1987. *American Vistas.* New York: Oxford University Press.

Dolan, E. F., Jr. and S. Finney. 1984. *Youth gangs.* New York: Julian Messner.

Dollard, J., L. Doob, N. Miller, O. Mowrer, and R. Sears. 1939 *Frustration and Aggression.* New Haven, CT: Yale University Press.

Donaldson, M. 1993. What is hegemonic masculinity? *Theory and Society* 22, 643-57.

Dowd Hall, J. 1983. The mind that burns in each body: Women, rape, and racial violence. In A. Snitow, C. Stansill, and S. Thompson eds., *Powers of desire: The politics of sexuality* 328-49. New York: Monthly Review Press.

———. 1979. *Revolt against chivalry: Jessie Daniel Ames and the women's campaign against lynching.* New York: Columbia University Press.

Driscoll, D. M. and C. R. Goldberg. 1993. *Members of the club: The coming of age of executive women.* New York: Free Press.

Dubinskas, F. A. 1988. Janus organizations: Scientist and managers in genetic engineering firms. In F. A. Dubinskas, ed., *Making time: Ethnographies of high-technology organizations,* 170-232. Philadelphia: Temple University Press.

Eagly, A. and V. Steffen. 1986 Gender and aggressive behavior: A meta-anaytic review of the social psychological literature. *Psychological Bulletin* 100, 309-30.

Elliott, D. 1988. *Gender, delinquency and society: A comparative study of male and female offenders and juvenile justice in Britain.* Aldershot, England: Avebury/Gower Publishing Company.

Elliott, D. S., D. Huizinga, and S. S. Ageton. 1985. Explaining delinquency and drug use. Beverly Hills, CA: Sage.

Esbensen, F. and E. P. Deschenes. 1998a. A multisite examination of youth gang membership: Does gender matter? *Criminology* 36:4, 799-827.

Esbensen, F and E. P. Deschenes. 1998b. Boys and girls in gangs: Are there gender differences in attitudes and behavior? Unpublished manuscript.

Esbensen, F. and D. Huizinga. 1993. Gangs, drugs, and delinquency in a survey of urban youth. *Criminology* 31:4, 565-90.

Esbensen, F. and L. T. Winfree. 1996. Race and gender differences between gang and non-gang youth: Results from a national survey. Paper presented at the 1996 Annual meeting of the Academy of Criminal Justice Sciences.

Esbensen, F., D. Huizinga, and A. Wieher. 1993. Gang and non-gang youth: Differences in explanatory factors. *Journal of Contemporary Criminal Justice* 9:2, 94-116.

Esbensen, F., E. P. Deschenes, and T. Winfree. Forthcoming. Differnces between gang girls and gang boys: Results from a multisite survey. *Youth and Society.*

Eysenck, H. J. 1964. *Crime and Personality.* London: Routledge and Kegan Paul.

Fagan, J. 1996. Gangs, drugs and neighborhood change. In C. R. Huff, ed., *Gangs in America,* 2nd ed., 39-74. Thousand Oaks, CA: Sage Publications.

———. 1990. Social processes of delinquency and drug use among urban gangs. In C. R. Huff, ed., *Gangs in America,* Newbury Park, CA: Sage Publications, 183-219.

———. 1989. The social organization of drug use and drug dealing among urban gangs. *Criminology* 27, 633-67.

Fagot, B. I. 1985 Beyond the reinforcement principle: Another step toward understanding sex role development. *Develomental Psychology* 21, 1097-1104.

Fagot, B. I. and R. Hagan. 1985. Aggression in toddlers: Responses to the assertive acts of boys and girls. *Sex Roles* 12, 341-51.

Faires, N. 1989. Transition and turmoil: Social and Political development in Michigan. In R. Hathaway, ed., *Michigan: Visions of Our Past.* East Lansing: Michigan State University Press.

Faith, K. 1993. *Unruly women.* Vancouver, BC: Press Gang Publishers.

Faludi, S. 1991. *Backlash: The undeclared war against women.* New York: Crown Publishers.

Federal Bureau of Investigation. 1992. *Uniform crime reports 1991.* Washington, DC: U.S. Government Printing Office.

———. 1992. Crime in the United States. Washington, DC: U.S. Department of Justice.

———. 1978. Crime in the United States—1977. Washington, DC: U.S. Department of Justice.

———. 1973. Uniform Crime Reports. Washington, DC

Felson, R.B. 1982 Impression management and the escalation of aggression and violence. *Social Psychology Quarterly* 45, 245-54.

Ferguson, A. 1991. *Sexual democracy: Women, oppression, and revolution.* Boulder, CO: Westview.

Ferrell, J. 1995. Style matters: Criminal identity and social control. In J. Ferrel and C. R. Sanders, eds., *Cultural Criminology,* 169-89. Boston: Northeastern University Press.

Ferrell, J. and C. R. Sanders. 1995. Culture, crime, and criminology. In J. Ferrell and C. R. Sanders, eds., *Cultural criminology* 3-21. Boston: Northeastern University Press.

———. 1995. Toward a cultural criminology. In J. Ferrell and C. R. Sanders eds., *Cultural criminology,* 297-326. Boston: Northeastern University Press.

Fields, A. and J. M. Walters. 1985. Hustling: Supporting a heroin habit. In B. Hanson, G. Beschner, J. M. Walters, and E. Bovelle, eds., *Life with heroin: Voices from the Inner City,* 49-73. Lexington, MA: Lexington Books.

Figueria-McDonough, J. and W. H. Barton. 1985. Attachments, gender and delinquency. *Deviant Behavior* 6, 119-44.

Fishman, L. T. 1997. Black female gang behavior: an historical and ethnographic perspective. Unpublished manuscript. University of Vermont.

———. 1995. The vice queens: an ethnographic study of black female gang behavior. In M. W. Klein, C. L. Maxson and J. Miller, eds., *The Modern Gang Reader.* Los Angeles: Roxbury.

———. 1988. The vice queens: an ethnographic study of black female gang behavior. Paper presented at the annual meeting of American Society of Criminology, Chicago, Illinois.

Fitzpatrick, J. P. 1971. *Puerto Rican Americans: The meaning of migration to the mainland.* Englewood Cliffs, NJ: Prentice Hall.

Florman, S. C. 1976. *The existential pleasure of engineering.* New York: St. Martin's Press.

Flowers, R. B. 1987. *Women and criminality.* New York: Greenwood Press.

Foner, E. 1988. *Reconstruction: America's unfinished revolution, 1863-1877.* New York: Harper and Row.

Forbes, G. 1923. Girl, twenty-one, tells how she ruled Holdup gang. Chicago Tribune, January 3.

Fox-Genovese, E. 1988. *Within the plantation household: Black and white women of the old South.* Chapel Hill: University of North Carolina Press.

Fraiman, S. 1994. Geometries of race and gender: Eve Sedgwick, Spike Lee, and Charlayne Hunter-Gault. *Feminist Studies* 20:1, 67-84.

Frankenberg, R. 1993. *White women, race matters: The social construction of whiteness.* Minneapolis: University of Minnesota Press.

Freud, S. 1950. Warum krieg? In *Gesammelte Werke.* Volume 16. London: Imago.

Friedman, S. S. 1995. Beyond white and other: Relationality and narratives of race in feminist discourse. *Signs* 21:1, 1-49.

Frodi, A., J. Macauley, and P. Thome. 1977. Are women always less aggressive than men? A review of the experimental literature. *Psychological Bulletin* 84, 634-60.

Garbarino, J., C. Schellenbach, and J. Sebes. 1986. *Troubled youth, troubled families.* New York: Aldine.

Genovese, E. 1974. *Roll, Jordan, roll: The world the slaves made.* New York: Random House.

Georgakas D. and M. Surkin. 1975. *Detroit, I do mind dying: A study in urban revolution.* New York: St. Martin's Press.

Gibbons, D. C. and M. J. Griswold. 1957. Sex differences among juvenile court referrals. *Sociology and Social Research* 32, 106-13.

Giddens, A. 1989. A reply to my critics. In D. Held and J. B. Thompson eds., *Social theory of modern societies: Anthony Giddens and his critics.* 249-301. New York: Cambridge University Press.

———. 1984. *The constitution of society: Outline of the theory of structuration.* Berkeley: University of California Press.

———. 1976. *New rules of sociological method: A positive critique of interpretive sociologies.* New York: Basic Books.

Gilligan, C. 1982. *In a different voice: Psychological theory and women's development.* Cambridge, MA: Harvard University Press.

Gilroy, P. 1990. One nation under a groove: The cultural politics of race and racism in Britain. In D. T. Goldberg, ed., *Anatomy of racism,* 263-82. Minneapolis: University of Minnesota Press.

Ginzburg, R. 1988. *100 years of lynchings.* Baltimore: Black Classic.

Giordano, P. 1978. Research note: Girls, guys and gangs: The changing social context of female delinquency. *Journal of Criminal Law and Criminology* 69:1, 126.

Giordano, P. and S. Cernkovich. 1977. On complicating the relationship between liberation and delinquency. Unpublished paper presented at the annual meeting of the International Sociological Association, Research Committee for the Sociology of Deviance and Social Control, Dublin, Ireland.

———. 1976. Changing Patterns of Female Delinquency. Unpublished paper presented at the annual meetings of the Society for the Study of Social Problems in New York, August 1976.

Giordano, P., S. Cernkovich, M. Pugh. 1978. Girls, guys and gangs: The changing social context of female delinquency. *Journal of Criminal Law and Criminology* 69, 126-32.

Girl gangs, the. 1972, October 16. Time, 33-34.

Glasgow, D. G. 1980. *The black underclass: Poverty, unemployment and entrapment of ghetto youth.* New York: Vintage Books.

Glenn, E. N. 1992. From servitude to service work: Historical continuities in the racial division of paid reproductive labor. *Signs* 18:1, 1-43.

Glueck, S., and E. Glueck. 1934. *One thousand juvenile delinquents.* Cambridge, MA: Harvard University Press.

Goffman, E. 1959. *The presentation of self in everyday life.* New York: Doubleday Anchor Books.

Goldstein, A. 1991. *Delinquent gangs.* Champaign, IL: Research Press.

Gora, J. 1982. *The new female criminal: Empirical reality or social myth.* New York: Praeger Publishers.

Gottfredson, M. and T. Hirschi. 1993. *A General Theory of Crime.* Stanford, CA: Stanford University Press.

Griffith, B. 1948. *American me.* Boston: Houghton Mifflin.

Hacker, S. 1989. *Pleasure, power, and technology: Some tales of gender, engineering, and the cooperative workplace.* Boston: Unwin Hyman.

Hagan, J., J. Simpson, and A. R. Gillis. 1987. Class in the household: A power-control theory of gender and delinquency. *American Journal of Sociology* 92, 788-816.

———. 1979. The sexual stratification of social control: A gender-based perspective on crime and delinquency. *British Journal of Sociology* 30, 25-28.

Hagan, J., A. R. Gillis, and J. Simpson. 1985. The class structure of gender and delinquency: Toward a power-control theory of common delinquent behavior. *American Journal of Sociology* 90:6, 1151-78.

Hagedorn, J. M. 1998a. *People and Folks: Gangs, Crime, and the Underclass in a Rustbelt City.* 2nd ed. Chicago: Lakeview Press.

———. 1998b. As American as apple pie: A case study of gang violence. In M. W. Watts, ed., *Cross-cultural perspectives on youth, radicalism, and violence.* Hartford CN: JAI Press.

———. 1998c. Gang violence in the post-industrial era. In Michael Tonry and Mark Moore, eds., *Youth violence: Crime and Justice 24: An Annual Review of Research,* 457-511. University of Chicago.

———. 1998d. Frat boys, bossmen, studs, and gentlemen: A typology of gang masculinities. In L. Bowker, ed., *Masculinities and Violence.* Beverly Hills: Sage.

———. 1996. The Emperor's new clothes: Theory and method in gang research. *Free Inquiry for a Cre-*

ative Sociology 24:2, 111-22.

———. 1994a. Neighborhoods, markets, and gang drug organization. Journal of Research in Crime and Delinquency 32, 197-219.

———. 1994b. Homeboys, dope fiends, legits and new jacks. Criminology 32:2, 197-219.

———. 1990. Back in the field again: Gang research in the nineties. In C. R. Huff, ed., Gangs in America. Beverly Hills: Sage.

———. 1988. People and folks: Gangs, crime and the underclass in a Rustbelt City. Chicago: Lake View Press.

Hagedorn, J. M. and J. W. Moore. 1987. Milwaukee and Los Angeles gangs compared. Paper presented at the annual meeting of the American Anthropological Society. Oaxaca, Mexico.

Hagedorn, J. M, J. Torres, and G. Giglio. 1998. Cocaine, kicks, and strain: Patterns of substance abuse in Milwaukee gangs. Contemporary Drug Problems 25:1, 113-45.

Hamid, A. 1992. The developmental cycle of a drug epidemic: The Cocaine smoking epidemic of 1981-1991. Journal of Psychoactive Drugs 24, 337-48.

Hammond, B. E. and J. Ladner. 1969. Socialization into sexual behavior in a Negro slum ghetto. In C. B. Broderick and J. Bernard, eds., The individual, sex, and society, 41-45. Baltimore: John Hopkins Press.

Hannerz, U. 1969. Soulside. New York: Columbia University Press.

Hanson, K. 1964. Rebels in the streets: The story of New York's girl gangs. Englewood Cliffs, NJ: Prentice Hall.

Harris, M. G. 1996 Aggression, gender and ethnicity. Aggression and Violent Behaviour 1, 123-46.

———. 1994. Cholas, Chicano girls and gangs. Sex Roles 30, 289-431.

———. 1988. Cholas: Latino girls and gangs. New York: AMS Press.

Harris, T. 1984. Exorcising blackness. Bloomington: Indiana University Press.

Healy, William, and Augusta Bronner. 1936. New light on delinquency, and its treatment. New Haven, CT: Yale University Press.

Hebdige, D. 1978. Subculture: The meaning of style. New York: Routledge.

Heller, C. S. 1966. Mexican American youth: Forgotten youth at the crossroads. New York: Random House.

Hindelang, M. J. 1971. Age, sex, and the versatility of delinquency involvements. Social problems 18, 522-35.

Hindelang, M., T. Hirschi, and J. G. Weis. 1981. Measuring delinquency. Beverly Hills, CA: Sage Publications.

Hine, D. C., ed. 1990. Multiple jeopardy, multiple consciousness: The context of a black feminist ideology. Brooklyn, New York: Carlson Publishing Inc.

Hirschi, T. 1969. Causes of Delinquency. Berkeley: University of California Press.

Hodes, M. E. 1991. Sex across the color line: White women and black men in the 19th-century American South. Unpublished doctoral dissertation. Princeton University.

Hooks, B. 1984. Feminist theory: From margin to center. Boston: South End.

Hopper, H. B. and J. Moore. 1990. Women in outlaw motorcycle gangs. Journal of Contemporary Ethnography 18:4, 363-87.

Horowitz, R. 1983. Honor and the American dream: Culture and identity in a Chicano community. New Brunswick, NJ: Rutgers University Press.

Horton, J. O. 1993. Free People of color: Inside the African American community. Washington, DC: Smithsonian Institution Press.

Howell, J. 1994. Recent gang research: Program and policy implications. Crime and Delinquency 40, 495-515.

Huff, C. R., ed. 1990/1996. Gangs in America. Newbury Park, CA: Sage.

Huizinga, D. 1991. Assessing violent behavior with self-reports. In Joel, ed., Neuropsychology of Aggression. Boston, MA: Kluwer.

Huizinga, D. and D. S. Elliott. 1987. Juvenile offenders: Prevalence, offender incidence, and arrest rates by race. *Crime and Delinquency* 33, 206-23.

Huizinga, D., F. Esbensen, and A. W. Wieher. 1991. Are there multiple paths to delinquency? *Journal of Criminal Law and Criminology* 82, 83-118.

Hutchinson, R. and C. Kyle. 1993. Hispanic street gangs in Chicago public schools. In S. Cummings and D. J. Monti, eds., *Gangs: The origins and impact of contemporary youth gangs in the United States.* Albany: State University of New York Press.

Hyde, J. 1986 Gender differences in aggression. In J. Hyde and M. Linn, eds., *The Psychology of Gender: Advances through Meta-Analysis.* Baltimore: Johns Hopkins University Press.

Inter-university Consortium for Political and Social Research. 1993. National archive of criminal justice data. Ann Arbor, MI: University of Michigan and Bureau of Justice Statistics.

Jarret, R. 1994. Living poor: Family life among single parent, African-American women. *Social Problems* 41, 30-49.

Jensen, G. J. and R. Eve. 1976. Sex differences in delinquency: an examination of popular sociological explanations. *Criminology* 13, 427.

Joe, K. A. and M. Chesney-Lind. 1993. Just every mother's angel: An analysis of gender and ethnic variations in youth gang membership. Paper presented at the annual meetings of the American Society of Criminology, Phoenix.

Joe, K. A. and M. Chesney-Lind. 1995. Just every mother's angel: An analysis of gender and ethnic variations in youth gang membership. *Gender and Society* 9, 408-31.

Johnson, M. M. 1988. *Strong mothers, weak wives.* Berkeley: University of California.

Johnston, J. H. 1970. *Race relations and miscegenation in the South, 1776-1860.* Amherst: University of Massachusetts Press.

Jones, J. 1986. *Labor of love, labor of sorrow: Black women, work, and the family from slavery to the present.* New York: Vintage.

Jordan, W. D. 1968. *White over black: American attitudes toward the Negro, 1550-1812.* Chapel Hill: University of North Carolina Press.

Juvenile Protective Association. 1921. Stag parties. *Bulletin,* May, 3:3.

Kanter, R. M. 1977. *Men and women of the corporation.* New York: Basic Books.

Kaplan, H. and A. D. Pokorny. 1971. Self derogation and childhood broken home. *Journal of Marriage and the Family* 33, 328-37.

Katz, J. 1988. *Seductions of crime: moral and sensual attractions of doing evil.* New York: Basic Books.

Keiser, R. L. 1969. *The vicelords: Warriors of the streets.* New York: Holt, Rinehart and Winston.

Kelley, R. D. G. 1992. The riddle of the zoot: Malcom Little and black cultural politics during World War II. In J. Wood, ed., *Malcom X: In our own image,* 155-82. New York: St. Martin's.

Kerfoot, D. and D. Knights. 1993. Management, masculinity, and manipulation: From paternalism to corporate strategy in financial services in Britain. *Journal of Management Studies* 30:4, 659-77.

Kimmel, M. S. 1987. Men's responses to feminism at the turn of the century. *Gender and Society* 1:3, 261-83.

King, D. K. 1988. Multiple jeopardy, multiple consciousness: The context of a black feminist ideology. *Signs* 14, 43-72.

Klein, D. 1973. The etiology of female crime: A review of the literature. *Issues in Criminology* 8, 3-30.

Klein, M. W. 1995. *The American street gang: Its nature, prevalence, and control.* New York: Oxford University Press.

Klemesrud, J. 1978 Women terrorists, sisters in crime. N.T. News Service. Honolulu Star Bulletin. January 16.

Knight, G., R. Fabes, and D. Higgins. 1996. Concerns about drawing causal inferences from meta-analysis: An example in the study of gender differences in aggression. *Psychological Bulletin* 119, 410-21.

Konopka, G. 1966. *The adolescent girl in conflict*. Englewood Cliffs, NJ: Prentice Hall.

Kotlowitz, A. 1991. *There are no children here: The story of two boys growing up in the other America*. New York: Anchor.

Kramer, R. C. 1992. The space shuttle Challenger explosion: A case study of state-corporate crime. In K. Schlegel and D. Weisburg, eds., *White-collar crime reconsidered*, 214-43. Boston: Northeastern University Press.

Ladner, J. 1972. *Tomorrow's tomorrow: The black woman*. Garden City, New York: Doubleday.

Laidler, K. J. and G. Hunt. 1997. Violence and social organization in female gangs. *Social Justice* 24:4, 148-69.

Lauderback, D., J. Hansen, and D. Waldorf. 1992. Sisters are doin' it for themselves: A Black female gang in San Francisco. *The Gang Journal* 1, 57-72.

Lebra, J. 1991. *Women's voices in Hawaii*. Niwot, CO: University Press of Colorado.

Lee, F. R. 1991. For gold earrings and protection, more girls take the road to violence. New York Times. November 25.

Leonard, E. 1983. *Women, Crime, and Society*. New York: Longman.

Lerman, P. 1967. Gangs, networks, and subculture delinquency. *American Journal of Sociology* 13, 63-72.

Lewis, D. K. 1981. Black women offenders and criminal justice: Some theoretical considerations. In M. Q. Warren, ed., *Comparing female and male offenders*. Beverly Hills: Sage Publications.

Lewis, N. 1992. Delinquent girls achieving a violent equality in D.C. *Washington Post*, December 23.

Lewis, O. 1965. *La Vida: A Puerto Rican family in the culture of poverty: San Juan and New York*. New York: Vintage Books.

Linnekin, J. 1990. *Sacred queens and women of consequence*. Ann Arbor: University of Michigan Press.

Lorenz, K. 1971. *On Aggression*. New York: Bantam Books.

Lorber, J. 1994. *Paradoxes of gender*. New Haven, CT: Yale University Press.

Lorber, J. and S. A. Ferrel, eds. 1991. *The social construction of gender*. Newbury Park, CA: Sage Publications.

Luce, G. 1971. Delinquent girl gangs. In J. Sergel, ed., *The mental health of the child*. Washington, DC, U.S. Government Printing Office.

Luckenbill, D. 1977. Criminal homicide as a situated transaction. *Social Problems* 25, 176-86.

Luhman, N. 1993. *Risk: A sociological theory*. New York: Aldine.

Madsen, W. 1973. *The Mexican-Americans of south Texas*. 2nd ed. New York: Holt-Rinehart and Winston.

Maher, L. 1997. *Sexed Work: Gender, Race, and Resistance in a Brooklyn Drug Market*. Oxford: Clarendon Press.

Majors, R. and J. M. Billson. 1992. *Cool pose: The dilemmas of black manhood in America*. New York: Touchstone.

Malcolm X with A. Haley. 1964. *The autobiography of Malcolm X*. New York: Ballantine.

Mancini, J. 1980. *Strategic styles: Coping in the inner city*. Hanover, NH.: University Press of New England.

Mann, C. R. 1993. Sister against sister: Female intrasexual homicide. In C. C. Culliver, ed., *Female criminality: The state of the art*, 195-223. New York: Garland.

———. 1984. *Female crime and delinquency*. University, AL: University of Alabama Press.

March, J. G. and Z. Shapira. 1987. Managerial perspectives on risk and risk taking. *Management Science* 33:11, 1404-18.

Marin, M. D. 1991. *Social protest in an urban barrio: A study of the chicano movement, 1966-1974*. Lanham, MD: University Press of America.

Marsh, P. and A. Campbell, eds. 1982. *Female aggression: Aggression and violence*. New York: St. Martin's Press, 137-50.

Martin, S. and N. Jurik. 1996. *Doing justice, doing gender*. Thousand Oaks, CA: Sage

Maxson, C. L. and M. W. Klein. 1990. Street gang violence: Twice as great, or half as great. In C. R. Huff, ed., *Gangs in America*. Newbury Park, CA: Sage.

McCarthy, K. and R. B.Valdez. 1986. *Current and future effects of Mexican immigration in California.* Santa Monica, CA: Rand Corporation.

McConnell, M. 1987. *Challenger: A major malfunction.* Garden City, NY: Doubleday.

McCray, C. A. 1980. The black woman and family roles. In L. F. Roders-Rose, ed., *The Black woman.* Beverly Hills: Sage Publications.

McDermott, L. 1985. Analysis of serious crime by young black women. *Criminology* 23, 81-98.

McKay, H. D. 1967. A note on trends in rates of delinquency in certain areas in Chicago. In *President's Task Force Report: Juvenile Delinquency and Youth Crime, 114-18.* Washington, DC: U.S. Govt. Printing Office.

McRobbie, A. 1978. *Jackie: An ideology of adolescent femininity.* Birmingham, England: Centre for Contemporary Culture Studies.

McRobbie, A. and J. Garber. 1975. Girls and subcultures. In S. Hall and T. Jefferson, eds., *Resistance Through Rituals: Youth Subculre in Post-War Britain.* New York: Holmes and Meier.

Meissner, H. H. 1966. *Poverty and the affluent society.* New York: Harper and Row.

Merton, R. K. 1938. Social structure and anomie. *American Sociological Review* 3, 672-82.

Messerschmidt, J. W. 1997. *Crime as structured action: Gender, race, class, and crime in the making.* Thousand Oaks, CA: Sage Publications.

———. 1995. From patriarchy to gender: Feminist theory, criminology, and the challenge of diversity. In N. H. Rafter and F. Heidensohn, eds., *International Feminist Perspectives in Criminology.* Philadelphia: Open Unversity Press.

———. 1993. *Masculinities and crime: critique and reconceptualization of theory.* Lanham, MD.: Rowman and Littlefield.

———. 1986. *Capitalism, patriarchy, and crime.* Totowa, NJ: Rowman and Littlefield.

Messner, M. 1995. Boyhood, organized sports, and the construction of masculinities. In M. S. Kimmel and M. A. Messner, eds., *Men's lives,* 102-114. Boston: Allyn and Bacon.

Miller, J. A. 1996. Female gang involvement in a midwestern city. Unpublished Ph.D. dissertation. Department of Sociology, University of Southern California, Los Angeles.

Miller, W. 1980. The Molls. In S. K. Datesman and F. R. Scarpitti, eds., *Women, crime, and justice.* New York: Oxford University Press.

———. 1975a. *Violence by youth gangs and youth groups as a crime problem in major American cities.* Washington, DC: U.S. Government Printing Office.

———. 1975b. Race, sex and gangs: The Molls. *Trans-Action* 11, 32-35.

———. 1973. The Molls. *Society* 2: 11, 32-35.

———. 1966. Violent crimes in city gangs. *Annuals of the American Academy of Political and Social Science* 364, 96-112.

———. 1958. Lower class culture as a generating milieu of gang delinquency. *Journal of Social Issues* 3, 5-19.

Mitchell, D. 1992. Adolescent female gang prevention in public housing: females obtaining resources and cultural enrichment: The next level. Proposal to Association for Children, Youth and Families, U.S. Department of Health and Human Services. 90CL1034. Boston.

Monti, D. J. 1993. Origins and problems of gang research in the United States. In S. Cummings and D. J. Monti, eds., *Gangs: The origins and impact of contemporary youth gangs in the United States.* Albany: State University of New York Press.

Moore, J. and H. B. Hopper. 1990. Women in outlaw motorcycle gangs. *Journal of Contemporary Ethnography* 18:4, 363-87.

Moore, J. W. 1994. The *chola* life course: Chicana heroin users and the barrio gang. *International Journal of the addictions* 29:9, 1115-26.

———. 1993. Gangs, drugs, and violence. In S. Cummings and D. J. Monti, eds., *Gangs: the origins and impact of contemporary youth gangs in the United States..* Albany: State University of New York Press.

————. 1991. *Going down to the Barrio: Homeboys and homegirls in change.* Philadelphia: Temple University Press.

————. 1990. Mexican-American women addicts: The influence of family background. In R. Glick and J. W. Moore, eds., *The ecology of crime and drug use in inner cities.* New York: Social Science Research Council.

————. 1989. Is there an Hispanic underclass? *Social Science Quarterly* 70:2, 265-83

————. 1988. Changing Chicano Gangs: Acculturation, generational changes, evolution of deviance or emerging underclass? In J. H. Johnson Jr. and M. L. Oliver, eds., *Proceedings of the Conference on Comparative Ethnicity.* Los Angeles: Institute for Social Science Research, UCLA.

————. 1978. *Homeboys.* Philadelphia: Temple University Press.

————. 1970. *Mexican Americans.* Englewoods Cliff, NJ: Prentice Hall, 99-118.

Moore, J. W. and M. L. Devitt. 1989. The paradox of deviance in addicted Mexican-American mothers. *Gender and Society* 3:1, 53-70.

Moore, J. W. and J. M. Hagedorn. In press. Female Gangs. Washington, DC: Office of Juvenile Justice and Delinquency Prevention.

————. 1996. What happens to girls in the gang? In C. R. Huff, ed., *Gangs in America.* 2nd ed. 99-118. Thousand Oaks, CA: Sage Publications.

Moore, J. W. and A. Mata. 1981. *Women and heroin in Chicano communities. Final Report for NIDA.* Los Angeles: Chicano Pinto Research Project.

Moore, J. W. and D. Vigil. 1987. Chicano gangs: Group norms and individual factors related to criminality. *Aztlan* 18, 27-44.

Moore, J, W., D. Vigil and J. Levy. 1995. *Huisas* of the street: Chicana gang members. *Latino Studies Journal* 6:1, 27-48.

Morash, M. 1986. Gender, Peer Group Experiences, and Seriousness of Delinquency. *Journal of Research in Crime and Delinquency* 23, 43-59.

Morgan, D. H. J. 1992. *Discovering men.* New York: Routledge.

Morgen, S. 1990. Conceptualizing and changing consciousness: Socialist feminist perspectives. In K. V. Hansen and I. J. Philipson, eds., *Women, class, and the feminist imagination: A socialist feminist reader,* 277-91. Philadelphia: Temple University Press.

Morris, R. R. 1965. Attitudes toward delinquency by delinquents, non-delinquents, and their friends. *British Journal of Criminology* 5, 249-61.

————. 1964. Female delinquency and relational problems. *Social Forces* 43, 82-89.

Moscovici, S. 1984. The phenomoneon of social representations. In R. Farr and S. Moscovici, eds., *Social Representations.* Cambridge: Cambridge University Press.

Moynihan, D. P. 1965. The Negro family: the case for national action. Washington: Government Printing Office.

Mulvihill, D., J. M. Tumin, and L. Curtis. 1969. *Crimes of violence.* Vol. 12. A staff report submitted to the National Commission on the Causes and Prevention of Violence. Washington, DC: Government Printing Office.

Muwakkil, S. 1993, April 5. Ganging together. *In these times.* Chicago.

Naffine, N., ed. 1995. *Gender, crime, and feminism.* Aldershot: Dartmouth.

————. 1987. *Female crime: The construction of women in criminology.* Sydney, Australia: Allen and Unwin.

National Institute of Justice. 1992. *Action plan development for the gangs initiative.* Washington, DC.

National Institute of Mental Health. 1975. The contemporary woman and crime. Public Health Service, Pub. No 161.

NBC. 1993. D. Koricke in East Los Angeles. *World News Tonight.* March 29.

Newburn, T. and E. Stanko. 1994. eds. *Just boys doing business? Men, masculinities, and crime.* London: Routledge.

Nye, F. I. and J. P. Short. 1957. Sealing delinquent behavior. *American Sociological Review* 22, 326-32.

Office of Youth Services, State of Hawaii. 1993. An Interim Report to the Legislature on the Gang Response System. Honolulu: Office of Youth Services, State of Hawaii.

Orenstein, P. 1994. *School girls*. New York: Doubleday.

Ostner, I. 1986. Die Entdeckung der Madchen. Neue Perspecktiven fur die. *Kolner-Zeitschrift-fur Soziologie und Sozialpsychologie* 38, 352-71.

Owen, Barbara. 1998. "In the mix": Struggle and survival in a women's prison. Albany: State University of New York Press.

Padilla, F. 1992. *The gang as an American enterprise*. New Brunswick, NJ: Rutgers University Press.

Palmer, C. T. and C. F. Tille. 1995. Sexual access to females as a motivation for joining gangs: An evolutionary approach. *The Journal of Sex Research* 32:3, 213-17.

Parsons. T. 1942. Age and sex in the social structure of the united states. *American Sociological Review* 7, 604.

Penalosa, F. 1967. The changing Mexican-American in Southern California. *Sociology and Social Research,* 51:4, 405-17.

Pescatello, A. 1973. Female and male in Latin America. Pittsburgh: University of Pittsburgh Press.

Pinkney, A. 1976. Red, black, and green: Black nationalism in the United States. New York: Cambridge University Press.

Plummer, K. 1983. *Documents of life*. Boston: Allen and Unwin.

Pollak, O. 1950. *The criminality of women*. New York: Barnes.

Portillos, E. L., N. C. Jurik, and M. Zatz. 1996. Machismo and chicano/a gangs: Symbolic resistance or oppression? *Free Inquiry in Creative Sociology* 24:2, 175-84.

President's Commission. 1986. *Report of the presidential commission on the space shuttle Challenger accident*. Washington DC: Government Printing Office.

Prothrow-Stith, D. and M. Weissman. 1991. *Deadly consequences*. New York: Harper Collins.

Puffer, J. A. 1912. *The boy and his gang*. Boston: Houghton Mifflin Co.

Quicker, J. C. 1983. *Homegirls: Characterizing Chicana gangs*. San Pedro, CA: International University Press.

Rable, G. C. 1984. *But there was no peace: The role of violence in the politics of reconstruction*. Athens, GA: University of Georgia Press.

Rainwater, L. 1960. *And the poor get children: Sex, contraception and family planning in the working class*. Chicago: Quadrangle.

Ramirez, S. 1970. Employment problems of Mexican American youth. In John Burma, ed., *Mexican Americans in the United States*. Cambridge, MA: Schenkman Pub. Co.

Raper, A. F. 1969. *The tragedy of lynching*. New York: Negro University Press.

Reckless, W. C. 1933. The natural history of vice areas in Chicago. Manuscript, University of Chicago Library.

Reckless, W., S. Dinitz, and B. Kay. 1957. The self component in potential delinquency and potential non-delinquency. *American Sociological Review* 22, 566-70.

Reiner, I. 1992. Gangs, crime and violence in Los Angeles. Findings and Proposals from the District Attorney's Office. Executive Summary. Los Angeles: District Attorney, County of Los Angeles.

Report of the Detroit Strategic Planning Project, the. 1987. Detroit. November. 79.

Report of the Detroit Strategic Planning Committee, the. 1988. Detroit.

Rice, R. 1963. A reporter at large: The Persian Queens. *The New Yorker* 39, 153-87.

Roberts, S. 1972. Crime rate of women up sharply over men's. *New York Times,* June 13.

Robinson, R. 1990. *Violations of girlhood: A Qualitative study of female delinquents and children in need of services in Massachusetts*. Unpublished Ph.D. dissertation. Brandeis University.

Rockhill, A., M. Chesney-Lind, J. Allen, N. Batalaon, E. Gerwin, K. Joe, and M. Spina. 1993. *Surveying Hawaii's youth: Neighborhoods, delinquency, and gangs*. Honolulu: Social Science Research Dept., University of Hawaii.

Rodriquez, L. J. 1993. *Always running, la vida loca: Gang days in L.A.* New York: Touchstone.

Rosenbaum, M. 1988. *Women on heroin.* New Brunswick, NJ: Rutgers University Press.

Rubel, A, J. 1966. The family. In Arthur J. Rubel, ed., *Across the tracks.* Austin, TX: Univ. of Texas Press.

Rubin, G. 1984. Thinking sex: Notes for a radical theory of the politics of sexuality. In C. E. Vance, ed., *Pleasure and Danger: Exploring female sexuality,* 267-319. Boston: Routledge.

Russett, C. E. 1989. *Sexual science: The Victorian construction of womanhood.* Cambridge, MA: Harvard University Press.

Ryan, W. 1972. *Blaming the victim.* New York: Vintage Books.

Salisbury, H. E. 1958. *The shook-up generation.* New York: Harper and Bros.

Sampson, R. J. and J. H. Laub. 1993. *Crime in the making: Pathways and turning points through life.* Cambridge, MA: Harvard University Press.

Sanchez-Jankowski, M. 1991. *Islands in the street: Gangs and American urban society.* Berkeley, CA: University of California Press.

Sandhu, H. S. and D. E. Allen. 1969. Female delinquency: goal obstruction and anomie. *Canadian Review of Sociology and Anthropology* 6, 107-10.

Saner, H. and P. Ellickson. 1996. Concurrent risk factors for adolescent violence. *Journal of Adolescent Health* 1: 2, 94-103.

Santiago, D. 1992, February 23. Random victims of vengeance show teen crime. *Philadelphia Inquirer.*

Scott, M and S. Lyman. 1968. Accounts. *American Sociological Review* 33, 46-62.

Schwarz, P. J. 1988. *Twice condemned: Slaves and the criminal laws of Virginia, 1705-1865.* Baton Rouge: Louisiana State University.

Schwendinger, H. and J. Schwendinger. 1985. *Adolescent subcultures and delinquency.* New York: Praeger.

Scott, A. F. 1970. *The southern lady: From pedestal to politics, 1830-1930.* Chicago: University of Chicago Press.

Segal, L. 1990. *Slow motion: Changing masculinities, changing men.* New Brunswick, NJ: Rutgers University Press.

Sellin, T. 1938. *Culture conflict and crime.* New York: Social Science Research Council.

Shacklady-Smith, L. 1978. Sexist assumptions and female delinquency. In Carol Smart and Barry Smart, eds., *Women and social control.* London: Routledge and Kegan Paul.

Shaw, C. 1938. *Brothers in crime.* Chicago: University of Chicago Press.

———. 1930. *The jack roller: A delinquent boy's own story.* Chicago: University of Chicago Press.

Shaw, C. and H. McKay. 1942a. Social factors in juvenile delinquency. In *National Commission on Law Observance and Enforcement. Report on Causes of Crime,* vol. 2. Washington, DC: U. S. Government Printing Office.

———. 1942b. *Juvenile delinquency in urban areas.* Chicago: University of Chicago Press.

Shaw, M. 1995. Conceptualizing violence by women. In R. E. Dobash, R. P. Dobash, and L. Noaks, eds., *Gender and crime,* 115-31. Cardiff: University of Wales Press.

Sheehan, S. 1976. *A welfare mother.* Boston: Houghton Mifflin.

Shelden, R. and M. Chesney-Lind. 1993. Gender and race differences in delinquent careers. *Juvenile and Family Court Journal* 44: 73-90.

Shelden, R. G., T. Snodgrass, and P. Snodgrass. 1993. Comparing gang and non-gang offenders: Some tentative findings. *The Gang Journal* 1, 73-85

Short, J. F. 1996. Foreword: Diversity and change in U.S. gangs. In C. R. Huff, ed., *Gangs in America,* 2nd ed., vii-xvii. Thousand Oaks, CA: Sage Publications.

———. 1990 Gangs, neighborhoods, and youth crime. *Criminal Justice Research Bulletin* 5, 1-11.

———. 1968. *Gang delinquency and delinquent subcultures.* New York: Harper and Row.

Short, J. F. and L. Clarke, eds. 1992. *Organizations, uncertainties, and risk.* Boulder, CO: Westview.

Short, J. F. and F. Strodtbeck. 1965. *Group process and gang delinquency.* Chicago: University of Chicago Press.

Sifakis, C. 1987. *The mafia encyclopedia.* New York: Facts on File.

Sikes, G. 1997. *8 ball chicks.* New York: Doubleday.

Simon, R. J. 1975. *Women and crime.* Lexington, MA: Lexington Books.

Simons, R. L., M. G. Miller, and S. M. Aigner. 1980. Contemporary theories of deviance and female delinquency: An empirical test. *Journal of Research on Crime and Delinquency* 20, 42-57.

Simpson, S. S. 1991. Caste, class, and violent crime: Explaining difference in female offending. *Criminology* 29:1, 115-35.

Skolnick, J. H. 1990. The social structure of street drug dealing. *American Journal of Police* 9, 1-41.

Skolnick, J., T. Correl, E. Navarro, and R. Rabb. 1989. *The social structure of street drug dealing.* Sacramento, CA: Office of the Attorney General, State of California.

Slawson, J. 1926. *The delinquent boy.* Boston: Badger Press.

Smart, C. 1977. *Women, crime and criminology: A feminist critique.* London: Routledge and Kegan Paul.

———. 1976. *Women, crime and criminology.* London: Routledge and Kegan Paul.

Smith, D. and R. Paternoster. 1987. The gender gap in theories of deviance: Issues and evidence. *Journal of Research in Crime and Delinquency* 24, 140-72,

Smith, L. S. 1978. Sexist assumptions and female delinquency: an empirical investigation. In C. Smith and B. Smart, eds., *Women, sexuality and social control,* 74-86. London: Routledge and Kegan Paul.

Smith-Rosenberg, C. 1985. *Disorderly conduct: Visions of gender in Victorian America.* New York: Oxford University Press.

Smith, T. E., M. Perie, N. Alsalem, R. Mahoney, Y. Bae, and B. A. Young. 1995. *The condition of education 1995.* Washington, DC: Department of Education.

Sommers, I. and D. R. Baskin. 1994. Factors related to female adolescent initiation into violent street crime. *Youth and Society* 25, 468-89.

———. 1993. The situational context of violent female offending. *Crime and Delinquency* 30, 136-62.

———. 1992. Sex, race, age, and violent offending. *Violence and Victims* 7:3, 191-201.

Spence, J.T. 1985 Gender identity and its implications for the concepts of masculinity and femininity. *Nebraska Symposium on Motivation 1984, Volume 32: Psychology and Gender.* Lincoln, Nebraska: University of Nebraska Press.

Spergel, I.A. 1995. *The youth gang problem.* New York: Oxford University Press.

———. 1990. Youth gangs: continuity and change. In N. Morris and M. Tonry, eds., *Crime and Justice: An annual review of research.* Chicago: University of Chicago Press.

———. 1964. *Racketville, Slumtown, Haulburg.* Chicago: University of Chicago Press.

Spergel, I. A. and G. D. Curry. 1990. *Survey of youth gang problems and programs in 45 cities and sites.* Chicago: School of Social Service Administration, University of Chicago, and Office of Juvenile Justice and Delinquency Prevention.

Spergel, I.A., R. Chance, and G. D. Curry. 1991. National youth gang suppression and intervention program. *Office of Juvenile Justice and Delinquency Prevention Bulletin.* Washington, DC: U.S. Department of Justice.

Spindel, D. J. 1989. *Crime and society in North Carolina, 1663-1776.* Baton Rouge: Louisiana State University Press.

Stack, C. B. 1974. *All our kin: Strategies for survival in a black community.* New York: Harper and Row.

Staples, R. 1973. *The black woman in America.* Chicago: Nelson-Hall Publishers.

———, ed. 1971. *The Black family: Essays and studies.* Belmont, CA: Wadsworth.

Starbuck, W. H. and F. J. Milliken. 1988. Challenger: Fine-turning the odds until something breaks. *Journal of Management Studies* 25:4, 319-40.

Steffensmeier, D. 1983. Organization properties and sex-segregation in the underworld: Building a sociological theory of sex differences in crime. *Social Forces* 4:61, 1010-32.

Steffensmeier, D. and E. Allan. 1996. Gender and crime: Toward a gendered theory of female offending. *Annual Review of Sociology* 22, 459-87.

———. 1991. Gender, age, and crime. In J. F. Sheley, ed., *Criminology: A contemporary handbook*, 67-93. Belmont, CA: Wadsworth.

Steffensmeier, D. and R. Steffensmeier. 1980. Trends in female delinquency: An examination of arrest, juvenile court, self report and field data. *Criminology* 18, 62-85.

Stokes, R. and J. P. Hewitt. 1976. Aligning actions. *American Sociological Review* 41, 838-45.

Strouse, J. 1972. To be minor and female. *Ms* August, 70-75.

Sullivan, M. L. 1985. *Teen fathers in the inner city: An exploratory ethnographic study.* New York: Vera Institute of Justice.

Sutherland, E. 1937. *The professional thief.* Chicago: University of Chicago Press.

———. 1934. *Principles of criminology.* Philadelphia: Lippincott.

Suttles, G. 1968. *The social order of the slum.* Chicago: University of Chicago Press.

Sykes, G. M. and D. Matza. 1957. Techniques of neutralization: A theory of delinquency. *American Sociological Review* 22, 664-70.

Takaki, R. 1982. *Iron cages: Race and culture in 19th-century America.* New York: Alfred A. Knopf.

Tannen, D. 1990. *You Just Don't Understand: Men and Women in Conversation.* New York: Morrow.

Taylor, C. S. 1993. *Girls, gangs, women, and drugs.* East Lansing: Michigan State University Press.

———. 1990. *Dangerous society.* East Lansing, MI: Michigan State University Press.

———. 1990. Gang imperialism. In C. R. Huff, ed., *Gangs in America.* Newbury Park, CA: Sage.

Taylor, I., P. Walton, and J. Young. 1973. *The New Criminology: For a Social Theory of Deviance.* New York: Harper and Row.

Taylor, R. D., R. Casten, S. M. Flickinger, D. Roberts, and C. D. Fulmore. 1994. Explaining the school performance of African-American adolescents. *Journal of Research on Adolescence* 4, 21-44.

Taylor, S. L. and A. Edwards. 1992. Loving and losing Malcolm. *Essence* 50-54, 104-110. February.

Tedeschi, J., R. Smith, and R. Brown. 1974. A reinterpretation of research on aggression. *Psychological Bulletin* 81, 540-62.

Thomas, F. 1992. Adolescent female gang project: Girls' leadership project. Proposal to Association for Children, Youth and Families, U.S. Department of Health and Human Services, 90CL1103. Washington, DC.

Thomas, W. I. and F. Znaniecki. 1958. *The Polish peasant in Europe and America.* New York: Dover.

Thompson, D. 1974. *Sociology of the black experience.* Westport, CN: Greenwood Press.

Thompson, H. 1967. *Hell's Angels.* New York: Ballantine.

Thompson, R. J. and J. Lozes. 1976. Female gang delinquency. *Corrective and Social Psychiatry and Journal of Behavior Technology Methods and Therapy* 22, 1-5.

Thomsen, G. 1996. *Perceptions of school and the future: A case study of 12th grade Latino students' perceptions of their adult opportunities and their current school experiences.* Unpublished Ph.D dissertation, University of Wisconsin-Milwaukee.

Thornberry, T., M. Krohn, A. Lizotte, and D. Chard-Wierschem. 1993. The role of juvenile gangs in facilitating delinquent behavior. *Journal of Research in Crime and Delinquency* 30:1, 55-87.

Thorne, B. 1993. *Gender play: Girls and boys in schools.* New Brunswick, NJ: Rutgers University.

Thorpe, E. E. 1967. *Eros and freedom in Southern life and thought.* Durham, NC: Seeman.

Thrasher, F. M. 1927/1966. *The gang: A study of 1,313 gangs in Chicago.* Chicago: University of Chicago Press.

Toch, H. 1969. *Violent Men.* Chicago: Aldine.

Tolnay, S. and E. M. Beck. 1995. *A festival of violence: An analysis of Southern lynchings, 1882-1930.* Chicago: University of Illinois Press.

Tolson, A. 1977. *The limits of masculinity.* New York: Harper and Row.

Tracy, P. and E. S. Piper. 1984. Gang membership and violent offending: Preliminary results from the 1958 cohort study. Paper presented at the 1982 annual meetings of the American Society of Criminology, Cincinnati, OH.

Trelease, A. W. 1971. *White terror: The Klu Klux Klan conspiracy and Southern reconstruction.* New York:

Harper & Row.

Tuck, R. 1946. *Not with the Fist*. New York: Harcourt, Brace and Co.

Turner, R. H. and S. J. Surace. 1956. Zoot suiters and Mexicans: Symbols in crowd behavior. *American Journal of Sociology* 62:1, 14–20.

Tyler, B. M. 1989. Black jive and white repression. *Journal of Ethnic Studies* 16:4, 31–66.

U. S. Congress. 1871. *The condition of affairs in the late insurrectionary states: Report and testimony to the Joint Select Committee*. 42d. Cong., 2d. Sess. 13.

U.S. Department of Health and Human Service. 1993. *Health, United States, 1992*. Washington DC: Government Printing Office.

Valentine, B. 1978. *Hustling and other hard work: Life styles in the ghetto*. New York: The Free Press.

Vaughan, D. 1996. *The Challenger launch decision: Risky technology, culture, and deviance at NASA*. Chicago: University of Chicago Press.

———. 1994. Risk, workgroup culture, and the normalization of deviance: NASA and the space shuttle Challenger. Paper presented at the annual meeting of the American Sociological Association, Los Angeles. August.

———. 1989. Regulating risk: Implication of the Challenger accident. *Law and Policy* 11:3, 330–49.

Vedder, C. B. and D. B. Somerville. 1973/1975. *The delinquent girl*. Springfield, IL: Charles C. Thomas.

Vigil, J. D. 1996. Street baptism: Chicano gang initiation. *Human organization* 55:2, 149–53.

———. 1990. Cholos and gangs: culture change and street youth in Los Angeles. In C. R. Huff, ed., *Gangs in America*. Newbury Park, CA: Sage Publications.

———. 1988. *Barrio gangs: Street life and identity in Southern California*. Austin: University of Texas Press.

Wajcman, J. 1991. *Feminism confronts technology*. University Park: Pennsylvania State University Press.

Waldorf, D.. 1993. *Final report on crack sales, gangs and violence to the National Institute on Drug Abuse*. San Francisco: Institute for Scientific Analysis.

Watters, J. K. and P. Biernacki. 1989. Targeted sampling: Options for the study of hidden populations. *Social Problems* 36, 416–30.

Webster, D. W., P. S. Gainer, and H. R. Champion. 1993. Weapon carrying among inner-city junior high-school students: Defensive behavior vs. Aggressive delinquency. *American Journal of Public Health* 83, 1604–08.

Weisfeld, G. 1980. Social dominance and human motivation. In D. Omark, F. Strayer and D. Freedman, eds., *An Ethological View of Human Conflict and Social Interaction*. New York: Garland STPM Press.

Welfare Council of New York City. 1950. *Working with teenage groups: A report on the central Harlem project*. New York: Welfare Council of New York City.

Werner, Emmy E. 1983. Vulnerability and resiliency among children at risk for delinquency. Unpublished manuscript.

West, C. and S. Fenstermaker. 1993. Power, inequality, and the accomplishment of gender: An ethnomethodological view. In P. England, ed., *Theory on gender/feminism on theory*, 151–74. New York: Aldine.

———. 1993. Doing difference. *Gender and Society* 9:1, 8–37.

West, C. and D. H. Zimmerman. 1987. Doing gender. *Gender and Society* 1:2, 125–51.

White, J. W. and R. M. Kowaski. 1994. Deconstructing the myth of the nonagressive woman: a feminist analysis. *Psychology of Women Quarterly* 18, 487–508.

Whyte, W. F. 1943. *Street corner society: The social structure of an Italian slum*. Chicago: University of Chicago Press.

Wiegman, R. 1993. The anatomy of lynching. *Journal of the History of Sexuality* 3:3, 445–67.

Wilkerson, I. 1988. Detroit crack empire shows all earmarks of big business. *New York Times*. December 18.

Williams, C. L. 1989. *Gender differences at work*. Berkeley: University of California Press.

Williams, T. M. and W. Kornblum. 1985. *Growing up poor*. Lexington, MA: Lexington Books.

Willis, P. E. 1979. Shop-floor culture, masculinity and the wage form. In J. Clarke, C. Critcher and R. Johnson, eds., *Working-class culture,* 185-98. London: Hutchinson.

Wilson, D. 1978. Sexual codes and conduct: A study of teenage girls, In Carol Smart and Barry Smart, eds., *Women, sexuality and social control,* 65-73. London: Routledge and Kegan Paul.

Wilson, W. J. 1987. *The truly disadvantaged: The inner city, the underclass, and public policy.* Chicago: University of Chicago Press.

Winant, H. 1995. Symposium. *Gender and Society* 9:4, 503-06.

Winfree, L. T., F. Esbensen, and D. W. Osgood. 1996. Evaluating a school-based gang prevention program: A theoretical perspective. *Evaluation Review* 20, 181-203.

Winfree, L. T., K. Fuller, T. Backstrom, and G. L. Mays. 1992. The definition and measurement of gang status: Policy implication for juvenile justice. *Juvenile and Family Court Journal* 43, 29-37.

Winfree, L.T., G. L. Mays, and T. Vigil-Backstrom. 1994a. Youth gangs and incarcerated delinquents: Exploring the ties between gang membership, delinquency and social learning theory. *Justice Quarterly* 11, 229-55.

————. 1994b. Social learning theory, self-reported delinquency, and youth gangs: A new twist on a general theory of crime and delinquency. *Youth and Society* 26, 147-77.

Wolfgang, M. E. and M. Riedel. 1975. Rape, racial discrimination, and the death penalty. In H. A. Bedau and C. M. Pierce, eds., *Capital punishment in the United States,* 99-121. New York: AMS Press.

Wright, G. C. 1990. *Racial violence in Kentucky, 1865-1940: Lynchings, mob rule, and legal lynchings.* Baton Rouge: Louisiana State University Press.

Yablonsky, L. 1966. *The violent gang.* New York: Macmillan Press.

Young, I. M. 1990. Justice and the politics of difference. Princeton: Princeton University Press.

Zatz, M. 1985. Los cholos: Legal processing of Chicano gang members. *Social Problems* 33, 13-30.

Zatz, M. and E. L. Portillos. n.d. *Voices from the barrio: Chicano gangs, families, and communities.* Unpublished Manuscript.

Zinn, H. 1980. *A people's history of the United States.* New York: Harper & Row.

Index

Horowitz, R.: on Chicano gangs in Chicago, 64, 110; on disputes over men as source of aggression, 115; on female gang involvement, 138–39; on identity as good mother, 111; on motherhood and reputation, 181; on social monitoring of Chicanas, 106; and stereotypes of female gang members, 234; on virginity in Chicano culture, 101

Howell, J. C., 133, 277

Huff, C. Ron, 133, 149, 187

Huizinga, D., 140, 151, 258, 277, 283

Hunt, G., 154

Hunt, Ronald, 199

hustling, 68, 76–77, 83, 107

Hyde, J., 248

hydraulic drive theory, 249

immigrants: in Hawaii, 225; Mexicans, 160, 315n.3; Puerto Rican gang members on, 106–7; Thrasher on social control among, 159, 176

immoral gangs, 15–17

impression management perspective, 249

incest, 155, 170–72, 173, 175, 251

infidelity, 114–15

initiation: in black female gangs in Philadelphia, 59–60; in Chicana gangs, 50–52, 236–39; exclusiveness provided by, 252–53; "fair fight," 52, 60; in Hawaiian gangs, 219; "jumping in," 51, 126, 236–37; "training in," 237–39, 244; violence in, 126; "walked in," 52

instinct theory, 249

instrumental violence, 245–46, 249, 250, 254, 272

integrity, fights over issues of, 75

Inter-university Consortium for Political and Social Research, 144

Jackson, Willie, 202

Jailbait (Bernard), 7, 45

James, Roy, 201

Jay, Melinda, 205–7

JEMA (gang), 224

Jensen, 92

Joe, Karen: on class and race in gang involvement, 120; on criminalizing female gang involvement, 151; on female gang involvement as coping, 152; on female gang members as seeking peer familial group, 280; on female gang violence, 262, 281; on group

solidarity in marginalized neighborhoods, 157; Hawaii study, 141–42; on media interest in female gangs, 277; on reasons why women join gangs, 290, 293; on social injury hypothesis, 256

Johnson, M. M., 259, 261, 262

Jones, Mike, 202

"jumping in," 51, 126, 236–37

Jurik, N. C., 234

Kalihi district (Oahu), 221

Kaplan, H., 315n.1

Katz, J., 213, 254

Kay, B., 159

Keiser, R. L., 49, 312n.1

Kelly, Kitty, 22

King, D. K., 68

Klein, M.W.: on delinquency in gang and nongang girls, 208; on drug dealing by male gangs, 270; on female gangs and violence, 81, 83; on female peer groups, 259; on female role in gangs, 258; on gangs having positive functions, 88; gang typology of, 264; on girls' effect on delinquent activity, 67, 82; on hustling, 68; on psychology of female gang members, 100, 139–40; on variation in female gangs, 258

Knight, G., 248

Kornblum, W., 123

Kowalski, R. M., 89

Ku Klux Klan (KKK), 189–90

Ladner, J., 69

Laidler, K. J., 154

Latina gangs: as auxiliaries of male gangs, 265–68; as carrying weapons, 67; in drug sales, 156, 180, 270; fighting by, 273; as lost between two worlds, 280; men as leaders of, 266; in Milwaukee, 179–81, 262–75. See also Chicana gangs; Puerto Rican female gangs

Latinas: female-headed families, 188; on marriage, 185–86; traditional gender norms affecting, 155–56, 267. See also Latina gangs

Lauderback, D., 120, 125, 142, 154, 156, 184, 214, 303–4

law enforcement: criminology, 85, 87, 119, 216, 247, 257, 258–59, 296–97; police, 75, 110, 190, 230; response to gangs, 143–46

leadership: in black female gangs, 71; in Chi-

Meda Chesney-Lind is Professor of Women's Studies at the University of Hawaii at Manoa. Her books include *Girls, Delinquency and Juvenile Justice*, which was awarded the American Society of Criminology's Michael J. Hindelang Award for the "outstanding contribution to criminology," and *The Female Offender: Girls, Women and Crime*. A fellow and former Vice President of the American Society of Criminology, she has received the American Society of Criminology's Herbert Block Award for service to the society and the profession and the Donald Cressey Award from the National Council on Crime and Delinquency.

John M. Hagedorn is the author of *People and Folks: Gangs, Crime and the Underclass in a Rustbelt City*, and *Forsaking Our Children: Bureaucracy and Reform in the Child Welfare System*. He has studied gangs in Milwaukee for 15 years, most recently as principal investigator in the Posse and Homegirl Studies at the University of Wisconsin-Milwaukee's Urban Research Center. He is now investigating the business of drugs and the underground economy. He is Associate Professor in the Criminal Justice Department of the University of Illinois-Chicago.